Key Issues

GROUP RIGHTS
Perspectives Since 1900

Acknowledgements

I am most grateful to Professor D. P. O'Brien for his advice and encouragement in connection with this book. I am particularly indebted to him for the translations in the piece by Maitland and for suggesting improvements to the Introduction.

I have also benefited from Dr Stefan Collini's comments on the Introduction and from the general assistance of the series editor, Dr Andrew Pyle.

— Julia Stapleton

CONFLICTING SOCIAL OBLIGATIONS
Reprinted courtesy of the Editor of the Aristotelian Society, © 1915.

THE ERUPTION OF THE GROUP
Reprinted with kind permission from Oxford University Press.

THE MASSES IN REPRESENTATIVE DEMOCRACY
Reprinted by permission of Eugen Rentsch Verlag ag
& Kluwer Academic Publishers,
© D. Reidel Publishing Company, Dordrecht, Holland.

THE ATAVISM OF SOCIAL JUSTICE
Reprinted by permission of Routledge, The University of
Chicago Press, and Mr Stephen Kresge, © F. A. Hayek.

COLLECTIVE ENTITIES AND MORAL RIGHTS
Reprinted by permission of the author and the University of
Texas Press, © The Southern Political Science Association.

CAPITALISM, CITIZENSHIP AND COMMUNITY
Reprinted by permission of Blackwell Publishers.

LIBERALISM AND THE
POLITICIZATION OF ETHNICITY
Reprinted by permission of the author.

ARE THERE ANY CULTURAL RIGHTS?
Reprinted by permission of Sage Publications Inc.,
© Sage Publications Inc.

THE CIVIL SOCIETY ARGUMENT
Reprinted by permission of Verso/New Left Books.

Key Issues

GROUP RIGHTS

Perspectives Since 1900

Edited and Introduced by
JULIA STAPLETON
University of Durham

Series Editor
ANDREW PYLE
University of Bristol

THOEMMES PRESS

© Thoemmes Press 1995

Published in 1995 by
Thoemmes Press
11 Great George Street
Bristol BS1 5RR
England

ISBN
Paper : 1 85506 402 2
Cloth : 1 85506 403 0

Group Rights: Perspectives Since 1900
Key Issues No. 3

British Library Cataloguing-in-Publication Data

A catalogue record of this title is available
from the British Library

Printed in Great Britain by Antony Rowe Ltd., Chippenham

ABA-1347

CONTENTS

The pieces reprinted in this book have been taken from original copies and the different grammatical and stylistic arrangement of each has been preserved.

INTRODUCTION

In his book *Politics and Vision* published in 1961, Sheldon Wolin argued that the last three centuries had been marked by a decline of the 'political' and rise of the 'social' sphere in western political thought. Prior to this development, he maintained, Hobbes' work constituted a landmark: it presupposed a distinct *Res Publica* in which the identity of citizens qua citizens was separate from and prior to all other roles and loyalties. Artificial though the parameters of 'the political' might be they were nevertheless sharply defined, providing the foundation of all society and civilization. This was the outcome of Hobbes' conception of the basic task of political philosophy: 'to identify and define what was truly political . . . a specific type of authority and its province of activity.'[1]

However, following Locke's conception of the political order as the 'rediscovery' of the natural world by a 'self-subsistent society', the sense of the political became 'sublimated' and fractured. The political world progressively became the domain of 'organisational man' who nevertheless still yearned for the 'community' of pre-modern times. The ensuing challenge to political society – detached, unitary, and sovereign – was rooted in forces which had been regarded previously as 'private' and peripheral, that is, belonging to the realm of civil society. Such forces derived from the industrial, professional, and class divisions wrought by the fluidity of modern society. The associations which emerged from these divisions, according to Wolin, provided more satisfactory forms of group inclusion than the state and became the new, diffused repositories of the sense of the political. This was the modern form which a long-established 'anti-politicism' had taken in western political thought.[2]

---

[1] S. Wolin, *Politics and Vision: Continuity and Innovation in Western Political Thought* (London, 1961), 289.

[2] *Ibid.*, 414.

It is important to recognize despite Wolin's thesis that the sovereign state continued to be upheld in the nineteenth century, particularly in the Idealist tradition following Hegel[3] and among legal positivists who had been influenced by John Austin. However, it does remain true that the idea of an all-inclusive public realm has been greatly eroded by the rise of group consciousness in the modern world. This tendency has been especially pronounced in the twentieth century, at its beginning and end in particular, the state enjoying considerable loyalty in the middle as a result of two world wars. Moreover, the upsurge of groups has often been accompanied by an insistence that they, as well as individuals, be recognized as bearers of 'rights'. Both developments form the subject of this book.

This introduction examines the different kinds of groups and collectivities which have attracted the sympathy – and also the antipathy – of political thinkers since 1900. It further considers the various cultural and political threats to which the doctrine of 'group rights' has been a response, together with the reservations and hesitations which its protagonists have elicited. Finally, it emphasizes the wider philosophies of group life which have always informed discussion of the 'rights' of human communities. This includes questions such as the attitudes which groups breed among their members, for better or worse, and the merits or otherwise of the loyalties they inspire.

These dimensions of the idea of group rights have necessitated a broad selection of articles. However, no suggestion is made here that the contributions included in this volume form part of a single debate; the groups concerned are too variegated in the human identities they represent. In general, they change from the 'voluntary' associations which preoccupied political thinkers earlier in the century to the cultural, linguistic, and 'oppressed' groups whose interests are widely upheld at present. However, the articles do illustrate the recurrence, albeit in very different guises, of a key issue in modern political thought – the role of groups in political life, and the measures to enhance or restrict their liberty which have been considered appropriate.

3 S. Collini, 'Political Theory and the "Science of Society" in Victorian Britain', *The Historical Journal*, 23, 1 (1980), 204.

1. English Pluralism.

Any discussion of the development of the idea of group rights must begin with the movement in which it first took recognizable shape – that of English Pluralism in the early years of the twentieth century. The chief stimulus here was F. W. Maitland (1850–1906) – a distinguished legal historian and Downing Professor of the Laws of England at Cambridge from 1888 until his death. He was greatly influenced by a contemporary legal theorist in Germany, Otto Von Gierke (1841–1921) who applied the ideas of German Romanticism to the sphere of law. Gierke opposed the form of Romanization of German Law advocated in the nineteenth century by Savigny and others. Instead, inspired by the Germanists Eichorn and Beseler, he sought to recover the indigenous German 'folk-law'; as such, he played an instrumental role in tilting the balance of Germany's new civil code of 1896 in favour of Germanism.[4]

An essential part of Germany's native legal inheritance stressed by Gierke was a theory of groups which saw them as free-forming and free-developing. This was in contradiction to what became known as the Roman theory of groups in which they were regarded as a mere 'fiction', created by a 'concession' of the sovereign and having no independent existence. In fact, as Gierke pointed out, this theory of associations was only articulated in the thirteenth century by Pope Innocent IV, the texts in the Roman Digest being extremely ambiguous on the matter. Maitland wrote:

> In Dr. Gierke's view Innocent, the father of 'the Fiction Theory', appears as a truly great lawyer. He really understood the texts; the head of an absolute monarchy, such as the Catholic Church was tending to become, was the very man to understand them; he found the phrase, the thought, for which others had sought in vain.[5]

In essence, groups were seen in this perspective as nothing more than a collection of the particular individuals who composed them.

For Gierke, the idea of groups as mere 'fictions' was completely at odds with Germany's rich associational life

---

[4] E. Barker, Introduction to his translation of O. Gierke, *Natural Law and the Theory of Society, 1500–1800* (Cambridge, 1934), l-lvi.

[5] F. W. Maitland, Introduction to his translation of O. Gierke, *Political Theories of the Middle Age* (Cambridge, 1900), xix.

which had arisen and developed quite spontaneously. It was
rooted in the *Gemeinde* (local community) and the *Genossenschaft* (Fellowship), among other organisations, which had
provided the cement of early German society and had survived
into the Middle Ages before the Reception of Roman Law at
around 1500. It was this spectacle of free communities,
originating in a tribal spirit, which captured Maitland's
imagination.

An avid Germanophile, Maitland brought
Gierke's reconstruction of the flourishing group life of Germany's past to the attention of English readers in 1900 in his
translation of Gierke's *Political Theories of the Middle Ages*.
Yet Maitland had English 'national' interests at heart in
doing so, as well as a warm appreciation of German antiquity.
For his concern was to emphasize England's own strengths in
the matter of voluntary organisation, strengths which – he
intimated at one point – exceeded those of Germany.[6] These
strengths needed emphasizing because they were so much taken
for granted. This in turn was due to the fact that England's
social (and political) development had not been truncated by
the Roman Reception: the peculiarly English device of the
'trust' had saved the country from the fate of the Roman theory
of Corporations which had effectively deadened the associative
impulse wherever it took root. The trust provided a 'wall' or
'screen' of trustees, behind which a society could develop
freely; it would be unconstrained by the founding principles by
which legal corporations were tied, and shielded from the
'assaults of individualistic theory'.[7]

Maitland berated English lawyers for treating the trust in a
highly technical way. The fact that it represented a cardinal
force in English history, constituting the main agent of 'social
experimentation', completely passed them by.[8] In several
important instances trusts had provided a channel for practices, the success of which provided the basis of subsequent
legislation. Such was the case of the Married Women's
Property Act of 1882, enabling all married women and not just
wealthy married women to hold property; and the Companies
Act of 1862, which recognized joint-stock companies with

6   F. W. Maitland, Introduction to Gierke, xxvii.

7   F. W. Maitland, 'Moral Personality and Legal Personality' (1903), in *The
Collected Papers of Frederick William Maitland*, edited by H. A. L. Fisher,
3 volumes, III (Cambridge, 1911), 317.

8   F. W. Maitland, 'The Unincorporate Body', in *Collected Papers*, 278.

limited liability after much trading had been effectively carried on in that form under the mantle of the trust for years. But there were many important functions performed by trusts, and not all of these led to legislation. Maitland gave further examples of the work done by the trust since its origins in fifteenth-century land law in his article entitled 'Trust and Corporation'. This was published in 1904 in response to the growing interest of German lawyers in the English trust, and extracts of which are reprinted here. Trusts, he claimed, had provided the legal framework for the Inns of Court (no wonder that the lawyers had smiled indulgently on trusts)[9], Lloyds insurance company, the Stock Exchange, religious denominations, the Jockey Club, the London clubs, and many other institutions. Resistance to the opportunity of incorporation afforded by the Companies Act of 1862 derived from a sense among such organisations that, in taking advantage of it, they would 'forfeit some of [their] liberty, some of [their] autonomy, and would not be so completely the mistress of [their] own destiny as [they are] when [they have] asked nothing and obtained nothing from the state'.[10]

However, Maitland's accentuation of the role of the trust was not just intended as a lesson on a missing but important dimension of English history. Taking the issue of trust and corporation into the sphere of social and political theory, Maitland came close to an articulation of group rights. He wrote:

> Some [friendly critics] would warn us that in the future the less we say about a supralegal, suprajural plenitude of power concentrated in a single point at Westminster – concentrated in one single organ of an increasingly complex commonwealth – the better for that commonwealth may be the days that are coming.[11]

Maitland's choice of language indicates his belief that John Austin's theory of sovereignty – which had carried much conviction in legal-political circles since its publication in 1832 – was the modern equivalent of the Innocentian doctrine of the subordinate status of groups to some higher and more inclusive

[9] F. W. Maitland, 'Trust and Corporation', in *Collected Papers*, III, 371.

[10] *Ibid.*, 388, 374.

[11] F. W. Maitland, Introduction to Gierke, xliii.

power. But the suggestive tone of his remark in favour of groups and at the expense of the state was replaced by a far more insistent one in the next two decades. In this, Gierke's (Hegelian) view that groups, while self-generating and self-developing, were nonetheless 'contained' within the larger whole of the state went by the board.

This 'Pluralist' turn in English political thought was prompted by two important court cases which made it highly topical. These were the Free Church of Scotland Appeals of 1904 and the Taff Vale Case of 1901. As well as underlining the high political relevance of Pluralism, they also emphasized the limitations of the English trust.

In the Free Church of Scotland Appeals, the House of Lords decided that the majority in the Church who had joined the United Presbyterians were not entitled to take the Church's property with them: they had acted *Ultra Vires* relative to the Church's original trust and therefore the minority 'wee frees' were entitled to retain the property. Subsequently, an Act of Parliament was passed, distributing the property of the Church fairly between its two contending parts.

The Taff Vale case was equally important in bringing issues of corporateness to the fore. Here, a trade union was held liable for damages arising from a strike, despite the fact that it was an unincorporate body and recognized as such in the Trades Disputes Act of 1876. In nonetheless treating the union as a legal person, subject to liabilities as well as rights, the courts blurred the lines between corporateness and unincorporateness in English law still further. The fact that, again, an Act of Parliament – the Trades Disputes Act – was needed to salvage the situation by giving trade unions immunity from certain consequences of their actions emphasized the lack of clarity concerning legal corporations and unincorporate bodies.

Maitland wryly commented of this confusion, '. . . our national law . . . muddles along with semi-personality and demi-semi-personality towards convenient conclusions'.[12] Because of the unobtrusiveness of the trust, the theory of groups was wildly out of step with legal practice. This did not matter while the members of all the various groups protected by trusts were reluctant to engage in litigation against them, a

---

12   F. W. Maitland, 'Moral Personality and Legal Personality', 319.

disposition with which trusts had historically been blessed.[13] Trusts were eminently effective in providing a 'hard exterior shell'[14] in litigation with outsiders. But as the Free Church of Scotland case indicated only too well, a searing internal dispute taken to court would spell the collapse of the trust's 'wall', revealing only the individual trustees behind (and not the 'moral personality' it otherwise so effectively concealed and protected).

This shortcoming of the English trust was seized upon by J. N. Figgis (1866–1919), an historian of political thought and keen disciple of Maitland. While he appreciated the great benefits yielded by the trust, he recognized its inferiority to 'the living communal society, the true corporation, with its basis in the *Genossenschaft* . . .'.[15] Figgis used Maitland's work chiefly in support of the disestablishment of the Anglican Church. But he was concerned with the freedom of all voluntary societies, which he took the Church of England to be now, a cause he vigorously fought in his book entitled *Churches in the Modern State* (1913). Targetting the concession theory as the arch-enemy of the associative spirit, he sought in the article reprinted here to identify its institutional and cultural origins. In doing so, he hoped to accentuate its nature as an inheritance from an age whose needs and beliefs were incompatible with those of the present. In Figgis's view that inheritance stemmed from the 'single society' that constituted western christendom. That is to say, there were not two societies, church and state, for the two were indistinguishable in the eyes of medieval christendom's inhabitants: baptism was synonymous with citizenship. The Reformation did not disturb this conception of the single society but merely placed the temporal power in ascendancy, a position of dominance which had issued in the theory of state sovereignty. But that theory had become a millstone around the neck of the 'complex group-life' which was the reality of modern society. For Figgis, the sooner the modern state recognized the fact that groups were 'separate societies with inherent rights', the better. The idea of sovereignty was now a 'venerable superstition', founded upon a

13   F. W. Maitland, 'Trust and Corporation', 368.
14   *Ibid.*, 368.
15   J. N. Figgis, 'Respublica Christiana', *Transactions of the Royal Historical Society*, 3rd Series, V (1911), 64.

persistent but futile and dangerous belief in 'the republic, one and indivisible'.

It is this notion of the desirability and possibility of complete social unity which all theorists of group rights have attempted to combat. At the turn of the century in Britain, such an animus was directed as much against the influence of Idealism on political thought as against the Austinian doctrine of sovereignty. The former had undergone a significant revival in late-nineteenth century Britain, associated with T. H. Green and Bernard Bosanquet. At its core was a theory of moral sovereignty in which the supremacy of the state rested upon an ideal of the common good, internalized by each citizen and expressed in a 'general will'. Certainly in Bosanquet's thought – which was much inspired by Plato and Rousseau – all social as well as political institutions were taken up in the state. He described the state in his *The Philosophical Theory of the State* of 1899 as 'the fly-wheel of our life': it was not merely a system of government but included 'the entire hierarchy of institutions by which life is determined, from the family to the trade, and from the trade to the Church and the University'.[16] It was this lack of distinction in Idealism between the state, on the one hand, and all the diverse organisations which constituted society, on the other, which R. M. MacIver (1882–1970) emphasized in his article of 1911.

MacIver had been educated in *Literae Humaniores* at Oxford in the early years of the century, an examination School upon which Idealism had a firm hold.[17] This was because Idealism, and certainly British Idealism, regarded the ancient world, particularly the world of Greek antiquity, as a beacon in the development of political society; the degree of homogeneity achieved in the Greek city-state was a model for the emergent ideal of citizenship in late-Victorian and Edwardian Britain. However, MacIver questioned the relevance of both the study of antiquity and philosophical Idealism to the problems of what he called the 'tangled' society of his own day.[18] His frustration with Idealism is evident in an article he wrote in 1911 which is reprinted here. Therein, he attacks

16 B. Bosanquet, *The Philosophical Theory of the State* (London, 1899, 4th edition, 1923), 143, 140.
17 P. Robbins, *The British Hegelians: 1875–1925* (New York, 1982), 46.
18 R. M. MacIver, *As a Tale that is Told: the Autobiography of R. M. MacIver* (Chicago, 1968), 61.

contemporary 'Hellenist' writers such as L. T. Hobhouse and Bosanquet, two thinkers he bracketed together despite Hobhouse's criticism of Idealism which culminated in his indictment of the philosophy of Hegel and Bosanquet in 1918.[19] Their error was to imagine that they were still living in 'the Aristotelian state four thousand citizens strong'.[20] It was true, argued MacIver, that the state represents an ideal of the common good. However, the common good it sought to bring about was partial not total. Striking a similar note to that of Figgis, MacIver argued that citizenship was no longer commensurate with all interests in society, but something that was distinct and determinate. The state, in effect, was simply a convenient territorial boundary. Therefore its claim upon an individual's loyalty was limited and something for which it had to compete strongly with other associations.

MacIver himself did not advance a theory of group rights. However, his writings were much in sympathy with the current Pluralist concern to cut the (sovereign) state down to size, particularly in view of the heterogeneity of modern society and the conflicting loyalties created by wide group membership. This problem was specifically addressed by G. D. H. Cole (1889–1959), who used Pluralist theory to underpin a decentralist form of socialism – Guild socialism.[21] Cole was much exercised by an inveterate hostility in recent political theory towards groups at sub-state level. At the very least, such theory manifested a low regard for them as the 'private' acts of individuals and thereby not fully 'social' (or 'public'). He saw Rousseau as the main culprit here, a view which he outlined in 1915 in his article reprinted below. Cole found Rousseau's theory of the general will as the cement of society quite feasible. However, he attacked Rousseau's translation of the concept into political terms; the general will, Cole argued, is primarily social not political in character, that is, expressed through a welter of private associations which collectively comprise the locus of sovereignty. The state could not possibly be the mouthpiece of the general will as it is only a 'mechanism' for

19 L. T. Hobhouse, *The Metaphysical Theory of the State* (London, 1918).

20 R. M. MacIver, 'Society and State', *The Philosophical Review*, XX (1911), 41.

21 On Cole's life and thought see A. W. Wright, *G. D. H. Cole and Socialist Democracy* (Oxford, 1979).

governing the affairs of a particular geographical area. It is sovereign, therefore, only with regard to those matters which affect individuals as members of that geographical grouping, for example, national defence. Indeed, the 'general will' cannot be confined to the machinery of any association, small or large. Ultimately, it falls upon individuals, using their judgement based upon a welter of social attachments, to decipher the requirements of the general will and act accordingly.

Cole argued for a devolution of power to particular associations in accordance with the 'function' they represented: where 'broad functional differences' manifested themselves, special associations were justified in 'controlling' these spheres, 'no doubt in relation to, but not under the domination of the geographical group'.[22] Another mistake of Rousseau was, he argued, to suspect that all associations were potentially, if not actually political associations, 'inevitably becom[ing] political in defence of [their] vested interests and privileges'. Cole, perhaps rather naively, claimed that associations – certainly the kind that had arisen since the nineteenth-century – were based upon 'functions' to counter this suspicion of groups as inherently 'political' in a negative sense. It was only eighteenth-century groups (ie., the survivals of feudalism) which were grounded in unwarranted 'privilege' and represented 'conspiracies against the public', he maintained. Cole's deep bias towards trade unions as the foundation of the guild socialist society to which he looked forward is evident in this belief. In his view, the recent types of associations held what privileges they possessed 'from the public on the ground that they are in the public interest: it is not privileged in the bad sense of constituting a vested interest irrespective of the common good.'[23]

Given his confidence in the integrity of such 'functional' organisations – whose authority the sovereign state had usurped in the interests of some mythical universality in public policy – Cole was, not surprisingly, vague on the difficulties of co-ordinating the various 'partial' wills which constituted complex modern societies. He brushed aside these difficulties as a problem for 'science', not 'philosophy'.

---

[22] G. D. H. Cole, 'Conflicting Social Obligations', *Proceedings of the Aristotelian Society*, n.s. XV (1915), 153.

[23] *Ibid.*, 144.

2. Reactions to Pluralism.

Cole's claim that groups should be sovereign within the functional sphere which concerns them – whether in the realm of industry, religion, or education – represented one extreme of the Pluralist movement in England. Most Pluralist thinkers who defended the idea of group personality recognized the liabilities as well as the rights to which groups were subject. This is why Figgis, Laski, and Maitland welcomed the Taff Vale decision. On the other hand there were some thinkers who, while otherwise sympathetic to Pluralist ideas, rejected the notion of group rights altogether as leading dangerously towards a belief in the priority and superiority of groups to the state. This was despite the qualification of the doctrine of group rights – by Figgis, for example, – that the 'inherent rights' of groups did not mean 'absolute rights'.[24]

One such thinker was Ernest Barker (1874–1960) who, at the time of the First World War when he entered the controversy stirred up by Pluralism, was a lecturer in Modern History at Oxford.[25] Like MacIver although a little earlier, Barker had encountered Idealism in his undergraduate education in *Literae Humaniores*. Idealism – in its moderate, Greenian form – proved an enduring influence upon him. In particular, its concern with the unity and coherence of society achieved through the state led Barker to approach Pluralism with a good deal of caution. Another factor in his sceptical approach to Pluralism was a Nonconformist upbringing which left him permanently on his guard against threats to personal liberty, threats which were as likely to emerge from groups as from the state itself. His 1915 article entitled 'The Discredited State', reproduced here, is often regarded as one which was written in overall support of Pluralism.[26] Certainly, he noted a traditional lack of enthusiasm for the state in England and also

24 D. Nichols, *The Pluralist State* (London, 1975), 81. There is now a second edition of this work entitled *The Pluralist State: the Political Ideas of J. N. Figgis and his Contemporaries* (London, 1994).

25 I have explored Barker's work in J. Stapleton, *Englishness and the Study of Politics: the Social and Political Thought of Ernest Barker* (Cambridge, 1994).

26 For example, A. Vincent, *Theories of the State* (Oxford, 1987), 188; D. Nicholls, *The Pluralist State*, 47. On Barker's own perception of his relationship to Pluralism, see Stapleton, *Englishness and the Study of Politics*, 70-71.

recognized that the state would not always secure a citizen's primary loyalty. However, he argued that this was a sign that the state had 'done its work well, and is doing its work well', that is, that the indispensable condition for a 'polyarchic' life – law and order – was being fulfilled.[27] As for Gierke and Maitland's definition of a group as 'a real person, with . . . a will of its own', this was an assertion from which Barker kept a considerable distance. He preferred to think of groups in terms of the 'organising ideas' on which they were based and which permeated all their members. These 'organising ideas' were related to, and competed with, one another, but the competition was quite unlike that which could be expected from 'real collective personalities'. This theory of groups as 'organising ideas' originated in a term which Bosanquet had applied to the dominant, unifying ideas of the individual mind, the structure of which was identical to, and confluent with, that of social groups and indeed organised society at large.[28] Barker's conception of voluntary associations as 'organising minds' was an attempt to obviate the concession theory of groups, on the one hand, and the spectre of inter- and intra-group feuds that was raised by 'realism' (the Gierke-Maitland concept) on the other. In particular, it meant that

> . . . we are rid of the idea of an internecine struggle between the real personality of the State and the real personality of other groups. We cease to feel murder in the air.[29]

Barker's staunch individualism would have made him less sanguine than Bosanquet that the great variety of voluntary groups in any society were simply 'the organs of a single pervading life'. Optimistic though he was about the prospects of social harmony in what he believed to be an integrated country like his own at the turn of the century, he would have considered that harmony possible only as the outcome of free political activity and not as a pre-existing given.

The Pluralist movement raised but did not resolve the issue of group rights; neither did it produce any cogent theories of the state, once the latter had been stripped of its absolute

---

27   E. Barker, 'The Discredited State: Thoughts on Politics before the War', in *Political Quarterly* (old series), 2 (February 1915), 121.

28   A. Vincent, *Theories of the State*, 209; B. Bosanquet, *Philosophical Theory of the State*, chapter VII.

29   E. Barker, 'The Discredited State', 113.

sovereignty. Many Pluralist writers simply re-introduced the
state by the back door – for example, Cole's notion of a
supreme authority in the form of a 'National Commune'
charged with the role of co-ordinating all the various 'functional' associations in society.[30] Similarly, Figgis's idea of the
state as a 'community of communities' whose role was to
control although not create groups left open the question of the
distinction between legitimate and illegitimate intervention.[31]

However, the work of the English Pluralists stimulated much
reflection upon the nature, virtues and vices of group life,
reflection which is central to the recognition or otherwise of
groups as the subject of rights. Accordingly it gave British and
American political thought a new issue with which to wrestle in
the search for a 'new state' after the First World War. The
impact of Pluralism in America is well illustrated in the writings
of the political philosopher, Miss M. P. Follett (1868–1933). A
philosopher, historian and practical reformer with strong
Idealist sympathies, Follett helped the Idealist counter-
offensive against Pluralism in Britain.[32] Follett's major book
entitled *The New State: Group Organisation the Solution of
Popular Government* appeared in 1918. Its thesis was that
future political organisation must steer a middle way between
the 'monism' of the absolute state and the 'diversity' of a
decentralized group life. Follett was enthusiastic about groups
which she regarded as the building-blocks of contemporary
society. She denounced the American distrust of the group in
the form of the 'corporation' and 'trust'; equally, however, she
lamented the 'apotheosization' of groups in Pluralist thought.[33]
The error of the Pluralists was to 'atomize' not only the state
but the groups which they attempted to elevate at the state's
expense. They were correct in thinking that only groups, not
individuals, may be the subject of rights ('. . . man's only rights

30 A. Vincent, *Theories of the State*, 212–13.

31 D. Nichols, *The Pluralist State*, 82.

32 On Follett's life and work see the introduction to the second edition of her
Dynamic Administration: The Collected Papers of Mary Parker Follett,
edited by E. M. Fox & L. Urwick (London, 1973). On Bosanquet's use of
Follett's work to combat the Pluralists, see his introduction to the third
edition of his *The Philosophical Theory of the State* (London, 1920),
xlv–lxii.

33 M. P. Follett, *The New State: Group Organisation the Solution of Popular
Government* (1918; Gloucester, Mass., 1965), 10.

are group-rights'); what they failed to see was that rights evolve through the unifying process of social co-operation, not through abstract declarations.

The ideal of 'unifying' was crucial for Follett; she contrasted it with the pretensions to 'unity' which Pluralists claimed to find in classical state theory. Her emphasis upon the 'unifying' power of groups when they engaged in public activities and conversation was founded on a cogent criticism of the Pluralists – that

> If it is possible for the members of a group to evolve a unified consciousness, a common idea, a collective will, for the many to become really one . . . this process can be carried on through group and group . . . .[34]

Hence, she could conclude her article reprinted here – entitled 'Community is a Process' – with a call to groups to 'carry on that activity by which alone [they] themselves have come into existence', instead of standing on their rights against it.

Follett recognized that groups had a propensity to become closed because constituted by the 'like-minded'; hence the menace of modern social life – 'the trade union man', the 'church man', and so on. However, she fervently believed that they could be opened up by exposure to wider influences through 'the practice of community', extending all the way to the League of Nations.[35] It was only fallacious Pluralist thinking which regarded groups as self-contained wholes existing in a state of confrontation with one another. The idea of 'conflicting obligations' which so concerned the Pluralists rested upon the reduction of the social process to a 'mechanical simplicity', impervious to its essential integrating activity in the creation of the self.

3. Group Rights and Politics in the Interwar Period.

Follett's conception of personal integration through group activity derived from some very selective utilization of Freudian psychology. She enlisted the latter's support for an optimistic view of society as entailing the creative harmonizing of individual and group, and group with group. Yet it was one

---

[34] M. P. Follett, *The New State: Group Organisation the Solution of Popular Government* (1918; Gloucester, Mass., 1965), 282–3.

[35] M. P. Follett, 'Community is a Process', *The Philosophical Review*, 28 (1919), 587.

thing to emphasize Freud's belief in the possibility of achieving the integration of an individual's 'wishes' in a 'working whole'.[36] It was another to overlook the fact that this idea was accompanied by a very pessimistic approach to society as entailing inherent frustration and unhappiness. The darker, more destructive and atavistic themes of Freud's writings, especially those relating to group psychology, also escaped Follett's notice. In Freud's view, groups – particularly nationalities – provided a vital channel for the satisfaction of mankind's aggressive instincts, the latter being directed towards outsiders and thereby providing the only effective basis of a group's internal cohesion.[37]

These two attitudes towards groups – optimistic and pessimistic – competed for intellectual favour in the interwar period. The kind of groups which then dominated the political imagination were national, ethnic, and racial groups. These groups had not been the primary concern of the English Pluralists who were mostly interested in voluntary, spontaneous associations for the pursuit of recreational, devotional, occupational, local and business ends. However, 'involuntary' or 'ascriptive' groups had preoccupied a previous generation – Victorian thinkers like John Stuart Mill, who stressed the right of all nations to self-determination as a paramount condition of political freedom.[38] (Significantly, however, Mill had little to say on the nature of groups more generally. As A. V. Dicey remarked of Mill, he devoted a few lines only to 'combined action' in *On Liberty*, stressing its importance to personal liberty but apparently oblivious to its dangers.)[39] Mill's view on the problem of nationality was opposed by Lord Acton, in particular, for whom diversity within national societies, rather than cultural uniformity, was the only safeguard of national and individual freedom, and general political stability.[40]

36 M. P. Follett, 'Community is a Process', *The Philosophical Review*, 28 (1919), 576.

37 S. Freud, 'Civilization and its Discontents', in *Civilization, Society and Religion* (Harmondsworth, 1985), 305.

38 J. S. Mill, *Considerations on Representative Government* (1861; London, 1972), chapter XVI.

39 A. V. Dicey, 'The Combination Laws as Illustrating the Relation between Law and Opinion in England during the Nineteenth Century', *Harvard Law Review*, XVII (1904), 526; J. S. Mill, *On Liberty* (1859; London, 1972), 75.

40 Lord Acton, 'Nationality' (1862), in J. N. Figgis (ed.), *The History of Freedom and other Essays* (London, 1907).

The aftermath of the First World War brought the question of minority rights within national and multinational cultures to the foreground of international debate. In the League of Nation's minority protection scheme – which recognized the separate political status of many European minority cultures in the interests of international peace and harmony – Mill's 'nationality principle' triumphed. However, the League's approach to nationalities was greatly undermined by the success of the Nazis in manipulating the German minorities in Czechoslovakia and Poland, encouraging them to make impossible demands upon their governments and thereby providing a pretext for aggression. Consequently, the United Nations dropped the commitment of its predecessor to promoting the 'rights' of 'subject' nationalities.[41] Yet even before international events turned world opinion against the notion of group rights in the form of minority rights, there were considerable doubts in some quarters about encouraging the self-consciousness of communities formed by blood, history and tradition, let alone granting 'rights' to them.

A leading sceptic in this respect was the British political theorist, Ernest Barker, who transferred all his wariness of the group rights being promoted by his Pluralist compatriots before 1914 to the new group politics of the interwar period. His fear that the assertion of the 'real personality' and 'inherent rights' of groups would lead to a declaration of their 'autonomy, and even, in the last resort, of the sovereignty, of their own particular group' formed the basis of his explanation of totalitarianism in the 1930s.[42] Totalitarianism, for Barker, was essentially bound up with the cult of the group in modern times, a theory he expounded in several places, including the chapter reprinted here from his *Reflections upon Government* (1942). It was a cult which he found rooted in German Romanticism (a 'great tide' which had risen to a *'fluctus decumanus* [floodgate] in this year of grace 1933')[43] and which more recently represented the revenge of new social elements upon the German and Italian states after the first steps towards

41 W. Kymlicka, 'Liberalism and the Politicization of Ethnicity', in *Canadian Journal of Law and Jurisprudence*, 4 (1991), 245-6; and *Liberalism, Community, and Culture* (Oxford, 1989), chapter 10.

42 E. Barker, *Natural Law and the Theory of Society*, lxxxi.

43 *Ibid.*, liii.

unification in the nineteenth century. That development – according to Barker – had been curtailed by the rise of democracy and socialism, forces which were viewed in the two countries concerned as dangerously divisive. In order to halt their advance, movements arose which appealed to some mystical idea of the 'Folk' whose salvation lay in mass submission of the populace to its will – incarnated in the will of a leader. This, for Barker, was the acme of the 'personalization' of groups which had been gathering strength since the nineteenth century and which swept away all traditional bonds and loyalties.

There were several versions of the totalitarian phenomenon, all rooted in the escape they offered to those who were 'weary of the burden of individual responsibility'.[44] First, the variety of German Fascism was premised upon the transformation of 'folk into race', a criterion of inclusion (and more importantly, exclusion) rooted in the purportedly indisputable factor of 'nature'. Second, the variety of Italian Fascism absorbed all social elements into the 'transcendent' group of the nation, whose 'spirit' was concentrated in the state and did not exist outside of the state. Third, Barker included Russian Communism in his analysis of the totalitarian groups of modern times, despite the Communist dismissal of the sort of Romanticism upon which fascism rested as 'idealistic' fantasy. In the Communist interpretation of 'Folk' as 'Class', however, Barker recognized deep parallels at an ideological level between Fascism and Communism and a common historical source. In its efforts towards total iron control, he argued, the Communist form of Romanticism

> . . . creates a romance of tractors and power-stations; it imposes it on the imagination, by the method of propaganda, as the aim of the hive is imposed by instinct on the motions of the bee. Next, and because machinery is not enough, the creative being of 'Folk into Class' produces its own proletarian art and literature, and its own total scheme of proletarian culture.[45]

The parallels between Fascism and Communism were especially clear in their positing of a group which stood above and

---

44 E. Barker, *Reflections on Government* (London, 1942), 148.

45 *Ibid.*, 163.

beyond its individual members, which not only invited but
demanded idolatry, and which was sharply differentiated from
other groups. This latter feature of the totalitarian group
formed the basis of Carl Schmitt's 'friend-foe' characterization
of modern politics in the 1920s, the significance of which
Barker was quick to grasp.

Against these modern totalitarian movements, Barker
elevated the liberal state as providing a legal framework
within which a wide spectrum of groups could be tolerated.
Here, he continued his earlier attempt to steer a middle way
between what the Pluralists regarded as the odious 'concession' theory of groups and – to him – the equally perilous
alternative of 'realism' which they put in its place. In his
view, groups may not owe their being to the state; but they
could not exist, or rather co-exist, in the absence of the
'operative criticism' provided by the state, mutually adjusting
each group purpose to a common legal scheme.[46] This meant
that groups possessed merely legal personality, while moral
personality and responsibility belonged solely to the
individuals who constituted them.[47] Barker's attitude illustrates the suspicion with which groups (let alone a notion of
their 'innate' civil rights) are held in the English Common
Law, a system on which the Roman theory of Corporations
has exercised much influence in this respect. Here Barker was
undoubtedly influenced by A. V. Dicey earlier in the
century.[48] In response to the controversy which enveloped
trade unions at the time of the Taff Vale decision, Dicey
perceptively pointed to the paradox raised by the right of
association: 'a right which from one point of view seems to be
a necessary extension of individual freedom is, from another
point of view, fatal to that individual freedom of which it
seems to be a mere extension.' A workman who refuses to
join a trade union may just as much endanger his employment prospects (now controlled by the union) as one who
takes part in a strike when union activity is outlawed.
Similarly, the strength of groups depends upon a significant
sacrifice of liberty on the part of its individual members.
How to maintain free association without giving unlimited

[46]   E. Barker, *Natural Law and the Theory of Society*, lxxix.

[47]   *Ibid.*, lxxv.

[48]   See J. Stapleton, *Englishness and the Study of Politics*, 63.

scope to groups and hence destroying personal freedom was, he believed, a most difficult balance for the law to strike.[49]

4. Groups and Postwar Political Thought.

Barker was confident that the dark shadow cast upon his era by the current enthusiasm for groups (and which underlay totalitarianism) was but a temporary blip in a three centuries old struggle. This was to develop 'the open order of a society of free individuals freely determining their common purposes, and the methods of their execution, in the forum of discussion'.[50]

This distrust of groups was sustained, although with less confidence, after the Second World War. Such unease was by no means widely prevalent – for example, groups, in the form of 'interest-groups' elicited much enthusiasm in the 1950s and '60s from 'behaviouralist' political scientists, anxious to celebrate the 'pluralist' nature of American democracy in particular.[51] However, these and other social groups and communities – even, and perhaps especially nations exhibiting an unusually high level of self-consciousness – continued to be regarded with deep disfavour, particularly along the liberal-conservative axis of political thought. Thinkers of this hue regarded groups as malign influences upon the politics of the period, which seemed dominated by the pursuit of 'social justice'. We here encounter a different type of concern in relation to groups. It concerned groups that were created not by the accidents of nature or historical tradition, or any kind of 'voluntary' association, but through what their protagonists deemed to be the injustices of the social and economic system. These groups hence sought to use the state as an instrument for their personal material betterment. Both Michael Oakeshott (1901–1990) and Friedrich Hayek (1899–1992) offered the same analysis and criticism of the many variants of modern 'welfarism' – that it was rooted in the atavistic mentality of a pre-modern communal order of society that humanity had failed to shake off. It was the resort of those who found the

---

[49] A. V. Dicey, 'The Combination Laws', 513–14.

[50] E. Barker, Reflections on Government, 167.

[51] On R. A. Dahl, leader of the post-war American Pluralists, see L. Tivey, 'Robert Dahl and American Pluralism', in L. Tivey & A. Wright (eds.), Political Thought since 1945: Philosophy, Science, Ideology (Aldershot, 1992).

unprecedented opportunities for exercising choice and asserting individuality offered by modernity a terrible burden.
Immersion in the comfort and security of a mass identity,
which would usurp the powers of government to raze to a
common level the capabilities and wealth of all members of
society, became the great escape of those to whom the Open
Society was an unmitigated disaster.

For Oakeshott, writing in 1961 in the article reprinted here,
the group mentality of modern times was of the nature of a
mass mentality. While it appealed to the 'morality of a defunct
communal order' – an order constituted by primary allegiances
to guilds, families, churches, and local communities – it was
essentially *sui generis* in attempting to destroy individuality.
Moreover, the morality of the 'anti-individual' was based upon
submission to leaders, who fed the resentment of their
followers while at the same time evincing every contempt for
them. Individual inadequacy on the part of the ruled was hence
joined by lust for power on the part of rulers to ensure that
government became 'not the referee of the collisions of
individuals, but the moral leader and managing director of "the
community" '.[52]

A similar diagnosis of the rejection of a 'free' market order in
favour of the 'mirage' of social justice was made by Hayek in an
article of 1976 which is reprinted here. This rejection entailed
an attempt to reverse the substitution of 'common rules of
conduct' for 'particular common ends as the foundations of
social order and peace' which is an ineluctable element of
modernity. The roots of this attempt lay in the sustained
transmission of the 'tribal' instincts of solidarity, which were
crucial to the survival of primitive hunter-gathering societies
but which were a hindrance to the present order of 'catallaxy'
rooted in anonymity and personal responsibility. The essence
of 'catallaxy' was a game of exchange, designed to elicit from
each player 'the highest worthwhile contribution to the
common pool from which each will win an uncertain share'.
But the full advantages of this system had been forestalled by
the falsification by governments of 'the market price signals,
whose appropriateness they had no means of judging . . . in the

---

[52]   M. Oakeshott, 'The Masses in Representative Democracy', in A. Hunold
(ed.), *Freedom and Serfdom: An Anthology of Western Thought*
(Dordrecht, 1961), 164.

hope of thereby giving benefits to groups claimed to be
particularly deserving . . . .'[53]

Clearly, both Oakeshott and Hayek regard groups as the
nemesis of an order constituted by self-determining individuals.
The resurgence of groups in modern society represented the
return to older, tribal ways by people for whom personal
responsibility was unwelcome and to whom the success of
others in this realm was a source of resentment. Hayek clearly
differs from Oakeshott in envisaging a free society as leading to
high productivity and hence prosperity. But for both thinkers,
modern morality belongs inextricably to the morality of free
individual choice, with which the clamouring for social justice
in the form of state benefits by alienated groups was deeply
incongruous.

5. Groups and Identity Politics in the Last Quarter of the Twentieth Century.

In the last two decades yet another type of group has become
the focus of political theory – not the voluntary, functional
organisation which was the principal concern of the English
Pluralists, nor the groups constituted by a dominant race,
nation and class which so unnerved Barker, nor the great
'masses' or majorities whose drives towards material and
cultural uniformity were castigated by Oakeshott and Hayek.
Rather, the kind of group which has been much discussed in
recent political thought has been first, national minorities who
have been forcibly integrated into a dominant culture and,
second, 'disadvantaged' groups who identify with the national
culture but whom society is held to have stigmatized or
'marginalized' or discriminated against on racial, cultural, or
sexual grounds. Much of recent liberal political theory, in
particular, has revolved around this issue of minority rights (as
has a new, 'radical' Pluralism which now provides the main
vehicle for egalitarianism with the substitution of 'identity' for
'class' politics.)[54]

There are two points of significance in this development.
First, it marks a turning away from the relative indifference

53 F. A. Hayek, 'The Atavism of Social Justice' (1976), in *New Studies in Philosophy, Politics, Economics and the History of Ideas* (London, 1978), 63.

54 A good guide to the 'new Pluralism' is A. Phillips, *Democracy and Difference* (Oxford, 1993).

towards groups that had dominated liberal political theory
after the Second World War. This is well illustrated in Van
Dyke's critique of Rawls' *A Theory of Justice* (1970), a work
whose starting-point in abstract individuals – and particularly
their speculative political preferences – marked a renaissance in
classical political philosophy. For Van Dyke, the two principles
of justice that would emerge from Rawls' 'original position' – in
which the 'veil of ignorance' concealed the group identities of
individuals – were impervious to the question of the status and
rights of 'endangered' or disadvantaged groups. In presuming
an homogenous society, devoid of cultural and other divisions,
Rawls' theory was, Van Dyke asserted, a travesty of reality.[55]
The second point of significance in the interest that has been
taken in minorities during the last two decades is that it is
substantially different from that which is found in the classic
liberal theory of John Stuart Mill. Principally, the difference
lies in the far wider conception of what constitutes a minority
in democratic theory today. In his *Considerations upon
Representative Government* Mill, like Rawls after him, presumed a country that was not divided by race, language and
nationality. Thus he conceived of a minority in terms of
intellectual dissidents, setting their 'instructed minds' against
the majority opinion founded upon mere sectional prejudice,
whether that of 'employees' or 'employers'. Such a minority (Mill
more often than not used this term in the singular) possessed no
automatic right to representation; rather their presence in
legislatures would result from the votes gained under a system of
proportional representation. This would be far more favourable
to minorities than a first-past-the-post system, giving them the
'moral power' afforded by their knowledge out of all proportion
to their numbers.[56] This conception of political minorities
prevailed, with only minor adaptation, throughout much of the
twentieth century. For example, Barker defined minorities in his
Reflections upon Government as a political opposition in
conventional Left/Right terms.[57]
In recent political thought, however, minorities have come to
be seen as many and varied. Furthermore, their identity is

[55]   V. Van Dyke, 'Justice as Fairness: For Groups?', in *American Political
Science Review*, 69 (1975), 607–614.
[56]   J. S. Mill, *Considerations on Representative Government*, 269.
[57]   E. Barker, *Reflections upon Government*, 203.

found in the 'oppression' they suffer at the hands of the majority, not – as in Mill's conception of minorities – the (educational) privileges they enjoy over it. Moreover, demands are increasingly heard for such minorities to be accorded special rights to representation in the form of reserved seats in legislatures or a guaranteed place in the process of consultation and decision-making, not simply in relation to the amount of votes they might muster under a favourable electoral system.

Such militant crusading on behalf of allegedly 'oppressed' groups is exemplified in an article by Iris Marion Young published in 1989. Young rejects the 'universalist' assumptions that have traditionally informed theories of citizenship – that the civic identity of citizens overrides their particular affiliations and that just laws can be formulated on this general basis. She advocates instead the establishment of 'mechanisms for the effective representation' of 'marginalized' groups. This recognition of the 'differentiated' nature of citizenship would lead to 'special rights' supplanting 'equal treatment' in public policy-making, thereby 'undermining oppression and disadvantage'. Young sees this requirement as temporary, lasting only so long as the oppressed group is unable to assert its needs and interests of its own accord in the mainstream culture. Nevertheless, her demands are large and contentious ones; they effectively treat often new, unstable and non-homogenous political groups such as the disabled, women, homosexuals, old people and immigrants in the same manner as long-established ones like churches and nations; her apparent criterion for the representation of an 'oppressed group' is the problematic one of 'self-identification'; her demand that public resources be made available to assist the organisation of 'oppressed groups' puts even the most liberal of sympathies to the test; and her grant of 'veto powers' to groups over issues which affect them 'directly' is tantamount to the dictatorship rather than the representation of minorities. Perhaps most questionable of all, Young protests against the view that the kind of group membership which concerns her is akin to something casual like membership of a voluntary society. The fact of the matter is, she asserts, that unlike the contractual relations which underpin such an association, membership of a 'group' 'defines one's very identity'.[58]

---

[58]   Iris Marion Young, 'Polity and Group Difference: A Critique of the Ideal of Universal Citizenship', *Ethics*, 99 (1989), 260.

Other modern theorists of 'group rights' – where the groups in question are not just voluntary associations but those into which one has been born or ascribed by dominant groups in society – have been anxious to limit the discussion to ethnic or cultural communities. The demand for group rights hence becomes a means of protecting such communities from the decisions of the wider, majority culture. Will Kymlicka has defended this form of group rights, not against but within traditional liberal ideas.[59] He has done so in response to the charge of Communitarian political theorists that liberalism is a bankrupt creed because it fails to take account of the individual's 'embodiedness' in membership of particular cultures. He argues that the recognition of group rights is not in conflict with individual liberty and autonomy but constitutes a vital means to the fulfilment of the latter. In a joint article with Wayne Norman, Kymlicka has pointed out that Young's 'oppressed groups' amount to around eighty per cent of the American population – a figure which makes a nonsense of the idea of 'special' rights.[60] But Kymlicka himself does not make a cogent case for distinguishing the historic cultural communities within majority cultures which he wishes to support from Young's extended list of ascribed and oppressed groups. In what sense do those minority communities, and those communities only, pursue their projects in 'unequal circumstances' – as opposed to 'assorted racial, religious, class, or gender groups'?[61]

Moreover, as Stephen Macedo persuasively argues in his article included here, it is not at all clear – contrary to both Young and Kymlicka – that voluntary associations can be written off as regards groups that form what Communitarians like to call 'constitutive' (or integral) features of a person's identity.[62] (It is certainly not clear why self-identity always is, or should be, a function of 'oppression', or even whether it is beneficial when it does take this form.) Macedo does not return to the argument of the English Pluralists, that voluntary societies must thus be accorded 'inherent rights'. But, like

59   See his *Liberalism, Community, and Culture*.

60   W. Kymlicka & W. Norman, 'Return of the Citizen: A Survey of Recent Work on Citizenship Theory', in *Ethics*, 104 (1994), 373-4, f26.

61   W. Kymlicka, *Liberalism, Community, and Culture*, 241.

62   S. Macedo, 'Capitalism, Citizenship and Community', *Social Philosophy and Policy*, 6 (1988), 128.

them, he sees voluntary groups as the foundation of a healthy, vigorous, liberal polity, one in which the 'self-confidence', autonomy and self-government of citizens can be maximized. Macedo's revival of the Tocquevillian ideal of democracy sets at arm's length the vogue for 'community' and 'integration' in both Communitarianism and the work of some of its liberal critics alike. Defending capitalism as the handmaiden of local, voluntary effort, he sees economic energy and the drive for self-direction in social affairs as mutually reinforcing, both eliciting but at the same time ennobling self-interest. Once the springs of voluntary effort are dried up by the state – as is threatened by the Communitarian attempt to create a more cohesive public culture than liberal capitalism allegedly makes possible – the result, as Tocqueville correctly foresaw, is widespread slavish uniformity and passive acquiescence in society.

We can discern significant differences in Macedo's response to the problem of 'group closure' which is characteristic of the twentieth-century argument for group rights, and that of Mary Follett earlier in the century. Both applaud the rich diversity of ends which groups – voluntary groups, that is – make possible in modern life. However, whereas Follett saw groups as forming an interlocking system of co-operative social purpose from the smallest neighbourhood association to the League of Nations, Macedo is anxious to stress the competing, independent nature of such societies, and to endorse them as such. In his view the attempt to engage people's interest in large impersonal concerns will merely thwart their need and capacity for 'personal accomplishment'. It is not that voluntary associations are 'private' – confined to the achievement of some limited objective of a limited number of individuals. On the contrary, these purposes are eminently 'public' – the spontaneous endeavours of individuals to pursue collectively determined ends.

Macedo's refusal to see voluntary societies as the concentric circles of some larger and homogenous social whole – despite insisting upon their public rather than private nature – also distances him from Michael Walzer. For Walzer, these 'particularized' societies provide essential vehicles for combating increasing public disorder reflected in a range of social problems – divorce, homelessness, violence and so on. Democratized and rejuvenated, voluntary associations are vehicles for the rebirth of 'civility' in an 'independent and active' rather than the 'subordinate' form which currently prevails. But the purpose of the revitalizing of 'civil society' here is the enhancement of 'connectedness and responsibility [for one another]'.[63] Consequently, Walzer is anxious to emphasize the *duties* which the state owes towards the various associations which constitute civil society, rather than the rights which they hold against it.[64] This is because he rejects the idea that civil society can provide an *alternative* to identification with, and reliance upon the state, whether in Eastern Europe or the West. Walzer's use of groups to promote a (liberalized) Communitarian vision is well illustrated in his view – expressed in a rather unfortunate phrase – that they will sometimes stand in need of 'political correction'. Such a provision leaves the autonomy of groups in his scheme of things open to question. This is particularly the case in the light of his revision of the liberal theory of the state which supported earlier defences of a plural 'civil society' – that it merely furnishes a legal framework in which diverse social purposes may be pursued. For Walzer this provides too weak a basis of social cohesion, the function of the state being instead 'to give a particular shape to the common life'.[65] Finally, the larger, more ambitious project to which Walzer has linked his support for the revival of voluntary social ties is manifested in his simultaneous call for a redistribution of wealth and the socialization of the economy.[66]

The politicization of voluntary organisations in the style envisaged by Walzer takes us in the opposite direction from English Pluralism, in which the activities of such groups were, broadly speaking, divorced from the political sphere and the fulfilment of any wider social end than their own. As mentioned above, this ideal is still embraced today but mostly on behalf of minority cultures rooted in ethnicity. Whether or not they are distinguishable from voluntary societies or other *in*voluntary societies determined by their alleged 'oppressed' status, their case for special political recognition has been much

---

63 M. Walzer, 'The Civil Society Argument', in C. Mouffe (ed.), *Dimensions of Radical Democracy: Pluralism, Citizenship, Community* (London, 1992), 107.

64 *Ibid.*, 104.

65 *Ibid.*, 105.

66 *Ibid.*, 105.

pressed (and resisted) recently. For example, Kymlicka's defence of such recognition has been forcefully rejected by Chandran Kukathas in his article reprinted here. Once again, the question of group rights is underpinned by debate concerning the nature of the group and an individual's relation to it. Thus, Kukathas denies that groups are part of any 'natural order', being the products solely of history, tradition and mutable political arrangements. Devoid of any fixed, inherent, interests themselves, their claims cannot be accorded the status of entrenched rights. Often, these claims represent the good of the minority culture as seen by its leaders, who may have particular interests of their own at odds with a minority or even the majority within their own community. Kukathas maintains that the problem of an elite-mass divergence within minorities can be overcome by regarding them simply as voluntary societies. The only provision which a liberal society need make with regard to minorities – so conceived – is to insist on the right of all members to leave, should they no longer find the culture to their needs or taste. This requirement entails no adjustment to liberal theory, while at the same time recognizing the valuable role which cultural communities make to personal fulfilment and self-determination. Once this provision has been made, a liberal society can safely allow a group to manage its own affairs as it sees fit, following a policy of non-interference.

It is because Kukathas recognizes the tyranny which groups may practice over their members that he insists upon a right of individuals to leave and also refuses to accord groups the kind of special protection implicit in the idea of collective rights. This is a valuable corrective to those, like Kymlicka, who argue that a consistent liberalism would extend rights to integrity from individuals to groups, groups providing the structures within which individuals make vital choices about their lives. Kukathas' objection to the idea of group rights is also built upon the valid point that such a recognition would have to apply to all groups, regardless of their size and influence. This would give small groups inordinate power, and begs the question of when a group should be singled out for special political treatment. Attempts to lay down precise criteria in this regard seem to favour some at the expense of others in a quite arbitrary manner. For example, in the article reprinted here, Vernon Van Dyke's 'eight standards' for identifying groups entitled to special political rights are framed in such a way as to exclude social classes. But it is by no means obvious that one of his requirements, at least, would do so – that the group must be 'significant in the lives of its members' and be based upon more than one characteristic (be it class, race, religion, language or whatever).[67] Traditional working-class communities provide classic examples of strong group cohesion from which the self-identity and pride of their members cannot be detached.

Kymlicka's response to this problem in his article reprinted here is to reserve rights for minority nations who have lost their autonomy through colonization. He distinguishes such groups from immigrant communities who have voluntarily settled on foreign soil. He stresses the validity of the claim to 'national rights' of colonized groups like the American Indians while denying that of immigrant communities who pursue assimilation on equal terms with the majority culture. Colonized nations within mainstream cultures can lay claim to being a 'distinct' as well as a subdued people; therefore they are entitled to autonomous institutions, even secession, if they think this is necessary to preserve their identity.

Yet even granting this distinction, the problem remains of heterogeneity within national minorities themselves. Would there not be minorities within the minority whose interests would be ill-served by secession from the dominant culture? Even if guarantees of protection for its own minorities were extended at the time of independence, this would be of little value once the minority had become a sovereign community. The recent history of independence movements does not inspire much confidence in this regard. For example, the majority 'Shona' tribe in Zimbabwe have shown no compunction in suppressing the minority 'Ndebele'. Communal violence in India after independence offers a similar warning.

Kukathas convincingly argues that pragmatic arrangements in political systems are sufficient to ensure that 'significant' minorities are well represented, thus avoiding disaffection and eventually civil war.[68] But despite his qualification that groups must not subject their members to cruelty and degradation, Kukathas, in turn, offers no consistent principle governing

67   Vernon Van Dyke, 'Collective Entities and Moral Rights: Problems in Liberal-Democratic Thought', in *The Journal of Politics*, 44 (1982), 32–3.

68   C. Kukathas, 'Are there any Cultural Rights?', *Political Theory*, 20 (1992), 131.

relations between them and the wider community. For example, he deems the arranged marriages practised by Indian immigrant communities as non-enforceable in societies based upon free marriage. However, in his view, the gypsy preference for keeping children away from formal schooling, contrary to national legislation requiring children to be so educated, is quite acceptable and does not deprive a child of the basis of 'choice' – whether to leave or remain – in later life. His different attitudes towards minority traditions in these two cases again raises the problem of arbitrariness in allowing and disallowing minority claims.

One may also question whether a right to leave a group is sufficient to ensure individual autonomy and liberty. As Kymlicka rightly maintains in his reply, Kukathas exaggerates the ease of leaving a community which has limited ties with the outside world (and upon which one may be deeply dependent in a material sense).[69]

Yet it does not follow that the idea of 'group rights' helps us to solve these problems. It certainly does not follow – pace Kymlicka – that this is not only compatible with, but a requirement of liberalism.[70] While he correctly points to a certain strand within liberalism which has indeed endorsed the right of nations to self-determination and has endorsed the nation-state as the primary context of individual liberty, this has in no way outweighed an alternative strand in which groups of all kinds are viewed with considerable detachment. Liberals have rarely encouraged the kind of 'thick' identity of individuals with groups which underpins Kymlicka's defence of the latter's 'rights'. More often than not within the liberal tradition, it is free political institutions, above all else, that are seen as the condition of our ability to – in Kymlicka's words – 'autonomously choose which features of [our] cultural tradition are most worth developing, and which are without

69 W. Kymlicka, 'The Rights of Minority Cultures: Reply to Kukathas', *Political Theory*, 20 (1992), 143. Kukathas's rejoinder fails to meet this criticism, emphasizing, as it does, the extreme case of someone who is ignorant of possibilities outside of a closed, repressive minority. In this case there is indeed no infringement of rights. But what of the case of one who lives in no such ignorance yet still remains loyal, albeit with a strong urge to reform the practices of the minority? The absence of 'liberal' rights within the minority is then a severe deprivation. C. Kukathas, 'Cultural Rights Again', *Political Theory*, 20, 4 (1992), 677-8.

70 W. Kymlicka, 'The Rights of Minority Cultures', 142.

value'.[71] His concern that minorities be accorded a special status in order to 'equalize the circumstances'[72] between them and the larger community, but regardless of respect for individual rights within the minority community makes a mockery of liberalism. If, on the other hand, we insist that the liberal character of the wider society be accepted as a condition of group rights – a view to which Kymlicka himself is drawn at times[73] – then the communal autonomy implied by those rights is denied. The most effective means to achieving this end of group 'parity', while ensuring individual rights, is a commitment to tolerance and a willingness to allow groups to practise their own religion, speak their own language, organise their own education and so forth. Such a policy is by no means derisory given the numerous instances of modern states in which minorities have been persecuted and their cultural life destroyed. Such an approach suggests that in liberalism – contrary to Kymlicka's belief – group affiliations are secondary and private, the most politically significant relation being that of common citizenship.

6. Conclusion.

The belief in group rights rests upon shaky philosophical as well as political foundations. Central to their defence are certain questionable normative assumptions about the importance of the individual's identification with groups and active participation in the latter. Frequently, too, collective rights are inferred from a problematic assertion of the 'moral' nature of groups. In addition, the view that recognition of such rights will increase the stability of the wider society is overly optimistic. Finally, the idea that one can achieve a measure of detachment from one's associational ties without the liberalizing air of a larger community is unsound. Twentieth-century assertions of group rights have generated much useful discussion of the problem of achieving social and political cohesion amid the immense diversity of contemporary societies. However, this problem is merely suppressed, not resolved, by conceding groups the right to autonomous

---

71   W. Kymlicka, 'Liberalism and the Politization of Ethnicity', 256.

72   W. Kymlicka, 'Rights of Minority Cultures', 142.

73   W. Kukathas, 'Cultural Rights Again', 679.

existence and encouraging the immersion of individuals in collective life.

The best framework in which groups of all kinds may flourish is that of liberal constitutionalism. It allows for breadth as well as depth in group attachments, an ideal which its adherents positively embrace rather than constituting a 'problem' to which a (liberal) political solution must be found.[74] It also provides a strong, central focus of loyalty. As Barker noted of countries which enjoy an 'old and established unity' and in which liberal constitutionalism can typically be found, their political systems are sufficiently flexible to adapt in both structure and activity to the flux of group expectations, without allowing any one group to exercise dominance. This order was upheld by Lord Acton in the nineteenth century and his support has been maintained by Hayek, Barker, and Macedo in our own. Barker, at least, recognized the disturbing consequences of the intensification of group consciousness in the interwar period. Countries which had yielded to totalitarianism had been 'vexed by a long process of historical disintegration, from which they ha[d] only recently emerged, and of which they fear[ed] the recurrence . . .'. The liberal state is threatened with similar instability by the doctrine of group rights. Their proponents invariably favour a particular kind of group – national or ethnic, 'oppressed', and so on – without providing adequate assurance against a spiralling of demands on the part of those to whom group rights are denied. The outcome of this process would be similar to that which occurred in the Soviet Union, Italy and Germany between the wars: the suppression of the liberal ideal of 'identity in difference' by an identity 'which transcends all difference and has to wage a constant war with difference'.[75]

Julia Stapleton
University of Durham
1995

[74] The last attitude is held by Kukathas, 'Cultural Rights Again', 680.
[75] E. Barker, *Reflections on Government*, 143.

Further Reading

English Political Pluralism.

D. Nicholls, *The Pluralist State: The Political Ideas of J. N. Figgis and his Contemporaries* (London, 1994).
J. W. Burrow, *Whigs and Liberals: Continuity and Change in English Political Thought* (Oxford, 1988), chapter 6.
J. Stapleton, *Englishness and the Study of Politics: the Social and Political Thought of Ernest Barker* (Cambridge, 1994), chapter 3.
A. Vincent, *Theories of the State* (Oxford, 1987), chapter 6.
P. Q. Hirst, *The Pluralist Theory of the State: Selected Writings of G. D. H. Cole, J. N. Figgis, and H. J. Laski* (London, 1989).

Oakeshott and Hayek.

J. Birner & R. van Zijp (editors), *Hayek, Co-ordination and Evolution: His Legacy in Philosophy, Politics, Economics and the History of Ideas* (London, 1994).
M. Oakeshott, 'The Political Theory of Collectivism', in *Morality and Politics in Modern Europe: The Harvard Lectures* (1958), edited by S. R. Letwin (New Haven, 1993).
R. Grant, *Oakeshott* (London, 1990).

Group Rights in Recent Political Theory.

A. Phillips, *Democracy and Difference* (Oxford, 1993).
J. Baker, *Groups Rights* (Toronto, 1994).
W. Kymlicka (editor), *The Rights of Minority Cultures* (OUP, forthcoming).
W. Kymlicka, *Multicultural Citizenship: A Liberal Theory of Minority Rights* (OUP, forthcoming).

TRUST AND CORPORATION[1]

Not very long ago, in the pages of this Review, Dr Redlich, whose book on English Local Government we in England are admiring, did me the honour of referring to some words that I had written concerning our English Corporations and our English Trusts.[2] I have obtained permission to say with his assistance a few more words upon the same matter, in the hope that I may thereby invite attention to a part of our English legal history which, so far as my knowledge goes, has not attracted all the notice that it deserves.

Perhaps I need hardly say that we on this side of the sea are profoundly grateful to those foreign explorers who have been at pains to investigate our insular arrangements. Looking at us from the outside, it has been possible for them to teach us much about ourselves. Still we cannot but know that it is not merely for the sake of England that English law, both ancient and modern, has been examined. Is it not true that England has played a conspicuous, if a passive, part in that development of historical jurisprudence which was one of the most remarkable scientific achievements of the nineteenth century? Over and over again it has happened that our island has been able to supply just that piece of evidence, just that link in the chain of proof, which the Germanist wanted but could not find at home. Should I go too far if I said that no Germanistic theory is beyond dispute until it has been tested upon our English material?

Now I know of nothing English that is likely to be more instructive to students of legal history, and in particular to those who are concerned with Germanic law, than that *Rechtsinstitut* [legal institution] of ours which Dr Redlich described in the following well chosen words : "das Rechtsinstitut des Trust, das ursprünglich für gewisse Bedürfnisse des englischen Grundeigenthumsrechtes enstanden, nach und nach

[1] *Grünhut's Zeitschrift für das Privat- und Öffentliche Recht*, Bd. xxxii.

[2] *Ibid.*, Bd. xxx, S. 167.

zu einem allgemeinen Rechtsinstitute ausgebildet worden ist und auf allen Gebieten des Rechtslebens praktische Bedeutung und eine ausserordentlich verfeinerte juristische Ausbildung erlangt hat." [The legal institution of Trust, that originally for certain needs of English land law existed, little by little into a general legal institution was built, and upon all fields of legal life practical significance and an extraordinarily sophisticated judicial apparatus has achieved.]

It is a big affair our Trust. This must be evident to anyone who knows – and who does not know? – that out in America the mightiest trading corporations that the world has ever seen are known by the name of "Trusts." And this is only the Trust's last exploit. Dr Redlich is right when he speaks of it as an "allgemeine Rechtsinstitut." It has all the generality, all the elasticity of Contract. Anyone who wishes to know England, even though he has no care for the detail of Private Law, should know a little of our Trust.

We may imagine an English lawyer who was unfamiliar with the outlines of foreign law taking up the new Civil Code of Germany. "This," he would say, "seems a very admirable piece of work, worthy in every way of the high reputation of German jurists. But surely it is not a complete statement of German private law. Surely there is a large gap in it. I have looked for the Trust, but I cannot find it; and to omit the Trust is, I should have thought, almost as bad as to omit Contract." And then he would look at his book-shelves and would see stout volumes entitled "Law of Trusts," and he would open his "Reports" and would see trust everywhere, and he would remember how he was a trustee and how almost every man that he knew was a trustee.

Is it too bold of me to guess the sort of answer that he would receive from some German friend who had not studied England? "Well, before you blame us, you might tell us what sort of thing is this wonderful Trust of yours.["]

[I]n the second half of the fourteenth century we see a new Court struggling for existence. It is that Court of Chancery whose name is to be inseparably connected with the Trust. The old idea that when ordinary justice fails, there is a reserve of extraordinary justice which the king can exercise is bearing new fruit. In civil (*privatrechtliche*) causes men make their way to the king's Chancellor begging him in piteous terms to intervene "for the love of God and in the way of charity." It is not of any defect in the material law that they complain; but somehow or another they cannot get justice. They are poor and helpless; their adversaries are rich and powerful. Sheriffs are partial; jurors are corrupt. But, whatever may be the case with penal justice, it is by no means clear that in civil suits there can be any room for a formless, extraordinary jurisdiction. Complaints against interference with the ordinary course of law were becoming loud, when something was found for the Chancellor to do, and something that he could do with general approval. I think it might be said that if the Court of Chancery saved the Trust, the Trust saved the Court of Chancery.

And now we come to the origin of the Trust. The Englishman cannot leave his land by will. In the case of land every germ of testamentary power has been ruthlessly stamped out in the twelfth century. But the Englishman would like to leave his land by will. He would like to provide for the weal of his sinful soul, and he would like to provide for his daughters and younger sons. That is the root of the matter.[3] But further, it is to be observed that the law is hard upon him at the hour of death, more especially if he is one of the great. If he leaves an heir of full age, there is a *relevium* [feudal succession duty] to be paid to the lord. If he leaves an heir under age, the lord may take the profits of the land, perhaps for twenty years, and may sell the marriage of the heir. And then if there is no heir, the land falls back ("escheats") to the lord for good and all.

Once more recourse is had to the *Treuhänder* [Trustee]. The landowner conveys his land to some friends. They are to hold it "to his use (*a son oes*)." They will let him enjoy it while he lives, and he can tell them what they are to do with it after his death.

I say that he conveys his land, not to a friend, but to some friends. This is a point of some importance. If there were a single owner, a single *feoffatus*, he might die, and then the lord would claim the ordinary rights of a lord; *relevium, custodia haeredis, maritagium haeredis, escaeta*, all would follow as a matter of course. But here the Germanic *Gesammthandschaft* [collective ownership] comes to our help. Enfeoff five or perhaps ten friends *zu gesammter Hand* ("as joint tenants"). When one of them dies there is no inheritance; there is merely accrescence. The lord can claim nothing. If the number of the *feoffati* is running low, then indeed it will be prudent to

---

[3] I do not wish to deny that there were other causes for trusts; but comparatively they were of little importance.

introduce some new ones, and this can be done by some transferring and retransferring. But, if a little care be taken about this matter, the lord's chance of getting anything is very small.

Here is a principle that has served us well in the past and is serving us well in the present. The *"Gesammthandprincip"* [collective ownership principle] enables us to erect (if I may so speak) a wall of trustees which will not be always in need of repair. Some of those "charitable" trusts of which I am to speak hereafter will start with numerous trustees, and many years may pass away before any new documents are necessary. Two may die, three may die; but there is no inheritance; there is merely accrescence; what was owned by ten men, is now owned by eight or by seven; that is all[4] . . .

It is always interesting, if we can, to detect the point at which a new institute or new concept enters the field of law. Hitherto the early history of our "feoffments to uses" has been but too little explored: I fear that the credit of thoroughly exploring it is reserved for some French or German scholar. However, there can be little doubt that the new practice first makes its appearance in the highest and noblest circles of society. . . .

Apparently the new fashion spread with great rapidity. We have not in print so many collections of wills as we ought to have; but in such as have been published the mention of land held to the testator's "use" begins to appear somewhat suddenly in the last years of the fourteenth century and thenceforward it is common. We are obliged to suppose that the practice had existed for some time before it found legal protection. But that time seems to have been short. Between 1396 and 1403 the Chancellor's intervention had been demanded.[5]

When we consider where the king's interest lay, it is somewhat surprising that the important step should be taken by his first minister, the Chancellor. It seems very possible, however, that the step was taken without any calculation of loss and gain.[6] We may suppose a scandalous case. Certain

---

4   Our "joint ownership" is not a very strong form of Gesammthadschaft. One of several "joint owners" has a share that he can alienate *inter vivos*; but he has nothing to give by testament.

5   *Select Cases in Chancery* (Selden Society), p. 69.

6   It may have been of decisive importance that at some critical moment the King himself wanted to leave some land by will. Edward III had tried ineffectually to do this. In 1417 Kind Henry V had a great mass of land in

persons have been guilty of a flagrant act of dishonesty, condemned by all decent people. Here is an opportunity for the intervention of a Court which has been taught that it is not to intervene where the old Courts of Common Law offer a remedy. And as with politics, so with jurisprudence. I doubt whether in the first instance our Chancellor troubled his head about the "juristic nature" of the new *Rechtsinstitut* [legal institution] or asked himself whether the new chapter of English law that he was beginning to write would fall under the title *Sachenrecht* or under the title *Obligationenrecht* [law of property]. In some scandalous case he compelled the trustees to do what honesty required. Men often act first and think afterwards. . . .

The *Billigkeitsrecht* [Equity] of the new Court moved slowly forward from precedent to precedent: but always towards one goal: namely, the strengthening at every point of the right of the destinatory. . . .

To complete the picture we must add that a very high degree not only of honesty but of diligence has been required of trustees. In common opinion it has been too high, and of late our legislature, without definitely lowering it, has given the courts a discretionary power of dealing mercifully with honest men who have made mistakes or acted unwisely. The honest man brought to ruin by the commission of "a technical breach of trust," brought to ruin at the suit of his friend's children, has in the past been only too common a figure in English life. On the other hand, it was not until lately that the dishonest trustee who misappropriated money or other movables could be treated as a criminal. Naturally there was a difficulty here, for "at law" the trustee was owner, and a man cannot be guilty of stealing what he both owns and possesses. But for half a century we have known the criminal breach of trust, and, though we do not call it theft, it can be severely punished.

Altogether it is certainly not of inadequate protection that a foreign jurist would speak if he examined the position of our destinatory. Rather I should suppose that he would say that this lucky being, the spoilt child of English jurisprudence, has been favoured at the expense of principles and distinctions that ought to have been held sacred. At any rate, those who would understand how our "unincorporate bodies" have lived and

the hands of feoffees (including four bishops, a duke and three earls) and made a will in favour of his brothers. See Nichols, *Royal Wills*, 236.

flourished behind a hedge of trustees should understand that the right of the destinatory, though we must not call it a true *dominium rei* [ownership of a thing], is something far better than the mere benefit of a promise. . . .

Soon the Trust became very busy. For a while its chief employment was "the family settlement." Of "the family settlement" I must say no word, except this, that the trust thus entered the service of a wealthy and powerful class: the class of great landowners who could command the best legal advice and the highest technical skill. Whether we like the result or not, we must confess that skill of a very high order was applied to the construction of these "settlements" of great landed estates. Everything that foresight could do was done to define the duties of the trustees. Sometimes they would be, as in the early cases, the mere depositaries of a nude *dominium*, bound only to keep it until it was asked for. At other times they would have many and complex duties to perform and wide discretionary powers. And then, if I may so speak, the "settlement" descended from above: descended from the landed aristocracy to the rising monied class, until at last it was quite uncommon for any man or woman of any considerable wealth to marry without a "marriage settlement." Trusts of money or of invested funds became as usual as trusts of land. It may be worthy of notice that this was, at least in part, the effect of an extreme degree of testamentary freedom. Our law had got rid of the *Pflichttheil* [legal portion] altogether, and trusts in favour of the children of the projected marriage were a sort of substitute for it. However, in this region, what we have here to notice is that the trust became one of the commonest institutes of English law. Almost every well-to-do man was a trustee; and though the usual trusts might fall under a few great headings, still all the details (which had to be punctually observed) were to be found in lengthy documents; and a large liberty of constructing unusual trusts was both conceded in law and exercised in fact. To classify trusts is like classifying contracts.

I am well aware that all this has its dark side, and I do not claim admiration for it. But it should not escape us that a very wide field was secured for what I may call social experimentation. Let me give one example. In 1882 a revolutionary change was made in our *eheliches Güterrecht* [matrimonial law]. But this was no leap in the dark. It had been preceded by a prolonged course of experimentation. Our law about this matter had become osseous at an early time, and, especially as regards *Fahrnis* [chattels] was extremely unfavourable to the wife. There was no *Gemeinschaft* [community of goods]. The bride's movables became the husband's; if the wife acquired, she acquired for her husband. Now *eheliches Güterrecht* [matrimonial law], when once it has taken a definite shape, will not easily be altered. Legislators are not easily persuaded to touch so vital a point, and we cannot readily conceive that large changes can be gradually made by the practice of the courts. You cannot transfer ownership from the husband to the wife by slow degrees.

But here the Trust comes to our help. We are not now talking of ownership strictly so called. Some trustees are to be owners. We are only going to speak of their duties. What is to prevent us, if we use words enough, from binding them to pay the income of a fund into the very hands of the wife and to take her written receipt for it? But the wedge was in, and it could be driven home. It was a long process; but one successful experiment followed another. At length the time came when four well-tested words ("for her separate use") would give a married woman a *Vermögen* [means] of which she was the complete mistress "in equity"; and if there was no other trustee appointed, her husband had to be trustee. Then, rightly or wrongly we came to the conclusion that all this experimentation had led to satisfactory results. Our law of husband and wife was revolutionized. But great as was the change, it was in fact little more than the extension to all marriages of rules which had long been applied to the marriages of the well-to-do.

But the liberty of action and experimentation that has been secured to us by the Trust is best seen in the freedom with which from a remote time until the present day *Anstalten* [institutions] and *Stiftungen* [charitable foundations/institutions] of all sorts and kinds had been created by Englishmen.

. . .

I believe that the English term which most closely corresponds to the *Anstalt* or the *Stiftung* of German legal literature is "a charity." It is very possible that our concept of "a charity" would not cover every *Anstalt* or *Stiftung* that is known to German lawyers: but it is and from a remote time has been enormously wide. For example, one of our courts had lately to decide that the mere encouragement of sport is not "charity." The annual giving of a prize to be competed for in a yacht-race is not a "charitable" purpose. On the other hand, "the total suppression of vivisection" is a charitable purpose, though it implies the repeal of an Act of Parliament, and though the judge who decides this question may be fully persuaded that this so-called "charity" will do much more harm than good. English judges have carefully refrained from any exact definition of a "charity"; but perhaps we may say that any *Zweck* [purpose] which any reasonable person could regard as directly beneficial to the public or to some large and indefinite class of men is a "charitable" purpose. Some exception should be made of trusts which would fly in the face of morality or religion; but judges who were themselves stout adherents of the State Church have had to uphold as "charitable," trusts which involved the maintenance of Catholicism, Presbyterianism, Judaism.

To the enforcement of charitable trusts we came in a very natural way and at an early date. A trust for persons shades off, we might say, into a trust for a *Zweck* [purpose]. We are not, it will be remembered, speaking of true ownership. Ownership supposes an owner. We cannot put ownership into an indefinite mass of men; and, according to our English ideas, we cannot put ownership into a *Zweck* [purpose]. I should say that there are vast masses of *Zweckvermögen* [special purpose funds] in England, but the owner is always man or corporation. As regards the trust, however, transitions are easy. You may start with a trust for the education of my son and for his education in a particular manner. It is easy to pass from this by slow degrees to the education of the boys of the neighbourhood, though in the process of transition the definite destinatory may disappear and leave only a *Zweck* [purpose] behind him.[7]

At any rate, in 1601 there was already a vast mass of *Zweckvermögen* [special purpose funds] in the country; a very large number of *unselbstständige Stiftungen* [non-independent foundation] had come into existence. A famous *Gesetz* [statute] of that year became the basis of our law of Charitable Trusts, and their creation was directly encouraged. There being no problem about personality to be solved, the courts for a long while showed every favour to the authors of "charitable" trusts.

7   In the oldest cases the Court of Chancery seems to enforce the "charitable" trust upon the complaint of anyone who is interested, without requiring the presence of any representative of the State.

In particular, it was settled that where there was a "charitable" *Zweck* [purpose] there was to be no trouble about "perpetuity." The exact import of this remark could not be explained in two or three words. But, as might be supposed, even the Englishman, when he is making a trust of the ordinary private kind, finds that the law sets some limits to his power of bestowing benefits upon a long series of unborn destinatories; and these limits are formulated in what we know as "the rule against perpetuities." Well, it was settled that where there is "charity," there can be no trouble about "perpetuity[8]."

It will occur to my readers that it must have been necessary for English lawyers to make or to find some juristic person in whom the benefit of the "charitable" trust would inhere and who would be the destinatory. But that is not true. It will be understood that in external litigation - *e.g.* if there were an adverse claim to a piece of land held by the trustees - the interests of the trust would be fully represented by the trustees. Then if it were necessary to take proceedings against the trustees to compel them to observe the trust, the *Reichsanwalt* (Attorney-General) would appear. We find it said long ago that it is for the king "ut parens patriae" to intervene for this purpose. But we have stopped far short of any theory which would make the State into the true destinatory (*cestui que trust*) of all charitable trusts. Catholics, Wesleyans, Jews would certainly be surprised if they were told that their cathedrals, chapels, synagogues were in any sense *Staatsvermögen* [state property]. We are not good at making juristic theories, but of the various concepts that seem to be offered to us by German books, it seems to me that *Zweckvermögen* [special purpose funds] is that which most nearly corresponds to our way of thinking about our "charities."

That great abuses took place in this matter of charitable trusts is undeniable. Slowly we were convinced by sad experience that in the way of supervision something more was necessary than the mere administration of the law (technically of "equity") at the instance of a *Staatsanwalt* [public prosecutor] who was casually set in motion by some person who happened to see that the trustees were not doing their duty. Since 1853 such supervision has been supplied by a central

[8]   An Englishman might say that § 2109 of the B.G.B. contains the German "rule against perpetuities" and that it is considerably more severe than is the English.

Behörde [public authority] (the Charity Commissioners); but it is much rather supervision than control, and, so far from any check being placed on the creation of new *Stiftungen* [foundations/charitable institutions], we in 1891 repealed a law which since 1736 had prevented men from giving land to "charity" by testament[9] . . .

And here it should be observed that many reformers of our "charities" have deliberately preferred that "charitable trusts" should be confided, not to corporations, but to "natural persons." It is said – and appeal is made to long experience – that men are more conscientious when they are doing acts in their own names than when they are using the name of a corporation. In consequence of this prevailing opinion, all sorts of expedients have been devised by Parliament for simplifying and cheapening those transitions of *Eigenthum* [property] which are inevitable where mortal men are the *Stützpunkt* [fulcrum] of an *unselbstständige Stiftung* [non-independent foundation]. Some of these would shock a theorist. In the case of certain places of worship, we may see the *dominium* [ownership] taken out of one set of men and put into another set of men by the mere vote of an assembly – an unincorporated congregation of Non-conformists[10] Of course no rules of merely private law can explain this; but that does not trouble us.

This brings us to a point at which the Trust performed a signal service. All that we English people mean by "religious liberty" has been intimately connected with the making of trusts. When the time for a little toleration had come, there was the Trust ready to provide all that was needed by the barely tolerated sects. All that they had to ask from the State was that the open preaching of their doctrines should not be unlawful . . . [T]here were among the Nonconformists many who would have thought that even toleration was dearly purchased if their religious affairs were subjected to State control. But if the State could be persuaded to do the very minimum, to repeal a few persecuting laws, to say "You shall not be punished for not going to the parish church, and you shall not be punished for going to your meeting-house," that was all that was requisite.

---

[9]   In some cases the land will have to be sold, but the "charity" will get the price.

[10]   Trustees Appointment Acts, 1850-69-90.

Trust would do the rest, and the State and *das Staatskirchen-thum* [the established church] could not be accused of any active participation in heresy and schism. Trust soon did the rest. I have been told that some of the earliest trust deeds of Nonconformist "meeting-houses" say what is to be done with the buildings if the Toleration Act be repealed. After a little hesitation, the courts enforced these trusts, and even held that they were "charitable."

And now we have in England Jewish synagogues and Catholic cathedrals and the churches and chapels of countless sects. They are owned by natural persons. They are owned by trustees.

Now I know very well that our way of dealing with all the churches, except that which is "by law established" (and in America and the great English colonies even that exception need not be made), looks grotesque to some of those who see it from the outside. They are surprised when they learn that such an "historic organism" as the Church of Rome, *"einem Privatverein, einer Ballspielgesellschaft rechtlich gleichsteht*[11]" [a private organisation, {and} a ballgame club enjoy equal legal standing]. But when they have done laughing at us, the upshot of their complaint or their warning is, not that we have not made this historic organism comfortable enough, but that we have made it too comfortable.

I have spoken of our "charity" as an *Anstalt* [Institution] for *Stiftung* [foundation], but, as might be expected in a land where men have been very free to create such "charitable trusts" as they pleased, *anstaltliche* [institutional] and *genossenschaftliche* [co-operative] threads have been interwoven in every conceivable fashion. And this has been so from the very first. In dealing with charitable trusts one by one, our Courts have not been compelled to make any severe classification. *Anstalt* [Institution] or *Genossenschaft* [co-operative], was not a dilemma which every trust had to face, though I suppose that what would be called an *anstaltliches element* [institutional element] is implicit in our notion of a charity. This seems particularly noticeable in the ecclesiastical region. There is a piece of ground with a building on it which is used as a place of worship. Who or what is it that in this instance stands behind the trustees? Shall we say *Anstalt* [institution] or shall we say *Verein* [society].

[11] Hinschius, op. cit. S. 222-4.

No general answer could be given. We must look at the "trust deed." We may find that as a matter of fact the trustees are little better than automata whose springs are controlled by the catholic bishop, or by the central council ("Conference") of the Wesleyans; or we may find that the trustees themselves have wide discretionary powers. A certain amount of *Zweck* [purpose] there must be, for otherwise the trust would not be "charitable." But this demand is satisfied by the fact that the building is to be used for public worship. If, however, we raise the question who shall preach here, what shall he preach, who shall appoint, who shall dismiss him, then we are face to face with almost every conceivable type of organization from centralized and absolute monarchy to decentralized democracy and the autonomy of the independent congregation. To say nothing of the Catholics, it is well known that our Protestant Non-conformists have differed from each other much rather about Church government than about theological dogma: but all of them have found satisfaction for their various ideals of ecclesiastical polity under the shadow of our trusts.

V

This brings us to our "unincorporated bodies," and by way of a first example I should like to mention the Wesleyans. They have a very elaborate and a highly centralized constitution, the primary outlines of which are to be found in an *Urkunde* [charter] to which John Wesley set his seal in 1784. Thereby he declared the trusts upon which he was holding certain lands and buildings that had been conveyed to him in various parts of England. Now-a-days we see Wesleyan chapels in all our towns and in many of our villages. Generally every chapel has its separate set of trustees, but the trust deeds all follow one model, devised by a famous lawyer in 1832 – the printed copy that lies before me fills more than forty pages – and these deeds institute a form of government so centralized that Rome might be proud of it, though the central organ is no pope, but a council.

But we must not dwell any longer on cases in which there is a "charitable trust," for, as already said, there is in these cases no pressing demand for a personal destinatory. We can, if we please, think of the charitable *Zweck* [purpose] as filling the place that is filled by a person in the ordinary private trust.

When, however, we leave behind us the province, the wide province, of "charity," then – so we might argue *a priori* – a question about personality must arise. There will here be no *Zweck* [purpose] that is protected as being "beneficial to the public." There will here be no intervention of a *Staatsanwalt* [public prosecutor] who represents the "*parens patriae*" [parent of the country]. Must there not therefore be some destinatory who is either a natural or else a juristic person? Can we have a trust for a *Genossenschaft* [co-operative], unless it is endowed with personality, or unless it is steadily regarded as being a mere collective name for certain natural persons? I believe that our answer should be that in theory we cannot, but that in practice we can.

If then we ask how there can be this divergence between theory and practice, we come upon what has to my mind been the chief merit of the Trust. It has served to protect the unincorporated *Genossenschaft* [co-operative] against the attacks of inadequate and individualistic theories.

We should all agree that, if an *Anstalt* [institution] or a *Genossenschaft* [co-operative] is to live and thrive, it must be efficiently defended by law against external enemies. On the other hand, experience seems to show that it can live and thrive, although the only theories that lawyers hold about its internal affairs are inadequate. Let me dwell for a moment on both of these truths.

Our *Anstalt* [institution] or our *Genossenschaft* [co-operative] or whatever it may be, has to live in a wicked world: a world full of thieves and rogues and other bad people. And apart from wickedness, there will be unfounded claims to be resisted: claims made by neighbours, claims made by the State. This sensitive being must have a hard, exterior shell. Now our Trust provides this hard, exterior shell for whatever lies within. If there is theft, the thief will be accused of stealing the goods of Mr A. B. and Mr C. D., and not one word will be said of the trust. If there is a dispute about a boundary, Mr A. B. and Mr C. D. will bring or defend the action. It is here to be remembered that during the age in which the Trust was taking shape all this external litigation went on before courts where nothing could be said about trusts. The judges in those courts, if I may so say, could only see the wall of trustees and could see nothing that lay beyond it. Thus in a conflict with an external foe no question about personality could arise. A great deal of ingenuity had been spent in bringing about this result.

But if there be this hard exterior shell, then there is no longer any pressing demand for juristic theory. Years may pass by, decades, even centuries, before jurisprudence is called upon to decide exactly what it is that lies within the shell. And if what lies within is some *Genossenschaft* [co-operative], it may slowly and silently change its shape many times before it is compelled to explain its constitution to a public tribunal. Disputes there will be; but the disputants will be very unwilling to call in the policeman. This unwillingness may reach its highest point in the case of religious bodies. Englishmen are a litigious race, and religious people have always plenty to quarrel about. Still they are very reluctant to seek the judgment seat of Gallio. As is well known, our "Law Reports," beginning in the day of Edward I, are a mountainous mass. Almost every side of English life is revealed in them. But if you search them through in the hope of discovering the organization of our churches and sects (other than the established church) you will find only a few widely scattered hints. And what is true of religious bodies, is hardly less true of many other *Vereine* [societies], such as our "clubs." Even the "*kampflustige Engländer*," [pugnacious Englishman] whom Ihering admired, would, as we say, think once, twice, thrice, before he appealed to a court of law against the decision of the committee or the general meeting. I say "appealed," and believe that this is the word that he would use, for the thought of a "jurisdiction" inherent in the *Genossenschaft* [co-operative] is strong in us, and I believe that it is at its strongest where there is no formal corporation. And so, the external wall being kept in good repair, our English legal *Dogmatik* [dogmatics] may have no theory or a wholly inadequate and antiquated theory of what goes on behind. And to some of us that seems a desirable state of affairs. Shameful though it may be to say this, we fear the petrifying action of juristic theory.

And now may I name a few typical instances of "unincorporated bodies" that have lived behind the trustee wall?

I imagine a foreign tourist, with Bädeker in hand, visiting one of our "Inns of Court": let us say Lincoln's Inn[12]. He sees the chapel and the library and the dining-hall; he sees the

---

[12]   In Latin documents the word corresponding to our *inn* is *hospitium*.

external gates that are shut at night. It is in many respects much like such colleges as he may see at Oxford and Cambridge. On inquiry he hears of an ancient constitution that had taken shape before 1422, and we know not how much earlier. He learns that something in the way of legal education is being done by these Inns of Court, and that for this purpose a federal organ, a Council of Legal Education, has been established. He learns that no man can practise as an advocate in any of the higher courts who is not a member of one of the four Inns and who has not there received the degree of "barrister-at-law." He would learn that these Inns have been very free to dictate the terms upon which this degree is given. He would learn that the Inn has in its hands a terrible, if rarely exercised, power of expelling ("disbarring") a member for dishonourable or unprofessional conduct, of excluding him from the courts in which he has been making his living, of ruining him and disgracing him. He would learn that in such a case there might be an appeal to the judges of our High Court: but not to them as a public tribunal: to them as "visitors" and as constituting, we might say, a second instance of the domestic forum.

Well, he might say, apparently we have some curious hybrid – and we must expect such things in England – between an *Anstalt des öffentlichen Rechies* [institution of Public Law] and a *privilegierte Korporation* [privileged corporation]. Nothing of the sort, an English friend would reply; you have here a *Privatverein* [private organisation] which has not even juristic personality. It might – such at least our theory has been – dissolve itself tomorrow, and its members might divide the property that is held for them by trustees. And indeed there was until lately an Inn of a somewhat similar character, the ancient Inn of the "Sergeants at Law," and, as there were to be no more serjeants, its members dissolved the *Verein* [society] and divided their property. Many people thought that this dissolution of an ancient society was to be regretted; there was a little war in the newspapers about it; but as to the legal right we were told that there was no doubt.

It need hardly be said that the case of these Inns of Court is in a certain sense anomalous. Such powers as they wield could not be acquired at the present day by any *Privatverein* [private organisation], and it would not be too much to say that we do not exactly know how or when those powers were acquired, for the beginning of these societies of lawyers was very humble and is very dark. But, before we leave them, let us remember that the English judges who received and repeated a great deal of the canonistic learning about corporations, *Fiktionstheorie, Concessionstheorie* [fiction theory, concession theory] and so forth, were to a man members of these *Körperschaften* [corporations] and had never found that the want of juristic personality was a serious misfortune. Our lawyers were rich and influential people. They could easily have obtained incorporation had they desired it. They did not desire it.

But let us come to modern cases. To-day German ships and Austrian ships are carrying into all the seas the name of the keeper of a coffee-house, the name of Edward Lloyd. At the end of the seventeenth century he kept a coffee-house in the City of London, which was frequented by "underwriters" or marine insurers. Now from 1720 onwards these men had to do their business in the most purely individualistic fashion. In order to protect two privileged corporations, which had lent money to the State, even a simple *Gesellschaft* [society] among underwriters was forbidden. Every insurer had to act for himself and for himself only. We might not expect to see such individualistic units coalescing so as to form a compactly organized body – and this too not in the middle age but in the eighteenth century. However, these men had common interests: an interest in obtaining information, an interest in exposing fraud and resisting fraudulent claims. There was a subscription; there was a small "trust fund"; the exclusive use of the "coffee house" was obtained. The *Verein* [society] grew and grew. During the great wars of the Napoleonic age, "the Committee for regulating the affairs of Lloyd's Coffee House" became a great power. But the organization was still very loose until 1811, when a trust deed was executed and bore more than eleven hundred signatures. I must not attempt to tell all that "Lloyd's" has done for England. The story should be the better known in Germany, because the hero of it, J. J. Angerstein, though he came to us from Russia, was of German parentage. But until 1871 Lloyd's was an unincorporated *Verein* [society] without the least trace (at least so we said) of juristic personality about it. And when incorporation cam in 1871, the chief reason for the change was to be found in no ordinary event, but in the recovery from the bottom of the Zuyder Zee of a large mass of treasure which had been lying there since 1799, and which belonged – well, owing to the destruction of records by an accidental fire, no one could exactly say to whom it belonged. In the life of such a *Verein* [society] "incorporation" appears as a mere event. We could not even compare it to the attainment of full age. Rather it is as if a "natural person" bought a type-writing machine or took lessons in stenography.[13]

Even more instructive is the story of the London Stock Exchange.[14] Here also we see small beginnings. In the eighteenth century the men who deal in stocks frequent certain coffee-houses: in particular "Jonathan's." They begin to form a club. They pay the owner an annual sum to exclude those whom they have not elected into their society. In 1773 they moved to more commodious rooms. Those who used the rooms paid sixpence a day. In 1802 a costly site was bought, a costly building erected, and an elaborate constitution was formulated in a 'deed of settlement." There was a capital of £20,000 divided into 400 shares. Behind the trustees stood a body of "proprietors," who had found the money; and behind the "proprietors" stood a much larger body of "members," whose subscriptions formed the income that was divided among the "proprietors." And then there was building and always more building. In 1876 there was a new "deed of settlement"; in 1882 large changes were made in it; there was a capital of £240,000 divided into 20,000 shares.

Into details we must not enter. Suffice it that the organization is of a high type. It might, for example, strike one at first that the shares of the "proprietors" would, by the natural operation of private law, be often passing into the hands of people who were in no wise interested in the sort of business that is done on the Stock Exchange, and that thus the *genossenschaftliche* [co-operative] character of the constitution would be destroyed. But that danger could be obviated. There was nothing to prevent the original subscribers from agreeing that the shares could only be sold to members of the Stock Exchange, and that, if by inheritance a share came to other hands, it must be sold within a twelvemonth. Such regulations have not prevented the shares from being valuable.

In 1877 a Royal Commission was appointed to consider the Stock Exchange. It heard evidence; it issued a report; it made

[13]   F. Martin, *History of Lloyd's*, 1876.

[14]   C. Duguid, *Story of the Stock Exchange*, 1901.

recommendations. A majority of its members recommended that the Stock Exchange should be incorporated by royal charter or Act of Parliament.

And so the Stock Exchange was incorporated? Certainly not. In England you cannot incorporate people who do not want incorporation, and the members of the Stock Exchange did not want it. Something had been said about the submission of the "bye-laws" of the corporation to the approval of a central *Behörde* [public authority], the Board of Trade. That was the cloven hoof. *Ex pede diabolum* [from the foot of the devil].[15]

Now, unless we have regard to what an Englishman would call "mere technicalities," it would not, I think, be easy to find anything that a corporation could do and that is not being done by this *nicht rechtsfähige Verein* [organisation without legal capacity, ie., the Trust]. It legislates profusely. Its representative among the Royal Commissioners did not scruple to speak of "legislation." And then he told how it did justice and enforced a higher standard of morality than the law can reach. And a terrible justice it is. Expulsion brings with it disgrace and ruin, and minor punishments are inflicted. In current language the committee is said to "pronounce a sentence" of suspension for a year, or two years or five years.

The "quasi-judicial" power of the body over its members – *quasi* is one of the few Latin words that English lawyers really love – is made to look all the more judicial by the manner in which it is treated by our courts of law. A man who is expelled from one of our clubs, – or (to use a delicate phrase) whose name is removed from the list of members – will sometimes complain to a public court. That court will insist on a strict observance of any procedure that is formulated in the written or printed "rules" of the club; but also there may be talk of "natural justice." Thereby is meant an observance of those forms which should secure for every accused person a full and fair trial. In particular, a definite accusation should be definitely made, and the accused should have a sufficient opportunity of meeting it. Whatever the printed rules may say, it is not easy to be supposed that a man has placed his rights beyond that protection which should be afforded to all men by "natural justice." Theoretically the "rules," written or unwritten, may only be the terms of a contract, still the thought

15   London Stock Exchange Commission, *Parliamentary Papers*, 1878, vol. XIX.

that this man is complaining that justice has been denied to him by those who were bound to do it, often finds practical expression. The dread of a *Vereinsherrschaft* [society with power] is hardly represented among us.

I believe that in the eyes of a large number of my fellow-countrymen the most important and august tribunal in England is not the House of Lords but the Jockey Club; and in this case we might see "jurisdiction" – they would use that word – exercised by the *Verein* [society] over those who stand outside it. I must not aspire to tell this story. But the beginning of it seems to be that some gentlemen form a club, buy a race-course, the famous Newmarket Heath, which is conveyed to trustees for them, and then they can say who shall and who shall not be admitted to it. I fancy, however, that some men who have been excluded from this sacred heath ("warned off Newmarket Heath" is our phrase) would have much preferred the major excommunication of that "historic organism" the Church of Rome.

It will have been observed that I have been choosing examples from the eighteenth century: a time when, if I am not mistaken, corporation theory sat heavy upon mankind in other countries. And we had a theory in England too, and it was of a very orthodox pattern; but it did not crush the spirit of association. So much could be done behind a trust, and the beginnings might be so very humble. All this tended to make our English jurisprudence disorderly, but also gave to it something of the character of an experimental science, and that I hope it will never lose.

But surely, it will be said, you must have some juristic theory about the constitution of the *Privatverein* [private organisa-tion]: some theory, for example, about your clubs and those luxurious club-houses which we see in Pall Mall.

Yes, we have, and it is a purely individualistic theory. This it must necessarily be. As there is no "charity" in the case, the trust must be a trust for persons, and any attempt to make it a trust for unascertained persons (future members) would soon come into collision with that "rule against perpetuities" which keeps the *Familienfideicommiss* [family entailed estate] within moderate bounds. So really we have no tools to work with except such as are well known to all lawyers. Behind the wall of trustees we have *Miteigenthum* [co-ownership] and *Vertrag* [contract]. We say that "in equity" the original members were the only destinatories: they were *Miteigenthümer* [co-owners] with *Gesammthandschaft* [collective ownership]; but at the same time they contracted to observe certain rules.

I do not think that the result is satisfactory. The "ownership in equity" that the member of the club has in land, buildings, furniture, books etc. is of a very strange kind. (1) Practically it is inalienable. (2) Practically his creditors cannot touch it by execution. (3) Practically, if he is bankrupt, there is nothing for them.[16] (4) It ceases if he does not pay his annual subscription. (5) It ceases if in accordance with the rules he is expelled. (6) His share – if of a share we may speak – is diminished whenever a new member is elected. (7) He cannot demand a partition. And (8) in order to explain all this, we have to suppose numerous tacit contracts which no one knows that he is making, for after every election there must be a fresh contract between the new member and all the old members. But every judge on the bench is a member of at least one club, and we know that, if a thousand tacit contracts have to be discovered, a tolerable result will be attained. We may remember that the State did not fall to pieces when philosophers and jurists declared that it was the outcome of contract.

There are some signs that in course of time we may be driven out of this theory. The State has begun to tax clubs as it taxes corporations.[17] When we have laid down as a very general principle that, when a man gains any property upon the death of another, he must pay something to the State, it becomes plain to us that the property of a club will escape this sort of taxation. It would be ridiculous, and indeed impossible, to hold that, whenever a member of a club dies, some taxable increment of wealth accrues to every one of his fellows. So the property of the "unincorporated body" is to be taxed as if it belonged to a corporation. This is a step forward.

Strange operations with *Miteigenthum* [co-ownership] and *Vertrag* [contract] must, I should suppose, have been very familiar to German jurists in days when corporateness was not to be had upon easy terms. But what I am concerned to remark is

---

16   In a conceivable case the prospective right to an aliquot part of the property of a club that was going to be dissolved might be valuable to a member's creditors; but this would be a rare case, and I can find nothing written about it. Some clubs endeavour by their rules to extinguish the right of a bankrupt member.

17   Customs and Inland Revenue Act, 1885, sec. 11.

that, owing to the hard exterior shell provided by a trust, the inadequacy of our theories was seldom brought to the light of day. Every now and again a court of law may have a word to say about a club; but you will find nothing about club-property in our institutional treatises. And yet the value of those houses in London, their sites and their contents, is very great, and almost every English lawyer is interested, personally interested, in one of them.

A comparison between our unincorporated *Verein* [society] and the *nicht rechtsfähige Verein* [organisation without legal capacity] of the new German code might be very instructive; but perhaps the first difference that would strike anyone who undertook the task would be this, that, whereas in the German case almost every conceivable question has been forestalled by scientific and controversial discussion, there is in the English case very little to be read. We have a few decisions, dotted about here and there; but they have to be read with caution, for each decision deals only with some one type of *Verein* [society], and the types are endless. I might perhaps say that no attempt has been made to provide answers for half the questions that have been raised, for example, by Dr Gierke. And yet let me repeat that our *Vereine ohne Rechtsfähigkeit* [societies without legal capacity] are very numerous, that some of them are already old, and that some of them are wealthy.[18]

One of the points that is clear (and here we differ from the German code) is that our unincorporated *Verein* [society] is not to be likened to a *Gesellschaft* (partnership): at all events this is not to be done when the *Verein* [society] is a "club" of the common type.[19] Parenthetically I may observe that for the present purpose the English for *Gesellschaft* is "Partnership" and the English for *Verein* is "Society." Now in the early days of clubs an attempt was made to treat the club as a *Gesellschaft*. The *Gesellschaft* was an old well-established institute, and an effort was made to bring the new creature under the old rubric. That effort has, however, been definitely abandoned and we are now

---

[18] I believe that all the decisions given by our Courts in any way affecting our clubs will be found in a small book: J. Wertheimer, *Law relating to Clubs*, ed. 3, by A. W. Chaster, 1903.

[19] It was otherwise with the unincorporated *Actiengesellschaft* [joint-stock company]; but that is almost a thing of the past. A few formed long ago may still be living in an unincorporated condition, e.g. the London Stock Exchange.

taught, not only that the club is not a *Gesellschaft*, but that you cannot as a general rule argue from the one to the other. Since 1890 we have a statutory definition of a *Gesellschaft*:– "Partnership is the relation which subsists between persons carrying on a business in common with a view to profit."[20] A club would not fall within this definition.

The chief practical interest of this doctrine, that a club is not to be assimilated to a *Gesellschaft*, lies in the fact that the committee of an English club has no general power of contracting on behalf of the members within a sphere marked out by the affairs of the club. A true corporate liability could not be manufactured, and, as I shall remark below, our courts were setting their faces against any attempt to establish a limited liability. The supposition as regards the club is that the members pay their subscriptions in advance, and that the committee has ready money to meet all current expenses. On paper that is not satisfactory. I believe that cases must pretty frequently occur in which a tradesman who has supplied wine or books or other goods for the use of the club would have great difficulty in discovering the other contractor. We have no such rule (and here again we differ from the German code) as that the person who professes to act on behalf of an unincorporated *Verein* [society] is always personally liable;[21] and I think the tradesman could often be forced to admit that he had not given credit to any man, the truth being that he thought of the club as a person. I can only say that scandals, though not absolutely unknown,[22] have been very rare; that the members of the club would in all probability treat the case as if it were one of corporate liability; and that London tradesmen are willing enough to supply goods to clubs on a large scale. If there is to be extraordinary expenditure, if, for example, a new wing is to be added to the building, money to a large amount can often be borrowed at a very moderate rate of interest. We know a "mortgage without personal liability"; and that has been useful. Strictly speaking there is no debtor; but the creditor has various ways by which he can obtain payment: in particular he can sell the land.

Deliktsfähigkeit [The capability of committing an offence] is an interesting and at the present time it is perhaps a burning

---

20   Partnership Act, 1890, sec. I. For the meaning of these words, see F. Pollock, *Digest of the Law of Partnership*, ed. 6.

21   B. G. B. § 54.

22   See Wertheimer, op. cit. p. 73.

point. A little while ago English lawyers would probably have denied that anything resembling corporate liability could be established in this quarter. Any liability beyond that of the man who does the unlawful act must be that of a principal for the acts of an agent, or of a master for the acts of a servant, and if there is any liability at all, it must be unlimited. But this is now very doubtful. Our highest court (the House of Lords) has lately held that a trade union is *deliktsfähig* [capable of wrong]: in other words, that the damage done by the organised action of this unincorporated *Verein* [association] must be paid for out of the property held by its trustees. Now a trade union is an unincorporated *Verein* [association] of a somewhat exceptional sort. It is the subject of special Statutes which have conferred upon it some, but not all, of those legal qualities which we associate with incorporation. Whether this decision, which made a great noise, is attributable to this exceptional element, or whether it is to be based upon a broader ground, is not absolutely plain. The trade unionists are dissatisfied about this and some other matters, and what the results of their agitation will be I cannot say. The one thing that it is safe to predict is that in England *socialpolitische* [social policy] will take precedence of *rechtswissenschaftliche* [jurisprudential] considerations. As to the broader question, now that a beginning has once been made, I believe that the situation could be well described in some words that I will borrow from Dr Gierke:

> "Vielleicht bildet sich ein Gewohnheitsrecht das die nicht rechtsfähigen Vereine in Ansehung der Haftung für widerrechtliche Schadenszufügung dem Körperschaftsrecht unterstellt."[23] [Perhaps there develops a Common Law which, in view of the legal liability for unlawful harm, brings societies without legal capacity under corporate law.'

The natural inclination of the members of an English club would, so I think, be to treat the case exactly as it if were a case of corporate liability. It has often struck me that morally there is most personality where legally there is none. A man thinks of his club as a living being, honourable as well as honest, while the joint-stock company is only a sort of machine into which he puts money and out of which he draws dividends.

As to . . . [*Deliktsfähigkeit* of corporations] [corporations' capability of committing an offence] it may not be out of place to

---

[23]   Gierke, *Vereine ohne Rechtsfähigkeit*, zweite Auflage, S. 20.

observe that by this time English corporations have had to pay for almost every kind of wrong that one man can do to another. Thus recently an incorporated company had to pay for having instituted criminal proceedings against a man "maliciously and without reasonable or probable cause." In our theoretical moments we reconcile this with the *Fiktionstheorie* [fiction theory] by saying that it is a case in which a master (*personal ficta*) pays for the act of his servant or a principal for the act of an agent, and, as our rule about the master's liability is very wide, the explanation is not obviously insufficient. I am not sure that this may not help us to attain the desirable result in the case of the unincorporated *Verein* [association].

Our practical doctrine about the *Vermögen* [property] of our clubs seems to me to be very much that which is stated by Dr Gierke in the following sentence, though (for the reason already given) we should have to omit a few words in which he refers to a *Gesellschaft* [partnership].[24]

"Das Vereinsvermögen . . . gehört . . . den jeweiligen Mitgliedern; aber als Gesellschaftsvermögen [Vereinsvermögen] ist es ein für den Gesellschaftszweck [Vereinszweck] aus dem übrigen Vermögen der Theilhaber ausgeschiedenes, den Gesellschaftern [Vereinsmitgliedern] zu ungesonderten Antheilen gemeinsames Sondervermögen, das sich einem Körperschaftsvermögen nähert." [The society property . . . belongs to the respective members; but as the communal property it is a special property, excluded from the remaining property of the associates, for the purpose of the association. This special property is the communal property of the associates, with no separable parts attributable to an individual associate, and approaches a corporate property.]

And then in England the *Sonderung* [separation] of this *Vermögen* [property] from all the other *Vermögen* [property] of the *Theilhaber* [sharing] can be all the plainer, because in legal analysis the owners of this *Vermögen* [property] are not the *Vereinsmitglieder* [society members], but the trustees. It is true that for practical purposes this *Eigenthum* [property] of the trustees of a club may be hardly better than a *Scheineigenthum* [dummy, or fictitious property], and the trustees themselves may be hardly better than puppets whose wires are pulled by the

---

24 *Vereine ohne Rechtsfähigkeit*, S. 14.

committee and the general meeting. And it is to be observed that in the case of this class of trusts the destinatories are peculiarly well protected, for, even if deeds were forged, no man could say that he had bought one of our club-houses or a catholic cathedral without suspecting the existence of a trust: *res ipsa loquitur* [the matter speaks for itself]. Still the *nudum dominium* [bare possession] of the trustees serves as a sort of external mark which keeps all this *Vermögen* [property] together as a *Sondervermögen* [special property]. And when we remember that some great jurists have found it possible to speak of the juristic person as puppet, a not unimportant analogy is established.[25] . . . Since our lawyers explained away a certain statute of Henry VIII, which will be mentioned below, our *nicht rechtsfähiger Verein* [organisation without legal capacity] has stood outside the scope of those *Gesetze* which forbad corporations to acquire land (Statutes of Mortmain). And this was at one time a great advantage that our *nicht rechtsfähiger Verein* [organisation without legal capacity] had over the *rechtsfähige Verein* [organisation with legal capacity]. The Jockey Club, for example, could acquire Newmarket Heath without asking the King's or the State's permission. Even at the present day certain of our *nicht rechtsfähige Vereine* [organisations without legal capacity] would lose their power of holding an unlimited quantity of land if they registered themselves under the Companies Acts and so became corporations.[26]

As regards *Processfähigkeit* [process capacity], our doctrine regarded the capacity "to sue and be sued" as one of the essential attributes of the corporation. Indeed at times this capacity seems to have appeared as the specific *differentia* of the corporation, though the common seal also was an important mark. And with this doctrine we have not openly broken. It will be understood, however, that in a very large class of disputes the concerns of the *nicht rechtsfähiger Verein* [organisation without legal capacity] would be completely represented by the trustees. Especially would this be the case in all litigation concerning *Liegenschaft* [real property]. Suppose a dispute with a neighbour about a servitude ("easement") or about a boundary, this can be brought into court and decided as if there were no trust in existence and no *Verein* [association]. And so if the dispute is with some

---

[25]   Gierke, op. cit., S. 21.

[26]   Companies Act, 1862, sec. 21.

Pächter [tenant] or *Miether* [lessee] of land or houses that belong "in equity" to the *Verein* [association]. There is a legal relationship between him and the trustees, but none between him and the *Verein* [association], and in general it will be impossible for him to give trouble by any talk about the constitution of the *Verein* [association]. And then as regards internal controversies, the Court of Chancery developed a highly elastic doctrine about "representative suits." The beginning of this lies far away from the point that we are considering. It must suffice that in dealing with those complicated trusts that Englishmen are allowed to create, the court was driven to hold that a class of persons may be sufficiently represented in litigation by a member of that class. We became familiar with the plaintiff who was suing "on behalf of himself and all other legatees" or "all other cousins of the deceased" or "all other creditors." This practice came to the aid of the *Verein* [association]. Our English tendency would be to argue that if in many cases a mere class (e.g. the testator's nephews) could be represented by a specimen, then *a fortiori* a *Verein* [association] could be represented by its "officers." And we should do this without seeing that we were infringing the corporation's exclusive possession of *Processfähigkeit* [process capacity].[27]

But with all its imperfections the position of the unincorporate *Verein* [association] must be fairly comfortable. There is a simple test that we can apply. For the last forty years and more almost every *Verein* [association] could have obtained the corporate quality had it wished to do this, and upon easy terms. When we opened the door we opened it wide. Any seven or more persons associated together for any lawful purpose can make a corporation.[28] No approval by any organ of the State is necessary, and there is no exceptional rule touching *politische socialpolitische oder religiöse Vereine* [political, social-political, or religious society]. Many societies of the most various kinds have taken advantage of this offer; but many have not. I will not speak of humble societies which are going to have no property or very little: only some chess-men perhaps. Nor will I speak of those political societies which spring up in England whenever there is agitation: a "Tariff Reform Association" or a "Free Food League"

---

[27]   Our law about this matter is now represented by Rules of the Supreme Court of Judicature, XVI, 9.

[28]   Companies Act, 1862, sec. 66.

or the like. It was hardly to be expected that bodies which have a temporary aim, and which perhaps are not quite certain what that aim is going to be, would care to appear as corporations. But many other bodies which are not poor, which hope to exist for a long time, and which have a definite purpose have not accepted the offer. It is so, for example, with clubs of what I may call the London type: clubs which have houses in which their members can pass the day. And it is so with many learned societies. In a case which came under my own observation a society had been formed for printing and distributing among its members books illustrating the history of English law. The question was raised what to do with the copyright of these books, and it was proposed that the society should make itself into a corporation; but the council of the society – all of them lawyers, and some of them very distinguished lawyers – preferred the old plan: preferred trustees. As an instance of the big affairs which are carried on in the old way I may mention the London Library, with a large house in the middle of London and more than 200,000 books which its members can borrow.

Why all this should be so it would not be easy to say. It is not, I believe, a matter of expense, for expense is involved in the maintenance of the hedge of trustees, and the account of merely pecuniary profit and loss would often, so I fancy, show a balance in favour of incorporation. But apparently there is a widespread, though not very definite belief, that by placing itself under an incorporating *Gesetz* [statute], however liberal and elastic that *Gesetz* [statute] may be, a[n] *Verein* [association] would forfeit some of its liberty, some of its autonomy, and would not be so completely the mistress of its own destiny as it is when it has asked nothing and obtained nothing from the State. This belief may wear out in course of time; but I feel sure that any attempt to drive our *Vereine* [associations] into corporateness, any *Registerzwang* [compulsory registration], would excite opposition. And on the other hand a proposal to allow the courts of law openly to give the name of corporations to *Vereine* [associations] which have neither been chartered nor registered would not only arouse the complaint that an intolerable uncertainty was being introduced into the law (we know little of Austria) but also would awake the suspicion that the proposers had some secret aim in view: perhaps nothing worse than what we call "red-tape," but perhaps taxation and "spoliation."

Hitherto (except when the Stock Exchange was mentioned) I have been speaking of societies that do not divide gain among their members. I must not attempt to tell the story of the English *Aktiengesellschaft* [joint-stock company]. It has often been told in Germany and elsewhere. But there is just one point to which I would ask attention.

In 1862 Parliament placed corporate form and juristic personality within easy each of "any seven or more persons associated together for any lawful purpose." I think we have cause to rejoice over the width of these words, for we in England are too much accustomed to half-measures, and this was no half-measure. But still we may represent it as an act of capitulation. The enemy was within the citadel.

In England before the end of the seventeenth century men were trying to make joint-stock companies with transferable shares or "actions" (for that was the word then employed), and this process had gone so far that in 1694 a certain John Houghton could issue in his newspaper a price list which included the "actions" of these unincorporated companies side by side with the stock of such chartered corporations as the Bank of England. We know something of the structure of these companies, but little of the manner in which their affairs were regarded by lawyers and courts of law. Then in 1720, as all know, the South Sea Bubble swelled and burst. A panic-stricken Parliament issued a law, which, even when we now read it, seems to scream at us from the statute book. Unquestionably for a time this hindered the formation of joint-stock companies. But to this day there are living among us some insurance companies, in particular "the Sun," which were living before 1720 and went on living in an unincorporate condition.[29] And then, later on when the great catastrophe was forgotten, lawyers began coldly to dissect the words of this terrible Act and to discover that after all it was not so terrible. For one thing, it threatened with punishment men who without lawful authority "presumed to act as a corporation." But how could this crime be committed?

From saying that organization is corporateness English lawyers were precluded by a long history. They themselves were members of the Inns of Court. Really it did not seem clear that men could "presume to act as a corporation" unless they said in so many words that they were incorporated, or unless they usurped that

29   F. R. Relton, *Fire Insurance Companies*, 1893.

sacred symbol, the common seal. English law had been compelled to find the essence of real or spurious corporateness among comparatively superficial phenomena.

Even the more definite prohibitions in the Statute of 1720, such as that against "raising or pretending to raise a transferable stock," were not, so the courts said, so stringent as they might seem to be at first sight. In its panic Parliament had spoken much of mischief to the public, and judges, whose conception of the mischievous was liable to change, were able to declare that where there was no mischievous tendency there was no offence. Before "the Bubble Act" was repealed in 1825 most of its teeth had been drawn.

But the *unbeschränkte Haftbarkeit* [unlimited liability] of partners was still maintained. That was a thoroughly practical matter which Englishmen could thoroughly understand. Indeed from the first half of the nineteenth century we have Acts of Parliament which strongly suggest that this is the very kernel of the whole matter. All else Parliament was by this time very willing to grant: for instance, active and passive *Process-fähigkeit* [process capacity], the capacity of suing and being sued as unit in the name of some secretary or treasurer. And this, I may remark in passing, tended still further to enlarge our notion of what can be done by "unincorporated companies." It was the day of half-measures. In an interesting case an American court once decided that a certain English company was a corporation, though an Act of our Parliament had expressly said that it was not.

And if our legislature would not by any general measure grant full corporateness, our courts were equally earnest in maintaining the unlimited liability of the *Gesellschaftsmitglieder* [members of the organisation].

But the wedge was introduced. If a man sells goods and says in so many words that he will hold no one personally liable for the price, but will look only to a certain subscribed fund, must we not hold him to his bargain? Our courts were very unwilling to believe that men had done anything so foolish; but they had to admit that personal liability could be excluded by sufficiently explicit words. The wedge was in. If the State had not given way, we should have had in England joint-stock companies, unincorporated, but contracting with limited liability. We know now-a-days that men are not deterred from making contracts by the word "limited." We have no reason to suppose that they would have been deterred if that word were expanded into four or five lines printed at the head of the company's letterpaper. It is needless to say that the directors of a company would have strong reasons for seeing that due notice of limited liability was given to every one who had contractual dealings with the company, for, if such notice were not given, they themselves would probably be the first sufferers. . . .

In England the State capitulated gracefully in 1862. And at the same time it prohibited the formation of large unincorporated *Gesellschaften* [partnerships]. No *Verein* [association] or *Gesellschaft* [partnership] consisting of more than twenty persons was to be formed for the acquisition of gain unless it was registered and so became incorporate. We may say, however, that this prohibitory rule has become well-nigh a *caput mortuum* [dead letter], and I doubt whether its existence is generally known, for no one desires to infringe it. If the making of gain be the society's object, the corporate form has proved itself to be so much more convenient than the unincorporate that a great deal of ingenuity has been spent in the formation of very small corporations in which the will of a single man is predominant ("one-man companies"). Indeed the simple *Gesellschaft* [partnership] of English law, though we cannot call it a dying institution, has been rapidly losing ground.[30]

In America it has been otherwise. As I understand, the unincorporate *Aktiengesellschaft* [joint-stock company] with its property reposing in trustees lived on beside the new trading corporations. I am told that any laws prohibiting men from forming large unincorporated partnerships would have been regarded as an unjustifiable interference with freedom of contract, and even that the validity of such a law might not always be beyond question. A large measure of limited liability was secured by carefully-worded clauses. I take the following as an example from an American "trust deed."

---

[30] A distinction which, roughly speaking, is similar to that drawn by B. G. B. §§ 21, 22 was drawn by our Act of 1862, sec. 4:– "No company, association or partnership consisting of more than twenty persons [ten persons, if the business is banking] shall be formed for the purpose of carrying on any business that has for its object the acquisition of gain by the company, association or partnership, or by the individual members thereof unless it is registered." I believe that in the space of forty years very few cases have arisen in which it was doubtful whether or not a *Verein* [association] fell within these words.

The trustees shall have no power to bind the shareholders personally. In every written contract they may make, reference shall be made to this declaration of trust. The person or corporation contracting with the trustees shall look to the funds and property of the trust for the payment under such contract . . . and neither the trustees nor the shareholders, present or future, shall be personally liable therefor.

The larger the affairs in which the *Verein* [association] or *Gesellschaft* [partnership] is engaged, the more securely will such clauses work, for (to say nothing of legal requirements) big affairs will naturally take the shape of written documents.

Then those events occurred which have inseparably connected the two words "trust" and "corporation." I am not qualified to state with any precision the reasons which induced American capitalists to avoid the corporate form when they were engaged in constructing the greatest aggregations of capital that the world had yet seen; but I believe that the American corporation has lived in greater fear of the State than the English corporation has felt for a long time past. A judgment dissolving a corporation at the suit of the *Staatsanwalt* [public prosecutor] as a penalty for offences that it has committed has been well-known in America. We have hardly heard of anything of the kind in England since the Revolution of 1688. The dissolution of the civic corporation of London for its offences in the days of Charles II served as a *reductio ad absurdum*. At any rate "trust" not "corporation" was the form that the financial and industrial magnates of America chose when they were fashioning their immense designs.

Since then there has been a change. Certain of the States (especially New Jersey) began to relax their corporation laws in order to attract the great combinations. A very modest percentage is worth collecting when the capital of the company is reckoned in millions. So now-a-days the American "trust" (in the sense in which economists and journalists use that term) is almost always if not quite always a corporation.

And so this old word, the "trustis" of the Salica, has acquired a new sense. Any sort of capitalistic combination is popularly called a "trust" if only it is powerful enough, and Englishmen believe that Germany is full of "trusts."

VI

And let me once more repeat that the connection between Trust and Corporation is very ancient. It is at least four centuries old. Henry VIII saw it. An Act of Parliament in which we may hear his majestic voice has these words in its preamble.[31]

> Where by reason of feoffments . . . made of trust of . . . lands to the use of . . . guilds, fraternities, comminalties, companies or brotherheads erected . . . by common assent of the people without any corporation . . . there groweth to the King . . . and other lords and subjects of the realm the same like losses and inconveniences . . . as in case where lands be aliened into mortmain.

We see what the mischief is. The hedge of trustees will be kept in such good repair that there will be no *escaeta* [escheat], no *relevium* [feudal duty], no *custodia* [watch], for behind will live a *Genossenschaft* keenly interested in the maintenance of the hedge, and a *Genossenchaft* which has made itself without asking the King's permission. Now no one, I think, can read this Act without seeing that it intends utterly to suppress this mischief.[32] Happily, however, the Act also set certain limits to trusts for obituary masses, and not long after Henry's death Protestant lawyers were able to say that the whole Act was directed against "superstition." Perhaps the members of the Inns of Court were not quite impartial expositors of the King's intentions. But in a classical case it was argued that the Act could not mean what it apparently said, since almost every town in England – and by "town" was meant not *Stadt* [town] but *Dorf* [village] – had land held for it by trustees. Such a statement it need hardly be said, is not to be taken literally. But the trust for a *Communalverband* [communal association] or for certain purposes of a *Communalverband* [communal association] is very ancient and has been very common: it is a "charity." There was a manor (*Rittergut*] near Cambridge which was devoted to paying the wages of the knights who represented the county of Cambridge in Parliament.[33]

---

[31] Stat. 23 Hen. VIII, c. 10.

[32] The trust is to be void unless it be one that must come to an end within twenty years.

[33] Porter's Case, I Coke's *Reports*, 60: "For almost all the lands belonging to the towns or boroughs not incorporate are conveyed to several inhabitants of the parish and their heirs upon trust and confidence to employ the

It is true that in this quarter the creation of trusts, though it was occasionally useful, could not directly repair the harm that was being done by that very sharp attack of the *Concessionstheorie* [concession theory] from which we suffered. All our *Communalverbände* [communal associations] except the privileged boroughs, remained at a low stage of legal development. They even lost ground, for they underwent, as it were, a *capitis diminutio* [loss of civil rights] when a privileged order of *communitates* [communities], namely the boroughs, was raised above them. The county of the thirteenth century (when in solemn records we find so bold a phrase as "die Grafschaft kommt und sagt") was nearer to clear and unquestionable personality than was the county of the eighteenth century. But if the English county never descended to the level of a governmental district, and if there was always a certain element of "self-government" in the strange system that Gneist described under that name, that was due in a large measure (so it seems to me) to the work of the Trust. That work taught us to think of the corporate quality which the King kept for sale as a technical advantage. A very useful advantage it might be, enabling men to do in a straightforward fashion what otherwise they could only do by clumsy methods; but still an advantage of a highly technical kind. Much had been done behind the hedge of trustees in the way of constructing *Körper* ("bodies") which to the eye of the plain man looked extremely like *Korporationen* [corporations], and no one was prepared to set definite limits to this process.

All this reacted upon our system of local government. Action and reaction between our *Vereine* [association] and our *Communalverbände* [communal associations] was the easier, because we knew no formal severance of Public from Private Law. One of the marks of our *Korporation* [corporation], so soon as we have any doctrine about the matter, is its power of making "bye-laws" (or better "by-laws"); but, whatever meaning Englishmen may attach to that word now-a-days, its original meaning, so etymologists tell us, was not *Nebengesetz*

profits to such good uses as defraying the tax of the town, repairing the highways . . . and no such uses (although they are common almost in every town) were ever made void by the statute of 23 H. 8." Some of the earliest instances of "representative suits" that are known to me are cases of Elizabeth's day in which a few members of a village or parish "on behalf of themselves and the others" complain against trustees.

[supplementary law] but *Dorfgesetz* [village, i.e. tribal law].[34]
And then there comes the age when the very name "corporation" has fallen into deep discredit, and stinks in the nostrils of all reformers. Gierke's account of the decadence of the German towns is in the main true of the English boroughs, though in the English case there is something to be added about parliamentary elections and the strife between Whig and Tory. And there is this also to be added that the Revolution of 1688 had sanctified the "privileges" of the boroughs. Had not an attack upon their "privileges," which were regarded as *wohlerworbene Rechte*, "vested rights," cost a King his crown? The municipal corporations were both corrupt and sacrosanct. And so all sorts of devices were adopted in order that local government might be carried on without the creation of any new corporations. Bodies of "commissioners" or of "trustees" were instituted by *Gesetz* [statute], now in this place, and now in that, now for this purpose, and now for that; but good care was taken not to incorporate them. Such by this time had been the development of private trusts and charitable trusts, that English law had many principles ready to meet these "trusts of a public nature." But no great step forward could be taken until the borough corporations had been radically reformed and the connection between corporateness and privilege had been decisively severed.

A natural result of all this long history is a certain carelessness in the use of terms and phrases which may puzzle a foreign observer. I can well understand that he might be struck by the fact that whereas our borough is (or, to speak with great strictness, the mayor, aldermen, and burgesses are) a corporation, our county, after all our reforms, is still not a corporation, though the County Council is. But though our modern statutes establish some important distinctions between counties and boroughs, I very much doubt whether any practical consequences could be deduced from the difference that has just been mentioned, and I am sure that it does not correspond to any vital principle.

[34] Murray, *New English Dictionary*. It will be known to my readers that in English books "Statute" almost always means *Gesetz* (Statutum Regni) and rarely *Statut*. Only in the case of universities, colleges, cathedral chapters and the like can we render *Statut* by "Statute." In other cases we must say "by-laws," "memorandum and articles of association" and so forth, varying the phrase according to the nature of the body of which we are speaking.

I must bring to an end this long and disorderly paper, and yet I have said very little of those *Communalverbände* [communal associations], which gave Dr Redlich occasion to refer to what I had written. I thought, however, that the one small service that I could do to those who for many purposes are better able to see us than we are to see ourselves was to point out that an unincorporated *Communalverband* [communal association] is no isolated phenomenon which can be studied by itself, but is a member of a great genus, with which we have been familiar ever since the days when we began to borrow a theory of corporations from the canonists. The technical machinery which has made the existence of "unincorporated bodies" of many kinds possible and even comfortable deserves the attention of all who desire to study English life or any part of it. What the foreign observer should specially remember (if I may be bold enough to give advice) is that English law does not naturally fall into a number of independent pieces, one of which can be mastered while the others are ignored. It may be a clumsy whole; but it is a whole, and every part is closely connected with every other part. For example, it does not seem to me that a jurist is entitled to argue that the English county, being unincorporate, and having no juristic personality, can only be a "passive" *Verband* [association], until he has considered whether he would apply the same argument to, let us say, the Church of Rome (as seen by English law), the Wesleyan "Connexion," Lincoln's Inn, the London Stock Exchange, the London Library, the Jockey Club, and a Trade Union. Also it is to be remembered that the making of grand theories is not and never has been our strong point. The theory that lies upon the surface is sometimes a borrowed theory which has never penetrated far, while the really vital principles must be sought for in out-of-the-way places.

It would be easy therefore to attach too much importance to the fact that since 1889 we have had upon our statute-book the following words:– "In this Act and in every Act passed after the commencement of this Act the expression 'person' shall, unless the contrary intention appears, include any body of persons corporate or unincorporate."[35] I can imagine a country in which a proposal to enact such a clause would give rise to vigorous controversy; but I feel safe in saying that there was

[35] Interpretation Act, 1889, sec. 19.

nothing of the sort in England. For some years past a similar statutory interpretation had been set upon the word "person" in various Acts of Parliament relating to local government.[36] Some of our organs of local government, for example, the "boards of health" had not been definitely incorporated, and it was, I suppose, to meet their case that the word "person" was thus explained. It is not inconceivable that the above cited section of the Act of 1889 may do some work hereafter; but I have not heard of its having done any work as yet; and I fear that it cannot be treated as evidence that we are dissatisfied with such theories of personality as have descended to us in our classical books.

One more word may be allowed me. I think that a foreign jurist might find a very curious and instructive story to tell in what he would perhaps call the publicistic extension of our Trust *Begriff* [concept]. No one, I suppose, would deny that, at all events in the past, ideas whose native home was the system of Private Law have done hard work outside that sphere, though some would perhaps say that the time for this sort of thing has gone by. Now we in England have lived for a long while in an atmosphere of "trust," and the effects that it has had upon us have become so much part of ourselves that we ourselves are not likely to detect them. The trustee, "*der zwar Rechtsträger aber nur in fremdem Interesse ist*" [the legal entity, indeed, but only in someone else's interest] is well known to all of us, and he becomes a centre from which analogies radiate. He is not, it will be remembered, a mandatory. It is not *Vertrag* [contract] that binds him to the *Destinatär* [beneficiary]. He is not, it will be remembered, a guardian. The *Destinatär* [beneficiary] may well be a fully competent person. Again, there may be no *Destinatär* [beneficiary] at all, his place being filled by some "charitable" *Zweck* [purpose]. We have here a very elastic form of thought into which all manner of materials can be brought. So when new organs of local government are being developed, at first sporadically and afterwards by general laws, it is natural not only that any property they acquire, lands or money, should be thought of as "trust property," but that their governmental powers should be regarded as being held in trust. Those powers are, we say, "intrusted to them," or they are "intrusted with" those powers. The fiduciary character of the *Rechtsträger*

---

[36] Public Health Act, 1872, sec. 60.

[legal entity] can in such a case be made apparent in legal proceedings, more or less analogous to those which are directed against other trustees. And, since practical questions will find an answer in the elaborate statutes which regulate the doings of these *Körper* [bodies], we have no great need to say whether the trust is for the State, or for the *Gemeinde* [community], or for a *Zweck* [purpose]. Some theorists who would like to put our institutions into their categories, may regret that this is so; but so it is.

Not content, however, with permeating this region, the Trust presses forward until it is imposing itself upon all wielders of political power, upon all the organs of the body politic. Open an English newspaper, and you will be unlucky if you do not see the word "trustee" applied to "the Crown" or to some high and mighty body. I have just made the experiment, and my lesson for to-day is, that as the Transvaal has not yet received a representative constitution, the Imperial parliament is "a trustee for the colony." There is metaphor here. Those who speak thus would admit that the trust was not one which any court could enforce, and might say that it was only a "moral" trust. But I fancy that to a student of *Staatswissenschaft* [political science] legal metaphors should be of great interest, especially when they have become the commonplaces of political debate. Nor is it always easy to say where metaphor begins. When a Statute declared that the *Herrschaft* [ruling power] which the East India Company had acquired in India was held "in trust" for the Crown of Great Britain, that was no idle proposition but the settlement of a great dispute. It is only the other day that American judges were saying that the United States acquired the sovereignty of Cuba upon trust for the Cubans.

But I have said enough and too much.[37]

---

37 It did not seem expedient to burden this slight sketch with many references to books; but the following are among the best treatises which deal with those matters of which I have spoken:– Lewin, *Law of Trusts*, ed. 10 (1898); Tudor, *Law of Charities and Mortmain*, ed. 3 (1889); Lindley, *Law of Partnership*, ed. 6 (1893); Lindley, *Law of Companies*, ed. 6 (1902); Pollock, *Digest of the Law of Partnership*, ed. 6 (1895); Buckley, *Law and Practice under the Companies Act*, ed. 8 (1902); Palmer, *Company Law*, ed. 2 (1898); Wertheimer, *Law relating to Clubs*, ed. 3 (1903); Underhill, *Encyclopædia of Forms*, vol. 3 (1903), pp. 728–814 (Clubs). As regards the early history of "uses" or trusts, an epoch was made by O. W. Holmes, "Early English Equity," *Law Quarterly Review*, vol. 1, p. 162.

RESPUBLICA CHRISTIANA
By the Rev. J. Neville Figgis, Litt.D.
Read December 15, 1910

I think it was Lord Halsbury, in the Scotch Church case, who stopped one of the advocates in his use of the word Church,[1] saying that they as a Court had nothing to do with that, and that they could only consider the question as one concerning a trust. In other words, with a religious society as such they could not deal, but only with a trust or a registered company. This is only one instance of a fact exhibited in the whole of that case: namely, the refusal of the legal mind of our day to consider even the possibility of societies possessing an inherent, self-developing life apart from such definite powers as the State, or the individuals founding the body under State authority, have conferred upon them explicitly. In this view, apart from the State, the real society – and from individuals the living members of the State – there are no active social unities; all other apparent communal unities are directly or indirectly delegations, either of State powers or of individuals. To such a view the notion is abhorrent of a vast hierarchy of interrelated societies, each alive, each personal, owing to the State loyalty, and by it checked or assisted in their action no less than are private individuals, but no more deriving their existence from Government concession than does the individual or the family. In other words, these phrases of Lord Halsbury are but the natural expression of the concession theory of corporate life which sees it as a fictitious personality, the creation by the State for its own purposes, and consequently without any natural or inherent powers of its own. This theory is not so universally accepted as was once the case, but Professor Geldart's inaugural lecture on 'Legal Personality' shows how great are the obstacles still to be encountered by that theory of realism

---

[1]   Cf. Orr, *Free Church of Scotland Appeals*. All the speeches and judgments are there set forth in full. It is to be noted that Lord Macnaughten did take the more liberal view, advocated by modern writers.

which is for most of us associated with the name of Gierke,[2] and was popularised by Maitland. The latter, moreover, has shewn how this very English institution of the *trust* has preserved us from the worse perils of the rigid doctrinaire conception of the civilian.[3] For under the name of a trust many of the qualities of true personality have been able to develop unmolested. But this has not been all to the good. It has probably delayed the victory of the true conception, by enabling us to 'muddle through' with the false one. Moreover, the trust is and assimilates itself always rather to the *Anstalt* or the *Stiftung* than to the living communal society, the true corporation, with its basis in the *Genossenschaft*; and consequently, as was proved in this Scotch case, the necessary independence of a self-developing personality is denied to it, and its acts are treated as invalid on this very ground – that it is only a trust tied rigidly to its establishing terms, and not a true society with a living will and power of change.

However, it is not the truth or falsehood of the concession theory, or its realist adversary, that I am to discuss here, but rather its origin. I want to try for a little to see what lies behind it. The doctrine of which we speak could hardly be of modern origin. In the infinitely complex life of modern civilisation and its religious heterogeneity we observe, as a matter of actual fact, the phenomenon of vast numbers of societies all acting as though they were persons. They do manage to do all or most of the things which they would do even if the concession theory

[2]   Gierke, *Das Deutsche Genossenschaftsrecht*, especially vols. ii. and iii., is the prime authority for the discussion of this topic in reference alike to historical development in the ancient medieval world and in the post-Renaissance state, and to theoretical truth. In another work, *Das Genossenschafts Theorie*, Dr. Gierke shows, by an elaborate analysis of recent decisions both in state and federal courts in Germany, how entirely impossible it is to work with the rigid civilian theory; and how the courts and judges, while often paying lip-service to 'Romanist' notions, are driven in spite of themselves to make use of the more vital Teutonic notions. The whole matter is intimately connected with that conflict described by Beseler in *Das Volksrecht und das Juristenrecht*. There is a short lecture of Gierke, *Das Wesen des Menschlichen Verbandes*, which is also very illuminative. Professor Jethro Brown in an Appendix to the *Austinian Theory of Law and Government* is worthy of study. There is a somewhat meagre account of the various theories in Carr, *The Law of Corporations*.

[3]   Cf. Maitland, *Collected Papers*, vol. iii. Other papers in this volume are also important on this topic. But valuable above all is Maitland's long introduction to his translation of Gierke's *Political Theory of the Middle Ages*.

were not dominant. Indeed, it is only by a series of very transparent fictions that their activities are brought under this rubric. To all intents and purposes they act, not as fictitious but as real legal personalities. Of course the metaphysical question, what this personality really means, lies outside our limits, just as the question whether the will is free or determined has nothing to do with the State in its treatment of the individual. No one is debarred from believing determinism because the State treats its citizens as free agents. Further than this the *Taff Vale* decision is significant, for it tended to show that corporate life was a thing natural and arising of itself in bodies of men associated for permanent objects, and that it could not be destroyed by the process of ignoring it; in other words, that Trades Unions were personalities, in spite of their own wishes, and in spite of the Act of Parliament which had allowed to them much of the liberty of corporate personality while preserving them from its liabilities. That the House of Lords upheld Mr. Justice Farwell in this case, and at the cost of much odium, is also evidence that the concession theory is not really congruous with the facts of life, and that it is not of modern origin, but is in some way an inheritance from the past. We see, in fact, the horizons of the legal mind changing, and we gather that this mentality must relate to some time when, to speak of the two great bodies whose clash has been unending, State and Church were so bound together in unity that they could not be conceived, either of them, as a separate society with a separate life, but each appeared as different aspects or functionings of one and the same body. Such a time is, of course, remote from the world we live in.

Let us now take an instance from a Continental country, France. In France the concession theory has long reigned practically unchecked, alike as a legal theory and even as a political maxim. It burst into renewed activity only the other day in the Associations 'Loi.' Rousseau and his followers have always been opposed to allowing any inherent rights to bodies other than the sovereign people. There were, at least in earlier theory, rights of man and there were rights of the State. There were no rights of any other society. But for their obsession with this doctrine, the statesmen of the Revolution could never even have dreamt of such a project as the *Constitution Civile* of the clergy. Now, however, men have gone even farther, and deny all rights at all except those of the Republic one and indivisible.

M. Emile Combes put it, writing in an English review, 'There are no rights but the rights of the State; there is no authority but the authority of the Republic.' As I said, it is the origin, not the validity, of this conception with which I am concerned this evening. On this very controversy there was published a volume of collected speeches by M. Combes, with a preface by M. Anatole France. It is called 'Une Campagne Laïque.' That title contains, in my view, the key to the mystery. Consider for a moment that M. Combes is not a layman, but an unbeliever; he is a fanatical anti-Christian, and would repudiate with scorn any notion that he was a lay member of the Catholic Church. He is a Secularist, pure and simple, and the whole campaign for the laicisation of the schools, whether in France, or Spain, or Portugal, is a campaign for their entire secularisation, as we well know and is never denied. The ludicrous difficulties into which the need of removing all Christian and Theistic reference sometimes leads the compilers of text-books have been frequently observed. Laicisation might very well describe the Kenyon-Slaney clause in England and is a not unfair description of some parts of the undenominationalist movement, for that is, at least in name, a Christian movement, and is directed to removing education from clerical control, direct or indirect, and substituting a purely lay authority – still Christian. In France, of course, no such aim was ever suggested, and the Extremists have never made any difficulty about declaring that their object was to de-Christianise the nation. Why, then, should M. Combes use a term so essentially ecclesiastical as lay to describe his campaign? I answer that it was because he could not help it; the distinction that has ruled Europe for so many centuries had been a distinction, not between Christian and non-Christian societies, but between cleric and layman, between the spiritual and the temporal power, each of them exercised within the Church; between the ecclesiastical and the secular governments, each of them functioning within the body politic. M. Combes used the word laïque as an unconscious survival of the day when an attitude similar to his own could have been rightly described by that term. He slipped into it, because the categories of our thought are still ruled by influences that breathe of a different world. He was unconsciously, and in spite of himself, recalling a time when troubles between Church and State were not troubles between two societies, but between two departments of one society; not between Church and State conceived as separate social entities facing one another, like the College and the University, but rather as between Churchmen, i.e. ecclesiastics and statesmen, between the King's Court and the Papal Curia, between lawyers and bishops, between kings or emperors and popes. Only some sort of odd historical survival affords any explanation of the use of such a term as *laïque* (which has no meaning except in relation to the Church and the clergy) by so violent an anti-Christian as M. Emile Combes. But this is not all. It seems to point to a narrower use of the term Church than that in vogue to-day. In common parlance the Church in the Middle Ages meant not the *congregatio fidelium* – though, of course, no one would have denied this to be the right meaning – not the whole body of baptised Christians as distinct from those who were not, but rather the active governing section of the Church – the hierarchy and, I suppose, the religious orders. The common use of any term, especially a collective name, is to be found, not by what it sometimes means nor by what it ought to mean by that for which the society stands, but by what other set of people it is used to distinguish from – and this is the case with the word Church. In the Middle Ages the Church is used to distinguish the spirituality from the laity, and in nine cases out of ten it means the ecclesiastical body; in modern times the word Church is used to distinguish Churchmen from Dissenters of one kind or another; so that, whereas in the Middle Ages 'I am a Churchman' would mean I am *not* a layman, nowadays the same phrase means I am not a Dissenter.

When we talk of the Church we commonly mean the body of Churchmen as against those who are not Churchmen. The reason is that we live in a society which is religiously heterogeneous; so that no one nowadays thinks of everybody as *ipso facto* in one Church, but as a member of this or that Christian community, all equally tolerated; or, indeed, of many other bodies semi-religious or secular, like the Theistic Church, the Positivist body, the Labour Church, the Theosophists, the Christian Scientists, and so forth.

But even here we are not consistent. In common speech men are always dropping quite unconsciously into the older habit of talk, which treats the Church as primarily the clergy. Let me give an instance common in nearly all our experience. How many a youth has been rebuked by some stiff Churchman, probably an uncle, an archdeacon home from Barbadoes, for

saying that he 'is going into the Church,' when he means taking
Holy Orders? He is bidden to remember that he is in the
Church as a baptised and confirmed member; that the Church
does not mean the clergy; that if that is the sort of doctrine he is
going to preach he had better adopt some other calling, etc.,
etc.

Now I cannot help feeling that the unfortunate schoolboy
has a far better defence than he commonly imagines. He might
reply in something of this sort: 'True, my dear uncle, I made a
slip, and I regret it. It is less important than you think. For
since you left England for the Barbadoes, thirty years ago,
things have greatly changed. We live in days of religious chaos,
when no one is likely to think Churchmanship a matter of
course. But I should like to point out to you that if the phrase I
have used is theologically heretical, which I do not deny, it is
historically orthodox, and by my use of it (a pure slip, due to
the uprush of the subliminal consciousness) I am witnessing to
the unity of history in a way which, with all your correct
Tractarianism, you fail to comprehend. In the Middle Ages,
and indeed a very long time since the Middle Ages, as you may
see if you will study novels, the Church did mean in ordinary
speech the Church as an effectively organised body, a hierarchy
(there were no Houses of Laymen in those days), and
nonconformity to the established religion was either non-
existent or a crime. If you and I had been living in the
thirteenth, fourteenth, or even the sixteenth century, and I had
ventured to say to a person of your dignity [for your dignity
was as great as your chances of salvation were said to be small
in those days], "I belong to the Church," meaning by it I belong
to that branch of the Church established in this realm, what
would have happened? You would have been surprised, nay
shocked. You would have charged me with incipient heresy
because to say I am a Churchman in that sense implies that I
have my choice, and that, if I chose, I might be something else.
Even to contemplate such a possibility borders upon heresy. If
not treason, it is very near akin to *misprision of treason* to Holy
Church. And as your nephew I should have been fortunate to
have escaped with a sound avuncular whipping. If, however, I
had said I belong to the Church, meaning by it what you have
just rebuked me for – meaning, namely, I am a clerk in Holy
Orders, or in minor orders going on to greater things – then
you would have quite understood me. You would have

strongly approved, and you would doubtless have given me, though only sixteen and a half years old, a couple of livings and one prebend to be held in plurality, and *in commendam* with a *non-obstante* dispensation from the Holy Father permitting absence, in view of the other livings and offices which a person so important as an archdeacon's nephew would certainly have held. So I'll trouble you, after all, for that five-pound note you threatened to withdraw.'

That is the point. The word Churchman means to-day one who belongs to the Church as against others. In the Middle Ages there were no others, or, if there were, they were occupied in being burnt. A Churchman meant one who belonged to the Church in the narrower sense of its governing body – an ecclesiastic, as the word implies; just as statesman to-day means not a member but an officer, actual or potential, of the State. In medieval Europe folk would be more doubtful whether you were an Englishman or Bavarian than whether you were or were not a Churchman in our sense, but they might be greatly concerned to know whether you were clerk or layman. Churchmanship was co-extensive with citizenship, and, indeed, with more than citizenship, but the Church as a hierarchy was not; it was not the realm, but an estate of the realm.

When the Church came in conflict, as it often did, with the State, it meant the clash of the ecclesiastical with the civil hierarchy of officials. Both these bodies were composed of Churchmen, in our sense, and both existed in the one society – the commonwealth.

All this leads to the main thesis of this paper – that in the Middle Ages Church and State in the sense of two competing societies did not exist; you have instead the two official hierarchies, the two departments if you will: the Court and the *Curia*, the kings' officials and the popes'. But in these controversies you have practically no conception of the Church, as consisting of the whole body of the baptised set over against the State, consisting of the same people, only viewed from a different standpoint and organised for a different end. It is a quarrel between two different sets of people – the lay officials and the clerical, the bishops and the justices, the pope and the kings; it is not thought of under that highly complex difficult form of a quarrel between two societies, each of which was composed of precisely the same persons, only one is called the State, for it deals with temporal ends, and the other Church, as the Christian community. Such a notion would only be possible if the sense of corporate personality in Church and State had been fully developed. This was not the case. The conception of the State was indeed very inchoate, and there was very little power of distinguishing it from its officials; and even in the Church this weakness led to the increasing power of the popes, for the Church took over its conceptions of government from the ancient world, and the Republic had latterly been entirely identified with the emperors.[4] There was no personal substratum behind of which he was the mere representative.

4   Cf. the notion of the Church when 'von der Kirche als Rechtssubjekt die Rede sei. Dies sei die Bedeutung von Ecclesia im Sinne des lokalen Verbandes. *Einen solchen aber konnte man bei der damaligen Verfassung naturgemäss nicht in der Gemeinde, sondern lediglich in der klerikalen Genossenschaft finden.* Und so kam man zu einer Definition, wie sie Placentinus aufstellt: *ecclesia dicitur collectio vel coadunatio virorum vel mulierum in aliquo sacro loco constitutorum vel constitutarum ad serviendum Deo.* So war in der That die Kirche als Rechtssubjekt in das korporative Schema gebracht und man konnte ohne Weiteres die *Ecclesia* zu den *Universitates* und *Collegia* rechnen und den für diese geltenden Rechtssätzen unterstellen. Ja es sollte ihr, weil sie die privilegiirteste unter den Korporationen sei, kein bei irgend einer Korporation vorkommendes Recht fehlen können, weshalb sie namentlich der *respublica* und *civitas* gleichgestellt wurde.' – Gierke, iii. 195.
    Again, 'Si enim aliqua universitas privilegiata est, hodie, potius privilegiata est ecclesia.' 'Ecclesia aequiparatur reipublicae.' But this is of individual churches. 'Weniger als je wurde den Gemeinden irgend ein aktives kirchliches Recht verstattet, immer entschiedener trat die Kirche, als ein fremder und äusserer körper dem Volk gegenüber Erschien sie dem Deutschen dieser Zeit vorzugsweise als eine grosse Innung oder Zunft, so war sie ihm doch keineswegs eine Innung aller Gläubigen, eine Gemeinschaft, die jeder Laie mit einem Teil seiner Persönlichkeit bilden half, sondern sie war ihm die Zunft des geistlichen Standes. . . . Freilich war es dem Laien unerlässlich für sein Seelenheil, an dem von der Kirche besessenen und verwalteten Heilsschatz Anteil zu erlangen; aber zu diesem Behuf verhandelte und verkehrte er mit ihr *wie mit einer dritten Person*, kaum anders wie mit der Kaufmannsoder Gewerbezunft, wenn er ihrer Waaren bedurfte. *Die Kirche war in Allem ein geistlicher Staat für sich*, in welchem der Laie keines Bürgerrechts genoss.' – Gierke, i. 427 (cf. also 287). 'Bei dieser Auffassung der staatlichen Rechtssubjectivität konnten es die Römer zu Wort und Begriff der Staatspersönlichkeit nicht bringen. Sie blieben bei der Subjectivität des *populus*, und später des Kaisers stehen. Diese Subjectivität aber unterstellten sie, weil einzig in ihrer Art, keinem höheren Gattungsbegriff.' – Gierke, iii. 50 ('Das Deutsche Genossenschaftsrecht). Cf. also the following passage in regard to the Church. After describing the Church as God-planted, 'Wenn einer so konstruirten Gesammtkirche Rechtspersönlichkeit beigelegt wird, so kann Quelle

To make my meaning clear let me quote two passages from Maitland's 'Lectures on Constitutional History.' On pp. 101-2 we read:-

> 'While we are speaking of this matter of sovereignty, it will be well to remember that our modern theories run counter to the deepest convictions of the Middle Ages - to their whole manner of regarding the relation between Church and State. *Though they may consist of the same units, though every man may have his place in both organisms, these two bodies are distinct. The State has its king or emperor, its laws, its legislative assemblies, its courts, its judges; the Church has its pope, its prelates, its councils, its laws, its courts.* That the Church is in any sense below the State no one will maintain, that the State is below the Church is a more plausible doctrine; but the general conviction is that the two are independent, that neither derives its authority from the other. Obviously, when men think thus, while they more or less consistently act upon this theory, they have no sovereign in Austin's sense; before the Reformation Austin's doctrine was impossible.'

In regard to the theory of sovereignty, this statement is doubtless true of the smaller States. It is not true of the papacy; the *plenitudo potestatis* being simply sovereignty in the Austinian sense, developed by the canonists from Roman law and applied to the pope. It is not true of the more extreme Imperialist doctrine; the lawyers who told Frederic Barbarossa that the property of all his subjects was really his, and the normal civilian were, in theory at least, strong Austinians. Indeed, it is from Rome, first imperial and then papal: i.e. from

derselben nicht *die den Körper bildende Gesammtheit, sondern lediglich Gott und mittelbar dessen irdischer Stellvertreter sein.* In der That hat daher nach der Lehre der Kanonisten der göttliche Stifter selbst seiner Kirche zugleich mit der Heilsvollmacht die für deren Durchführung erforderliche Rechtssubjektivität verliehen. Und allein von Gott und seinem Vikar sind fort und fort alle einzelnen Privilegien und Rechte abzuleiten, welche der Gesammtkirche um ihres geistlichen Berufes willen zustehen, während auch die höchste weltliche Macht diese Rechte nicht zu mindern, sondern ur rein weltliche Privileginen hinzuzufügen vermag. Ebenso aber findet die einheitliche Kirchenpersönlichkeit ihren obersten Träger und Repraesentanten nicht in der Gesammtheit, sondern in Gott selbst und mittelbar in dessem irdischem Statthalter, so dass sogar als Subjekt der Rechte, welche für die *ecclesia universalis* in Anspruch genommen werden, Gott oder Christus selbst und vertretungsweise dann auch der Papst bezeichnet werden kann.' - G. iii. 250.

civil and canon law, that the modern doctrine of sovereignty derives. In its modern form it goes through the medieval canonists to Renaissance thinkers like Bodin, thence through Hobbes and the supporters of Divine Right to Austin. Even in the fourteenth century it is applied to the minor States. Baldus, I believe, was the first to say that *rex est imperator in regno suo*, and we find one of our own kings claiming to be *entier empereur dans son royaume*, and this, the claim to sovereignty, is the true meaning of the preamble to the great statute of appeals 'this realm of England is an Empire.' Moreover, it is not quite true to assert that no one said that the Church ought to be below the State. For that is the exact argument of the twelfth-century Erastian treatise by Gerard of York, printed by Böhmer in the 'Libelli de Lite.' He declares, indeed, not that the Church is below the State, but that, in the one commonwealth, which you can call either kingdom or church at your pleasure, the secular power is above the ecclesiastical. Still, of course, it is true that in the main Austinian doctrine is not applicable to the feudal commonwealth of the Middle Ages.

It is not of this matter that I want to speak at length, but of the sentences in italic. Later on in the book there is an even more emphatic expression of the same view:-

The medieval theory of the relation between Church and State seems this, that they are independent organisms consisting nevertheless of the same units. - p. 506.

To that statement I say *quod non*. I make this criticism with much diffidence, for every word that Maitland wrote is worth its weight in gold. Yet we must remember that these lectures were not written to be published, and that they were delivered in 1887, before he entered upon those studies which resulted in his work on 'The Canon Law' and his translation of Gierke. To say the very least, it is not certain that he would have written thus fifteen years later. Nor, again, do I desire to assert an 'absolute not.' I do not deny that such a view of Church and State was possible to acute minds in the Middle Ages, any more than I assert that because men normally meant by the Church the hierarchy they did not quite frequently mean the *congregatio fidelium*. I think that in the later Middle Ages men were moving in that direction. Judging by his letters and manifestoes, I think it not impossible that Frederic II held this view or something like it. What I do think is that this view in no way represented the ruling thought of the Middle Ages, that it was not the necessary background of their minds, that all, or nearly all, the evidence points the other way, and that, if we accepted Maitland's view, we should be left with no intelligible explanation of certain phenomena in the sixteenth century, to say nothing of existing controversies and modes of thought.

When we do find one pope speaking of God's vicar as master both of the terrene and the spiritual empire, he shows by his words that he cannot think them apart. The notion of a single society is so universal that, even where in words the popes admit two, it is in order to deny it in fact and to claim for themselves the lordship of both.

Moreover, when the Inquisition handed a heretic over to the secular arm, what was intended by the figure? Surely, that the two arms, the secular and spiritual powers, were arms of the same body – or else the metaphor makes nonsense. Yet the view we combat would make two different bodies.

Let me put before you the following considerations:– Is it not rather improbable that this difficult position of two corporate bodies, each of the same individual persons though totally distinct as corporate personalities, should have been thought of in a world whose ideals were symbolised in the Holy Roman Empire, whose true respublica is the *civitas Dei*? Even in our own day, when there is so much to favour it, views of this sort, at least in regard to established Churches, are not accepted readily or without argument. How would it have been in a world where the unbaptised and the excommunicate were outlaws, and citizenship and Christianity were inextricably bound up? Nobody in the Middle Ages denied that the king was God's minister, or that the bishops were great lords in the commonwealth. Pope and emperor, when they quarrelled, quarrelled like brothers, as members of the same society, the *civitas Dei*.

The fact is, *ecclesia* and *respublica* are more often than not convertible terms in medieval literature. One writer, who is well known, describes much in Maitland's way, viz. 'a system of two sets of law and courts'; but it is of two sets of people that he is thinking – the clergy and the laity, and it is within the whole – the one society, the *civitas*, which he says is the *ecclesia* – that these two bodies are to be found. I do not say but that later on, after the crystallisation of national states and the development through S. Thomas of the habit of arguing about the Church as one among a class of political societies, some such view as Maitland suggests may not have been now and then discernible. But I think it was very rare.

And what we want to know is not how some theorist formulated the matter, but what were the 'common thoughts of our forefathers.' Supposing that I had graduated, not at Cambridge but at Bologna in the thirteenth century, that I was a *doctor in utroque jure*, a protonotary apostolic and an auditor of the rota, should I have declared the kingdom or the empire to be a society quite distinct from the Church, though containing the same units? I trow not. I am much more likely to have said that the limits of the kingly power were determined by the Church, meaning the hierarchy, and that the king must do his duty because he was the minister of God and must therefore be subject to His vicar. So far from denying the king *qua* king to be a member of the same society as my own, I should have made his membership the ground of a due reverence for *protonotaries apostolic*. Supposing again, I had been a clerk of the king's court or a royal justice or one of the barons at Merton, who were not going to have the laws of England changed to suit the bishops, should I have asserted that they were members of a different State; should I not rather have claimed that, though specially and even reprehensibly privileged, though forming a distinct order in the commonwealth, they were yet English lieges and should be made, willy-nilly, to do and forbear those things lawful to English lieges, and none others? Even if – pardon the impertinence – I had been either a pope on the one hand or an emperor on the other, should I have thought of my rival as the head of another society with which my own relations were strictly international? Hardly. I should rather have deemed him a 'dear colleague' and felt it as a God-imposed duty to prevent him injuring his character by attempting a dictation over me, which for God's cause and solely as a matter of duty, I was determined to resist. Nor was there warrant in antiquity for this notion of the two societies. The conception of a religious society as distinct from the State had not dawned upon the unified civilisation of Greece and Rome. It was alien alike from the City-State and the Pagan Empire. When it did dawn upon some men's minds, what was the universal response? *Christiani ad leones*. Sir William Ramsay has made it clear that the persecution of the early Church was a matter of policy, and that it was directed against this very notion, the claim to be a separate society, while still remaining Roman citizens. It was the Church as upholding 'a new non-Roman unity' that men feared. That primitive Church was without question a society distinct from the Roman State.[5] As she grew to strength and threatened to absorb the whole population there was every likelihood of the view arising, outlined by Maitland.

But it did not arise. The old conception that of Pagan and Jew, was too strong for it. After Constantine granted the peace of the Church, it was not long, at most three-quarters of a century, before the old conception ruled again of a great unity in which civil and ecclesiastical powers were merely separate departments. Had the world been ripe for toleration of rival bodies things might have been very different. But it was not ripe. The emperors, as you know, were treated almost as ecclesiastical powers; coercion was employed on both sides in the Arian controversy; finally the Catholics conquered under Theodosius the Great. Arianism was made a crime; Paganism was suppressed; and the world was ripe for that confusion of baptism and citizenship which ruled the Middle Ages. True, there were many struggles between the different authorities, and their issues varied with time and place. But neither emperors nor prelates were treated as rulers of rival societies. The code of 'Justinian' was compiled subsequently to the 'De Civitate Dei' of S. Augustine. The whole spirit of both is to identify Church and State. The Pagan State was also a Church, and the medieval Church was also a State; *the* Church and *the* State in theory. Each governs the whole of life and the problem

---

[5] 'Dagegen lag allerdings von vornherein eine gewaltige negative Umwälzung der antiken Anschauungen von Staat und Recht in *den vom Wesen des Christenthums untrennbaren Principien* welche dem staatlichen Verbande einen grossen Theil seines bisherigen Inhalts zu Gunsten der religiösen Gemeinschaft und des Individuums entzogen. Einmüthig bekannte man sich zu dem Glauben, dass das innere Leben der Einzelnen und ihrer religiös-sittlichen Verbände keiner weltlichen Macht unterworfen und über die Sphäre der staatlichen Daseinsordnung erhaben sei. *Damit entschwand die allumfassende Bedeutung des Staats.* Der Mensch gieng nicht mehr im Bürger, die Gesellschaft nicht mehr im Staat auf. Das grosse Wort, dass man Gott mehr gehorchen soll als den Menschen, begann seinen Siegeslauf. Vor ihm versank die Omnipotenz des heidnischen Staats. Die Idee der immanenten Schranken aller Staatsgewalt und aller Unterthanenpflicht leuchtete auf. Das Recht und die Pflicht des Ungehorsams gegen staatlichen Gewissenszwang wurden verkündigt und mit dem Blute der Märtyrer besiegelt.' – Gierke, op. cit. iii. 123. Cf. also the author's remarks on the effect of S. Augustine's *De Civitate Dei*. Ibid. 124–7.

is not whether you take power from one society and give it to the other, but where you tilt the balance of authority – on to the side of the lay officials or to that of the clerics. Shall power belong to him who wields the sword or to him who instructs the wielder? Roman law, as it entered the medieval world, is the law of a medievalised empire, and the code begins with the rubric, *De Summa Trinitate et Fide Catholica*. Much of the liberty afterwards claimed by canonists could be supported by adroit quotations from the imperial law.

All this was crystallised in the ideal of the *Holy Roman Empire*, the governing conception of a great world, Church-State, of which it is hard to say whether it is a religious or a temporal institution. Half the trouble came from the fact that popes and emperors were heads, in theory co-equal, of the same society. The argument so constantly repeated, that the unity of the society needs a single person as the centre, and that, therefore, the secular power must be subject to the spiritual, owes its force to the very fact that men were incapable of seeing two societies, and that the theory of two co-equal heads under Christ as King did not work in practice. The pope, we must remember, is the emperor's archbishop, foreign he might be to England and France as nationality crystallised, but no emperor could afford to treat him as foreign. That would have been to give up all claims to Italy.

The lesser conflicts were all conducted under the shadow of this conception. Although in countries like England or France it may have been easier to see the distinctions of the two powers, its meaning was not grasped till later, and men did not talk of two societies separate, though composed of the same individuals.

But it will be said, what of the Canon Law? Here is a separate body of legal rules modelled in its form on the civil law and claiming sometimes to override it, possessed of a higher sanction, so that towards the close of the Middle Ages a French writer can say that *omnia jura civilia sunt canonica*.[6]

---

[6] The following passages are a fair indication of the common view: 'Si auctoritas sacra pontificum et potestas imperialis vere glutino caritatis adinvicem complerentur; nihil est enim in praesenti seculo pontifice clarius, nihil rege sublimius.' Cf. also Henry IV to Greg. VII, Jaffé Bib. Rer. Ger. ii. 46: 'Cum enim regnum et sacerdotium, ut in Christo rite administrata subsistant, vicaria sua ope semper indigeant.' From the following sentence from the Deposition of Frederic II, it can readily be seen how intimately connected are canon and civil law: 'Nonne igitur hec non levia, sed efficacia

Now it is true that in so far as the Canon Law governed the laity, and existed by the side of national laws, its existence points towards a belief in two distinct social organisms; yet I do not think that this inference was drawn at the time. The passage I alluded to above treats it as mainly *law for the clergy*, and so far as that was usual, this view would tally with all I have been saying. The popes, however, doubtless thought they were legislating for all Christians, but these popes were claiming a *plenitudo potestatis* over kings and princes, which implied that all secular law was merely allowed by them. Moreover, in those days of feudal courts, men were in the habit of seeing every kind of competing jurisdiction without definitely claiming that it destroyed such unity in the State as they were accustomed to see. The very looseness of structure of the medieval State, if we are to use the term, enabled the canonists to do their work alongside of the secular courts without drawing all the conclusions we should do. Unification was the work of the Renaissance and the Reform, and it was not till then that men would come to argue that it must either exist by the allowance, express or tacit, of the prince, or else that the prince must be in reality a subject.

Moreover, I do not think people sufficiently realise how systems, apparently competing, went on together in practice. Legal writers, like Bartolus on the one hand or Innocent IV on the other, quote the canon law and the civil law indiscriminately, and never seem conscious of them as being the laws of two separate societies. I cannot find this conception in Innocent's great commentary on the 'Decretale of Gregory IX.' Bartolus wrote a treatise on the differences between the two systems, but there is no hint that he regarded them as the laws of two different States.[7] The fact is that it was the two together, treated as an ideal rather than coercive law, which ruled men's minds; and out of this amalgam arose modern politics and international law.

sunt argumenta de suspicione heresis contra eum, cum tamen hereticorum vocabulo *illos jus civile contineri asserat*, et latis adversus eos sentenciis debere subcumbere qui vel levi argumento a judicio catholice religionis et tramite detecti fuerint deviare?' (Deposition of Frederick II. Huillard-Bréholles, *Historia Diplomatica F. II*, vi. 326.) Elsewhere he is accused of treason towards the pope. 'Non sine proditionis nota, et lese crimine majestatis.' Ibid. 322.

7   It is not certain that this attribution is correct. But it makes no difference to this point, whether the book was by Bartolus or another lawyer.

Again, if you take the 'Unam Sanctam' of Boniface VIII, that
does not assert the power of the Church over the State. Rather it
asserts the power of the Pope over every human being.[8] In fact
the personalisation of authority in popes, kings, and feudal lords
and prelates was one of the causes that retarded the growth of
such theory as that of the two kinds of *societas perfecta*. The
conflicts between the two powers are habitually spoken of as
struggles between the *sacerdotium* and the *regnum*; although the
wider terms *respublica* and *ecclesia* are not unknown, it is surely
reasonable to interpret them by the former. I give one or two
stanzas of a doggerel[9] poem by Gualterus de Insula from the
'Libelli de Lite.' They represent the natural categories into which
men's thoughts fell when they discussed the topic.

'Per Noe colliginius summum patriarcham
Totius ecclesiae caput et monarcham.

'Ergo vel ecclesiae membrum non dicatur
Caesar, vel pontifici summo supponatur.

'Major et antiquior est imperialis
Dignitas quam cleri sit vel pontificalis,
"Major" dico tempore, semper enim malis
Regibus subiacuit terra laycalis.

'Imperator Esau major quidem natu,
Papa quidem Jacob est, minor enim statu:
Ille sceptro rutilat, este potentatu,
Ille major viribus, iste dominatu.

'Caesar habet gladium sed materialem,
Hunc eundem pontifex sed spiritualem.
Caesar ergo suscipit usum temporalem
Ab eo, qui possidet curam pastoralem.

'Igitur si vera sunt ista quae promisi
Nichil habet penitus imperator, nisi
Ab eo, qui possidet claves paradisi,
At Petri vicarius; *non est sua phisi*.'

8   Cf. Henry of Cremona's interesting treatise on behalf of Boniface VIII,
    printed in Scholz, *Die Publizistik zur Zeit Philipps des Schönen*, App. 475;
    'Sunt diversi ordines,' etc. Is it possible that a passage like this would have
    been written in a day when Church and State were conceived as two
    societies, each consisting of the same units?

9   iii. 559-60.

The famous passage of Pope Gelasius about the two powers, so often quoted, is no evidence the other way; it refers to the two governing authorities of the *mundus*, which one writer declares to mean the State, not two separate societies. Its date alone is sufficient proof that it had reference to the Christianised ancient empire, when such a decision was not to be thought of.

John of Salisbury, in his 'Policraticus,' holds very high views of the function of the priest in the State, but it is a power within, not outside, the State that is to rule it, like the soul in the body.

One writer, Jordan of Osnabruck, equates the three powers, the *sacerdotium*, the *imperium*, and the *studium*, as all equally needful for the health of the Church. The *sacerdotium* he assigns to the Romans as the senior, the *imperium* to the Germans, and the *studium* to the French as being more perspicacious. That such a view could even be thought of is evidence how far asunder were the mediaeval notions on the subject from those natural to us.[10]

Wyclif, in his 'Speculum Militantis Ecclesiae,' declares that the ecclesia or commonwealth consists of three sections – lords, clergy, and commons. The argument of the book is that if the Church were disendowed the nobles would be richer and have less motive to oppress the poor. Whether that result followed the dissolution of the monasteries we need not here determine. What is certain is that it never occurred to him to conceive of Church and State as two distinct societies composed of the same units. The same is the case with Marsilius; but his Erastianism is so marked that it may be thought that his evidence is not to the point. It is notable, however, that he states (while disapproving the fact) that in ordinary use the Church meant the clergy and not the whole Christian people, at least, he says, that is the most common usage.

Lastly, let us note the surprise of Archbishop Whitgift at the doctrine of two societies. Cartwright, the Presbyterian protagonist, was strongly imbued with the notion of two kingdoms, Whitgift seems hardly able to believe his eyes as he reads it. This comes out *passim* in Whitgift's answer to Cartwright.

---

10   Cf. Jordanus von Osnabruck, *Buch über das Römische Reich* (Ed. Waitz, p. 71).

I need hardly point out that this is also the view of Hooker. And that is the point; how did that view arise? The very general Erastianism of most of the Reformers is well known. It came from this very fact. Society being conceived as fundamentally one, and the clergy in their eyes not having done their part in removing abuses, recourse must be had to the other power in the Church, the secular government. When Luther appealed to the German princes to take up the work of Reform he did not mean that he was appealing from the Christian Church to a secular State, but merely from the clerical to the civil authority. Any other view is preposterous.

My point is that this distinction of the two societies is either very primitive, dating from the days of persecution, or else very modern, dating from the religious divisions of Europe. I think that it came about in some such way as this:

(1) The analysis of political forms, begun by S. Thomas on the Aristotelian basis, set on foot the habit of reasoning about political societies. The facts of the great schism and the conciliar movement drove men to discuss the character and constitution of the Church, considered as a community, and comparable to states and kingdoms.

(2) This tendency was furthered by the growth of compact national states, by the decay of feudalism, and by the practical abeyance of the Holy Roman Empire; although, even after Constance, the concordats are not between Church and State, but between pope and king, bishops and nobles, etc., of France or other countries.

(3) Then came the Reformation. So far as this was political and princely it made no difference, save that it tilted the balance of power from the clerical to the lay officials. On the other hand in the Empire, as a whole, religious unity was destroyed and after the Religious Peace of Augsburg the Church could no longer be identified with the Empire. But where either prince or people were not able to make their own religion supreme or universal within the territorial state, the conception of two distinct societies tends to grow up. It is not really in the thought of Calvin, but the organisation of the Huguenots was very important in influencing men's minds. It was so local, so compact, so distinct, that it helped to forward the idea among all persons placed as they were. I do not think that Knox, any more than the other reformers, had any real notion of this distinction. But towards the end of Elizabeth's

reign it is certainly to be found in Cartwright and the whole English Presbyterian movement. Andrew Melville developed it in Scotland; and Robert Browne, the originator of the Independents, was inspired by this notion in the pamphlet 'Reformation without tarrying for any.'

In England both the Laudian and the Puritan party were medievalist; they believed in a State which was also a Church and were essentially theocratic. What developed the contrary notion was the non-juring schism. This compelled its adherents, and many High Churchmen who were not its adherents, to think of the Church as the body of all the faithful with rights and powers inherent and unconnected with the State. Union with Scotland increased this tendency, for there was thus before men's eyes the spectacle of two different established Churches. Thus Hoadly gives no hint of any other notion than the old, and his idea of toleration was merely a comprehensive Erastianism, very similar to certain schemes we hear of now. Warburton, on the other hand, develops explicitly and in set terms, in his 'Alliance between Church and State,' the doctrine that the two are independent organisms consisting of the same individuals, but existing for different ends, each to be treated as a *corporate personality*. His theory comes at the end, not at the beginning of the development I have been describing, and I cannot help feeling it would have been incomprehensible to men such as Gerard of York or S. Thomas of Canterbury. I should also add that the Jesuits, who had to consider the question of the relations of Church and State in reference to the changed conditions of a divided Europe, were forward in developing the notion of the two societies. In Gierke's view they were the first to develop a frankly secular theory of the State. On the other hand, royalists like Barclay in France, who were yet strong Catholics, in order to combat Bellarmine's doctrine of the indirect temporal sovereignty of the Pope were driven to be equally explicit as to the State being a *societas perfecta* no less than the Church, and to claim that the two societies were in a sense distinct.

But it may be asked, What difference does all this make? Nobody denies that Henry IV went to Canossa,[11] or that Boniface VIII issued the 'Unam Sanctam,' or that Frederic

---

[11]   At least I do not. I understand that doubt has been thrown even on this event.

Barbarossa held the papal stirrup, or that his grandson was deposed by a Church council. What difference can it possibly make whether we assert that these incidents were the result of conflicts between two separate societies, each of them a State, or between two sets of officials in one and the same society? If what has been said is well founded, we must view these conflicts as of the nature of civil war. Does that get us any 'forrarder'? If I were a scientific historian I should use great and desolate words about truth, and say that the less it mattered the better was it worth studying. However, instead of this I shall make the modest claim that such view helps us to understand better both history and ourselves.

(1) It explains the quick drop into Erastianism all over Europe in the sixteenth century. The campaign of the Reformers was just *une campagne laïque*. They were not attempting to take power out of the Christian society, but merely out of its clerical officials. All coercive power was to be rested in the prince, but in theory it was always the godly prince, 'most religious.' So long as they had him on their side, men so different as Laud and Luther felt that they were safe. The sixteenth century witnessed an undoubted victory of the secular over the ecclesiastical power; but it was not for the secular power as a society distinct from the Church, it was a victory for the temporal authority within the one society which can be called either Church or State according to the aspect prominent at the moment. Erastus himself declared that he was only discussing the case of a State which tolerated but a single religion *eamque veram*, a statement which shows how far he is removed from the modern form of the system, which derives its name from him.

(2) Many problems and controversies of modern times are rendered more intelligible to us, if we adopt the view which I suggest. Slowly, but only very slowly, has the notion of separate societies with inherent rights developed, just as it is only now that the doctrine of true corporate personality is being realised. The *Kulturkampf* was simply due to the incapacity of Bismarck to realise that there could be any corporate life with inherent powers of its own, unwilling to accept the *sic volo, sic jubeo* of the State. As we saw, the same notion was at bottom of the difficulties in the 'Free Church of Scotland Appeals.' Nor does it take much ingenuity to discover it lurking in recent judicial pronouncements about the

Deceased Wife's Sister Act, or about the controversy between Churches and undenominationalism in regard to education.[12]

(3) The unity of history is a cant phrase and is often made to bear a burden too heavy. But it may be pointed out how strong a testimony to this doctrine is afforded by the persistent notion of the republic, one and indivisible, which has come down to the modern world by descent through the medieval papacy, the Christianised ancient empire, the pagan empire, whither it migrated from the compact all-absorbing city-state. Mr. Carlyle, in the first chapter of his history of political theory in the West, was able to show us how the doctrines of Rousseau anent the fundamental equality of man and modern democracy can be found implicit in the Roman jurists, in Cicero, and to witness to a change in feeling between the aristocratic doctrine of Aristotle and the universalist theories of the great republic. This view has been encountered in our own day by the revival of aristocracy proclaimed by Nietzsche, and the doctrines of the fundamental inequality of men based partly on the subjugation of the tropics, partly on Darwinian theories of natural selection and the struggle for existence. The doctrine, however, which I have been considering is even more venerable than that of human equality. For it goes back, with hardly a

---

[12] 'Hinsichtlich der Enstehung der Korporation geht das Corpus Juris durchweg von der Auffassung aus, dass aus der natürlichen oder gewollten Vereinigung von Individuen zwar das thatsächliche Substrat, niemals jedoch die rechtliche Existenz einer Verbandseinheit hervorzugehen vermag. Vielmehr stammt zunächst die publicistische Verbandswesenheit während der Staat selbst als die mit und über den Individuen gegebene Allegemeinheit keiner Zurückführung auf einen besonderen rechtlichen Begründungsakt bedarf, auf allen übrigen Stufen vom Staat. *Staatliche Verleihung gilt als die Quelle der publicistischen Existenz auch solcher Gemeinwesen*, welche vor ihrem Eintritt in das römische *jus publicum* als selbständige Staaten bestanden haben; aus staatlicher Verleihung fliesst die Korporationsqualität auch derjenigen Verbände, deren thatsächliches Dasein freier Vereinigung verdankt wird; auf staatliche Verleihung gründet sich die publicistische Verbandseinheit auch der christlichen Kirche, welche selbst ihren Bestand aus göttlicher Stiftung herleitet. Überall aber verfährt hierbei der Staat hinsichtlich des rechtlichen Elementes der engeren Verbandswesenheiten wahrhaft constitutiv. *Alle körperschaftliche Existenz erscheint als das Werk frei schaffender Gesetzgebung*, durch welche der Staat, sei es in der Form der *lex specialis* für das einzelne Gebilde, oder sei es in der Form genereller Regeln für einen Komplex gleichartiger Verbände, seine eigne Gliederung setzt und ordnet. Darum bedarf es in keiner Weise einer Normirung bestimmter Voraussetzungen für die Errichtung einer Korporation.' - Gierke, op. cit. iii. 142-3.

break, to the omni-competent and universally penetrating supervision of Sparta and Athens. It is only when we have traced it right back to its origin that we see its inapplicability to the complex life of a modern world-empire.

The theory of sovereignty, whether proclaimed by John Austin or Justinian, or shouted in conflict by Pope Innocent or Thomas Hobbes, is in reality no more than a venerable superstition. It is only true to the facts in a cosy, small and compact State, although by a certain amount of strained language and the use of the maxim, 'whatever the sovereign permits he commands,' it can be made not logically untenable for any conditions of stable civilisation. As a fact it is as a series of groups that our social life presents itself, all having some of the qualities of public law and most of them showing clear signs of a life of their own, inherent and not derived from the concession of the State.

The State may recognise and guarantee (and demand marks for so doing) the life of these societies – the family, the club, the union, the college, the Church; but it neither creates that life any more than it creates the individual, though it orders his birth to be registered. It is the problem of the future, as Mr. A. L. Smith showed at the close of his lecture on Maitland, to secure from legal theory the adequate recognition of these facts, and in regard to religion the problem is raised in an acute form, and it will be the service of multiplied sectarianism to a true, that is a realistic political, philosophy if it forces the recognition of the truth that smaller societies live by their own life, and exercise real authority over their members. The struggle for liberty nowadays is the struggle to secure that recognition. What I have tried to indicate is the causes of that struggle being arduous. The atmosphere in which law has lived for more than one millennium (apart from the Teutonic and feudal influences) has been all in favour of the doctrine which recognises two and only two social entities, the individual on the one hand and the State on the other. In that atmosphere law not only gets out of relation to living facts and precipitates struggles like the *Kulturkampf* and absurdities like those involved in the case of the *Free Church of Scotland*, but political philosophy, which is always largely dependent on law, oscillates between an unreal individualism and a wildly impossible socialistic ideal. The facts of life are hostile to both, but injury, both practical and theoretical, is always done by trying to ignore facts, especially facts so tremendous as the complex group-life which is to most of us more than the State. What I have tried to show is that this error is not of modern origin, that it did not come into our world at the Renaissance, though it may have been accentuated then, but that it is part of the *damnosa hereditas* from the Civil Law of the Roman Empire, of which Stubbs once said that, whenever it has been dominant, it destroyed any real idea of civil and religious freedom.[13]

[13] I do not claim to have proved the view here set forth; still less to have set out the whole evidence. I am not certain of any hard and fast categories in the topic. But I would ask the student to study the ecclesiastico-political controversies throughout this course, from the *Libelli de Lite* down to the modern newspaper and platform speaker, and to ask himself whether the view here put forward does not fit more readily into the words and modes of thought of thinkers on all sides than that which I have combated. Even if it be only a difference of emphasis, it seems to me one of those matters when the emphasis makes as much difference as the distinction between a stroke of the cat and a stroke of the cane.

SOCIETY AND STATE
The Philosophical Review, Volume XX

It is a noteworthy fact that most of the serious attempts, during the last century and a half, to reach a comprehensive political principle, have owed their inspiration to Hellenic ideas. This is as true for Rousseau, "citizen of Geneva," whose abstract love of "nature" transmuted itself into a very concrete affection for a city-state, as for certain writers of our own day, and especially Professor Bosanquet, with his ideal of "Christian Hellenism,"[1] itself inspired by the great Hellenic thought of Hegel. This Hellenism has indeed taught us so much that it may seem ungrateful to accuse it of misleading us. Yet the conditions of our modern life are in some respects very different from those of Hellenic society. In particular, within the small circles of the Greek world certain distinctions lay concealed which in the wider reach of the modern community are or should be manifest. An application to modern life of a purely Hellenic theory is on that account dangerous, and seems to the writer to have in fact misled many of those theorists who, from Rousseau onwards, have adopted it, – who have found in Hellenism the key to the modern state.

Within the small circle of the Greek city the distinction of state and society lay concealed. It might be interesting to trace the rise of this distinction in the political consciousness of later ages,[2] but here it must suffice to say that the distinction is an essential one and that its validity is shown by the incoherence of the logic which obscures or denies it. In particular, the theory of the general will is, in the hands of most of its interpreters, a virtual denial of this necessary distinction, and I propose before going further to examine briefly the forms of this doctrine held respectively by Rousseau, Hegel, and

---

[1]   *Essays and Addresses*, p. 48.

[2]   Ritchie (*Principles of 'State-Interference* p. 157) quotes an early instance, viz., St. Thomas Aquinas (*De regimine principum*) translates the πολιτικὸν ζῷον of Aristotle by *animal sociale et politicum*.

Professor Bosanquet, and to show that in every case they are vitiated by a too narrow Hellenism.

1. The General Will, said Rousseau, is the true sovereign and ultimate authority in a state, and, in its obvious sense, this is the accepted doctrine of all democratic states, whose machinery is so constructed that, in one way or another, the ultimate decision lies with the mass of voters, the "people." Politically, then, the "general will" is and must remain sovereign. So far Rousseau is justified. But Rousseau, not content with the necessary political sovereignty of the people, went on to show *not* that such a sovereignty was a moral thing, but that it was *identical* with a moral sovereignty. The general will, Rousseau explained, cannot err. The rightful sovereign *must* act rightfully. Now, that the sovereign "can do no wrong" is a logical and obvious legal position. Legality cannot transcend law; morality can, and it is just the necessary moral righteousness, not the legal rightness, of the sovereign that Rousseau was concerned to uphold. For him the political organization was in no way made distinct from the complex and indeterminate social structure and therefore the bonds of state were just the bonds that keep a society together, the moral sanctions of society. Thence arose the refinements of theory by which Rousseau vainly tries to maintain the identification. First, the general will is distinguished from the "will of all" – not in truth a distinction between two kinds of *political* willing – and then it is asserted that the former always wills the good, though it may be unenlightened. The legal formula asserts the legal rightness of the sovereign's action and leaves its moral rightness open, but the dictum of Rousseau asserts its moral rightness and thus makes the political sovereign an anomalous "person" liable, it may be, to intellectual error but in every other respect infallible, – a "person" absolutely good but somewhat short-sighted. It is the danger of modern Hellenism to confound the actual with the ideal, and in this strange conception of inerrant will united to fallible judgment we have a good instance of that confusion. Here already we find Rousseau losing hold of the political principle, seeking a political sovereign which no state can ever recognize because no state can ever find it.

Rousseau identified the common will with the good will, but without going into the difficult places of psychology we may say that, although it may be to the general interest or good that the general will should be fulfilled, the general will is not therefore the will for the general good. And the practical difficulty is no less than the psychological. A will which cannot be determined by any positive standard can never be a legislative authority or source of positive law. Will is liable to persuasion, and the persuading will is therefore sovereign over the persuaded. So the will of the people may be the will of a single individual, does sometimes mean the will of two or three. To analyze the complex of influences moral and social determining a given act of will, a specific act of legislation, is difficult in the extreme; to isolate among these determinants an original or sovereign will is impossible. For all practical purposes we must find a definitive sovereign, a political sovereign; we must ask not whether it is Pericles persuading the demos or Aspasia persuading Pericles, but what will it is that wills the decree, that actually commands or consents.

The whole attempt to identify the principle of democracy – as any other political principle – with that of morality is fore-doomed to failure, and ends in setting on the political throne a crowned abstraction. For a will that is not realized, that is no man's will, is meaningless. What profit is it that this "general will" does not err – if it does nothing at all? Even if on any occasion the "general will" as understood by Rousseau came into being, it would simply be an interesting social fact, a coincidence; for political purposes it would be identical with a *majority*-will. In every case, therefore, the majority-will – which extended far enough becomes the "will of all" – must be the political principle, and to determine political obligation in terms of any other is worse than useless.

It is his consistent attempt to identify the political with the social order that leads Rousseau into the vagaries of his political logic. Why cannot the people be represented or act through deputy? Logically there seems to be no reason why the general will should not will legislation by its representative. But Rousseau is thinking of the whole complex of ideals and interests and aims animating a society – and that cannot be represented. Why, again, does the *Contrat social*[3] afford us that strangest of all spectacles, the apostle of freedom prescribing "dogmas of civil religion," declaring that "if anyone, after publicly acknowledging those dogmas, acts like an unbeliever of them, he should be punished with death"?

[3] *Contrat social*, Bk. IV, c. 8.

Again the answer is that Rousseau has utterly failed to distinguish the sanctions of all social order from the proper bonds of the political organization.

2. Hegel[4] finds fault with Rousseau because, while rightly adhering to the principle of will, he "conceived of it only in the determinate form of the individual will and regarded the universal will not as the absolutely reasonable will (*an und für sich Vernünftige des Willens*) but only as the common will that proceeds out of the individual will as conscious." It is a little like accusing the author of a physiological treatise of not writing a work on psychology when the writer has in fact merely mixed up the two. After all, is there not a common will and is not this common will the basis of any state or institution? Behind the definite institution, the work of conscious will, the philosopher may look for a rationality or universality which that conscious will yet has not for itself. It is at least permissible to search. But no fact is explained away by the greater rationality of another fact, and for the state, for any *institution*, the fact of will is just the fact of "common will, proceeding out of the individual will as conscious." The will on which state-institutions are based must be a conscious will, the will of the citizens, or they would never come to be. State institutions are not built like the hexagons of a bee-hive, by an instinct of unconscious co-operation. Society in the wider sense is not an "institution" and there it may be permissible to look for a will or a reason that is greater than the will or the reason of the constituents. But though, in the construction of any institution, we may build wiser than we know, the plan of the building and the co-operation of the builders must be consciously resolved upon.

To Hegel as to Rousseau there was ever present the tendency to interpret the State in terms of Hellenism, and that in spite of his being credited with discovering the distinction of state and society. In reality his account of that distinction is neither clear not satisfactory. The society which he distinguishes from the state – what he calls *bürgerliche Gesellschaft* – seems to hang strangely between actuality and ideality. It is a community resting on the "particularity" of desires, on economic need, and yet in discussing this economic community which is "different" from the state

---

4 *Grundlinien der Philosophie des Rechts*, § 258.

Hegel treats of law and police, essentially state institutions. On the other hand, the economic system is not the only social grouping, though a primary one, which can be distinguished from the state organization; we might equally distinguish, *e.g.*, the institutions through which arts and sciences develop, the educational system, the church, charitable institutions, *le haut monde*, and so on, names which cover a kaleidoscopic variety of constantly re-forming elements.[5] But the state cannot be regarded as absorbing within itself the free and living interplay of all these social forces; for one thing they are many of them not bounded by the limits of any state; and therefore it is absurd to say, *tout court*, that the *State* is "developed spirit," "the world the spirit has made for itself," and so forth.

The foregoing argument bears directly on the misconception of the "general will," and I propose next to consider the more or less Hegelian account of that doctrine set forth in Professor Bosanquet's book *The Philosophical Theory of the State*. In no modern work are the inconsistencies and contradictions of applied Hellenism more apparent.

Professor Bosanquet's general position is as follows: Liberty is the condition of our "being ourselves" or willing ourselves, and this liberty is identified with the life of the state. "It is such a 'real' or rational will that thinkers after Rousseau have identified with the state. In this theory they are following the principles of Plato and Aristotle, no less than the indications which Rousseau furnished by his theory of the general will in connection with the work of the legislator. The State, when thus regarded, is to the general life of the individual much as we saw the family to be with regard to certain of his impulses. The idea is that in it, or by its help, we find at once discipline and expansion, the transfiguration of partial impulses, and something to do and to care for, such as the nature of a human self demands." He adds two considerations "to make this conception less paradoxical to the English mind." "(a) The State, as thus conceived, is not merely the political fabric. The term state accents indeed the political aspect of the whole, and is opposed to the notion of an anarchical society. But it includes the entire

<hr>

[5] Hegel's incidental treatment of those parts of the social system is bewildering. What is to be made of such a statement as the following: "Inasmuch as consciousness (*Wissen*) has its seat in the state, science (*Wissenschaft*) too has it there, and not in the church" (§ 270)?

hierarchy of institutions by which life is determined, from the family to the trade, and from the trade to the Church and the University. It includes all of them, not as the mere collection of the growths of the country, but as the structure which gives life and meaning to the political whole, while receiving from it mutual adjustment and therefore expansion and a more liberal air. The State, it might be said, is thus conceived as the operative criticism of all institutions – the modification and adjustment by which they are capable of playing a rational part in the object of human will. . . . (b) The State, as the operative criticism of all institutions, is necessarily force; and in the last resort, it is the only recognized justified force."[6]

The first and greatest confusion into which Professor Bosanquet falls is that he uses the term "state" in two quite different senses. We find him, on the one hand, defining the state as a "working conception of life" (p. 151) or even, after Plato, as "the individual mind writ large" (p. 154) – and it is clear that here he means by state the unity of all the social forces at work in a community of human beings; on the other hand, when he comes to talk of state-action, it is at once obvious that he is now using 'state' in its proper signification of '*political* society,' with its definite form, its definite and limited type of action. Hence we are told that the mans of the state are not *in pari materia* with the end (p. 187) and are left with the anomalous conclusion that the "real will," the "rational will," "the will that wills itself," can never will any positive action whatever, much less "itself," can only "hinder hindrances" (p. 191). Hindrances to what?

The same confusion underlies Professor Bosanquet's distinction of "real" and "actual" will, by means of which he attempts to solve the problem of political obligation. The distinction intended is itself a true and suggestive one, though wrongly expressed. It rests on the primary distinction of "good" and "seeming good." People will what, if they knew the case fully and truly, they would no longer will. They will the seeming good because it seems the good. It is an obvious fact enough, but I may set down as an illustration an instance mentioned by Balzac in the novel *Cousin Pons*. "The mortality in French hospitals," he declares, "caused by women who take food privately to their husbands has been so great that physicians

---

6   *The Philosophical Theory of the State*, Ed. 1, pp. 149–152.

have now resolved to enforce a rigid personal search of the patients on the days when their relatives come to see them." Now Professor Bosanquet's distinction of 'real' and 'actual' rather obscures the psychological relations here involved, and suggests a false antithesis of 'real' and 'actual' will. The opposition is not between two wills, a 'real' and an 'actual,' but within the single act of willing, between the motive and the intention, if we care to use such terms, or between the object intended, the giving of food, and the end it was meant to serve, the restoration to health of the husbands. There is but one object willed, the giving of food. We cannot say even that the health of the husbands was 'willed,' still less the death of those husbands. A motive or end is not an act of will, 'real' or otherwise. Would Professor Bosanquet say that these women 'really' willed the recovery of their husbands, but 'actually' willed the giving of food?[7]

It has to be remembered that Professor Bosanquet introduces this distinction of 'real' and 'actual' will in order to answer the question of political obligation. "We have thus far been attempting to make clear what is meant by the identification of the state with the real will of the Individual in which he wills his own nature as a rational being; in which identification we find the only true account of political obligation" (p. 154). But this in fact does not touch the real problem. It is only too obvious that an 'actual' state is not the 'real' state of Professor Bosanquet, and the question of political obligation is: "On what grounds and how far is a citizen bound to obey the actual laws of the state?" What might be the principle of political obligation in an ideal state – where the question would never arise – is very different from what must be the principle under actual political conditions. The will of an actual state, in respect of any definite act of legislation, is and must be based on a majority-will. It is not because he finds his 'real' will embodied in legislation from which he actually dissents that the citizen is obedient to the law. A thorough-going identity of will is in the nature of the case impossible, and we must look instead for some persistent identity of interest, giving unity to the fundamental will on which the state, like any other institution,

[7] It looks as if Professor Bosanquet's distinction rested on such an opposition as this – they "really" will the recovery of their husbands, they "actually" *cause* their death – not an opposition in terms of will at all.

must rest, and consent – no longer unanimity – to the secondary acts of will through which the state fulfills its end. We ask too much if we expect an identity of will. In an actual state no individual can have this ideal, this harmony of his will and the state-will, realized all the time. Granting the first unity – the primary will for political life resting on the primary good of political life – we must thereafter be content to rest political obligation on common *good*, and at most only directly, through that notion, on common will.

Professor Bosanquet in fact refuses to recognize the necessities of the situation. To avoid Rousseau's difficulty that where a portion of the people must accept the will of another portion there is no freedom. Professor Bosanquet would declare that the general will is the rational will and thus true freedom – a double confusion for, first, the *political* principle must be the majority-will, and second, supposing *per impossibile* that the majority-will were purely rational, yet to identify freedom with enforced subjection to reason or good and to call such subjection self-government is indeed a "paradox." Doubtless a man may be forced to be free – Rousseau's own dangerous paradox contains a certain truth – but to identify such enforcement with "self-government" is to strain language and meaning to the breaking point. It involves an impossible identification of good and will.

On both sides Professor Bosanquet's account fails to answer the concrete question of political obligation. The conception of an abstract self willing an abstract good will never be an explanation of why and when the actual citizen should loyally identify himself with the positive commands of a very concrete government, enforcing measures whose ultimate conformity to his own "true" nature he may not unreasonably refuse to take for granted.

The basal fallacy of all such views lies, as I have pointed out, in the identification of state and society, in the refusal to draw a clear distinction here. "We have hitherto," says Professor Bosanquet, "spoken of the State and Society as almost convertible terms. And in fact it is part of our argument that the influences of Society differ only in degree from the powers of the State, and that the explanation of both is ultimately the same" (p. 184). This position vitiates the whole of Professor Bosanquet's account of the state, and it may be well, therefore, if we attempt positively to distinguish the meanings of the two terms 'state' and 'society,' to point out so far as may be the relation of the political organization to the whole social order.[8] The difference involved is all-important, a difference of kind and not of degree, in fact almost the whole world of difference between an end and a means.

If the state does not absorb into its own life of organization the other forms of social life, the worlds of art, science, religion, and social intercourse, not to speak of the family life, in what relation does it stand to these? On the one hand, of course, the form of the state depends on the whole character of a society; it is just what it is because of the character and temperament of the people who make the state. But that is not the question. Relations of this character are not reciprocal. No doubt a hundred social forces have determined the present shape of an Englishman's hat, but that work of art does not equally determine those social forces. In fact, determination would lose all meaning if it worked equally in opposite directions. The state, however, does exercise a certain control over the individual and social centres of movement and influence. In the first place, because of what it stands for, because it preserves and upholds through its organization the very existence of society, that being its primary end, it has a certain superiority of control, not merely of influence, over alike the partial organizations and the free life of society, – a control which in no way contradicts the essential claim to spontaneity made by that life. Suppose the state thought a certain religion undermined the security of society, it would interfere with that religion; suppose it thought a certain industrial concern deprived its workers of the opportunity to live a social beings, again it might interfere. It would here be protecting one social grouping against another.

But of course state-action has a much wider area than that just indicated. Individualistic writers like Mill and Spencer limited the state to that type of action, and so gave away their case. The state as the central organization can come forward to organize when such organization is clearly of advantage, and in this way exercise direct control over – though here it would be

---

8   Logically the Hegelian argument involves a thorough-going socialism, and that is why some socialist writers have rightly claimed Hegel as one of themselves in spite of much if his teaching that seems directly opposed to their doctrine.

wrong to admit interference with – the various social activities. For one thing, the various and infinite societies which constantly arise within "society" develop secondary organizations, and these must be inter-organized. For another, the central protective organization can greatly further the partial organizations and thus the life which these support. Take, *e.g.*, the economic life of society. To a certain extent state-organization can develop that life without destroying its spontaneity, – and so we find the state regulating forms of contract, controlling coinage, determining the conditions of limited liability, establishing a bank, even assuming entire control of those industries which, so to speak, bind all other industries together and make their free development possible, the industries of intercommunication. Or again take family life. The family is not simply an element in the state – after the desiccated conception of socialism – but essentially something more. Yet the state does not merely recognize and protect the family. It claims a certain control. It regards marriage, *e.g.*, as a political institution so far as to insist on certain regulations, registration and so forth, and it defines to some degree the rights and duties of relatives, making them legal and not merely social rights and duties. It might reasonably prohibit the marriage of persons suffering from certain forms of disease, though here, as always, the limit of state-intervention becomes a difficult *practical* problem.

The state is thus determinate, a close organization of social life; while society is indeterminate, an ever-evolving system spreading beyond and only partially controlled by the definite network of the state. That network of organization, by enclosing within it a portion of society, gives that portion a certain unity and definition, but neither cuts it off from a wider society of which it is essentially part nor within that portion substitutes its own external mode of action, its necessity, for the spontaneity that is the mark of all life, social and other. Such a protective and controlling organization it would be better to think of as an enclosing and interpenetrating network than as, say, a shell, even a living and growing shell, – for it is essentially true that the whole social life of a community is not comprehended within the form of the state.

The question we are considering is in no sense "mere theory" – for political science there is no such thing – and we may finally turn briefly to consider certain important practical applications. I believe the answer to the socialist ideal must rest on the distinction just drawn, but into that larger question I shall not enter here.

1. Hellenistic writers such as Hobhouse[9] and Bosanquet often speak as if they were still living in the Aristotelian state four thousand citizens strong – as if a single centre of interests were still possible and the station and duties of the individual could be determined simply in terms of citizenship in a state. Such a view is wholly inadequate, not only because the modern state is too vast to serve such an end, but also because it is too much differentiated. The view in question overlooks the whole development of the political consciousness since Aristotle wrote his *Politics*. The state stands for an area of common good, not for the whole of common good. The life of the individual citizen cannot therefore be lived wholly in the light of the ideal for which the state stands. In modern conditions the ordinary citizen simply cannot live all the time for the state, though he can still die for it on occasion. For certain classes, indeed, for the politician, the civil servant, the soldier, social ends seem more nearly to identify themselves with the political end, but even for these, and in the attempt to serve such an end, there will arise in the very state-organization social groupings with narrower ideals, a political party, *e.g.*, or a military order. For an adequate social life smaller and nearer centres are necessary – the district, the city, the village, and the numerous associations they include. Social life can no longer in practice and should no longer in theory be centralized into state-life. The individual should not be summed up in his citizenship, otherwise the claim of citizenship will itself become a tyranny and its essential moral value be lost. "The modern wilderness of interests" will not be set in order by our pointing simply to the road of citizenship. For the main road of citizenship, which we must make straight as possible, though it intersects a

9   For the Hellenism of Mr. Hobhouse *cf.* the following passage from *Morals in Evolution*: "Untroubled by any conflict between the secular and the spiritual power the Greeks could readily conceive a political society as an association for all the principal purposes of life that are not covered by the smaller association of the household. On this side their ideal of the state has never since been equalled." On the contrary it has been the great beneficial result of the conflict between the secular and the spiritual power that more than anything else it has helped to make clear the essential distinction between state and society.

thousands paths of social interest, cannot and should not absorb them.

2. These paths of social interest do not stop at the frontiers of states. The political interest is determinate and has limits, the social has none. Here, therefore, for the proper understanding of international relations, it is most necessary to distinguish state and society. On the assumption of identity we can have no unity of peoples until they are absorbed in some world-state. For each state by its very definition is a determinate and self-sufficient unit. A man can belong to one alone, can owe allegiance to one alone. Citizenship has hard and fast limits. In respect to the sphere of its sovereignty every state is demarcated absolutely from every other. Consequently if political will were identical with social will, the members of one state would remain totally alien from those of every other state. States would stand to one another as Spinoza and Hobbes imagined them to stand, isolated as the pre-civil individuals of their imagination, totally independent until some contract is agreed upon, even then totally independent because there is no higher will to make agreement binding. But of course it is in international relations that the distinction of state and society is most clearly revealed and that the common interests of universal society most manifestly weave new unities in spite of political separation. A man may perhaps "denationalize" himself (though that is hardly the proper word) by leaving his country, but he cannot "desocialize" himself without leaving the world of men, or at least of civilized men.

Society, therefore, and not the state, is the "world the spirit has made for itself." "The spirit" does not isolate itself in states, as Hegel's argument assumes.[10] On the contrary, the growth of civilization means the growth of ever widening community, the "realization" of social interest beyond the limits of politically independent groups. Society widens and the sense of community grows. In particular, the privileged classes of the different peoples, the authors of most past wars, become more and more allied by social intercourse, by common commercial

[10] Hegel is rather confusing on this point. For instance he says (*Gr. der Phil. des Rechts*, § 330) that the state is "not a private person but a completely independent totality" and yet immediately adds that it is related to other states (§ 331) and instances the nations of Europe as "forming a family on account of the universal principles of their legislation, their ethical usages, and their civilisation" (§ 339). How can "completely independent totalities" form a family?

and intellectual interests. M. Tarde has pointed out how classes of men whose occupation, even if in a competitive way, brings them into constant association with one another develop a friendlier spirit towards one another than classes not subject to this socializing influence. The same holds of peoples. It is not civilization but inter-civilization that develops mutual sympathy between states. The highly socialized Greek cities, because each held to an ideal of autonomy and self-sufficiency, the ideal of "completely independent totality," were not inter-socialized, and accordingly displayed the intensest hostility to one another. But the aloofness of Greek states is impossible in the modern world, which is pervaded by intersocializing influences of literature and commerce. Common ideas and common trade[11] have formed everywhere social bonds which cut across the line of states, and have made western Europe, looked on as a whole, an effective society. Thus an educated Englishman comes to have more in common with an educated Frenchman than he has, say, with an English agricultural laborer. The alien, shut out from his state, has yet a closer social affinity to him than his fellow citizen.

We should note here that it is just on the sense of community that organization rests. Political organization, the completest and most self-sufficient of all organizations and indeed the most necessary. ultimately requires a definite kind and degree of felt community. But there are other degrees and forms of community. At a certain stage every society, every grouping founded on whatever sense of community, becoming conscious of its unity, strengthens or confirms it by some form of organization, makes for itself as it were an integument of organization, so there are as many types of organization as there are of society. The political society is based on the distinctive organization of law, other societies develop quasi-legal or contract organizations which in turn the political society, as possessing the supremest form of organization, tends to inter-organize. But when the community extends beyond the limits of a state, the single state can no longer of

---

11   For this reason universal Free Trade would be preferable to universal protection. I may quote Hobhouse on this point: "The doctrine of natural liberty, particularly as preached by Cobden and the Free Traders, also told heavily on the side of peace, just as the recrudescence of militarism in our own day has been associated, not in this country alone, with economic protection." *Morals in Evolution*, Vol. 1, p. 278.

itself ratify the society. So international relations arise, which are no longer strictly legal relations at all, but only approximations to these. There may be many degrees of approximation, representing many degrees of international social integration, from alliances and federations down to the minimal organization represented by Berlin treaties and Hague conventions, extradition laws, and so forth. A federation of Europe would therefore in no sense be a new thing. Europe is already federated.

At the same time we should perhaps further note that those writers are mistaken who assume as a logical development of this principle an ultimate world-empire.[12] The principle is that a felt community between men in course of time produces a contract organization in respect to all definitely recognized common elements, that every society, when it becomes conscious of itself, develops an institutional aspect. But community can be felt only in so far as community exists; and the amount of community necessary for a true political society, is, as experience has shown, a very large one. Community must, perhaps should, always be partial, is rendered partial at the outset by the ultimate fact that men and peoples are marked off from one another not only by their own necessary differences but also by their occupancy of different portions of the earth's soil. It is on this difference that the territorial state is immediately based, making certain boundaries, often not very obvious boundaries, the rigid dividing line where one sovereignty ends and another begins. In such territorial states it is at once obvious that the political line is not a social frontier as well. So far as the territorial principle goes, country is marked off from country just on the principle on which district is separated from district and parish from neighboring parish. Of course between districts, and even between parishes, further differences are found, and so between countries there are differences of national type, temperament, education, and language, sufficient to justify at once the community and the separation involved in political society, the determinations of government which constitutes a state. A world-state would mean that the world had become in certain definite respects an homogeneous society. But as a general rule community and separation, centralization and decentralization, both within

---

[12]   *Cf.*. Tarde, *Les lois de l'imitation*, Ed. 2, Ch. 8, p. 420.

and beyond the limits of the state, and just because of the social forces that underlie the state, must go hand in hand, must develop *pari passu*, the two being not antagonistic but complementary principles. Most empires have been failures because they pursued the principles of centralization alone: the Roman empire in particular, when at the last it became a world state and not simply an aggregation of states around one central state, showed how impossible it was for a completely centralized system to meet the needs of peoples of different temperaments and living under very different physical and social conditions. If centralization is necessary for peace and order, decentralization is equally necessary for development and life.

I have tried to point out one or two applications of this vital distinction of state and society. There are many others to be made, and of these the economic application is perhaps the most important. It is only by keeping this distinction in mind that we can hope to understand the difficult relations of political and economic forces. But to touch on this subject here would be unduly to extend the limits of this paper.

R. M. MacIver
King's College
Aberdeen

THE DISCREDITED STATE
Thoughts on Politics before the War

It is perhaps not an untrue saying, that the State has generally been discredited in England. Indeed, foreign lawyers have been known to say that the State has never existed in England. Notions of *imperium* and *majestas* have not flourished in these islands, except in the Byzantine days of Henry VIII. Austin, who, one is told, was not particularly skilled in English law, and could blunder shockingly in Roman law, may have theorized about *majestas*; but his own difficulties in fitting his theory of sovereignty into the framework of English politics seem to show that it is fairly remote from the *genius loci*. A sovereign and majestic State, a single and undivided *imperium*, lifted above the conflicts of society, neutral, mediatory, impartial, such as Hegel conceived and such as German theorists still postulate – this we have not known. Our State is on its executive side a bundle of officials, individually responsible for their acts, and only united by a mysterious Crown which is responsible for nothing and serves chiefly as a bracket to unite an indefinite series of $1 + 1 + 1$. Our State on its legislative side, as Hegel told us a hundred years ago, is no pure State, emancipated from society: it is trammelled in the bonds of *bürgerliche Gesellschaft*; and our legislature, composed of members of this society, 'sacrifices objective freedom or rational right to mere formal freedom and particular private interests' (*Philosophie des Geistes*, § 544).

With a bracket-enclosed bundle of officials, and a socially trammelled legislature, we cannot have a State, a German will say; or if we have a State, it can only be discredited. History cannot elucidate, but it may at any rate illustrate, this discredit. Let us take three illustrations. The feudal baronage of the days of Magna Carta were good syndicalists – and indeed the best syndicalists throughout history have been the upper classes. For organized labour like theirs they felt that the State had no message. They asserted a right of striking against the State:

they claimed a class-privilege of legalized rebellion whenever the class-privileges which they had defined in Magna Carta suffered infringement. Their syndicalism had a good mediaeval philosophy at its back. They could appeal to contract and natural law. The king ruled on contractual terms; if he transgressed the terms which he had promised in his coronation oath to observe, they were quit of their *fides* and might betake themselves to *diffidentia*. Moreover, natural law rules the world, including States and kings; and if class-privileges are included under that elastic head, class-privilege rules, or overrules, the world of States and kings. In other words, the feudal barons were not unacquainted with the eminent dominion of natural rights.

A second illustration follows logically, if not chronologically. 1688 is no far cry from 1215. Locke speaks of property instead of class-privilege; and since we all *may* have property, he seems more universally kind. Be that as it may, he inaugurated a long period of our history. The right of property, not only in things but in persons – not only for use, but also for power – has raised its head against the State for these last two centuries. Once more contract, always inimical to the State, has served as a philosophy; and in the name of freedom of contract a great organ of freedom has had its long winter of discredit. But two may play with the same doctrine. The natural rights of labour may be urged as well as the natural rights of property. They are being urged to-day. This revenge of labour on property has its ironies. The worst of the natural right of property was its want of logic. While it claimed immunity from the State, it could only exist by the protection of the State. Its motto was, You must keep your hands off me; but you must stand in front of me. Labour has learned its lesson from property; and with an almost equal want of logic, perhaps the more pardonable because it has good precedent, it claims immunity from the State for its trade unions in the same breath that it demands recognition by the State of the natural 'right to work'.

A third illustration touches different ground. Men may claim not a mere natural right to privilege, or property, or work, but a right divine to worship free. Robert Browne, of Corpus Christi College, Cambridge, had little use for the Elizabethan State. Henry Barrow, of Clare, was of the same way of thinking. Congregationalism, which ranks there two Cambridge men among its founders, simply turned its back on the State. Calvinism, in one sense more drastic, in another sense more complacent, recognized the State, but made it the organ of a spiritual consistory, and enlisted its secular arm for enforcing the final judgements of an ecclesiastical tribunal. It is Congregationalism, however, and not Calvinism, which has influenced English political thought most deeply. The first and most striking agent of that influence was Sir Harry Vane, Milton's contemporary. Vane, taught by his experience of religious intolerance in America, had early come by the principle of 'soul-liberty', which Roger Williams, father of toleration, had made the basis of his community at Providence in 1636. Soul-liberty, Vane urged, was exempt from and higher than the State. 'Magistracy', he wrote, 'is not to intrude itself into the office and proper concerns of Christ's inward government and rule in the conscience; but it is to content itself with the outward man, and to intermeddle with the concerns thereof in reference to the converse which man ought to have with man.' The doctrine may seem to us trite and conservative; it was new-minted and radical to an age which thought in terms of the one society, the church-state, whose membership was compulsory, and whose rules, alike the ecclesiastic and the politic, were equally binding on all its members. Milton celebrates Vane as a new Cortez who has seen a new Pacific:

> To know
> Both spiritual power and civil, what each means,
> What severs each, thou hast learned, which few have done.

Believing that the individual can never forfeit to the State his soul-liberty, Vane equally believed that the community can never alienate its own inherent if limited sovereignty. The responsibility of each individual for the saving alive of his own soul, the responsibility of each community for the determining of its own life, there are the two divine burdens of humanity. No wonder that Vane's philosophy had a deep influence on T. H. Green, who had a notable sympathy for English Nonconformists. Vane said on the scaffold, 'The people of England have long been asleep. I doubt they will be hungry when they awake.' 'If the people of England should yet awake and be hungry', Green writes, 'they will find their food in the ideas which, with much blindness and weakness, he vainly offered them, cleared and ripened by a philosophy of which he did not dream.'

English Nonconformity has been the main influence in the discrediting of the English State, just because it has been the noblest. Antigone has confronted Creon these 250 years with the declaration that his mortal decrees were not so strong as to outspeed the unwritten and unfailing law of God. The pity is that our English Antigone has had Midas for her ally. For the Nonconformist defiance of the State had been confirmed and corroborated by the defiance of the economic man, with his appeal to the unwritten and unfailing law of free contract and free competition. Our two distinctively English products in the sphere of the mind – and we may take these to be Nonconformity and political economy – have been shrewd enemies of the State. It is curious to notice that he who wrote *The Man versus the State* was reared in Nonconformist circles and nourished on political economy. It was for a paper called the *Nonconformist* that Herbert Spencer wrote his first essay on politics – *The proper sphere of Government*: it was in the agitation against the Corn Laws that he first took any active part in politics. And the whole assumption of the validity of natural rights which Spencer so largely drew from these two influences is an assumption that still lies at the back of ordinary English thought and prejudice. Few Englishmen might know what you meant if you spoke to them of natural rights; but most Englishmen believe in natural rights. Professor Halévy, a close observer of things English, noted, in a recent letter to the writer, that 'the old eighteenth-century idea, exploded as it is, of the abstract rights of the individual is quietly gaining ground in the world of actual English politics'.

The measure of the ground gained is the number of the new 'isms' that are current. Their number sometimes surprises, and men feel that they live in new and unstable days. The quiet Victorian peace of the last half of the nineteenth century has perhaps lulled us into forgetfulness. But there were many 'isms' abroad in the tumultuous years between 1789 and 1848; and there were ideas spreading even in the years of Victorian peace which are now sown broadcast. Two of these – Tractarianism and Marxianism – suggest some reflections. They have in some sense taken the place of the old Nonconformity and the old economics in resistance to the State. Curiously enough Nonconformity is now if anything conformist. It is Elizabethan: it will enforce a State definition of religion by State machinery in elementary schools. The real Nonconformist of these days is the high Anglican. Ever since 1833 he has felt the claim and urged the rights of the Church of his conception against the State and its menace. He has left that his Church is a substantive body independent of the State, with its own origin in divine foundation, its own continuity in virtue of apostolical descent, its own rights in virtue of its origin and continuity. Newman wrote to his fellow clergy in the first Tract for the Times: 'A notion has gone abroad that [the people] can take away your power. They think they have given and can take it away . . . Enlighten them in this matter. Exalt our holy fathers the bishops, as the representatives of the Apostles . . . and magnify your office as being ordained by them to take part in their ministry.' Here the protest is not the protest of Roger Williams for individual soul-liberty: it is a protest for group-liberty. And Marxianism, a philosophy which probably owes much to English inspiration, and certainly owes something to the inspiration of Thomas Hodgskin, indicates a similar change. The economic defiance of the State is no longer the individualist claim of the economic man for *laissez faire*: it is the cry of class consciousness, the collective voice of Labour. Interpreted and expanded by Sorel, Marxianism urges the need for the liberty of the proletariate consciousness and culture from the contamination of the bourgeois State, just as Catholicism demands the freedom of religious consciousness and the religious idea of life from the coercion of the secular State. Nonconformist soul-liberty and economic individualism have both surrendered the defiance of the State to new challengers. The challengers are now groups, challenging in the name of groups; but the challenge is still there.

The English State is thus accustomed to discredit. And to tell the truth it has never sought to take great credit to itself. It has not magnified its own office, or exalted its own dignity. It has left its officers to be responsible for their official doings to the ordinary courts and by the ordinary rules of the common law. Habeas Corpus enables the judges to review any act of the executive which has resulted in the imprisonment of a subject. No official can swell with pride as the embodiment of the State, or boast that the clothes he wears distinguish him from his civic brethren. Our forefathers at the end of the seventeenth century would not even allow the State, in the shape of the Crown, to contract our National Debt. The National Debt is owed, and the interest on the National Debt is paid, by 'the Publick'. While law has not been tender to the State, it has been tender enough, intentionally or no, to all manner of groups. Here we touch on that peculiarly English thing, the Trust. The State replied to Nonconformist defiance, at any rate in the eighteenth century, by turning the other cheek. For one thing it passed annual Acts of Indemnity to secure those Nonconformists who had violated its laws by taking office without the due subscription; for another, it permitted the conception of trust to shelter Nonconformity in possession of its chapels and funds. The trust, as Professor Maitland has shown, preserved religious liberty. And the trust has also served trades unions. It has permitted them to accumulate and to hold the funds without which their activities would have been impossible. It may indeed be urged that the trust has sheltered group-life more fully than any legal recognition of the 'real personality' of groups could have done. Hidden behind their trustees, groups have thriven and grown unnoticed. The recognition of their real personality would have meant their coming more fully under the public eye; and the public eye might have refused to wink at the doings of bodies which it could see, while it never even blinked at the activities of groups which were hidden by the screen of trust.

Nor have groups merely flourished in our country under the shelter of trusts. They have flourished anyhow and anywhere. England is a place where they seem always to have been budding and maturing. In this clubable country groups and associations are always arising freely and acting as freely. We have thrown off in an easy and light-hearted way groups like the East India Company, which, as we may read in our statute book, can have financial transactions with the English 'Publick' as an independent entity, so that in 1786 the Public stands indebted to the Company in a sum of more than four millions. In the same easy way this English State has thrown off groups like colonies, which manage to combine independence with allegiance; and within her own borders she has thrown up those associations called parties, which are well within the State, and yet so far from being altogether under the State, that they have a habit of taking the State in tow and 'running' it after their own devices. Nonconformist bodies, trades unions, great semi-sovereign companies, self-governing colonies, political parties – they have all budded freely, matured easily, and gone very much their own way. In some ways England is not unlike the University of Oxford – or for that matter any other amoeba. She can throw off by a ready process of fission colleges and delegacies; and some of these delegacies may even take to running the *universitas* itself.

It is curious that, while English thought and practice have never been particularly favourable to the claims of the State, two Englishmen, Hobbes and Austin, should have been preachers of a doctrine of *majestas* which recognizes and, one may almost say, consecrates those claims. The doctrine has a long history, and its history proves that it is not of English origin. As stated by Austin it runs as follows: 'Every positive law, or every law simply and strictly so called, is set by a sovereign person, or a sovereign body of persons, to a member or members of the independent political society wherein that person or body is sovereign or supreme.' In other words, all laws are the fiat of a sovereign; all sovereigns are persons or bodies of persons of a determinate character; each independent political society has one and only one such person or body of persons; and every such person or body of persons has indeterminate or unlimited power. This is a theory of an admirable simplicity; but it is not the theory of Bentham, who recognizes the possibility of a limited sovereignty;[1] it fails to square with the facts of English political life and structure; and it is, one may suspect, French in its immediate and perhaps papal in its ultimate origin. In the eighth chapter of his first book, the French legist, Bodin, defines *majestas* as *summa in cives ac subditos legibusque soluta potestas*. This majesty is the *differentia* of a State: 'a state transcends a corporation by the fact that it embraces a multitude of citizens and towns within the protection of the majesty of its power.' For support of the transcendence and omnipotence of this majesty Bodin appeals, and very naturally appeals, to the supremest of all sovereigns, the papal chair. Innocent IV, he writes, 'who understood best of all men the rights of sovereignty, and who had put under his

[1] Cf. the *Fragment on Government*, chapter iv, §§ 34–6. 'What difficulty there should be in conceiving a state of things to subsist in which the supreme authority is thus limited [by an instrument of convention, setting assignable bounds to its power], what greater difficulty in conceiving it with this limitation, than without any, I cannot see.' Bentham, writing in 1776, thus anticipated, more than ten years in advance, the principle of the United States Constitution. (I owe this reference to the kindness of Sir F. Pollock.)

feet the authority of almost all emperors and Christian princes, said that supreme power belongs to him who can take away from ordinary law'. It is indeed the high papal view of the *plenitudo potestatis* which really inspires Bodin, as Bodin inspires Austin. As the Papacy is the *fons et origo* of the government of the august commonwealth of Christian men, so the sovereign is the ἀρχή – the ἀρχή in both senses of the word – of the public conduct of the members of each independent political society.

A modern clerical writer – inspired by the teaching of Acton, who fought papal infallibility, and stimulated by the writings of Gierke, who champions the real personality of those corporations relegated by Innocent IV to the category of *fictae personae* – has set his lance against this high and dry doctrine of sovereignty. Dr. Figgis, representing those tendencies of advanced Anglicanism which have been mentioned before, has written more than one philippic against the Innocentine and Austinian notions of sovereignty. If one looks at the ecclesiastical community in itself, the Innocentine notion is fatal to the true federal character of the Catholic Church; if one looks at the ecclesiastical community as engaged in the life of a State, the Austinian notion is destructive of the rights of that community, because it is fatal to the true federal character of the State, through whose recognition alone the rights of its component communities can be preserved. Advocating a federalistic view alike of the Catholic Church and of the State, Dr. Figgis ingeminates the phrase 'inherent rights of associations'. He returns, in a word, to the old idea of natural rights, but he resuscitates that ghost by giving it blood to drink – the red blood of real corporate personality. It is in the name of real group-persons that Dr. Figgis can renounce the doctrine of an 'omnicompetent State' confronting and controlling a 'sum of atomistic individuals'; it is in this sign that he will victoriously instal the doctrine of a partially competent State of a federal character, embracing in a kind of co-partnership – and not, as Bodin says, in the transcendent majesty of power – real groups which have also their competence in their sphere.

II

The problem of resistance is in actual life always a problem of groups. Theorists may set limits to the State in the name of the individual; practical resistance is always a matter of group-consciousness. What is a group? Has it a personality beyond the persons of its members, and a will beyond their wills? Maitland, following and interpreting Gierke, has answered that 'the fellowship is a real person, with . . . a will of its own'. Professor Geldart, in an inaugural lecture on legal personality, cautiously writes that 'there seems to be at least a *prima facie* case for holding that our legal theory ought to admit the reality of a personality in permanent associated bodies, or at least of something so like personality that we may provisionally call it by that name for want of a better'. The problem is perhaps the simplest and most terrible of all problems. It is the problem of universals: the problem of identity and difference. It is as easy for a mind without the philosophic compass to drift into the *res praeter res*, and to see all identity, as it is to run up against the *nomen de rebus*, and to see all difference. Perhaps neither fits the facts; perhaps the Identical, in this matter of groups, is neither a real person nor a nominalist fiction. Let us call it an idea, and see into what dim port we drift with that pilot. William of Wykeham had an idea, somewhere about 1378; to-day there is a group, or fellowship, of St. Mary College of Winchester in Oxford, and this paper has been written in a room that belongs to this idea, and its writer is somehow, being Fellow of Wykeham's college, related to this same idea. What has happened is that this idea has entered into a continuous succession of persons. They have retained their personality, but they have coloured their personality with the idea: a new personality has not arisen, but a new organizing idea has served as a scheme of composition for existing personalities. We have it on Aristotelian authority that the State is the same as long as its scheme of composition is the same. Its identity resides not in any single transcendent personality but in a single organizing idea permeating simultaneously and permanently a number of personalities. As for the State, so for all fellowships; there may be oneness without any transcendent one. We may alter our organizing idea; we may turn a tragic chorus into a comic chorus. We do not kill a personality that existed before, or create a personality that did not exist before: we alter our organizing idea.

Law has to bring these permanent and organizing ideas, which unite persons together in lasting schemes, under some rubric or title – trust, contract, *persona ficta* or real person. The rubrics of law are not reality; they are cases in which to put reality; but the cases may fit reality well or badly, and since reality has a way of growing, they may help or hinder its growth. Apparently the cases called trust, contract, and *persona ficta* all hinder growth, and cramp the living texture of reality within the limits of a rigid trust-deed, or a hard bond of contract, or a limiting charter of delegation such as must go to the creation of a *persona ficta*. Much may be said for the rubric of real personality as a rubric of the lawyers and for the lawyers; and much might be said in this connexion on a fascinating problem – how far legal categories are created by the demands of social growth, and how far legal categories create or rather determine social growth itself. But to the plain man the simple necessity is the necessity of preserving the organizing idea fresh and growing, freshly apprehended as a motive by each mind in the organization, and freely growing with the growth of mind, as a wider outlook discovers fresh implications and fresh relations of the idea. Ideas have their pathology; and they suffer from two main diseases. They may become mere bundles of blue paper swathed in red tape: we may have trust-deeds in lieu of ideas; and the religious idea itself, which is the true and only unity of any Church, may pass from an idea to a creed, and from a creed to an empty formulary. Again, they may become office chairs and organizing secretaries. This is the tragedy that is always enacted when an institution becomes mere officialdom, or a Church mere sacerdotalism. Great is the magic of office chairs, and the hard-driven word organization too often covers an ample paucity of ideas. But we need not escape blue paper and office chairs by flying to real personalities which are perhaps, in any other sense than that of legal categories, the ghosts of imagination. Ideas are, and are not fictions: they have hands and feet; but they are not persons, any more than they are fictions.

We may eliminate personality and will – transcendent personality and transcendent will – from associations; we may be content to speak of associations as schemes in which real and individual persons and wills are related to one another by means of a common and organizing idea. We may conceive the State as such a scheme based on the political idea of law and order; we may conceive it as containing, or at any rate co-existing with, a rich variety of schemes based on a rich variety of ideas. We are all members of the one scheme and partakers of the one idea; most of us are also members of many other schemes, and partakers of many other ideas. The ideas are in relation to one another; perhaps they are in competition with one another. If it is so, it is a competition of ideas, not of real collective personalities. To apprehend this point of view is already a certain gain. We are rid of the idea of an internecine struggle between the real personality of the State and the real personality of other groups. We cease to feel murder in the air. Real ideas cannot be killed: they can only die by the suicide of their own excess, or the slow internal decay of their own life. Again, when we talk of real persons, we attach to them an intrinsic value as such, because we feel that all personality has value. At that rate we should see value in the Mafia[2] or Camorra. If one talks rather of ideas, one can keep something more of critical poise. One can argue with ideas: one can show that they are partial or erroneous; one can deflate a bubble idea with a prick of logic.

But the problem remains to be faced – if not to be solved, for it is perhaps theoretically insoluble – whether there is any graded hierarchy of associating ideas, and whether we can ascribe sovereignty to one associating idea. A passion for the *reductio ad unum*, such as inspired the *De Monarchia* of Dante, may urge us to seek a dominant One; and finding that One in the associating idea of the political community, we may speak of the sovereignty of public opinion. We may urge that there must be a single source of adjustment to determine the relations of associating ideas one with another, to criticize each scheme of associations on its merits, to abolish associating ideas that are dead, to reinvigorate associating ideas that are

---

2   It is curious to note that the word Mafia is applied both to the organizing (or disorganizing) idea, and to the society which it unites. Dr. Murray defines Mafia as 'the spirit of hostility to the law and its ministers prevailing among a large portion of the population (of Sicily) . . . also the body of those who share in this anti-legal spirit'. It would seem that the Sicilians are good enough philosophers to give the name of the organizing idea to the society which it constitutes.

dormant. Whether empirically or theoretically considered, the matter is by no means easy. Empirically we may see that other associating ideas than that of the political community have claimed, and – what is more important – have received a final and absolute allegiance. This is most conspicuously true of the religious idea, which political theory has a way of neglecting. The final allegiance of the thorough Romanist lies with Rome, and not with Westminster. The allegiance of Sir Harry Vane, 'in the office and proper concerns of Christ's inward government and rule in the conscience', lay not with the magistracy, nor even with the sacerdocy, but with the indwelling Christ. The mediaeval world knew no unitary political sovereignty. Mediaeval thinkers might indeed conceive of a final and ultimate law of nature, whether as an 'indicative law' and the dictate of reason as to what is right, or as an imperative rule and the will of God; but just because they ascribed sovereignty to this law of nature, insomuch that all laws and all executive acts contrary thereto were *ipso facto* null and void, they could not and did not ascribe any sovereignty to a political superior. It was possible for the associating idea of the feudal privilege of a class to erect itself into an ultimate value, and to claim and exercise the right of legal rebellion against the authority of the State. The conception of an ultimate State Sovereignty entered England with the Reformation. Its zenith is the year 1539, when Parliament ascribed to Henry VIII's proclamations the force of law, and by the Act of the Six Articles took the very ark of the religious idea itself into the sphere of its regulation. But State Sovereignty was shattered by Nonconformity and shot-ridden by the Great Rebellion. And if to-day some may see a new Henry VIII in the guise of a sovereign public opinion, the syndicalist will none the less claim exemption from the bourgeois State for his idea of class, the nationalist will claim immunity from the denationalized State for his idea of the nation, and the right hand of the churchman will lose its cunning if he forgets Jerusalem. Even a quiet and cautious scholar like the President of Harvard will tell us in his last book that public opinion, which is in effect the opinion of the majority, is only dominant within the sphere of those things in which the minority will voluntarily consent to the decision of the majority, and that outside this sphere there lies an area of issues which a prudent State will never raise, because it is impotent to decide.

Public opinion, the associating idea of the political community, would be uniquely sovereign if it were absolutely homogeneous. That it never is; and that, some of us may hope, it never will be. Any community is a field of competing ideas; and with the growth of mind we can only expect a richer competition. It may be urged that heterogeneity of opinion is a symptom of an imperfect community, which has never thought itself together. It may also be urged that the opposite is true. The pullulation of new organizing and associating ideas is not a sign of poverty of the mind. The formation of new idea-centres, and the organization of men round those centres, is not likely to cease. One may rejoice as well as grieve to see Ulstermen and Irishmen, labour-men and churchmen, swarming after new guiding ideas to new hives. The apiarist is troubled: he wants all his bees in his own private orchard. But there is something to be said for the bees. Their guiding idea may be imperfect. It may contain a narrow and imperfect synthesis of data; and the nationalist idea, for instance, may lead men to seek a life that is narrow and poor in comparison with the wider and richer life of a great culture-state. But ideas have also to be measured by their effects on persons – in a word, if a very loose word, by their subjective value. An idea may be one-sided, but it may enlist the whole personality in its defence as nothing else could. If it does, it has after all its value as a vital and energizing factor for the individual. One defends democracy not as a form of government but as a mode of spiritual expression – an eliciting and enlisting force, which draws from us energies of thought and of will which we should never otherwise expend. The same defence may also cover this sphere. And there is another thing to be said. Admitting for the moment that the State idea is the broader and wider synthesis, it may, just because of its breadth, be an imperfect synthesis, which only achieves success by neglecting factors for which it should find room. It may be a forced and bare universal, purchased at the cost of many of its individuals. The very attempt of factors which conceive themselves neglected to push themselves forward as absolute wholes on their own account may serve as an incentive to a truer synthesis. If bare unitary sovereignty is, as it seems to be, such a forced and bare universal, we should only rejoice in its practical criticism by the logic of fact.

III

On what lines men may achieve, if ever they can achieve, a single associating universal, it is difficult to see. Churches, at any rate, seem likely always to be recalcitrant elements. As things now are, the high Hegelian unification seems at least premature. When Hegel tells me that 'the being of the State (on its objective side) is the in-and-for-itself universal', and that yet 'the State, as self-knowing and self-acting, is pure subjectivity and *one* individual'; when I hear that I, 'seeking to be a centre for myself, am brought by the State back into the life of the universal substance' – I throw up my hands. When I take things as I find them, I cannot see that universality, sovereignty, call it what you will, is the unique property of any one association. Other times, other fashions; and again *tot sententiae, quot societates*. At different times different societies may claim a final allegiance; and at one and the same time two or more societies may tug at the same heart-strings with equally imperative demands. No associating idea seems to engulf the whole man; and any man may have to face that solemn conflict of duties, which his membership of two different societies, his divided allegiance to two divergent ideas, may at any moment awake. There is no set solution of the dilemma. One is thrown back on the leaden canon of Lesbian builders – 'for the canon of the indeterminate is itself also indeterminate'. Either way one seems bound to lose. Whether one unsheathes the sword for the idea of the political society – the idea which requires as its bare minimum the observance of law and order – or for the idea of the other and rival society of religion, or nation, or class, the thumb is turned down against the gladiator. Either the pains and penalties that attend outraged law and order, or the ostracism or excommunication which attends desertion of the other group.

The prospect seems desolating. And most of us are not Childe Rolands, nor do we come to the dark tower. From anxiety and suspense, from the condition of unstable equilibrium, we deliver ourselves into the obvious and primrose path towards the greener valleys of law and order. *Quod principi placuit legis habet vigorem.* No associating idea, we may comfort ourselves, can have absolute validity or inherent right save one. Men who live together in a community must have an ultimate source of adjustment of their relations. That ultimate adjusting force, itself unadjusted, gives all rights except its own; and all rights are therefore derivative, none are inherent. You may talk – and here you hit most shrewdly – of the inherent rights of Churches; but what of Mormonism? You may talk of the inherent rights of proletariate consciousness; do you also admit the inherent rights of capitalistic consciousness? You may talk of the inherent rights of nationality: what of Albania? After all, the Idea of the State is the idea *par excellence* – all-embracing, all-subsuming, all-adjusting. Other ideas are partial; other ideas need criticism and adjustment. One may praise famous associations such as did bear rule in their kingdoms; but the tyranny of the association over its own members may be greater than any coercion exercised by the State over associations; and the State may and will be an organ of the freedom of persons, which is the only freedom, if it curtails the freedom of associations, which is only a paper freedom.

Yet some may still set a lance against the State, however daunted. The State is the organ of freedom: it is also a vehicle of force. Its sphere is automatism; it does external acts to produce external results. Other associations need consent the more as they use force the less; they must act more in the spiritual sphere, and seek to supply motive ideas in order to produce spiritual reactions. Again, the State may be broader; but is it many-sided, or one-sided? It rests fundamentally on the idea of law and order in the external converse of man with man; and the cultural ideas which it has superadded, turning itself from a plain grocer's shop into a Whiteley's emporium, have not altered its foundations. And therefore it is perhaps after all no final source of adjustment. It may be that there is no other source of adjustment among the associating ideas of a many-sided community except omniscience, which we admittedly do not possess. It may be that the State-idea is but *primus inter pares* – as ultimate as, but hardly more ultimate in the last resort than, other ideas which can quicken the pulse and fire the heart. Our universal may thus turn out to be a federal sort of thing. The state may be an educator of citizens: the Church may also be an educator of churchmen with a right of entry as such. The State may have its Westminster Parliament: the nation may also have its Dublin Parliament. The State may be in an area of political action: the trades union may also be a field of political action. It hardly meets the point to urge that the Church will not have its right of entry, or Dublin its parliament, or trades unions a political levy, until the State has issued its permissive law. The State is not prior to law; and Gierke will tell us that 'law is the result not of a common will that a thing shall be, but of a common conviction that it is'. Browning can write

Justinian's Pandects only make precise
What simply sparkled in men's eyes before,
Twitched in their brow or quivered on their lip,
Waited the speech they called but would not come.

In a word, law, as it has already been said, makes cases to hold reality, though it may affect reality very vitally by the kind of case it makes.

The Austinian notion of sovereignty is such a case. The reality it seeks to contain is the associating and organizing idea of law and order. The difficulty is that reality is wider than the case, for there are other ideas, in practice equally ultimate with this idea; and reality is therefore cramped by its case. In foreign affairs, it is true, there is a point in emphasizing the independence or ultimacy of a determinate political authority: only upon such terms can it negotiate with any finality. Indeed, changing the venue of our metaphor, we may say that sovereignty is a lotion for external application. But it ought to be labelled 'Poison – not to be taken internally'. Internally, it leads to a false view of law, which it degrades into the mere will of the sovereign. 'The human mind', Professor Wallace wrote in one of his lectures, 'must be disabused of the delusion that it makes laws.' Sovereignty fosters the delusion. Internally, again, it leads to a false unification and simplification of the rich complexity of the fact. It substitutes unitarianism for federalism, a corner in lieu of competition.

This may seem anarchism. Really it is polyarchism. And as for the problem of polyarchism – the problem of unstable equilibrium – why, after all, *solvitur ambulando*, it is likely to be settled by the needs of mere ordered life. This is the ultimate necessity; but it is not an absolute or invariable necessity. It varies with times and seasons. The sixteenth century was a time and season for *salus populi lex suprema*. Within, there was need of taming fully a still half-tamed nobility, of laying securely the red spectre of social unrest: without, nations were assuming 'the state and posture of gladiators' in their dealings one with another. Machiavelli could preach the State ultimate, the State undivided: he could warn his new prince that he would 'often be forced, in order to maintain his state, to go to work against faith, against charity, against humanity, against religion'. Years of ordered life have permitted the germination of other ideas than the indispensable minimum idea of law and order; they have brought us polyarchism for monachism. If the indispensable basis of law and order has been well and truly laid in sound hard concrete, it is all for the good. If that basis is not secure, if the building of our common life shows cracks and signs of subsidences, if the enemy without should see a gaping opportunity for his battering-ram, the cry of 'Back to law and order' will be great, and will prevail. Perhaps the hour is not yet. But if it should strike, there is no fear for the State, or for the idea of law and order. There is rather fear for other societies, other ideas. The idea of law and order, when it is roused, is one of the cruellest things in history. Think of the suppression of the Parisian Commune in 1871.

The discredit of the State is a sign that it has done its work well, and is doing its work well. When the judge gets white gloves at assize after assize, we can afford to think of putting up the shutters of the jails. The State will come into credit again, with a rush, at the double, as soon as it is seen to be doing its work badly. In the use of my private income I like to support charity and all manner of good causes. If it comes to a pinch, I have to say to myself, as someone said to Napoleon, 'It is necessary to live'. In our social life we are swarming hither and thither after associating ideas not only of law and order, but of religion, nation, class. If it comes to a pinch, we shall forget that we are anything but citizens. Through our mouths the State, which is nothing but ourselves organized in an ordered life, will then say to itself, 'It is necessary to live'. And there is no Napoleon to say to the State, 'I do not see the necessity for it'.

[*This paper was written in May 1914. It has been left as it stood, without any but verbal alterations. It is curious to reflect how differently one would have written in January 1915. Germany has shown that the sixteenth century has not been altogether overpast – at any rate in her own case.*

And yet the fundamental questions remain, and will re-emerge when the waters abate. Meanwhile the State is proclaiming, 'It is necessary to live'. We have forgotten that we are anything but citizens, and the State is having its high midsummer of credit.]

E. Barker

CONFLICTING SOCIAL OBLIGATIONS
By G. D. H. Cole

"The body politic is a moral being possessed of a will; and this general will, which tends always to the preservation and welfare of the whole and of every part, and is the source of the laws, constitutes for all the members of the State, in their relation to one another and to it, the rule of what is just or unjust."

"Every political society is composed of other smaller societies of different kinds, each of which has its interests and its rules of conduct; but those societies which everyone perceives, because they have an external and authorised form, are not the only ones that actually exist in the State; all individuals who are united by a common interest compose as many others, either temporary or permanent, whose influence is none the less real because it is less apparent, and the proper observance of whose various relations is the true knowledge of public morals and manners. The influence of all these tacit or formal associations causes, by the influence of their will, as many different modifications of the public will. The will of these particular societies has always two relations; for the members of the association it is a general will; for the great society it is a particular will, and it is often right with regard to the first object, and wrong as to the second. An individual may be a devout priest, a brave soldier, or a zealous senator, and yet a bad citizen. A particular resolution may be advantageous to the smaller community, but pernicious to the greater. It is true that, particular societies being always subordinate to the general society in preference to others, the duty of a citizen takes precedence of that of a senator, and a man's duty of that of a citizen; but unhappily personal interest is always found in inverse ratio to duty, and increases in proportion as the association grows narrower and the engagement less sacred; which irrefragably proves that the most general will is always

the most just also, and that the voice of the people is in fact
the voice of God."

Rousseau: Political Economy

I have set these two passages at the head of this paper because I
believe that, both where they are right and where they are
wrong, they afford the most valuable guidance in approaching
the problem of conflicting social obligations. This problem, we
have no difficulty in seeing to-day, is closely bound up with the
whole question of the place of particular associations in Society
– a question which becomes increasingly urgent as the opposing
forces of philosophers and practical men meet in a conflict
which is at once theoretical and practical. During the
nineteenth century the theory of State Sovereignty won an
almost universal triumph in abstract political theory; it now
seems likely that, under pressure from religious and industrial
theorists, it will suffer during the twentieth century a defeat no
less decisive. It is the bearing of this controversy upon the
problem of social obligation that I propose to examine.

Rousseau's theory of the General Will is, in its profoundest
aspect, the expression of the truth that all social machinery is
the organisation of human will. Social organisation can be
studied only as a branch of conduct: it is neither more nor less
than the instrument of co-operative action, in whatever guise it
may manifest itself. Wherever two or three are gathered
together, a common will different from their individual wills
may emerge: wherever two or three form a coalition or
association, of whatever sort, a new corporate will comes into
being.

The effect of this theory on philosophy is two-fold: it both
breaks down a distinction and creates one. It breaks down the
hard and fast distinction between ethics and politics which
comes of treating the one as an interpretation of human will
and the other not as philosophy, but as science, mechanism. It
creates a distinction, not between governmental acts on the one
side and private acts on the other, but between all social or
corporate acts and all individual acts – a distinction between
will acting directly, without intervening mechanism, and will
that acts only through such a mechanism.

How comes it, then, that philosophers, who have set out
since Rousseau from a conception of both ethics and politics in
terms of will, have still treated private associative acts as rather

of the individual than of the social type? It is, I believe, this mistake that lies at the root of our failure to provide any satisfactory answer to the problem of conflicting obligations.

In the *Social Contract* Rousseau was discussing the general will only in one of its manifestations – in the City-State. In the passages I have quoted he is treating the subject universally, so that corporate will in general becomes evident as the basis of his whole theory. Every particular association within the State, he assures us, has a general will of its own, and so far resembles the body politic, in which the pre-eminently general will is supposed to reside. But, he continues, while the will of any association is general in relation to its members, it is purely individual in relation to the State. And elsewhere, especially in the first book of the original draft of the *Social Contract* (published in the edition of M. Dreyfus-Brisac) he expressly declares that, in relation to a world-federation, the body politic itself would be purely individual.

Rousseau, in his City-State, decided, if possible, to banish associations altogether, on the ground that they would inevitably prove conspiracies against the public. He admitted, however, that there must be one important exception to this rule, since the people must appoint a government, and this government will inevitably use its corporate will in order to usurp Sovereignty, which belongs to the people. This is, in Rousseau's phrase, the inevitable tendency of the body politic to deteriorate.

Beginning, then, with an identification of the body politic with the ultimate sovereign people, Rousseau goes on to reduce to a minimum the number of conflicting wills within Society, and only admits the intrusion of any will other than those of the body politic and of the individuals composing it as a necessary imperfection of human societies. Similarly, the whole tendency of nineteenth century philosophy was to regard the association as, at the most, a necessary imperfection, to be tolerated rather than recognised, with no rights beyond those of expediency, and no powers beyond those conferred expressly by statute. From this point of view we are now struggling slowly back to a saner doctrine; but we have done this so far more on grounds of practical necessity than on grounds of philosophic theory. We are still too apt to take a view resembling Rousseau's as our basis, and to admit exceptions only as they arise.

What, then, was the fundamental error in Rousseau's presentation of the problem? We can best understand it by trying to envisage the types of particular association he conceived. As soon as we make this attempt, Rousseau's statement of the case cannot help appearing unnatural in view of the problems our century has to face. Rousseau states the difference between the body politic and the particular association as it if were simply a question of size, extent, membership. Just as the government consists of a select body, all of whom are also members of the sovereign people, so he seems to think of every association as consisting simply of so many persons who are also citizens. General wills within general wills, from the smallest possible association to the widest possible "confederation of the world," he envisages and fears: the division of one corporate will from another by function is a division he never seems to face, and one which he sweeps away merely by implication.

The corporate will of the government, or executive, is clearly a subordinate will of the kind of which Rousseau is thinking, and where the will of the government conflicts with that of the Sovereign, it will be universally admitted that the former should, in the end, give way. But, if we ask ourselves why this is so, we shall not, I think, reply with Rousseau that it is merely because it is smaller, but because it is both smaller and of the same kind.

Rousseau, in fact, as we can see most clearly in the famous chapter in which he dismisses particular associations, always thinks of them in terms of cliques, parties, conspiracies against the public. He does not distinguish between political and non-political associations, probably because he feels that every non-political association, from the Church to the city-guild, inevitably becomes political in defence of its vested interests and privileges. With a pessimism which the experience of France in the eighteenth century almost justified, he therefore declared in theory against every form of particular association.

When Rousseau's principle was put into practice by the *loi Chapelier* of 1791, there was, then, considerable reason, on grounds of mere expediency, for the general abolition of associations. But, as all students of French history know, the prohibition was never in effect complete, and it was not long before associations of various kinds, and especially workmen's societies, began to fight their way back to toleration and, at a later date, to recognition by the State. In practice, the revolutionary principle of the law of Chapelier broke down, and there came into existence new associations which were not conspiracies against the public, but natural human groupings with a specific function of their own.

If, then, the distinguishing feature of eighteenth century associations was privilege, passing easily into conspiracy against the public, the feature of nineteenth century association is speciality of function, which, though it may sometimes lead to controversy and prejudice the common good, is in no sense based on a conspiracy against the public. If it is privileged, it holds its privileges from the public on the ground that they are in the public interest: it is not privileged in the bad sense of constituting a vested interest irrespective of the common good.

What, we must now ask, is the relation between these particular associations and the State? Let me begin by defining my terms a little more exactly. By State I mean the governmental machine, national and local, with its various dependencies; by Association I mean any body which, whether or no it stands in a defined relation to the State, does not form part of the governmental machine; by Society I mean, for the time being, the whole complex of organised bodies within the national area, including both the State, national and local, and every organised association, of whatever kind; by Community I mean something wider still, the whole mass of desires, opinions, traditions, and possibilities which are, for the moment, incarnated in the citizens.

The State is thus itself a complex of institutions of a more or less uniform type, which, whatever else they may take into account, generally resemble one another in being based on geographical grouping. Society is a wider complex of institutions, which resemble one another throughout only as being one and all expressions of man's associative will. The Community, as I have used the word, is the sum total of social values, organised or unorganised, capable or incapable of organisation, within the national area.

I say "the national area," not because there is necessarily a magic in it, and still less because national grouping invariably determines the extent of associative grouping, but simply and solely in order to simplify the problem. The fact that some non-governmental groupings cover an area far larger than that of a single State is of the greatest practical importance, since it may immensely strengthen them in their conflicts with any State: it is none the less irrelevant to the discussion of the respective rights of governmental and non-governmental associations; and I am discussing, not expediency, but rights. I shall, therefore, assume an isolated national area, completely covered by a Nation-State and its various local governmental bodies, and including many functional associations of varying extent. What is the relation between these bodies, and, in the event of a conflict of principle between them, how ought the individual to determine his allegiance?

Philosophical writers on the general question (as distinguished from its particular applications) have answered in one of three ways. Either they have tried to define, absolutely and inclusively, the sphere of State action, or they have imposed certain theoretical limitations upon the otherwise universal Sovereignty of the State, or, thirdly, they have accepted the theory that the State is absolutely and universally sovereign.

In the first case, which has been as a rule the earliest in point of time, the State is regarded as an *ad hoc*, or at any rate an *ad hac*, authority, sovereign in certain defined spheres of action peculiarly its own, but elsewhere an interloper, wholly without right of intervention. This, roughly speaking, was the view of John Locke and of Herbert Spencer, much as they differed in many respects: it is the view which treats the State as primarily the upholder of something, whether it be property, law and order, liberty, religion, or morality, and not as the expression of any positive common will. Such a theory, in its old form, can have only an exceptional survival in face of modern social conditions. Those who hold it to-day are not philosophers, but practical men who wish to safeguard or to destroy some special interest. It still finds expression in the pamphlets of the Liberty and Property Defence League and in the pages of the *Spectator*: it also persists among Anarchists and Syndicalists, who still regard the State solely as the protector of property.

The second view, which became popular as the State, in the hands of opportunists, extended its sphere of activity, reverses the process of the argument: instead of defining inclusively what the State is and can do, it tries to define it by the exclusion of what it is not and cannot do. Its advocates often begin with a "bill of rights," a "declaration of the rights of humanity and citizenship," which lays down certain inalienable natural rights. The exclusion may be more or less comprehensive, and may even confine itself to excluding one special type of action from the jurisdiction of the State. It may attempt, as Mill attempted, to set up some general principle of division between actions with which the State is concerned, and actions with which it is not concerned. In any case, it accepts the view that the State is sovereign except where it is specially indicated not to be: it does not attempt an inclusive definition, and it excludes only by limitation. The further this theory removes itself from the *ad hoc* theory of the State, the nearer it comes to the acceptance of universal State Sovereignty, into which indeed most of its adherents have been forced by the breakdown of their attempted distinctions.

Just as the æsthetic philosopher goes in search of the ultimate principle of beauty, just as the moral philosopher tries to define the ultimate nature of moral obligation, so social philosophers are inevitably driven to seek out the ultimate principle of social obligation. Their failure lies, not in this attempt, but in the answer they have been induced to accept. For, driven from the two positions we have just defined, the philosophers have almost invariably accepted, as if it were the only alternative, a theory of complete State Sovereignty. They have been Austinian enough to shut their eyes to any Sovereign that might run the risk of being indeterminate, and Hobbist enough to accept the heroic simplification which merges all conflict of obligations into a single all-embracing State obligation.

Agreement on the theory of State Sovereignty has not led, indeed, to agreement on questions of practical policy, and herein lies the chief hope that this theoretical conversion is not final. The "limitation" theory was advocated by men who wished to save something they prized from the desecrating grip of the State. It may have been a communal value they were trying to conserve; but they were called, all the same, "individualists." Sooner or later a case would be bound to arise in which the common interest was clearly prejudiced by some action of the particular type which they had excluded from the jurisdiction of the State – at all events, they could never be sure that such a case might not arise. In such a case, they would be asked, should State interference be allowed? They might answer in the negative, and so save their consistency and nothing else; for they could offer no reason. Or they might throw up the sponge, and become, theoretically, advocates of State Sovereignty.

Thus we have, on the one hand, the author of *The Philosophical Theory of the State* (or should it be "of the Charity Organisation Society"?) coupling with a theory that amounts to State Sovereignty a note of solemn warning to the State not to presume too much upon its rights; and, on the other hand, we have Mr. Ramsey Macdonald and his like practically claiming the doctrine of State Sovereignty as a justification of Socialism, with which it has nothing to do.

If we ask what has led men who differ so in practice to agree upon their theoretical basis, if we ask, that is, why men accept the theory of State Sovereignty, even while they dislike and distrust the State, we shall find the answer if we understand the problem they were trying to face. Modern social theory was born in the period of political revolution, and is throughout both a reflection of existing political conditions and an attempt to justify various political opinions. When men studied in the eighteenth century the basis of human societies, what primarily interested them was not associative action as such, but State action: they were seeking, not so much the basis of human association, as the justification or refutation of the democratic argument. Rousseau's *Social Contract* appealed to his contemporaries, and even to himself, rather as a justification of democratic State Sovereignty than as an account of the fundamental nature of supra-individual will. The current political controversies turned social philosophy into political philosophy: thinking always of the State, philosophers sought, not the principle of social obligation, but the principle of political obligation.

This attitude has indeed persisted all through the nineteenth century, and up to our own times. That mid-Victorian Rousseau, T. H. Green, is infected, in an even greater degree than his predecessor, with a purely political bias. If anything besides the State creeps in, it is regarded as a form of association essentially different from the State, and in no sense the depository of ultimate social obligation.

We have seen that all modern social philosophy goes back to Rousseau, and that Rousseau's distinctive contribution lies in the recognition that social life, no less than individual life, is the expression of organised will. Rousseau set out to find the universal principle on which human society is based; almost as a bye-product he created the theory of the modern democratic State. We have only to read the *Political Economy* as well as the *Social Contract* to be quite sure that he was seeking, fundamentally, not a theory of the political State, but a statement of the life of the community as expressed in terms of will, individual and general, or rather individual, corporate, and general. But as a result of the political preoccupations of the time, instead of creating a philosophical theory of Society, Rousseau and his successors created a philosophical theory of the State, in which other associations found a position only on sufferance, if at all.

The main reasons which led to the triumph of the theory of State Sovereignty were three – two theoretical and one practical. Thinkers of every shade of opinion felt the need for some ultimate sovereign authority; their failure to regard associations as distinguished primarily by function led them to regard all association as a potential conspiracy against the public, and therefore to support the "democratic" State against the "privileged" association; and, thirdly, the immense political upheavals of the eighteenth and nineteenth centuries, by fixing men's eyes on the State, have tended to make all theories of social action chiefly theories of State action.

To-day, when most of us, however firmly we may retain our belief in political democracy, have at least lost the illusion of an inevitable democratic political progress, we may reasonably hope to reach a more inclusive conception of social action, and a better idea of the relation of particular associations to the State.

The key to Rousseau's whole social theory is to be found in his conception of the General Will. Nay more: the key to any rational social theory must be found in some conception of a General Will. Social science is the study, and social philosophy the interpretation, of the phenomena of collective personality. What right, then, has the State to claim a monopoly of such personality? Is not the very existence of particular associations a sufficient proof that the State cannot fully express the associative will of man? And is not the fact that these associations are the work of human volition a sufficient reason for crediting them with all the attributes of collective personality? Finally, if all these questions are answered in the affirmative, what superior claim has the State to the allegiance of the individual as against some particular association to which he belongs?

The General Will has been called an abstraction, and has been rejected as a guiding principle precisely by those who have felt this inadequacy on the part of the State to serve as collective "will of all work" to man's social consciousness. They have rejected the General Will because they have been always in search of a "determinate human superior," and the General Will has not seemed to form a natural attribute of any such superior. In fact, like Rousseau, they have conceived of the General Will as belonging only to the body politic, or State, and in such a connection the whole idea has seemed, as indeed it is, fantastic and abstract.

Yet what theory, in the freshness of youth, has not claimed too much for itself? The discoverers of the democratic State felt that in it they had found a method of expressing the whole civic consciousness of the individual, that political democracy was not only infallible, but omnipotent. Their ardent faith in democracy led them to an absolute trust in an absolutely generalised democratic machine, which, they believed, would equally express the common will whatever the matter in hand might be. At its best, this doctrine led to the repudiation by the State of all knowledge of distinctions of class; at its worst, it led to such absurdities as a State religion.

Yet we must not forget that, fundamentally, Rousseau's general principles were nearly always far more true than his ways of applying them. It makes no difference that the General Will cannot find complete expression through any single piece of social machinery. It is indeed precisely that universal will which all social machinery only partially expresses. The degree in which the General Will finds expression at all through organised machinery, governmental or non-governmental, the relative share borne in such expression by the State and by particular associations, and the actual intensity of the will itself, may vary from nation to nation and from generation to generation; but always and everywhere, all social machinery, alike in its agreements and in its conflicts, is a partial and more or less successful expression of a General Will which every community possesses.

The ultimate obligation of the individual is clearly not to any piece of mechanism, but to this General Will itself. How, then, is he to decide between conflicting claims to his allegiance, and how is he to answer the claim of the State to be served with a loyalty surpassing, and different in kind from, other loyalties?

The State is the national geographical grouping, and as such can claim to represent those elements in the common life which are best represented on a geographical basis, that is, by a general vote of all the persons resident in the national area, split up into such territorial subdivisions as may seem desirable.

This conception of the State as an essentially geographical grouping is, no doubt, a modern conception, and is perfectly true only of the purely democratic State. In so far as any privileged order retains special governmental rights or functions, the State is not purely geographical in its basis. But though perhaps no purely geographical State exists, the typical modern State is in the main a geographical grouping, and such rights as it possesses in a social system resting on popular Sovereignty must be founded on this geographical basis.

If we assume that a larger homogeneous group has always the ultimate right to override a smaller group *of the same kind*, it seems clear that geographical representation will serve to express those purposes which are distributed with some approximation to equality among all the citizens. If we assume that a national interest should, in the last resort, override a local interest, the supremacy of the National State over local governmental bodies follows. But this does nothing to mark out the proper sphere of action of either national or local government.

The State, national and local, should be the expression of those common purposes which affect all the citizens, roughly speaking, equally and in the same way. In those spheres of action in which a man's interest is determined by the fact that he lives and makes his home in a particular country or district, the geographical group can best express the desires which he shares with his fellows. Here, therefore, the State is sovereign.

The case is altogether different when we come to those spheres of action which affect men unequally, or in different ways. The power of the State adequately to represent the common will on such questions, so far from being demonstrated by experiment, becomes with every attempt more doubtful. The incursions of the State into the realm of organised religion have been invariably unhappy, and the attempts of State departments to run industry, while there is no evidence that they have been on the whole inefficient in the commercial sense, have wholly failed to satisfy the demand of the workers engaged in them for freedom and self-government at their work.

The reason for this failure is not far to seek. Religion is a disease which takes people in different ways, or not at all. It neither affects all men equally, nor affects them in the same way. It is therefore pre-eminently unfit to be governed by a body which has no principle of selection other than the geographical, and in which the irreligious man has an equal say with the religious, and men of different religions in the government of one another's churches. Similarly, industry affects different men in different ways, and would do so even in a community in which every man had his place in industry. Each industry has its special interests, and industry as a whole has an interest and an outlook of its own which no geographical group can adequately represent. In both cases, a broad functional difference is manifest which justifies the constitution of special associations to control the spheres of religion and industry, no doubt in relation to, but not under the domination of, the geographical group.

There is a further consideration which lends additional weight to this repudiation of universal State Sovereignty. Not only cannot an electorate gathered together on a geographical basis alone be fitted to deal with special questions which do not affect them all, or all alike, but also the persons whom they elect cannot possess this fitness. If we have learnt to distrust our politicians, is it not largely because we have allowed them to do things for which a geographical electorate is unfit to select the right representatives?

Strong as these arguments may seem, they will fall on deaf ears unless those who urge them do something to disprove the charge of individualism. Men have fallen into a theory of State Sovereignty, not because they like it, but because it has seemed the easiest, if not the only, way out of the slough of individualism. Half a hundred principles of social obligation, each binding us to a different social unit, cannot take the place of the unifying principle we set out to find. If this principle indeed proves not simple, but complex, its complexity can only be that of diversity in identity. The withdrawal, therefore, of some class of actions from the sphere of the State must not carry with it any denial of their social character, or even of their ultimate commensurability with social actions of another class. It must be simply a denial that the State is the right mechanism for the execution of certain types of social purpose. If we can keep this social element recognised in actions outside the sphere of the State, we may hope to avoid the theory of State Sovereignty.

It is, of course, universally admitted that individual acts have, as a rule, a social element. The tendency of social theory has been to treat the social element in associative acts as similar to the social element in individual acts, and to set both in contrast to State action, which is supposed to be wholly social. It is my whole point, not that associative acts are wholly social, but that State acts are not. The associative act has two relations: it is, as Rousseau says, general in relation to the association which performs it; but it is particular in relation to the Society of which the association forms a part. It may be general in the second case, in the sense that it may be directed to the good of the community as a whole; but it is still the act of an individual in relation to that Society. The State, I contend, even if it includes everybody, is still only an association among others, because it cannot include the whole of everybody.

The object, then, of my argument is not to generalise the association, but to particularise the State. Rousseau, thinking, as we saw, always in terms of local, and not of functional, association, always conceived the body politic as the great association, claiming a loyalty before which all other loyalties faded. But as soon as we make a clear distinction between the State and the community, and still more as soon as we make one between the State and Society, the body politic loses its omnipotence, and becomes at the most *primus inter pares*.

Let us here meet one difficulty which may make against the adoption of this idea. The historical fact that the State has, in modern times, secured a monopoly of law-making, and has kept in its hands the power to recognise or outlaw all other associations, proves nothing; for it may well, under the instigation of democratic or autocratic partisans of State Sovereignty, or from the mere pressure of events, have usurped a power to which it has no rightful title. We may repeat in this connection one of Rousseau's wisest sayings in dealing with social theory: *Écartons tous les faits!*

Even, however, if it is recognised that history is irrelevant to a discussion of right, it is not so easy to brush away the "tidy" logician, who does at least find in the universal Sovereignty of the state a theoretically ultimate resolution of all conflicts of obligation. Where, in effect, if we destroy State Sovereignty, is our ultimate Sovereign to be found? Is it not fair to answer that a dearth of good men is no reason for making a bad man king: it is rather a reason for a republic? There remains, however, the question whether this republic of obligations would not be in effect so loosely federal as to amount to anarchy. Would not obligations ceaselessly conflict, and would not the possibility of deciding such conflicts have been beyond remedy destroyed?

There are here in reality two questions. How far will functional devolution reduce the possibility of conflict to a minimum? And how far will there be any way of resolving such conflicts between two functional authorities, when they arise?

It is surely evident that the greater number of the conflicts of obligation which arise in the Society of to-day are due to an imperfect demarcation of spheres. The Ulster question was the result of fear concerning the religious effects of a political change. The most glaring failure of modern politics is in the sphere of industrial legislation. Inhumanity, arising from a lack of understanding, is the mark of the State in its dealings with man in his religious aspect, and in his capacity as worker. A division of spheres would obviate many of the conflicts of to-day, but, as both religion and, still more, industry, have their relations to men in their geographical groups, the possibility of conflict can never be altogether avoided.

We come back, then, to our second question. Where, in our view, does the ultimate Sovereignty lie? Clearly it cannot lie in any one piece of machinery: either it is not embodied in any machinery at all, or else it exists only as the resultant of a system including many pieces of machinery of varying kinds.

All machinery is necessarily imperfect, because all machinery tends to standardise what is, in its real nature, infinitely various. The individual who wills purely wills in and for the individual situation in which he is acting: as soon as he makes for his guidance a general rule, he detracts from the perfection and purity of his willing, because he tries to classify the essentially unique. Yet the individual must, in most cases, make such general rules, because he is not strong enough to trust his judgment of each situation as it arises. He can only aim at making his rules as little crude and machine-made as may be.

All associative will, save the unruly judgments of a mob, must act through general rules, and all associative will is therefore necessarily imperfect. But if in this case the necessity for some imperfection is absolute, the degree of imperfection is none the less relative. The General Will of the community must suffer some leakage as soon as the attempt is made to confine it: at once it becomes something less perfect, the General Will of Society, including only that part of the will of the community which the least imperfect rules and formulæ can cover. This General Will in its turn consists of a number of lesser wills, differentiated by function, all of which are essential to its fullest possible expression.

On this showing, ultimate Sovereignty clearly lies with the fullest possible organised type of will. The quest for a true "ultimate" is, no doubt, in some sense a wild goose chase, since behind all organisations lurks always the final voice of the community. We are, however, dealing with this last court of appeal only in so far as it expresses itself in a mechanism or mechanisms, and we may therefore pass by, with this tribute, the General Will of the community.

With Society, the complex of organised associations, rests the final more or less determinate Sovereignty. We cannot carry Sovereignty lower without handing it over to a body of which the function is partial instead of general. We must, therefore, reject the three theories of State Sovereignty, Theocracy, and Syndicalism, the theories of political, religious, and industrial dominance. All these mistake the part for the whole; our difficulty seems to be the making of a whole out of their parts.

The task of the social philosopher is to define the nature of social obligation; the task of the practical man is to make a Society to fit the philosopher's definition. It is mainly the philosopher's fault that the order of precedence has been so often reversed in the past. It remains, none the less, the philosopher's task to say where Sovereignty should lie, and the business of the practical man to find the requisite machinery. If, then, objection is taken to the Sovereignty of Society on the ground that it is, at best, only "more or less determinate," the philosopher's answer is clear. The determinateness is none of his business: it is for the practical man to make the Sovereign determinate. It is true that in the communities of to-day, which are permeated by the idea of State Sovereignty, the last determinate authority is the State. But, as man has made the

State, man can destroy it; and as man has made it great, man can again restrict it. Moreover, as man has made the State, man can make something greater, something more fitted to exercise a final Sovereignty, or at least to provide a final court of appeal.

The demand, then, for functional devolution is not a demand for the recognition of associations by the State, but a demand that the state itself should be regarded only as an association – elder brother, if you will, but certainly in no sense father of the rest. This, I take it, has been the real motive behind the demand for equality between Church and State – or, as I would rather say, religion and politics. This is certainly behind the new demand for an industrial democracy outside politics which has been put forward in the National Guild System of the *New Age*. It undoubtedly seems to complicate matters very considerably; but our philosophy should have taught us not to be afraid of necessary complications. We are too fond of counting heads to save the trouble, not of breaking, but of convincing them. We are too fond of patching up our quarrels without settling the principle that is at stake. Yet we know well that, though we may compose, we cannot settle a controversy between religion and politics or industry and politics merely by making one or other of them supreme. Attempts to avoid conflict by establishing the dictatorship of one of the contestants inevitably provoke, if not active conflict, at least passive discontent. Yet this is the "State Sovereignty" solution of the problem. A well-organised Society will admit the ultimate possibility of conflict, but will try to reduce the need for conflict to a minimum. Attempts to avoid conflict altogether merely end by making it inevitable.

We are left, then, with, at the strongest, a merely federal body including representatives both of the State and of the chief functional associations as the sole mechanism able to speak in the name of our Sovereign. When, therefore, differences arise between one great functional group and another, when, say, the individual finds himself torn between his loyalty to the State and his loyalty to the industrial body of which he is a member, how is he to make his choice? Simply, as Rousseau said, by means of the General Will that is in him, if he tries to choose either what is in the interest of his Church or his Trade Union or his State or municipality, he is "putting himself the wrong question," to use once again a phrase used by Rousseau. What he has to consider and what, in a case of corporate action, his association has to consider, is none of these things, but the good of the community as a whole, which is neither the State, nor the Church, nor the Trade Union, nor even quite the complex I have called Society, but something greater than all these. He has to decide, in fact, by falling back upon his judgment of the individual situation, guided, but not finally determined, by general precepts.

But if he has to make his choice, he has also to stand the racket. If a machine representing the will of Society can be devised to harmonise the occasional conflicts between the various functional authorities, that is no doubt all to the good. But the devising of such machinery is not philosophy, but science. Whether or no such a body can exist, Sovereignty remains with Society, and the State has no right to mount the throne, which, even if no determinate person or persons sit in it, is full of a presence which is none the less active for being indeterminate in an Austinian sense.

A last word, and I have done. Much that has gone before has been an attack on a theory which has animated political democrats; but none of it has been an attack upon democracy. Democrats have too often confused the ultimate equality, not of men's powers, but of their rights, with the sacredness of a mass vote on a purely geographical basis. Functional devolution involves, not the abandonment of democracy, but the substitution, for an omnipotent political democracy, of a functional democracy. The unit of self-government should be a functional unit: whatever a mass vote may be, a representative system on a geographical basis is certainly not the last word of democracy.

COMMUNITY IS A PROCESS
M. P. Follett

Community is a process. The importance of this as the
fundamental principle of sociology it is impossible to over-
estimate. Physical science based on the study of function is
today a study of process. The Freudian psychology, based on
the study of the 'wish,' is preëminently a study of process and
points towards new definitions of personality, purpose, will,
freedom. If we study community as a process, we reach these
new definitions.

For community is a *creative* process. It is creative because it
is a process of integrating. The Freudian psychology, as
interpreted and expanded by Holt,[1] gives us a clear exposition
of the process of integrating in the individual. It shows us that
personality is produced through the integrating of 'wishes,' that
is, courses of action which the organism sets itself to carry out.
The essence of the Freudian psychology is that two courses of
action are not mutually exclusive, that one does not 'suppress'
the other. It shows plainly that to integrate is not to absorb,
melt, fuse, or to reconcile in the so-called Hegelian sense. The
creative power of the individual appears not when one 'wish'
dominates others, but when all 'wishes' unite in a working
whole.

We see this same process in studying the group. It is the
essential life process. The most familiar example of integrating
as the social process is when two or three people meet to decide
on some course of action, and separate with a purpose, a will,
which was not possessed by anyone when he came to the
meeting but is the result of the interweaving of all. In this true
social process there takes place neither absorption nor compromise. Many of the political pluralists believe that we cannot
have unity without absorption. Naturally averse to absorption,
they therefore abandon the idea of unity and hit upon

---

[1] I am indebted to Professor Holt's very valuable book, *The Freudian Wish*,
for the references in this paper to the Freudian psychology.

compromise and balance as the law of association. But whoever thinks compromise and balance the secret of coöperation fails, insofar, to understand the social process, as he has failed to gather the fruits of recent psychological research. Our study of both individual and group psychology shows us the evolving individual. But when you advocate compromise, it means that you still see the individual as a *ding-an-sich*. If the self with its purpose and its will is even for the moment a finished product, then of course the only way to get a common will is through compromise. But the truth is that the self is always in flux weaving itself out of its relations.

Moreover, the Freudian psychology shows us that compromise is a form of suppression. And as the Freudians show us that a 'suppressed' impulse will be our undoing later, so we see again and again that what has been 'suppressed' in the compromises of politics or of labor disputes crops up anew to bring more disastrous results. I should like to apply the Freudian definition of the sane man to social groups. After having shown us that dissociation of the neural complex means dissociation of personality, it defines the sane man as one in whom personality is not split, as one who has no thwarted wishes, 'suppressions,' incorporated in him. Likewise the sane industrial group would be one in which there was no 'suppression,' in which neither workman nor employer had compromised. The sane nation would be one not based on logrolling. The sane League of Nations would be one in which no nation had made 'sacrifice' of sovereignty, but where each gains by the fullest joining of sovereignty. Suppression, the evil of the Freudian psychology, is the evil of our present constitution of society – politically, industrially and internationally.

What then is the law of community? From biology, from psychology, from our observation of social groups, we see that community is that intermingling which evokes creative power. What is created? Personality, purpose, will, loyalty. In order to understand this we must study actual groups. For instance, it is often discussed whether community may be a person. A recent book on ethics gives the arguments for and against. There is only one way to find out. My idea of ethics is to lock three people into a room and listen at the keyhole. If that group can evolve a common will, then that group is a 'real' person. Let us stop talking about personality in ethics and sovereignty in political science and begin to study the group. Wherever you have a genuine common will, you have a 'real' person; and wherever you have a common will and 'real' personality, you have power, authority, sovereignty.

As the process of community creates personality and will, freedom appears. According to Holt the individual is free as far as he integrates impulses, 'wishes.' His activity will be constantly frustrated by that part of him which is 'dissociated.' An individual misses of freedom by exactly as much as he misses of unity.

The same process must take place with a group of two, say of two people who live together. They have to stand before the world with joint decisions. The process of making these decisions by the interpenetrating of thought, desire, etc., transfers the centre of consciousness from the single I to the group I. The resulting decision is that of the two-self. It is the same with a three-self, a several-self, perhaps a village-self. Our conception of liberty depends upon where we put the centre of consciousness.

Freedom, however, is supposed by many to be the last stronghold in the individual which has not yielded to contacts, that impregnable stronghold which *will* not yield to contacts. These people are in grave danger of some day entering their Holy of Holies and finding it empty. I must each moment find my freedom anew by making a whole whose dictates, because they are integratings to which I am contributing, represent my individuality at that moment. The law of modern psychology is, in a word, achieving. We are achieving our soul, our freedom.

When we see community as process, at that moment we recognize that freedom and law must appear together. I integrate opposing tendencies in my own nature and the result is freedom, power, law. To express the personality I am creating, to live the authority I am creating, is to be free. From biology, social psychology, all along the line, we learn one lesson: that man is rising into consciousness of self as freedom in the forms of law. Law is the entelechy of freedom. The forms of government, of industry, must express this psychological truth.

I have said that community creates, that it creates personality, power, freedom. It also creates purpose, continuously creates purpose. No more fatally disastrous conception has ever dominated us that the conception of static ends.

The Freudian psychology shows us purpose as part of the process. Through the integrating of motor reflexes and objective stimuli we get specific response or behavior, which is purpose. The object of reference in the environment is not the end of behavior, but a constituent of behavior. In the same way we see that when in the social group we have the integrating of thought and overt action, purpose is a constituent of the process. As in the Freudian psychology the purpose about to be carried out is already embodied in the motor attitude of the neuro-muscular apparatus, so in the social process the purpose is a part of the integrating activity; it is not something outside, a prefigured object of contemplation toward which we are moving. Nothing will so transform economics and politics, law and ethics, as this conception of purpose, for it carries with it a complete revaluation of the notion of means and ends. Many who are making reconstruction plans are thinking of static ends. But you can never catch a purpose. Put salt on the tail of the European purpose today in 1919 – if you can! Ends and means truly and literally make each other. A system built about a purpose is dead before it is born.[2]

The conception of community as process affects materially our idea of loyalty and choice. When we are told to choose our loyalties, as the idealist would have us choose the universal community and the political realist[3] the 'nearest' group, the

2   The correspondence between Holt's Freudianism and the activity of social groups we see daily. Holt synthesizes idealism and realism by showing us one and only one evolving process which at different stages we call matter or mind. By showing us scientifically that the integrating whole is always more than the sum of all the parts, he clearly indicates that the appearing of the new is a moment in evolution. This corresponds perfectly to what we find in our study of groups. The genuine social will, or community, is always a moment in the process of integrating. The recognition that joint action of reflex arcs is not mere reflex action, the recognition of the law of *organised* response, and that behavior is not a function of the immediate stimulus, is as important for sociology as for biology. What Holt names "receding stimuli" is a term particularly felicitous for group psychology. Holt calls himself a pluralist – is this pluralism? Holt calls himself a realist – he expresses the *truth* of idealism in dynamic concepts and scientific language.

3   I say the political realist meaning the realist in his applications to politics, because the realists in their interpretation of recent biological research do not make this mistake: they show that the reaction *is* the picking out of a part of that which sets up the reaction. This makes the process of selection decidedly more complex than the political realists seem to realize. They forget that the self which they say chooses the stimuli is being made by reaction to these stimuli.

same error is being made: the individual is put outside the process. According to many of the pluralists there is an individual who stands outside and looks at his groups and there is something peculiarly sacred about this individual.[4] This individual is a myth. The fallacy of pluralism is not its pluralism, but that it is based on a non-existent individual. But Royce, who was not a pluralist (!) would have had us 'choose' a cause to be loyal to. Life is knit more closely than that. It is the complexity of life which both monists and pluralists seem not to reckon with just here. For a man to decide between his trade-union and the state is an impossibility, because by the time the decision comes to him it is already too late: I am part of the trade-union purpose; also the I that decides is a trade-union-I, in part. When the pluralist says that the individual is to choose between his group and his state, he has reduced the social process to a mechanical simplicity nowhere to be found in actual life. I am quite sure, for instance, that I should be capable in some instances of voting with my trade-union to-day in a trade-union meeting and with the state to-morrow in an election, even when the two votes might be opposed. Now what is the reason for this, if you are willing to assume that it is not moral depravity on my part? Are our groups wrong, is the relation of group to state wrong, is the relation of individual to group and of individual to state not yet synthesized, and if so what forms of government or what forms of association would tend to synthesize them? These questions cannot be answered without further study of the group.

To conclude this point of choice. Our loyalty is neither to imaginary wholes nor to chosen wholes, but is an integral part of that activity which is at the same time creating me. Moreover, choice implies that one course is 'right' and one 'wrong.' Freud has taken us beyond that simple rule of morals, that unproductive ethics, by teaching us integration.

We see the same mistake of putting the individual outside the process when it is said, by a pluralist: "The greatest contribution that a citizen can make to the state is certainly this, that he should allow his mind freely to exercise itself on its problems." But it seems to me that the greatest contribution a citizen can make to the state is to learn creative thinking, that is, to learn how to join his thought with that of others so that the issue

---

[4] This is the same as the outside God of the Old Testament.

shall be productive. If each of us exhausts his responsibility by bringing his own little piece of pretty colored glass, that would make a mere kaleidoscope of community.

The individualist says, Be true to thyself. The profounder philosophers have always said, Know thyself, which carries the whole process a step further back: what is the self, what integrations have I made? I am willing to say that the individual *is* the final judge, but who is the individual? My individuality is where my centre of consciousness is. From that centre of consciousness, wherever it may be, our judgments will always issue, but the wider its circumference the truer will our judgments be. This is as important for ethics as for political science. When modern instinct psychology tells us of the need of self-expression, the *group* psychologist at once asks, "What is the self I am to express?"

A man expands as his will expands. A man's individuality stops where his power of collective willing stops. If he cannot will beyond his trade-union then we must write upon his tombstone, "This was a trade-union man." If he cannot will beyond his church, then he is a church man. The soul of the process is always the individual, but the individual forever escapes the form. The individual always escapes, but it is no wayward self who goes from this group to that and slips from all bonds to sit apart and judge us. But also he is no methodical magistrate bent on 'order,' 'organization,' 'method,' 'hierarchy,' who rises from a lower group to a higher and then to a higher and finally to a 'highest.' Life is not a pyramid. The individual always escapes. Yes, but because his sustenance is relation and he seeks forever new relations in the ceaseless interplay of the One and the Many by which both are constantly making each other.

The study of community as process does away with hierarchy, for it makes us dwell in the qualitative rather than in the quantitative. Much of the pluralist objection to the state is because of the words often applied to it by the monists: it is 'superior,' it is 'supreme,' it is 'over and above.' What we need is to discard this quantitative way of thinking and speaking.

Unifying activity is changing its quality every moment. *La durée* does not abandon itself, but rolls itself into the new *durée* endlessly, the qualities interpenetrating so that at every moment the whole is new. Thus unifying activity is changing its quality all the time by bringing other qualities into itself. We must develop the language which will express continuous *qualitative* change. Those who speak of hierarchy deal with the quantitative rather than the qualitative: they jump from the making to the thing that is made; they measure quantitatively the results of the unifying principle. But what on the other hand are the groups of the pluralists? They are the mere creatures of the unifying and they are helpless. When we understand the principle of unifying taught by the latest psychology and the oldest philosophy, we shall no longer fear the state or deify the state. The state, as state, is not "the supreme object of my allegiance." The supreme object of my allegiance is never a thing, a 'made.' It is the very Process itself to which I give my loyalty and every activity of my life.

We see this error of hierarchy in ethics as well as in political philosophy. We hear there also much of conflicting loyalties, and while the pluralist is satisfied to let them fight or balance, others tell us, surely an equally repugnant idea, that we are to abandon the narrower for the wider loyalty, that we are to sacrifice the lesser for the larger duty. But the man who left his family to go to the Great War did not 'abandon' his allegiance to his family; he gathered himself and his family into the fullness of the answer he made to the new demand. The most ardent supporters of the League of Nations do not intend to abandon their nation when a difference arises between it and the League; they hope to find the true integration.

It is partly, I realize, a matter of emphasis. A noble passage in a recent book shows us Martin Luther standing on the Scala Santa facing away from the Roman church. I am sufficiently Bergsonian to see Martin Luther with all the richness and strength of the Roman Catholic church so incorporated into his being that he is capable of faith in Self-salvation. It was impossible for that *durée* to be lost, it rolled up and rolled up and created. The absolute impossibility of Martin Luther turning away from the Roman Catholic church is to me one of the splendid truths of life.

To sum up this point of hierarchy. There is no above and below. We cannot schematize men as space objects. The study of community as process will bring us, I believe, not to the over-individual mind, but to the inter-individual mind, an entirely different conception.

If the study of community as process might perhaps lead the monists to abandon the notion of hierarchy, it might give the pluralists another conception of unity. The pluralists are always speaking of the 'reduction to unity.' With many of the pluralists unity is synonymous with uniformity, identity, stagnation. This would be true of a static unity but never of the dynamic unity I am trying to indicate. The urge to unity is not a reduction, a simplification, it is the urge to embrace more and more, it is a reaching out, a seeking, it is the furthest possible conception of pluralism, it is pluralism spiritually not materially conceived. Not the 'reduction' to unity but the expansion towards unity is the social process. That is, the expanding process and the unifying process are the same. The same events have created a Czecho-Slav state and the League of Nations: they are not cause and effect, they are not mere concomitants, they are activities absolutely bound together as one process in the movement of world history. This is enormously significant. Our alternative is not between Royce's finished Absolute and James's strung-alongness. We create the beyond and beyond and so to be sure produce strung-alongness which, however, exists only as part of the unifying process.

The pluralist loves the apple best when it rots. Then he sees the seeds all scattering and he says, "This is Life, this is Truth." But many men see beyond the rotting apple, the scattering seeds, the fresh upspringings, the cross-fertilizations, to the new whole being created. If, on the other hand, some of the monists have tried to petrify the 'finished' fruit (as in the conception of the absolute state), life has never allowed them to do so.

To put the conception of unify*ing* the place of unity might help to bring monists and pluralists nearer together. Spontaneous unifying is the reality for humanity. But is not spontaneous unifying what the pluralists are already urging in their advocacy of groups? And is not spontaneous unifying the heart of a true monism? The activity of the pluralists' entities, the activity which is their only being, should be harmonious adjustment to one another – which is monism a-making.

The practical importance of an understanding of the nature of community can only be indicated, but its influence on our attitude towards present political and industrial problems is very great. We come to see that the vital matter is not methods of representation, as the menders and patchers fondly hope, nor even the division of power, as many of the pluralists tend to think, but *modes of association*. When the political pluralists propose a more decentralized form of government, I am entirely in sympathy with them; but what they propose will surely fail unless we are considering at the same time the modes of association through which we are to act within these different pluralities. The political pluralists are very much concerned with the question whether we need one authority or many. I think our hardest job is not to change the seat of power but to get hold of some actual power. And when we are told that the trade-union should be directly represented in the state, we must remember that we have at present little reason to think that a man will be more able to contribute his will to the trade-union will than he has been able to contribute it to the national or civic will. Whoever has watched for the last few years the struggle of the younger men to break the Gompers machine will not think that party politics vary greatly in labor organizations and political organizations. It is only through an understanding of the nature of community that we shall see clearly the fallacies involved in the 'consent of the governed': a preëxisting purpose (very insidious today in both industry and politics), a collective will as the will of the like-minded, and the denial of *participation*. One is sometimes a little struck by the Rip van Winklism of the pluralists: consent and balance, believed in a hundred or two years ago, we have now outgrown.

That labor problems should be studied in the light of our conception of community as process is of the utmost importance. We hear much at present of the application of instinct psychology to industry, but this I am sure is full of pitfalls unless we join to it a study of group psychology. Again, if the industrial manager is to get the fruits of the scientific management, he must understand the intricate workings of a group. If he is to have good reasons for his opinion as to whether a shop-committee should be composed of workmen alone or of workmen and management, he must study group psychology. It is impossible to work out sound schemes of compulsory compensation or compulsory insurance without understanding the group relations and group responsibility upon which these are based. And so on and so on. The study of community as process is absolutely necessary for the sound development of industry. And if we should have industrial democracy - but democracy is just this, productive inter-relatings.

It seems to me that jurisprudence has gone ahead of ethics or political science or economics in an understanding of community, as for instance in the notion of reciprocal relation. It is significant that the fact that the master has a relation to servant as well as servant to master has now general recognition. Moreover, the philosophical jurists see that it is the same process which produces the corporate personality and the social individual who is fast becoming the unit of law. Our progressive judges seek always the law of the situation, which means in the language of this paper the discovery and formulation of modes of unifying. Upon this point turns all progress for jurisprudence.[5] Less bound by the crowd illusion than the rest of us, and therefore better understanding community as process, jurists are showing us law as endlessly self-creating. I hope they will soon show us explicitly some of the errors involved in a teleological jurisprudence. It would be interesting to examine the decisions of judges to see how often in the case before them they accept a fossil purpose developed in bygone times, and how often, on the other hand, they see the purpose a-growing within the very situation.[6]

A criticism of pragmatism involved in the conception of community as process may be barely mentioned. The essence of pragmatism, as commonly understood, is testing. But whenever you 'test' you assume a static idea. With a living idea, however, truth may be created. If, for example, you try the pragmatic test and take 'coincident interest,' as between employer and employed, out to find its cash value, you will find it has very little. But coincident interest can be *created* through the process of interrelating: as, for instance, the employer often finds, after his patience has been exhausted in the joint committee, that the further education of the worker is

5   The importance of this for the development of "group-law" as advocated by the upholders of administrative syndicalism, I have not space to go into, but there are problems here to be worked at jointly by jurists and political scientists.

6   Many revaluations are involved in the conception of community as process. The functional theory of causation must be applied to every department of thought. Natural rights take on a new meaning. And the distinction between subjective and objective loses its significance, as it has with the realists through their interpretations of the results of recent biological research where they see the objective, as an integral part of the process of integration, becoming thereby the subjective, and the subjective becoming objective. The importance of this for jurisprudence and political science must be developed at some later time.

as much to his own interest as to that of the worker. And so on. We are told by a realist that according to pragmatism truth is "a harmony between thought and things." Is it not more 'realistic' to say that thought and things interpenetrate and that this is the creating activity? Rationalists 'verify' within the realm of reason. Pragmatists 'test' in the concrete world. The step beyond is to learn to *create* in both.[7]

To conclude: I wish to urge in this paper actual group association – the *practice* of community. I am thus in close sympathy with the pluralists because I too believe in the 'nearest' group; but while most of the pluralists believe in the 'nearest' group because they think the personal element gets thinner and thinner the further away you get from it, I believe in it just because I do *not* think this, because I think it is the path to a fuller and richer personality. This idea of the pluralists is I believe infinitely prejudicial to our national life for the practical harm such a conception can accomplish, witness many of the lectures last winter on the League of Nations. I know of a talk based on this idea given to an audience of working men with the consequence that that particular audience was left with very little interest in the League of Nations. The lecturer with this mistaken sociology and mistaken ethics was trying to urge his audience to rise above personal interests to impersonal considerations. We shouldn't, we don't, we can't. The larger interest must be made personal before it can be made real. That audience ought to have been told, and shown, how a league of Nations would change their own lives in every particular.

We build the real state, the vital and the moral state, by reinforcing actual power with actual power. No state can, forever, *assume* power. The present state has tried to do so and the pluralists have been the irrepressible child to cry out, "The King has on no clothes." But if the pluralists have seen the King, as in the fairy story, clad by the weavers who worked at empty looms, shivering in nakedness while all acclaimed the beauty of the robes of state, many of us do not intend to accept this situation, but believe in the possibility of ourselves weaving, from out our own daily experience, the garments of a genuine state.

---

7   I am speaking of course in a general way, not forgetting those pragmatists who do not hold the somewhat crude idea of testing.

Idealism and realism meet in the actual. Some of us care only for the workshop of life, the place where things are *made*. James says that critical philosophy is sterile in practical results. As far as this is true it is because critical philosophy remains in the concepts it evolves, instead of grasping the activity which produced them and setting it at concrete tasks. We must grip life and control its processes. Conscious achieving is leaping into view as the possibility of all. We are capable of creating a collective will, and at the same time developing an individual spontaneity and freedom hardly conceived of yet, lost as we have been in the herd dream, the imitation lie, and that most fatal of fallacies – the fallacy of ends.

This is the reality for man: the unifying of differings. But the pluralists balk at the unifying. They refuse to sweat and suffer to make a whole. They refuse the supreme effort of life – and the supreme reward. Yet the pluralists lead our thought today because they begin with the nearest group, with the actual. If they will add to this insight the understanding that the job of their actual groups is to carry on that activity by which alone these groups themselves have come into existence – they will have recognized community as process.

THE ERUPTION OF THE GROUP
E. Barker

§ 1. The Worship of the Group and its Causes

The eruption of the personal is not the only eruption of our
times. There is also another, which seems to be its opposite, but
which is really its complement – the eruption of the group and of
the worship of the group. The solitary personal leader who
claims to hold a representative position must find some body or
being which he can profess to represent. That body or being will
not be an electorate of individual voters. If it were, he would be
committed to ideas of his own election; of the giving and
withholding of free assent to his action; of the possibility of
dismissal. Indeed he would be committed to even more. An active
electorate is by its nature divided into a majority and a minority
part, and the leader who bases himself upon it will necessarily
find by his side an anti-leader with a similar basis who opposes
his claims and his policy. The single leader who stands alone in
the claim of a representative position must find some body or
being other than the electorate to serve as his basis. He will
therefore evoke some unity – something undivided and indivisible
– which he can claim to express and to represent. He may call it
nation: he may call it race: he may even call it by the name of
class, if the class be sufficiently large, and if it can be regarded
as destined to embrace all others in a final unity. Whatever it be
– race, nation, or class – the unity represented must be
something super-personal. It must be something other than,
and something which can be held to stand above, a definite
body of individual persons who can express their own views
and formulate their own wishes. The person who claims to
represent this super-personal entity has a far freer scope for his
own personality. He can claim to be the one organ of its views,
or rather of its necessities. Directing allegiance to it, and
claiming allegiance only on its behalf, he consolidates his own
position in the act of seeming to abnegate direct allegiance to
himself.

It would be absurd to believe that the leader invents the myth of the group. It would be hardly less absurd to believe that, finding it ready to his hand, he exploits it consciously in his own interest. He may be the pure and convinced prophet of what he believes to be absolute and ultimate reality. But it is true, none the less, that the mysticism of the group is a welcome ally to the personalism of the leader. It consecrates him, and it consecrates his party – no party in the ordinary sense of a section of the electorate, but a body of chosen believers in the unity, the reality, and the transcendency of the group. It may seem a paradox to connect the personality of the leader (and the personal allegiance of his party or following) with the cause of the super-personal group. If it be a paradox, it is, as we have seen, a paradox as old as the history of German Romantic thought. The leader who expresses the spirit of a group which is a person above the persons of its own members is not a figure of to-day, or even of yesterday. He is a figure of hoar antiquity.

When we consider the current idea of the unity, the reality, and the transcendency of the group, we may be struck by another paradox – a paradox which, on reflection, becomes an obvious truism. It is the countries of an imperfect actual unity which cultivate most ardently the idea of a perfect and transcendental unity. Where unity is in the very air, and is taken for granted without reflection, differences are tolerated, parties emerge, and individual variety of taste and opinion is accepted and even expected. Countries of an old and established unity, with a traditional form of State and a generally accepted scheme of law and order, can easily afford to follow the philosophy of 'identity in difference'. They will regard variety as a proof of vitality; they may even regard it as the normal and natural pattern of life, to which the State must adjust its structure and its activity. Countries vexed by a long process of historical disintegration, from which they have only recently emerged, and of which they fear the recurrence, will follow a different line of thought. For them identity will be something which cannot be found in difference, and cannot even be reconciled with difference. It will be something which transcends all difference and has to wage a constant war with difference. Local varieties become local particularisms which are a treason against the spirit of the whole; parties become factions which rend the unity of the nation; classes and their social aspirations become schisms in the body politic; churches and their claims on the allegiance of their members become secessions from the cause of national unanimity; and the idea of individual development becomes the idea of desertion.

It seemed, a generation ago, as if national unification had been definitely achieved in all the great countries of Europe. It seemed as if it only remained for historians to write the history of the achievement, and for statesmen (now provided with the necessary basis of unity) to pursue the democratic method of discussion of differences and compromise between them which the achievement had rendered possible. To-day we are beginning to realize that unification was not completed when it seemed to be. The past is not liquidated so easily; and the first and formal achievement of unity is only the beginning of actual unification. There is a sense in which we may say that Italian Fascism and German National Socialism are simply new phases of the still incomplete and still continuing process of Italian and German unification. Three causes have combined to provoke a new and vigorous reassertion of the cause of unity. In the first place, the old provincialisms and local particularisms, forgotten in the enthusiastic moment of the first and formal unification, but still surviving undiminished, have come to be felt as alien and irritating substances which must be eliminated from the body of the State. This, in itself, is a mere matter of the liquidation of an internal past; and by itself it would not provoke a passionate worship of unity. But, in the second place, the newly unified countries have found themselves confronted by general European movements, political and social – the movement of democracy and the movement of Socialism – which might be interpreted as invasions and disruptions of their unity. Democracy brought the conflict of parties: socialism preached the conflict of classes; and both of them could be regarded as the allies of local particularisms which could now be used as a cover for the interests of a political party or of a social creed.[1] Those who believed in the

[1] Herr Hitler, in a speech to his party at Nuremberg (1 September 1933) referred to 'the party egoists who made a cold and calculated identification of their perverse party interests with provincial traditions of particularism (*einzelstaatlich en Ländertraditionen*), and thus sought to bring the unity of the Reich into danger.'

cause of unity could plead that unless it conquered parties and creeds, thus allied with local divisions, and unless it absorbed them into a single national party professing a single creed, it would itself be conquered and lost. In the third place, and perhaps more powerful and more explosive than any other cause, there was the external corollary and sequel of national unification. Even if it *were* actually united at home, a newly united country would inevitably feel that it had not achieved its unification, or consolidated its unity before the world, until it had found a place in the sun proportionate to its new strength. 'When we were disunited, we did not count; now that we are united, we must count for all the worth of our unity'. This is instinctive feeling. It issues in a collective mood of sensitive pride, disturbing the old equilibrium of States (and with it all the old States which are content to sleep in an equilibrium), but rallying the members of each new State in a new devotion to a new and higher power of unity. It is in this sense, and from this point of view, that we say that the history of national unification is a process which was not, after all, completed in the nineteenth century, but is still active – and indeed more volcanically active than ever – in the twentieth. Our hopes were vain when we dreamed of the consummation of a national unity which would henceforth be content to follow the tranquil methods of national self-government. We did not know the strength of the national ferment, or how it would continue to work – without as well as within.

But there is another way in which men may press the idea of unity as something transcending, and therefore determining, the individual. They may not only start from the idea of a nation, and exalt the claims of national loyalty; they may also start from the idea of the class, and proclaim the duty of class solidarity. The two ways may seem, at first sight, to lead in opposite directions. The nationalist is ready enough to claim that his cause is the cause of unity; but he is equally ready to insist that the cause of class is the cause of disunity. His claim and insistence are just if we admit the assumption he makes – the assumption that his idea of unity is the only true idea, or at any rate the higher idea to which all others must be adjusted. But it is obvious that the idea of class is also a major idea of unity for those who believe only, or believe pre-eminently, in the unity of class; and if the idea of the unity of class be made a transcendent and determining unity, there will be no intrinsic difference between the high nationalist's conception of the claims of unity and that of the high socialist. There may of course be extrinsic differences. There may be differences in the number of persons who are united, or supposed to be united, in the group. The nation may include more persons, and may, in that merely quantitative sense, be said to be a greater unity. On the other hand a class which claims and attempts to be international may seek to surpass the nation even in point of quantity. Again there may be differences in the number of interests which one form of group includes in comparison with another. Here the nation, *prima facie*, is the more comprehensive group; and including a wider range of interests – more especially all the great interests which go by the name of national culture – it may claim a pre-eminence of quality. On the other hand a class may also vindicate for itself the possession of a culture which is peculiar to itself and gives it a peculiar quality. It may regard itself as equal to the nation in the number of interests which it comprehends, and superior, by virtue of its community of economic status and feeling, in the solidarity with which it supports those interests. The extrinsic differences between nation and class are not, after all, so great that only one of the two can claim to be the vehicle of unity. Both can make that claim; and both may press the claim to the ultimate conclusion in which unity becomes the dominating and determining principle of human life and action.

It is thus not only the unspent tide of national unification, but also a new and rising tide of class consciousness and class solidarity, which has led to the contemporary eruption of the group and the worship of the group. The liberal or democratic State, which simply assumes the existence of a national society, and directs itself by the policy of discussion between its members, is challenged on two fronts. There are those, on the one hand, who feel that the existence of national society cannot be simply assumed, and that its continuance is incompatible with the free play of discussion. To them national unity is an end which is still to be attained, and can only be attained by devotion and sacrifice: to them the leader, who inspires the devotion and claims the sacrifice, is the only form of government consistent with the end. On the other hand there are those who see no value in any form of national society, whether it be assumed as a tacit condition or exalted as an ultimate end; who substitute class for nation, and demand for the class the same devotion, and the same system of leadership, which the nationalist demands for the nation. In the triangular contest which is thus engaged it is not always clear which antagonist is opposed to which. From one point of view it may be said that the democrat is so far at one with the high nationalist that he accepts the nation as the normal unit of political organization, and on that ground is opposed to the theory of the high socialist. From this point of view, communism becomes the enemy of enemies, which must be opposed by all forms of State which are based on the idea of national society. From another point of view the Fascist form of State, which has arisen on the ruins of the democratic form and continues to denounce its disunity, may find more affinities with the unitary system of communist government than with any other; and democracy may thus appear as the common enemy of the planned authoritarian State in both of its forms. From still a third point of view the democratic and the community State may find that they have common principles, or at any rate a common antagonist. Both of them, if in different ways, pay homage to the principle of human equality; both of them, if for different reasons, oppose the fervent nationalism which claims total allegiance for the national State at the expense of all other groups.

§ 2. *The Totalitarian Group in its Relation to Individuals and to Societies of Individuals*

In this confusion of alliances and oppositions it is necessary to find and follow some guiding thread. The thread which has emerged from the previous argument is simple. It depends entirely on the idea of the relation of the individual to his community – whatever the community may be. It does not greatly matter (at any rate in comparison) whether the community is held to be primarily a nation, or primarily a class. Most of us would prefer to start from the nation, for the simple reason (if no other) that the nation is a great and given fact of history. But we should admit that the nation is coloured in some degree by a class or system of classes, just as we should also contend, in the same way but in the opposite sense, that a class which claims to be the whole of the community (as in Russia) at once colours itself with national characteristics and tends to become a nation. (The development of Russia, during the last quarter of a century, is the development of a would-be international proletariat into an actual national community.) The ultimate issue, therefore, is not the issue of nation versus class, though that issue has its own deep importance; it is an issue between what is nowadays called the totalitarian community, which transcends and determines its members, and the simple community of co-operation, which has no existence apart from its members and whose purposes and activities are determined by its members. In a word we have to decide whether we start from the conception of individual moral personality, with its moral claims on others and its moral responsibilities to others, or from that of the transcendent personality of the community (however it is held to be constituted), with its total claims on individual allegiance and its responsibility only to itself.

Totalitarianism, with its insistence on the rounded O of the whole society, has a deep appeal to some of the finer instincts of men. It summons the devoted spirit to service and sacrifice. It strikes the same strings of human nature which have always been struck by religion: indeed it may almost be called a form of religion – or of anti-religion. It is something which goes deeper than the mere assertion of unity against its enemies; and it is more than a negative protest against that 'atomism' of individuals, and that 'particularism' of parties, which it charges against the cause of contemporary democracy. It has its own positive quality. It makes an historic appeal, beyond the present, to an idealized past – here to the ancient Roman unity, when all were for the State; there to the old German tradition of the mystic unity of the Folk. It offers, through the resuscitation of that past, to provide a way of future salvation for those who are weary of the burden of individual responsibility. Vexed by fluctuations – of currency and income, of parties and ministries, of individual and of communal life – men are summoned to an assured stability. They are bidden home from their wanderings – back into the life of the universal substance; back into the historic tradition of their people; back into the comfort of community. There is something in totalitarianism which has a positive attraction both to the strong and to the weak – to the strong, because it commands a devotion of service and sacrifice; to the weak, because it promises the comfort and security of guidance. But paternalism, authoritarianism, absolutism – by whatever name it may be called, has always had that attraction. Charles I could rally to his cause both the vigorous Strafford and the unreflecting Royalist. It would be wrong to say that the only new thing about totalitarianism is its name. But it may perhaps be said, without error, that it only seeks to corroborate an old cause by giving it the support of a new idea. The cause of authority (and with it, of security) is strengthened when it is made to appear as the cause not of a person, or of a government, but of the whole. Each giving himself to the whole gives himself to no person. He gives himself to something which at once includes him and stands above him – his folk, his nation, his class. Immersed in its totality, he finds in its existence the reason for his own. He is content to be merged because he finds himself not only sustained, but also explained, by the body in which he is merged.

The old authoritarian governments, while they relied on the human passion for security, sought also to find their basis in the religious motive. They pleaded some form of divine right, vested by God in his vicar and vicegerent; and some of the greatest of their servants (among them Bismarck himself) were rallied to their service by this plea. The new totalitarianism has also its religious aspect and its connection with the religious motive; but the connection is different, and it raises different and graver questions. The authoritarian monarch who claimed a sanctity for his authority was not claiming that his authority was a religion, but only that it was a part of religion. Totalitarianism, in its strict logic, is not a part of religion, but a religion. Professing to be a whole, and to embrace the whole man, it leaves no room in its theory (though it may in its practice, which for reasons of convenience may fall short of its theory) for the area of religious life. If does not seek to find a place or a foothold for itself within that area: it seeks to penetrate and absorb it. A logical totalitarianism has no room for religion and churches. It may accommodate itself to them, but only on the condition that they accommodate themselves to it, by becoming parts of the whole and serving its purposes. It is true that in this respect totalitarianism is not absolutely unique. Any new political doctrine which claims and receives a passionate adhesion attracts to itself the religious motive and tends to become a religion. The creed of Liberty, Equality, and Fraternity, which swept through France in the days of the Revolution, was a creed which gravely affected religion and the

Churches. The Republic 'one and indivisible' implied, if it did not enunciate, the doctrine of totality; and the Civil Constitution of the clergy, which brought the organization of the Church into harmony with revolutionary principles, was an attempt to accommodate religious institutions to the spirit of an ardent and all-embracing republicanism. Monarchism, too, no less than republicanism, has sought to be all-embracing; and the reform of the Church by Henry VIII, if it followed a different direction, was in the same spirit as the French reforms of 1790. But though the totalitarianism of our own day has its analogies in the past, it has also its differences from the past. Just because it is definitely and avowedly totalitarian, it leaves less room for religion and the Churches. In one of its forms it eliminates them; in another, it assimilates them; in the third form, it consents to recognize them by a concordat, but still continues to claim a total allegiance for itself.

The relation of totalitarianism to religion and the Churches raises an even larger issue – the issue of the relation between society and the State. In our current English conception we draw a distinction between them. We regard a national society as a general body of different cohesions, or associations, existing for a number of different purposes – legal, religious, economic, charitable, educational, cultural. We regard the State as one, but only one, of the different cohesions or associations in and through which the national society acts. In our view the State is an association, which differs indeed from other associations in including all the members of the national society, as no other association does, and again in using a final power of legal coercion, as no other association can, but which is none the less an association like other associations, and like other associations has a particular and specific purpose – that of declaring and enforcing a scheme of legal order obligatory on its members in the sphere of external conduct. No doubt the purpose is particularly important; no doubt its achievement is the necessary basis and background of the achievement of other social purposes; no doubt the associations which are concerned with those other purposes will be affected, and even controlled, on all questions of legal order arising in the sphere of external conduct, by the rules of the legal association. But the purpose of a scheme of legal order is none the less particular and specific: it is not total and absolute. It does not include or abolish other social purposes; and the association which is its agent does not include or abolish the other associations which are the agents of other purposes. On this view, therefore, the State can never be totalitarian. It is, indeed, the whole society, so far as its membership goes: in other words it includes all the members of the national society on which it is based. But it is not totalitarian, so far as its purposes go: it is not the agent of all the purposes of the society: it has its own specific legal purpose, which will carry it, indeed, into the fields of other associations which seek to achieve other purposes, but will carry it into those fields only in so far as legal questions are raised which relate to matters of external conduct and are capable of solution by the methods of legal coercion.

It follows upon our argument that the worship of the group, in its modern form, involves two different, and yet connected, consequences. In the first place, the group is made to transcend, to explain, and to determine the existence of individuals. It becomes something above them and apart from them, for which they must live and to which they are means. In the second place, one form or aspect of the group – the form or aspect of legal regulation and coercive control – is made to absorb and abolish the rest. The State is identified with society; the coercive power of the legal association, extended beyond its legal purpose, is made to include all other purposes, and to serve as the general agent of every purpose. The idea of the transcendence of the group is thus accompanied by the idea of its pure and indifferentiated unity. The two ideas are naturally and logically connected. If the individual ceases to retain his own existence as a being who possesses an intrinsic value in himself, the voluntary associations in which he has sought to find expression and fulfilment will suffer a corresponding change. They too will cease to possess an inherent value and an independent title to existence. They will either be abolished (as Trade Unions, for example, have been abolished in Germany) on the ground that they are inimical to the cause of unity, or they will be absorbed and transformed (on the corporative plan adopted in Italy) into 'organs of State' which are charged by the State with the duty of achieving one of its purposes under its auspices. It is not merely political parties, or the democratic institutions with which they are connected, that perish or suffer a transformation in the totalitarian States. It is very much more. It is the whole idea and system of society, in the sense of the word in which it signifies something more than the State –

something broader and richer than the State – something of which the State is indeed a very necessary form or aspect, but of which there are other forms, and other aspects, with a necessity of their own. If we believe that there are Churches as well as States – and not only so, but also that there are other forms of society, and other associations, as well as Churches, which also serve in their way the expression and the fulfilment of the human spirit – we cannot but realize the gravity of the issue with which we are faced.

The idea of the transcendent and unitarian group – the idea which is expressed in the word 'totalitarianism' – is thus far more than a challenge to the idea of the democratic State. It is a challenge to a whole scheme of ideas in regard to the relation of society and the State. It affects society as well as the State; it affects any form of State (the authoritarian or non-democratic as well as the democratic) which conceives its function as specific, limits itself to the purpose of a legal association, and recognizes the existence and the purposes of other associations. There is, of course, point and sense in the antithesis which is currently made between the totalitarian State and democracy. The States which confront the totalitarian State are actually, for the most part, democratic. The apologists of the totalitarian State attack them on the ground of their democratic form of government; and the form of government adopted in the totalitarian State, while it is alleged to be 'pure' and 'true' democracy, is ostentatiously the opposite of actual democratic forms. It is natural enough, with such evidence before us, to speak of the antithesis of democracy and totalitarianism as if the issue were a simple issue between two forms or methods of government. But though it is natural, it is erroneous, or at any rate misleading. It is not the form of its government which makes the totalitarian State what it is. A State with an authoritarian form of government need not be totalitarian. What makes a totalitarian State is not the particular form of its government (though that will be generally, and even necessarily, authoritarian), it is the conception on which it acts of the whole purpose and function of the State. We know a totalitarian State much more by what it does than by the form of government which it employs. A totalitarian State is one which, whatever its form of government and its method of political action, acts on the principles (1) that the whole (however conceived, in terms of race, or of nationality, or of class) is a transcendent being or 'organism' which determines the life of its members, (2) that the whole is 'integrally realized', or entirely comprehended, in the one association called the State, and (3) that the State has therefore a complete and solitary control of human life and activity.

Before we turn to discuss the different terms in which the whole may be conceived, we may pause to consider a little further the relation of the idea of totalitarianism to the idea of democracy. Our view of the relation will depend upon our interpretation of the idea of democracy. If democracy is interpreted as the government of will – the will of the people, which means in effect the will of a majority of the people – it seems possible to believe, at any rate theoretically, in the combination of totalitarianism with democracy. A State organized on the basis of universal suffrage *might* claim to be the only association, and *might* seek to exercise total control over the lives of all its members. But it would be difficult for such a State to appeal to any transcendent being which warranted its activity and inspired its will. It would be too obviously itself to allege any impulse of its activity beyond itself; it could invoke no mysticism; and it would thus lack the crucial and essential ingredient of totalitarianism. The appeal to the will of the people, however devoutly it may be proclaimed by apostles of the sovereignty of that will, must always be, in the last resort, an appeal to the actual will of an actual people; and there is no transcendence in such a will. Even if we identify democracy with the will of number, we cannot, after all, reconcile it with totalitarianism. The will of number has not enough divinity for the purposes of totalitarianism.

It is even less possible to reconcile democracy with totalitarianism if it be identified not with the will of number, but with the process of discussion. A State which acts on that process makes the fundamental assumption that individuals, and groups of individuals, determine the lines of its action by the agreement or compromise which they finally attain after freely expressing, and freely debating, the different views from which they start about the lines to be followed. On this assumption there is no superior and separate whole, with its own inherent and dominant demands which have to be detected, and translated into effect, by an intuitive intelligence which emerges to act as their organ and commands and receives a general assent in that capacity. On this assumption, again, there is no given and pre-existent will of the people, which has to be elicited and registered by the method of voting and the election of representatives. There is a simple community of individuals, already organized in a number of groups or associations, who have to think out together, in common and open discussion, the rules of their common life. This common effort and process is the *primum mobile* of political action. By it the individuals, and the groups of individuals, who participate in its activity, determine their mutual relations, their common purposes, and the modes of the execution of those purposes. They determine the whole which is immanent in them and 'actuated' by them: they are not determined by it as something transcending them and 'actuating' their wills. The view of democracy which finds its essence in the power of discussion begins with free individuals and free groups of individuals, and trusts them, by the pooling of their thoughts, to construct a whole in which they can live together at peace and in liberty. The whole is their construction: it is a legal association, with common rules of law, which they have made for themselves; and though it could not exist unless there were a pre-existent society in which free individuals, and free groups of individuals, were already accustomed to act, it is something distinct from that society – something which has supervened upon it, by deliberate creation directed to a definite and limited purpose, and which is operated, for that purpose, by the deliberate will of its constituent members.[2]

---

[2] This may seem pure individualism. But if the line of argument here suggested were pursued to its conclusion, we should discover that it implies two corollaries which transcend individualism. (a) The individuals who determine the whole do not determine it as separate individuals, or isolated groups, from calculations of individual interest or of the interests of particular groups: they determine it as co-operating individuals and groups, engaged in a common effort of thought with a view to attaining and realizing a common conception of a common good. It is this co-operation of all, and not the separate action of each, which is the determining factor. (b) Before the common effort of thought can begin, it must necessarily be assumed that there is a common good to be discovered. Men cannot co-operate in a common effort of discussion unless they already entertain the idea that a common good exists, and that it can and must be discovered by common effort. In that sense the idea of a common good of the whole is prior to discussion, and is the cause of all discussion; and in that sense (but only in that sense) men may be said to be determined by the whole.
   On the other hand two notes must be added to these two corollaries. (i) The whole which determines individuals and groups to co-operate is simply and solely the *idea* of a common good of the whole community – an

§ 3. *The Different Ideas of the Totalitarian Group: Race, Nation, and Class*

The terms in which the dominant whole is conceived by the advocates of totalitarianism are various. They all proceed from the fertile thought of Germany, incessantly vexed by the problem of unity, and constantly impelled to fly from an actual world of local particularism and social cleavage to an ideal world in which the One comes by its own. When the unity of society is a simple fact which is taken for granted, there is little need to speculate about its nature, or to emphasize its claims. When its very existence seems in question, it provokes enquiry and invites assertion. German philosophy, traversing the hills of divided thought, has thus been naturally led to detect some great figure, looming in the mist, which might satisfy an urgent need. In the early history of Romanticism the figure was that of the Folk – the spirit of the Folk, with open arms ready to enfold and sustain. The romantic idea of the Folk was primarily the idea of a common spiritual substance, 'a community of values,' a common culture in which (however they might be divided otherwise) the 'folk-mates' who shared it were fundamentally united. But this common spiritual substance was also regarded as something more than substance, or rather as necessarily involving something beyond itself which alone would explain its existence. If there was a spiritual substance, there must be a creative spiritual being – a unit, like itself – which brought it into existence and continued to be its 'bearer'. The argument was not impeccable: a common spiritual substance may be the creation of co-operative individual minds, and may be carried and contained in the common thought of individuals. If, however, the argument be accepted, the Folk becomes a spirit and a being; and we have thus a world of different Folk-spirits or Folk-beings, each creating and each sustaining a spiritual substance or culture of its own. It is no ignoble conception; but it is somewhat tenuous. These spirits, who move in the sphere

idea resident and immanent in the minds of its individual members, and resident nowhere else. (ii) This idea, which forms or constitutes the whole, only determines individuals, as an idea, in so far as they freely accept it and determine themselves by it – just as all ideas only determine us, as ideas, in so far as we make them our own and act by our own faith in them. If we are determined by some other man's idea of the whole, we are not determined by the idea itself: we are determined by *him* – by the prestige *he* carries or the force *he* commands.

of culture, must drink blood before they can speak to us audibly. They must assume some physical shape. It is here that variety of interpretation begins.

One variety of interpretation, current in modern Germany, may be called by the name of 'Folk into Race'. On this interpretation the Folk, instead of being primarily conceived in terms of the spiritual culture which it creates and carries, is primarily and essentially conceived in terms of blood and physical attributes. In a sense this means a materialization of the conception of Folk-society and the nature of the Folk-being. They become a matter of physical rather than of spiritual substance. In another sense, since the factor of race is closely connected with that of culture, and since it can be contended that peculiarity of race is the primordial source of each peculiar culture, the theory of 'Folk into Race' continues the tradition of a common spiritual substance, but gives it a ground or basis in physical idiosyncrasy. It can be argued that the Folk-being, without this physical substratum, is vague and unexplained. The *Volksgeist* is supposed to live, and to produce its fruits of culture; but it has no attachment to the solid earth from which life ultimately springs. Race and blood provide the attachment. A Folk which is a simple system of culture, or simply produces a system of culture, has no very obvious or definite membership. Strangers may profess to share in the system, and may claim to be members: in any case culture, in itself and without a precise attachment, is a cosmopolitan sort of term, which may rally adherents indiscriminately. Blood is a known and definite sign; and a community which begins by being a community of blood, and then issues in its own and peculiar system of culture, is a known and definite community.

The idea of Race has thus a double advantage. It provides something prior to the Folk, which explains its peculiarity and its power of producing a peculiar culture; and again it provides a sign or note by which the true members of the Folk may be known and recognized. The vogue of the idea of Race in modern Germany is partly to be explained by the double advantage which it thus offers: it is also to be explained by historical facts and developments. Biological science, with its emphasis on the physical inheritance of natural characteristics, is a contributory cause; but it is a cause which is not peculiar to Germany, and which, by itself, will not explain the cult of the idea of race in Germany.[3] Anthropology, with its categories of races – Nordic, Alpine, Mediterranean, and as many others as each exponent of classification may find a reason for detecting – is a more proximate cause; but the study of anthropology is, again, not peculiar to Germany, and indeed the theory which assigns a peculiar virtue to the Nordic race is a theory which originated in France. The real causes which have produced a racial philosophy in Germany are practical rather than theoretical. It is the practical effort to find some final core of unity which has harnessed science to its needs. The formula of 'Folk into Race' is the answer to an urgent question of actual German life; 'What is our unity, and what is the sign by which we can know that we are one?' To the ardent nationalist, living in the days of the Weimar constitution, unity was not to be found in the fact of a common government and a common constitution. Government was a matter of multiple and conflicting parties; and each territory or *Land* had its own constitution as well as the *Reich*. Nor, again, was unity to be found in the common culture, the community of values, proclaimed by Möller van den Bruck. In a critical and self-conscious age the very idea of a common culture became a matter of doubt and uncertainty[4]; and in any case culture was a term too vague, and too comprehensive, to satisfy those who hungered for a definite and intimate unity. The unity of a common blood, proclaimed by a *Volkspartei* which identified Folk with Race, seemed a unity rooted in nature itself – a unity which could not be lost, like political unity; a unity which could not be shared, like cultural unity. It seemed an ultimate, on which all other forms of unity would follow, and without which no other form of unity could permanently exist. The historic memory of the old German 'stems' and 'tribes', knit (alleged to be knit) by the bond of blood, might be alleged in its favour. Anti-Semitic feeling, always latent, and always provocative of the idea of a profound and inescapable difference of blood and breed, might be elicited in its support. Whatever science might say (and German science might give a favourable testimony if the gospel of race were pragmatically established),

---

[3]   But I remember vividly a lecture on Race, with the recurrent theme of the *Erbmasse*, delivered by a scientific professor in one of the German universities, in the Spring of 1934, to a crowded audience of colleagues and university students.

[4]   See P. Viénot, *Incertitudes allemandes*, especially pp. 19 sqq.

the exigencies of life seemed to demand a saving idea; and race, backed by historic memories and contemporary feeling, became that idea.

The transformation of Folk into Race is from one point of view the raising of the Folk to a higher power. The Folk remains a creative spirit which produces the spiritual substance of a common culture; but it also becomes a body, breed, or blood. In this body the spirit finds its necessary residence; and through this body it will maintain its spiritual purity, by the mere process of heredity, if only the body itself maintains its physical purity. The racial theory thus makes a double assumption. It assumes that a folk has its ultimate unity in race, and is essentially a race: it also assumes that the racial factor is the cause of the culture of the folk. Both of these assumptions may be challenged.

Even if a folk *is* a race, it does not follow that the culture which it develops in the course of its history is determined purely by the factor of race. No culture develops in isolation. Every culture is an amalgam of ingredients, borrowed (or rather, diffused) as well as native – ingredients drawn from the long historical development of the Mediterranean world, in its Semitic, Greek, and Roman areas, as well as from the more recent development of Northern Europe. The racial genius of a Folk, even if we admit its existence, is only a colouring matter which gives a peculiar tincture to the common cultural inheritance of civilized humanity.

But there is no valid reason for admitting the existence of a racial genius in a Folk. The assumption that a folk is a race is a pure assumption, which is not warranted by any evidence. A folk or a nation is not a race, whatever else it may be, and whatever a race may be. Every nation of which we know is an amalgam of different racial ingredients, which the long process of historical migration has deposited on the national soil. The unity of a Folk is never the unity of a single race. To assert that it is, is to be oblivious of the simple fact of human movement and migration, and to create an abstraction based on oblivion. . . . We do not therefore, raise the Folk to a higher power when we transform it into a Race. We only give it a body which is even more imaginary than the creative spirit which it is imagined to possess. The elusive ideal of unity has eluded us once more.

Another variety of interpretation of the transcendent group, current in modern Italy, may be termed by the name of 'Folk into Nation'. This is a very simple transformation; indeed it may be said to be merely a verbal translation, which turns the German *Volk* into the Italian *Nazione*. Such a saying, however, would be an exaggeration. It is certainly true that the current Italian conception of the nation is deeply coloured by German ideas and German philosophy. But words have a magic of their own; and there is an Italian magic, or quality, about the word *Nazione*. The Italian Nation is different from the German Folk. It is not primarily a system of culture: still less is it a unity of race. 'Race – that is a sentiment, not a reality,' Signor Mussolini is reported to have said; '95 per cent is sentiment'.[5] The essence of the nation, in modern Italian thought, is 'spirit', issuing in the form of will: 'a will for existence and for power; self-consciousness; personality'.[6] A nation, therefore, is not race; it is not territory: it is not number: it is a personality with the supreme attribute of will, which expresses itself in willing its own continued existence and its own increase of power. 'For us the nation is above all spirit. . . . A nation is great when it translates into reality the force of its spirit'.[7] A consequence follows upon this emphasis of will as the supreme attribute of the personality of the nation. It is a consequence of primary and fatal importance. In order that it may will, the nation must have a will-centre. That will-centre is the State. The nation, on this view, cannot exist without the concurrent existence of the State; we may even say, if we follow this view, that it cannot exist without the previous existence of the State. 'The Nation does not exist to generate the State. The Nation is created by the State, which gives to the people, conscious of its own moral unity, a will, and thereby an effective existence.'[8] The Nation is indeed a personality; but it is a personality which could not exist, because it would not possess its essential attribute of will, unless it were brought into existence, and unless it were continually sustained, by the inspiration of the State.

---

[5]   B. Mussolini, *Scritti e Discorsi*, VIII, p. 95, note 19. But this saying belongs to an epoch earlier than that of the new racial idea later adopted in Italy in the course of 1938.

[6]   *Ibid.*, p. 72, § 9, *ad finem*.

[7]   *Ibid.*, p. 96.

[8]   B. Mussolini, *Scritti e Discorsi*, VIII, p. 72. But see p. 340, note 2.

Two conceptions are thus implied in the formula of 'Folk into Nation'. The first is the conception of the Nation as a self-conscious spirit which exists in the form of explosive will, and seeks to translate its force of will into action. Here the Romantic Folk-mind has become less of a mind, and more of a will; less a creator of culture, and more a doer of deeds. *Spirito*, after all, is different from *Geist*. But the Nation is still, like the Folk of German Romantic philosophy, a transcendent being, with an existence of its own distinct from that of its members. It is a personality: it is a personality of a higher order (*personalità superiore*): it has a being, and it has ends and means of action, superior to those of the individuals of whom it is composed. The second conception implied in the formula is that of the relation of this personality to the State. The personality cannot exist apart from the State, and except on the presupposition of the State. Its being consists in the exercise of will; and without the State it is without a will, and therefore without any real existence. The Nation without the State is a brute aggregate, and not a spirit. There must at least be a State *in fieri* – a political will already in action among the *élite*, and already inspiring an active sense of unity among the masses – before there can be the beginnings of a nation.

A national personality active in the area of will, and directing the activity of its will to the assertion of its force – a personality so connected with the State that it is fanned into being by it, and receives its will and its effective existence from it – this is the essence of the Italian version of the transcendent group. The nation is simply an Ego, with its own inevitable egoism; but the egoism is held to be 'sacred' because it is collective – or more exactly because, in seeking its own satisfaction, the national Ego seeks the satisfaction of all. This is a facile philosophy; but it depends on two assumptions. The first is that there can be no real conflict between the will of the national Ego and those of the individual members of the nation. The second is that the national Ego is moving in a bare universe in which it does not come into contact with other and similar beings, impinging on its egoism and necessarily limiting its will. Neither of these assumptions can be readily granted. It is true that the first assumption may not only be made in theory, but also asserted by force. Agreement between the will of the nation, 'given' to it by the State, in some particular form or constitution which the State has happened to assume, and the will of its individual members, may be secured by the way of fact. But a forcible identification is not the same as identity; and the egoism of the nation will not be sacred, even to its own members, if it simply imposes its purposes on their wills. In the sphere of external relations the sanctity of the virile affirmation of national will is still less obvious. Such an affirmation is indeed a fact. It may even be, in a given conjuncture, a fact which imposes itself. But the mere affirmation of national will can never be more than a fact, or acquire the dignity of a 'sacred' right, unless it adjusts itself to other wills, and until it enters a system of wills based on a common recognition of limits and a common respect for those limits.

Even if we admit the existence of a national personality, expressing itself in the area of will, we are thus left with a double problem – the problem of the adjustment of national personality to the personality of the individual members of the nation, and the problem of its adjustment to the personality of other nations. These problems are not solved, on the contrary, they are simply shelved – if we make the national person a lonely absolute which is entirely free to enforce, both within and without, its will for existence and power. We have simply added one supposition to another. We have first supposed a national personality; and we have then supposed a solitude in which it is free to operate. We may well be led to doubt, when we reflect on the unwarranted character of the second of these suppositions, whether the first supposition is any more warranted than the second, and whether we can really admit the existence of a national personality. Our doubts will be increased when we reflect that the national personality, as it is conceived in Italian theory, is not an original or self-existing personality. It is created by the State, and it derives its essential character of will from the State. The Nation as a personality (and not only a personality, but a 'higher personality') is thus a derivative fact. It has no inherent being and no original will. In its present form, it is the creation of the present form of the Italian State. Its being is what the Fascist party and its leader think it to be; its will is the will which is given to it by them. It is a shadow rather than a substance – a State-created shadow, in the name of which the creating State can subsequently profess to act. In the last resort, therefore, the formula of 'Folk into Nation' presents us, like the formula of 'Folk into Race', with an imagination. But the metaphysical nation of Italian

Fascist theory, with its higher being and its higher ends, is not only an imagination: it is a self-confessed imagination. The racial folk of German National Socialist theory, conceived as the creator and carrier of a peculiar Folk-culture and a corresponding and protecting Folk-State, may be criticized as imaginary, but it cannot be fairly criticized as a work of self-confessed imagination.If in either case a political party has erected an idol, or imaginary recipient of worship, the Fascist idol of the metaphysical nation, created by the State and posterior to the State, is even more fictitious than the National Socialist idol of the racial Folk.

The third interpretation of the transcendent group, prevalent in the scheme of Communism, may be called by the name of 'Folk into Class'. Here, indeed, we must begin by admitting that, at the first blush, Communism would seem to by the very antithesis of the whole Romantic tradition of the transcendent group. It does not, on its own showing, deal in mysticism: it is severely materialistic. The Communist does not start from any belief in the *Volksgeist*, or in the spirit of the nation: he starts from matter, the modes of acquiring material subsistence, and the system of classes which springs from those modes. On this basis he is led to deny the unity of the Folk or nation – so long as it is still distracted by the war of conflicting classes. The nation, in his view, is the product of a false idealism, intended to disguise and gloss the reality of class; and the true ideal – true because it is based on the essential material factor – is the international solidarity of the whole international proletariat. The whole of the Romantic theory, subjected to this corrosive, appears to be dissolved; and the solid residuum is the unromantic but poignant reality of economic class.

But Communism, after all, is only a form of Romanticism. It may be inverted Romanticism; but it is Romanticism none the less.[9] When it develops into action, as it has done in Russia, it displays this character more and more clearly in the successive stages of its development. In the first place, whatever its theory of internationalism may be, and however much it may seek to

---

[9] Marx (in the preface to the 1873 edition of *Das Kapital*), referring more particularly to the dialectic of Hegel, spoke of himself as having inverted the teaching of his master. 'With him it is standing on its head. It must be turned right side up again, if you would discover the rational kernel within the mystical shell.' But Hegel inverted is still Hegel; and inverted Romanticism is still Romanticism.

conduct international propaganda, it necessarily operates, under the conditions of modern life, in the area of a national State. In the second place, and within that area, it sets itself to create the unity which it fails to find, but is all the more resolved to make. The proletarian class (or more exactly a section of that class – the urban and industrial section) is assumed to be the core of unity: the capitalistic class is suppressed: the semi-proletarian classes, engaged on the land or in the professions, are incorporated into the core; and a single and homogeneous workers' society is substituted for the system of conflicting classes. Finally, this society assumes the romantic quality of a creative being which creates a new culture in its own image and inspires the whole life of every worker. The proletarian class, turned into a workers' society, inherits the mantle of the Folk.

Primarily, because it is primarily economic in its own basis and intention, it creates an economic ideal of rationalized mechanization – a new mode of acquiring material subsistence, congruous with its own unity and necessary to its own unity, by which each member of the society is made a contributory cog. It creates a romance of tractors and power-stations; it imposes it on the imagination, by the method of propaganda, as the aim of the hive is imposed by instinct on the motions of the bee. Next, and because machinery is not enough, the creative being of 'Folk into Class' produces its own proletarian art and literature, and its own total scheme of proletarian culture. Here the wheel has come full circle. The Folk, decomposed into classes, and then reconstituted on the basis of one (and one only) of these classes, has attained a new scheme of composition; and while, on this new scheme, it is engaged in doing new things, it is also doing the old. True, on the communist philosophy of material determination, it is doing them not as spirit, or at any rate as free spirit, but as a materially determined being which simply does what it must. But it is active none the less; and it is active as a being which transcends and controls individuals.

§ 4. *The Common Features of the Different Ideas of the Totalitarian Group*

It is difficult to compare the three idols, or to say which imposes the heaviest burden of worship. Class proscribes other classes; race proscribes other races; the metaphysical nation, though it seems to rally all to its service, proscribes none the less all those of its members who are not 'true' to the national spirit, and it also proscribes other nations. Each form of exclusive absolute makes its own particular exclusions; and when we make comparisons, we are apt to measure each absolute in terms of our own particular sympathies with the particular elements which it excludes – falling ourselves, to that extent, under the sway of our own class feeling, or our own racial sense, or our own national pride, and thus succumbing ourselves to our own form of counter-idol. Comparisons are idle, and even dangerous; we shall profit more and lose less if, instead of seeking to establish a hierarchy of these absolutes, we note their common features and the similarity of their results.

Each absolute weds itself to a State, which it makes equally absolute with itself. It finds a person who becomes its incarnation; he in his turn finds a party, on the basis of the absolute which he incarnates; he and his party then capture the State, and use its machinery to stamp their absolute on the community. First the absolute (the class, the race, the national organism); then the person of the leader; then the party; then the absolute party-State, dominated by the person – this is the logic of the development. Sometimes the logic may seem ideal rather than actual. It may be argued that, in Italy for example, the future leader had emerged, had founded his party, and had even captured the State, before he discovered the absolute which he and his party were destined to serve. It is certainly true that there is a large element of contingency in human affairs, and it is no less true that a dynamic personality is often an incalculable factor. But it is equally true that the Italian creed of nationalism was prior to the leader; and whatever the vicissitudes of his opinions may have been, there is as good a reason for saying that the creed chose him as there is for saying that he chose the creed. In Russia, at any rate, the sequence of history squares with the logic of development; and the same may be said of Germany. The leader is seldom, after all, the creator of the cause which he leads – though he may deify himself afterwards, or be deified afterwards by his followers, into the position of its creator. He is the user rather than the inventor. He uses the cause invented by thinkers as the basis of his own inventions (the party and the party-State) and the ground of his own position.[10]

The end of the absolute, when it has achieved its development, is political absolutism. But it is also something more. It is totalitarianism. Totalitarianism goes beyond absolutism. The absolute ruler is simply a ruler unlimited by any political constitution standing above him, or by any political organs of government (legislative of judicial) standing by his side. He has a giant's strength; but it is a strength which belongs to the political sphere, and he does not in his nature invade the field of society. Exigency may sometimes compel him to do so; but exigency will generally persuade him to purchase political power at the price of tolerating the general play of such social institutions as do not directly affect the exercise of his power. A totalitarian government follows a different policy. The absolute on which it is based must be carried into every domain of life – the social no less than the political: religion, education, economics, the methods of sport and the uses of leisure, as well as politics proper. Any form of group for any activity is a potential rival; it is a possible magnet of loyalty, which, however insignificant it may seem in comparison with the great loadstone, may none the less succeed in deflecting the quivering point of allegiance. From early life, and in every activity of life, the individual must be taught to point true: he will be enlisted early in the Octobrists or the Balilla or the Hitler Youth: his games, his holidays, the very life of his family, will be drawn into the field of the party, the party-State, the leader, the ultimate absolute. Zeal is more powerful, and more consuming, than power. The zeal of race, or class, or national spirit, can eat men up in its fire as no Leviathan, at his most 'dragonish', ever can.

Totalitarianism professes to be modern: to be a matter of scientific engineering: to be a system of deliberate planning. But it is an old idea that men should be engineered, and that their life should be made to move according to plan. There is a sense in which we may say that the totalitarian States are living in the sixteenth century.

10   Lenin is unique among leaders of the twentieth century (and perhaps in history) is being an inventor as well as a user. But even Lenin may be called the developer of an invention, rather than an inventor. He was the re-interpreter of Marx.

The Tudor period of our English history had its totalitarian features. One society, one State, one Church, one system of economics controlled by the King in Parliament – these were the ideals of that period. There were dissidents, there were rebellions, there were repressions; but a ground of unity was achieved sufficient to allow the subsequent growth, from the Great Rebellion onwards, of the spirit which tolerates difference and is ready to consider compromise. There are no exact parallels in history; but similar causes at any rate tend to produce similar results. Whenever a group of men is shaken by a nervous tremor, it will tend to draw closely together for comfort and reassurance. There were tremors and alarms in the England of the sixteenth century: there are tremors and alarms in Germany, Italy, and Russia to-day. Solidarity seems dearly precious in such times; its name is exalted, and it carries the day. Men are always apt, in each troubled moment, to see the eternal in the moment, and to find eternal verities in the occasions of the hour. Our own sophisticated age, troubled by old problems, has invented more imposing and high-sounding verities than ever occurred to the age of the Tudors. To explain and to expedite an instinctive closing up of the ranks, it has called into existence transcendent beings on which men can suppose themselves to be closing; it has constructed, in order to organize the movement, hurrying parties, urgent leaders, and a general system of tension. Faced by such tendencies, which are relative to particular occasions and the sentiments which they evoke, we may find comfort in seeking the perspective of history and remembering the relativity of our own human reactions. It is true that the closing up of the ranks in any one country, or set of countries, will tend to induce, by the force of contagious excitement, a similar movement in others. It is also true that a general tendency will appear, from its very generality, to be permanent as well as general. But if we seek the perspective of history, we shall see that such things have come – and gone – before now; and if we remember the relativity of human reactions, we shall see that they are answers to a particular stimulus, which may not always last, and which, if it is active in some countries, need not be active in all. Totalitarianism has happened before; and it may happen again. It is happening here; and it may also happen there. But it will not necessarily endure; nor will it necessarily spread.

Meanwhile it is good to arm ourselves against contagious excitement, and to ask ourselves, before we too begin to close up, whether there are any occasions in our life which demand it; whether there is any 'being' on which we can close; and whether the open order in which we are moving is not true to the best tactics of social life. For nearly three hundred years – ever since the New Model Army debated the ultimate foundations of politics – we have been trying to develop the open order of a society of free individuals freely determining their common purposes, and the methods of their execution, in the forum of discussion. We have assumed that this society was constituted and actuated by its members; we have assumed that they could freely debate a number of alternative purposes, or alternative schemes of social life, as well as alternative methods of realizing a single particular purpose or scheme; we have assumed that they could group themselves freely, in political parties and otherwise, for the advocacy both of alternative purposes and of alternative methods. A wide are of choice, among ends as well as among means; free discussion of the alternatives; free association for the purpose of formulating choices and advocating their adoption – these have been the tactics (sometimes clumsily followed, and sometimes sadly impeded by the prejudice of confessions and the bias of classes) which have controlled our general life. We shall hardly surrender them readily to the eruption of the group, and the worship of the group, which is connected with the eruption of the personal.

THE MASSES IN REPRESENTATIVE DEMOCRACY
Michael Oakeshott
London School of Economics

I

The course of modern European history has thrown up a character whom we are accustomed to call the 'mass man'. His appearance is spoken of as the most significant and far-reaching of all the revolutions of modern times. He is credited with having transformed our way of living, our standards of conduct and our manners of political activity. He is, sometimes regretfully, acknowledge to have become the arbiter of taste, the dictator of policy, the uncrowned king of the modern world. He excites fear in some, admiration in others, wonder in all. His numbers have made him a giant; he proliferates everywhere; he is recognized either as a locust who is making a desert of what was once a fertile garden, or as the bearer of a new and more glorious civilization.

All this I believe to be a gross exaggeration. And I think we should recognize what our true situation is in this respect, what precisely we owe to this character, and the extent of his impact, if we understood more clearly who this 'mass man' is and where he has come from. And with a view to answering these questions, I propose to engaged in a piece of historical description.

It is a long story, which has too often been made unintelligible by being abridged. It does not begin (as some would have us understand) with the French Revolution or with the industrial changes of the late eighteenth century; it begins in those perplexing centuries which, because of their illegibility, no historian can decide whether they should properly be regarded as a conclusion or a preface, namely the fourteenth and fifteenth centuries. And it begins, not with the emergence of the 'mass man', but with an emergence of a very different kind, namely, that of the human individual in his modern idiom. You must bear with me while I set the scene for the entry of the character we are to study, because we shall mistake him unless we prepare ourselves for his appearance.

II

There have been occasions, some of them in the distance past, when, usually as a consequence of the collapse of a closely integrated manner of living, human individuality has emerged and has been enjoyed for a time. An emergence of this sort is always of supreme importance; it is the modification not only of all current activities, but also of all human relationships from those of husband, wife and children to those of ruler and subject. The fourteenth and fifteenth centuries in western Europe were an occasion of this kind. What began to emerge, then, were conditions so pre-eminently favourable to a very high degree of human individuality, and human beings enjoying (to such a degree and in such numbers) the experience of 'self-determination' in conduct and belief, that it over-shadows all earlier occasions of the sort. Nowhere else has the emergence of individuals (that is, persons accustomed to making choices for themselves) either modified human rela-tionships so profoundly, or proved so durable an experience, or provoked so strong a reaction, or explained itself so elaborately in the idiom of philosophical theory.

Like everything else in modern Europe, achievement in respect of human individuality was a modification of medieval conditions of life or thought. It was not generated in claims and assertions on behalf of individuality, but in sporadic divergencies from a condition of human circumstance in which the opportunity for choice was narrowly circumscribed. To know oneself as the member of a family, a group, a corporation, a church, a village community, as the suitor at a court or as the occupier of a tenancy, had been, for the vast majority, the circumstantially possible sum of self-knowledge. Not only were ordinary activities, those concerned with getting a living, communal in character, but so also were decisions, rights and responsibilities. Relationships and allegiances nor-mally sprang from status and rarely extricated themselves from the analogy of kinship. For the most part anonymity prevailed; individual human character was rarely observed because it was not there to be observed. What differentiated one man from another was insignificant when compared with what was enjoyed in common as members of a group of some sort.

This situation reached something of a climax in the twelfth century. It was modified slowly, sporadically and intermittently over a period of about seven centuries, from the thirteenth to the twentieth century. The change began earlier and went more rapidly in some parts of Europe than in others; it penetrated some activities more readily and more profoundly than others; it affected men before it touched women; and during these seven centuries there have been many local climaxes and corresponding recessions. But the enjoyment of the new opportunities of escape from communal ties gradually generated a new idiom of human character.

It emerged first in Italy: Italy was the first home of the modern individual who sprang from the break-up of medieval communal life. 'At the close of the thirteenth century', writes Burckhardt, 'Italy began to swarm with individuality; the ban laid upon human personality was dissolved; a thousand figures meet us, each in his own special shape and dress'. The *uomo singolare*, whose conduct was marked by a high degree of self-determination and a large number of whose activities expressed personal preferences, gradually detached himself from his fellows. And together with him appeared, not only the *libertine* and the *dilettante*, but also the *uomo unico*, the man who, in the mastery of his circumstances, stood alone and was a law to himself. Men examined themselves and were not dismayed by their own want of perfection. This was the character which Petrarch dramatized for his generation with unmatched skill and unrivalled energy. A new image of human nature appeared – not Adam, not Prometheus, but Proteus – a character distinguished from all others on account of his multiplicity and of his endless power of self-transformation.

North of the Alps, events took a similar course, though they moved more slowly and had to contend with large hindrances. In England, in France, in the Netherlands, in Spain, in Switzerland, in Poland, Hungary and Bohemia, and particularly in all centres of municipal life, conditions favourable to individuality, and individuals to exploit them, appeared. There were few fields of activity untouched. By the middle of the sixteenth century they had been so firmly established that they were beyond the range of mere suppression: not all the severity

of the Calvinist *régime* in Geneva was sufficient to quell the
impulse to think and behave as an independent individual. The
disposition to regard a high degree of individuality in conduct
and in belief as the condition proper to mankind and as the
main ingredient of human 'happiness', had become one of the
significant dispositions of modern European character. What
Petrarch did for one century, Montaigne did for another.

The story of the vicissitudes of this disposition during the last
four centuries is exceedingly complex. It is a story, not of
steady growth, but of climaxes and anti-climaxes, of diffusion
to parts of Europe at first relatively ignorant of it, of extension
to activities from which it was at first excluded, of attack and
defence, of confidence and of apprehension. But, if we cannot
pursue it in all its detail, we may at least observe how
profoundly this disposition imposed itself upon European
conduct and belief. In the course of a few hundred years, it was
magnified into an ethical and even into a metaphysical theory,
it gathered to itself an appropriate understanding of the office
of government, it modified political manners and institutions,
it settled itself upon art, upon religion, upon industry and trade
and upon every kind of human relationship.

In the field of intellectual speculation the clearest reflection
of this profound experience of individuality is to be seen in
ethical theory. Almost all modern writing about moral conduct
begins with the hypothesis of an individual human being
choosing and pursuing his own directions of activity. What
appeared to require explanation was not the existence of such
individuals, but how they could come to have duties to others
of their kind and what was the nature of those duties; just as
the existence of other minds became a problem to those who
understood knowledge as the residue of sense experience. This
is unmistakable in Hobbes, the first moralist of the modern
world to take candid account of the current experience of
individuality. He understood a man as an organism governed
by an impulse to avoid destruction and to maintain itself in its
own characteristic and chosen pursuits. Each individual has a
natural right to independent existence: the only problem is how
he is to pursue his own chosen course with the greatest measure
of success, the problem of his relation to 'others' of his kind.
And a similar view of things appeared, of course, in the
writings of Spinoza. But even where an individualistic conclusion was rejected, this autonomous individual remained as

the starting point of ethical reflection. Every moralist in the seventeenth and eighteenth centuries is concerned with the psychological structure of this assumed 'individual': the relation of 'self' and 'others' is the common form of all moral theory of the time. And nowhere is this seen more clearly to be the case than in the writings of Kant. Every human being, in virtue of not being subject to natural necessity, is recognized by Kant to be a Person, an end in himself, absolute and autonomous. To seek his own happiness is the natural pursuit of such a person; self-love is the motive of the choices which compose his conduct. But as a rational human being he will recognize in his conduct the universal conditions of autonomous personality; and the chief of these conditions is to use humanity, as well in himself as in others, as an end and never as a means. Morality consists in the recognition of individual personality whenever it appears. Moreover, personality is so far sacrosanct that no man has either a right or a duty to promote the moral perfection of another: we may promote the 'happiness' of others, but we cannot promote their 'good' without destroying their 'freedom' which is the condition of moral goodness.

In short, whatever we may think of the moral theories of modern Europe, they provide the clearest evidence of the overwhelming impact of this experience of individuality.

But this pursuit of individuality, and of the conditions most favourable to its enjoyment, was reflected also in an understanding of the proper office of government and in appropriate manners of government and being governed, both modifications of an inheritance from the Middle Ages. We have time only to notice them in their most unqualified appearance, namely, in what we have come to call 'modern representative democracy'. This manner of governing and being governed appeared first in England, in the Netherlands and in Switzerland, and was later (in various idioms) extended to other parts of Western Europe and the United States of America. It is not to be understood either as an approximation to some ideal manner of government, or as a modification of a manner of government (with which it has no connection whatever) current for a short while in certain parts of the ancient world. It is simply what emerged in Western Europe where the impact of the aspirations of individuality upon medieval institutions of government was greatest.

The first demand of those intent upon exploring the intimations of individuality was for an instrument of government capable of transforming the interests of individuality into rights and duties. To perform this task government required three attributes. First, it must be single and supreme; only by a concentration of all authority at one centre could the emergent individual escape from the communal pressures of family and guild, of church and local community, which hindered his enjoyment of his own character. Secondly, it must be an instrument of government not bound by prescription and therefore with authority to abolish old rights and create new: it must be a 'sovereign' government. And this, according to current ideas, meant a government in which all who enjoyed rights were partners, a government in which the 'estates' of the realm were direct or indirect participants. Thirdly, it must be powerful – able to preserve the order without which the aspirations of individuality could not be realized; but not so powerful as itself to constitute a new threat to individuality. In an earlier time, the recognized methods of transforming interests into rights had been judicial; the 'parliaments' and 'councils' of the Middle Ages had been pre-eminently judicial bodies. But from these 'courts of law' emerged an instrument with more emphatic authority to recognize new interests by converting them into new rights and duties; there emerged legislative bodies. Thus, a ruler, and a parliament representative of his subjects, came to share the business of 'making' law. And the law they made was favourable to the interests of individuality: it provided the detail of what became a well-understood condition of human circumstance, commonly denoted by the word 'freedom'. In this condition every subject was secured of the right to pursue his chosen directions of activity as little hindered as might be by his fellows or by the exactions of government itself, and as little distracted by communal pressures. Freedom of movement, of initiative, of speech, of belief and religious observance, of association and disassociation, of bequest and inheritance; security of person and property; the right to choose one's own occupation and dispose of one's labour and goods; and over all the 'rule of law': the right to be ruled by a known law, applicable to all subjects alike. And these rights, appropriate to individuality, were not the privileges of a single class; they were the property of every subject alike. Each signified the abrogation of some feudal privilege.

This manner of governing, which reached its climax in the 'parliamentary' government which emerged in England and elsewhere in the late eighteenth and early nineteenth centuries, was concurrently theorized in an understanding of the proper office of government. What had been a 'community' came to be recognized as an 'association' of individuals: this was the counterpart in political philosophy of the individualism that had established itself in ethical theory. And the office of government was understood to be the maintenance of arrangements favourable to the interests of individuality, arrangements (that is) which emancipated the subject from the 'chains' (as Rousseau put it) of communal allegiances, and constituted a condition of human circumstance in which the intimations of individuality might be explored and the experience of individuality enjoyed.

Briefly, then, my picture is as follows. Human individuality is an historical emergence, as 'artificial' and as 'natural' as the landscape. In modern Europe this emergence was gradual, and the specific character of the individual who emerged was determined by the manner of his generation. He became unmistakable when the habit appeared of engaging in activities identified as 'private'; indeed, the appearance of 'privacy' in human conduct is the obverse of the desuetude of the communal arrangements from which modern individuality sprang. This experience of individuality provoked a disposition to explore its own intimations, to place the highest value upon it, and to seek security in its enjoyment. To enjoy it came to be recognized as the main ingredient of 'happiness'. The experience was magnified into an ethical theory; it was reflected in manners of governing and being governed, in newly acquired rights and duties and in a whole pattern of living. The emergence of this disposition to be an individual is the pre-eminent event in modern European history.

III

There were many modest manners in which this disposition to be an individual might express itself. Every practical enterprise and every intellectual pursuit revealed itself as an assemblage of opportunities for making choices: art, literature, philosophy, commerce, industry and politics each came to partake of this character. Nevertheless, in a world being transformed by the aspirations and activities of those who were excited by these opportunities, there were some people, by circumstance or by temperament, less ready than others to respond to this invitation; and for many the invitation to make choices came before the ability to make them and was consequently recognized as a burden. The old certainties of belief, of occupation and of status were being dissolved, not only for those who had confidence in their own power to make a new place for themselves in an association of individuals, but also for those who had no such confidence. The counterpart of the agricultural and industrial *entrepreneur* of the sixteenth century was the displaced labourer; the counterpart of the *libertine* was the dispossessed believer. The familiar warmth of communal pressures was dissipated for all alike – an emancipation which excited some, depressed others. The familiar anonymity of communal life was replaced by a personal identity which was burdensome to those who could not transform it into an individuality. What some recognized as happiness, appeared to others as discomfort. The same condition of human circumstance was identified as progress and as decay. In short, the circumstances of modern Europe, even as early as the sixteenth century, bred, not a single character, but two obliquely opposed characters: not only that of the individual, but also that of the 'individual *manqué*'. And this 'individual *manqué*' was not a relic of a past age; he was a 'modern' character, the product of the same dissolution of communal ties as had generated the modern European individual.

We need not speculate upon what combination of debility, ignorance, timidity, poverty or mischance operated in particular cases to provoke this character; it is enough to observe his appearance and his efforts to accommodate himself to his hostile environment. He sought a protector who would recognize his predicament, and he found what he sought, in some measure, in 'the government'. From as early as the sixteenth century the governments of Europe were being modified, not only in response to the demands of individuality, but in response also to the needs of the 'individual *manqué*'. The 'godly prince' of the Reformation and his lineal descendant, the 'enlightened despot' of the eighteenth century, were political inventions for making choices for those indisposed to make choices for themselves; the Elizabethan Statute of Labourers was designed to take care of those who were left behind in the race.

The aspirations of individuality had imposed themselves upon conduct and belief and upon the constitutions and activities of governments, in the first place, as demands emanating from a powerful and confident disposition. There was little attempt to moralize these demands, which in the sixteenth century were clearly in conflict with current moral sentiment, still fixed in its loyalty to the morality of communal ties. Nevertheless, from the experience of individuality there sprang, in the course of time, a morality appropriate to it – a disposition not only to explore individuality but to approve of the pursuit of individuality. This constituted a considerable moral revolution; but such was its force and vigour that it not only swept aside the relics of the morality appropriate to the defunct communal order, but left little room for any alternative *to itself*. And the weight of this moral victory bore heavily upon the 'individual *manqué*'. Already outmanoeuvred in the field (in conduct), he now suffered a defeat at home, in his own character. What had been no more than a doubt about his ability to hold his own in a struggle for existence, became a radical self-distrust; what had been merely a hostile prospect, disclosed itself as an abyss; what had been the discomfort of ill-success was turned into the misery of guilt.

In some, no doubt, this situation provoked resignation; but in others it bred envy, jealousy and resentment. And in these emotions a new disposition was generated: the impulse to escape from the predicament by imposing it upon all mankind. From the frustrated 'individual *manqué*' there sprang the militant 'anti-individual', disposed to assimilate the world to his own character by deposing the individual and destroying his moral prestige. No promise, or even offer, of self-advancement could tempt this 'anti-individual'; he knew his individuality was too poorly furnished to be explored or exploited with any satisfaction whatever. He was moved solely by the opportunity of complete escape from the anxiety of not being an individual, the opportunity of removing from the world all that convicted him of his own inadequacy. His situation provoked him to seek release in separatist communities, insulated from the moral pressure of individuality. But the opportunity he sought appeared fully when he recognized that, so far from being alone, he belonged to the most numerous class in modern European society, the class of those who had no choices of their own to make. Thus, in the recognition of his numerical superiority the 'anti-individual' at once recognized himself as the 'mass man' and discovered the way of escape from his predicament. For, although the 'mass man' is specified by his disposition – a disposition to allow in others only a replica of himself, to impose upon all a uniformity of belief and conduct that leaves no room for either the pains or the pleasures of choice – and not by his numbers, he is confirmed in this disposition by the support of others of his kind. He can have no friends (because friendship is a relation between individuals), but he has comrades. The 'masses' as they appear in modern European history are not composed of individuals; they are composed of 'anti-individuals' united in a revulsion from individuality. Consequently, although the remarkable growth of population in Western Europe during the last four hundred years is a condition of the success with which this character has imposed itself, it is not a condition of the character itself.

Nevertheless, the 'anti-individual' had feelings rather than thoughts, impulses rather than opinions, inabilities rather than passions, and was only dimly aware of his power. Consequently, he required 'leaders': indeed, the modern concept of 'leadership' is a concomitant of the 'anti-individual', and without him it would be unintelligible. An association of individuals requires a ruler, but it has no place for a 'leader'. The 'anti-individual' needed to be told what to think; his impulses had to be transformed into desires, and these desires into projects; he had to be made aware of his power; and these were the tasks of his leaders. Indeed, from one point of view, 'the masses' must be regarded as the invention of their leaders.

The natural submissiveness of the 'mass man' may itself be supposed to have been capable of prompting the appearance of appropriate leaders. He was unmistakably an instrument to be played upon, and no doubt the instrument provoked the *virtuoso*. But there was, in fact, a character ready to occupy this office. What was required was a man who could at once appear as the image and the master of his followers; a man who could more easily make choices for others than for himself; a man disposed to mind other people's business because he lacked the skill to find satisfaction in minding his own. And these, precisely, were the attributes of the 'individual *manqué*', whose achievements and whose failures in respect of individuality exactly fitted him for this task of leadership. He was enough of an individual to seek a personal satisfaction in the exercise of individuality, but too little to seek it anywhere but in commanding others. He loved himself too little to be anything but an egoist; and what his followers took to be a genuine concern for their salvation was in fact nothing more than the vanity of the almost selfless. No doubt the 'masses' in modern Europe have had other leaders than this cunning frustrate who has led always by flattery and whose only concern is the exercise of power; but they have had none more appropriate – for he only has never prompted them to be critical of their impulses. Indeed, the 'anti-individual' and his leader were the counterparts of a single moral situation; they relieved one another's frustrations and supplied one another's wants. Nevertheless, it was an uneasy partnership: moved by impulses rather than by desires, the 'mass man' has been submissive but not loyal to his leaders: even the exiguous individuality of the leader has easily aroused his suspicion. And the leaders' greed for power has disposed him to raise hopes in his followers which he has never been able to satisfy.

Of all the manners in which the 'anti-individual' has imposed himself upon Western Europe two have been pre-eminent. He has generated a morality designed to displace the current morality of individuality; and he has evoked an understanding of the proper office of government and manners of governing appropriate to his character.

The emergence of the morality of the 'anti-individual', a morality, namely, not of 'liberty' and 'self-determination', but of 'equality' and 'solidarity' is, of course, difficult to discern; but it is already clearly visible in the seventeenth century. The obscurity of its beginnings is due in part to the fact that its vocabulary was at first that of the morality of the defunct communal order; and there can be little doubt that it derived strength and plausibility from its deceptive affinity to that morality. But it was, in fact, a new morality, generated in opposition to the hegemony of individuality and calling for the establishment of a new condition of human circumstance reflecting the aspirations of the 'anti-individual'.

The nucleus of this morality was the concept of a substantive condition of human circumstance represented as the 'common'

or 'public' good, which was understood, not to be composed of
the various goods that might be sought by individuals on their
own account, but to be an independent entity. 'Self-love',
which was recognized in the morality of individuality as a
legitimate spring of human activity, the morality of the 'anti-
individual' pronounced to be evil. But it was to be replaced, not
by the love of 'others', or by 'charity' or by 'benevolence' (which
would have entailed a relapse into the vocabulary of individuality), but by the love of 'the community'.

Round this nucleus revolved a constellation of appropriate
subordinate beliefs. From the beginning, the designers of this
morality identified private property with individuality, and
consequently connected its abolition with the condition of
human circumstance appropriate to the 'mass man'. And
further, it was appropriate that the morality of the 'anti-
individual' should be radically equalitarian: how should the
'mass man', whose sole distinction was his resemblance to his
fellows and whose salvation lay in the recognition of others as
merely replicas of himself, approve of any divergence from an
exact uniformity? All must be equal and anonymous units in a
'community'. And, in the generation of this morality, the
character of this 'unit' was tirelessly explored. He was
understood as a 'man' *per se*, as a 'comrade', as a 'citizen'. But
the most acute diagnosis, that of Proudhon, recognized him as
a 'debtor'; for in this notion what was asserted was not only the
absence of distinction between the units who composed the
'community' (all are alike 'debtors'), but also a debt owed, not
to 'others' but to the 'community' itself: at birth he enters into
an inheritance which he had played no part in accumulating,
and whatever the magnitude of his subsequent contribution, it
never equals what he has enjoyed: he dies necessarily insolvent.

This morality of the 'anti-individual', the morality of a
solidarité commune, began to be constructed in the sixteenth
century. Its designers were mostly visionaries, dimly aware of
their purposes, and lacking a large audience. But a momentous
change occurred when the 'anti-individual' recognized himself
as the 'mass man', and perceived the power that his numerical
superiority gave him. The recognition that the morality of the
'anti-individual' was, in the first place, the morality not of a
sect of aspirants, but of a large ready-made class in society (the
class, not of the 'poor', but of those who by circumstance or by
occupation had been denied the experience of individuality),

and that in the interests of this class it must be imposed upon all mankind, appears unmistakably first in the writings of Marx and Engels.

Before the end of the nineteenth century, then, a morality of 'anti-individualism' had been generated in response to the aspirations of the 'mass man'. It was, in many respects, a rickety construction: it never achieved a design comparable to that which Hobbes or Kant or Hegel gave the morality of individuality; and it has never been able to resist relapse into the inappropriate concepts of individuality. Nevertheless it throws back a tolerably clear reflection of the 'mass man', who by this means became more thoroughly acquainted with himself. But we are not concerned with its merits or defects, we are concerned only to notice it as evidence of the power with which the 'mass man', has imposed himself on modern Europe over a period of about four centuries. 'Anti-individuality', long before the nineteenth century, had established itself as one of the major dispositions of the modern European moral character. And this disposition was evident enough for it to be recognized unequivocally by Sorel, and to be identified by writers such as Nietzsche, Kierkegaard and Burckhardt as the image of a new barbarism.

From the beginning (in the sixteenth century) those who exerted themselves on behalf of the 'anti-individual' perceived that his counterpart, a 'community' reflecting his aspirations, entailed a 'government' active in a certain manner. To govern was understood to be the exercise of power in order to impose and maintain the substantive condition of human circumstance identified as 'the public good'; to be governed was, for the 'anti-individual', to have made for him the choices he was unable to make for himself. Thus, 'government' was cast for the rôle of architect and custodian, not of 'public order' in an 'association' of individuals pursuing their own activities, but of 'the public good' of a 'community'. The ruler was recognized to be, not the referee of the collisions of individuals, but the moral leader and managing director of 'the community'. And this understanding of government has been tirelessly explored over a period of four and a half centuries, from Thomas More's *Utopia* to the Fabian Society, from Campanella to Lenin. But the leaders who served the 'mass man' were not merely theorists concerned to make his character intelligible in a moral doctrine and in an understanding of the office of government; they were also practical men who revealed to him his power and the manner in which the institutions of modern democratic government might be appropriated to his aspirations. And if we call the manner of government that had been generated by the aspirations of individuality 'parliamentary government', we may call the modification of it under the impact of the 'mass man', 'popular government'. But it is important to understand that these are two wholly different manners of government.

The emergent individual in the sixteenth century had sought new rights, and by the beginning of the nineteenth century the rights appropriate to his character had, in England and elsewhere, been largely established. The 'anti-individual' observed these rights, and he was persuaded that his circumstances (chiefly his poverty) had hitherto prevented him from sharing them. Hence the new rights called for on his behalf were, in the first place, understood as the means by which he might come to participate in the rights won and enjoyed by those he thought of as his better placed fellows. But this was a great illusion; first, because in fact he had these rights, and secondly because he had no use for them. For the disposition of the 'mass man' was not to become an individual, and the enterprise of his leaders was not to urge him in this direction. And what, in fact, prevented him enjoying the rights of individuality (which were as available to him as to anyone else) was not his 'circumstances' but his character – his 'anti-individuality'. The rights of individuality were necessarily such that the 'mass man' could have no use for them. And so, in the end, it turned out: what he came to demand were rights of an entirely different *kind*, and of a kind which entailed the abolition of the rights appropriate to individuality. He required the right to enjoy a substantive condition of human circumstance in which he would not be asked to make choices for himself. He had no use for the right to 'pursue happiness' – that could only be a burden to him: he needed the right to 'enjoy happiness'. And looking into his own character he identified this with Security – but again, not security against arbitrary interference in the exercise of his preferences, but Security against having to make choices for himself and against to meet the vicissitudes of life from his own resources. In short, the right he claimed, the right appropriate to his character, was the right to live in a social protectorate which relieved him from the burden of 'self-determination'.

But this condition of human circumstances was seen to be impossible unless it were imposed upon all alike. So long as 'others' were permitted to make choices for themselves, not only would his anxiety at not being able to do so himself remain to convict him of his inadequacy and threaten his emotional security, but also the social protectorate which he recognized as his counterpart would itself be disrupted. The Security he needed entailed a genuine equality of circumstances imposed upon all. The condition he sought was one in which he would meet in others only a replica of himself: what he was, everybody must become.

He claimed this condition as a 'right', and consequently he sought a government disposed to give it to him and one endowed with the power necessary to impose upon all activities the substantive pattern of activity called 'the public good'. 'Popular government' is, precisely, a modification of 'parliamentary government' designed to accomplish this purpose. And if this reading is correct, 'popular government' is no more intimated in 'parliamentary government' than the rights appropriate to the 'anti-individual' are intimated in the rights appropriate to individuality: they are not complementary but directly opposed to one another. Nevertheless, what I have called 'popular government' is not a concrete manner of government established and practised; it is a disposition to impose certain modifications upon 'parliamentary government' in order to convert it into a manner of government appropriate to the aspirations of the 'mass man'.

This disposition has displayed itself in specific enterprises, and in less specific habits and manners in respect of government. The first great enterprise was the establishment of universal adult suffrage. The power of the 'mass man' lay in his numbers, and this power could be brought to bear upon government by means of 'the vote'. Secondly, a change in the character of the parliamentary representative was called for: he must be not an individual, but a *mandataire* charged with the task of imposing the substantive condition of human circumstances required by the 'mass man'. 'Parliament' must become a 'work-shop', not a debating assembly. Neither of these changes was intimated in 'parliamentary government'; both, in so far as they have been achieved, have entailed an assembly of a new character. Their immediate effect has been twofold: first, to confirm the authority of mere numbers (an authority alien to the practice of 'parliamentary government'); and secondly, to give governments immensely increased power.

But the institutions of 'parliamentary government' proved to have only a limited eligibility for conversion into institutions appropriate to serve the aspirations of the 'mass man'. And an assembly of instructed delegates was seen to be vulnerable to a much more appropriate contrivance – the *plébiscite*. Just as it lay in the character of the 'mass man' to see everyman as a 'public official', an agent of 'the public good', and to see his representatives not as individuals but instructed delegates, so he saw very voter as the direct participant in the activity of governing: and the means of this was the *plébiscite*. An assembly elected on a universal adult suffrage, composed of instructed delegates and flanked by the device of the *plébiscite* was, then, the counterpart of the 'mass man'. They gave him exactly what he wanted: the illusion without the reality of choice; choice without the burden of having to choose. For, with universal suffrage have appeared the massive political parties of the modern world, composed not of individuals but of 'anti-individuals'. And both the instructed delegate and the *plébiscite* are devices for avoiding the necessity for making choices. The 'mandate' from the beginning was an illusion. The 'mass man', as we have seen, is a creature of impulses, not desires; he is utterly unable to draw up instructions for his representative to follow. What in fact has happened, whenever the disposition of 'popular government' has imposed itself, is that the prospective representative has drawn up his own mandate and then, by a familiar trick of ventriloquism, has put it into the mouth of his electors: as an instructed delegate he is not an individual, and as a 'leader' he relieves his followers of the need to make choices for themselves. And similarly, the *plébiscite* is not a method by which the 'mass man' imposes his choices upon his rulers; it is a method of generating a government with unlimited authority to make choices on his behalf. In the *plébiscite* the 'mass man' achieved final release from the burden of individuality: he was told emphatically what to choose.

Thus, in these and other constitutional devices, and in less formal habits of political conduct, was generated a new art of politics: the art, not of 'ruling' (that is, of seeking the most practicable adjustments for the collisions of 'individuals'), nor even of maintaining the support of a majority of individuals in a 'parliamentary' assembly, but of knowing what offer will collect most votes and making it in such a manner that it appears to come from 'the people'; the art, in short, of 'leading' in the modern idiom. Moreover, it is known in advance what offer will collect the most votes: the character of the 'mass man' is such that he will be moved only by the offer of release from the burden of making choices for himself, the offer of 'salvation'. And anyone who makes this offer may confidently demand unlimited power: it will be given him.

The 'mass man', as I understand him, then, is specified by his character, not by his numbers. He is distinguished by so exiguous an individuality that when it meets a powerful experience of individuality it revolts into 'anti-individuality'. He has generated for himself an appropriate morality, an appropriate understanding of the office of government, and appropriate modifications of 'parliamentary government'. He is not necessarily 'poor', nor is he envious only of 'riches'; he is not necessarily 'ignorant', often he is a member of the so-called *intelligentsia*; he belongs to a class which corresponds exactly with no other class. He is specified primarily by a moral, not an intellectual, inadequacy. He wants 'salvation'; and in the end will be satisfied only with release from the burden of having to make choices for himself. He is dangerous, not on account of his opinions or desires, for he has none: but on account of his submissiveness. His disposition is to endow government with power and authority such as it has never before enjoyed: he is utterly unable to distinguished a 'ruler' from a 'leader'. In short, the disposition to be an 'anti-individual' is one to which every European man has a propensity; the 'mass man' is merely one in whom this propensity is dominant.

IV

Of the many conclusions which follow from the reading of the situation the most important is to dispose of the most insidious of our current political delusions. It has been said, and it is commonly believed, that the event of supreme importance in modern European history is 'the accession of the masses to complete social power'. But that no such event has taken place is evident when we consider what it would entail. If it is true (as I have contended) that modern Europe enjoys two opposed moralities (that of individuality and that of the 'anti-individual'), that it enjoys two opposed understandings of the office of government, and two corresponding interpretations of the current institutions of government, then, for the 'mass man' to have won for himself a position of undisputed sovereignty would entail the complete suppression of what, in any reading, must be considered the strongest of our moral and political dispositions and the survival of the weakest. A world in which the 'mass man' exercised 'complete social power' would be a world in which the activity of governing was understood *solely* as the imposition of a single substantive condition of human circumstance, a world in which 'popular government' had altogether displaced 'parliamentary government', a world in which the 'civil' rights of individuality had been abrogated by the 'social' rights of anti-individuality – and there is no evidence that we live in such a world. Certainly the 'mass man' has emerged and has signified his emergence in an appropriate morality and an appropriate understanding of the office of government. He has sought to transform the world into a replica of himself, and he has not been entirely unsuccessful. He has sought to enjoy what he could not create for himself, and nothing he has appropriated remains unchanged. Nevertheless, he remains an unmistakably derivative character, an emanation of the pursuit of individuality, helpless, parasitic and able to survive only in opposition to individuality. Only in the most favourable circumstances, and then only by segregating him from all alien influences, have his leaders been able to suppress in him an unquenched propensity to desert at the call of individuality. He has imposed himself emphatically only where the relics of a morality of communal ties survived to make plausible his moral and political impulses. Elsewhere, the modifications he has provoked in political manners and moral beliefs have been extensive, but the notion that they have effaced the morality of individuality and 'parliamentary government' is without foundation. He loves himself too little to be able to dispose effectively of the only power he has, namely, his numerical superiority. He lacks passion rather than reason. He has had a past in which he was taught to admire himself and his antipathies; he has a present in which he is often the object of the ill-concealed contempt of his 'leaders'; but the heroic future forecast him is discrepant with his own character. He is no hero.

On the other hand, if we judge the world as we find it (which includes, of course, the emergence of the 'mass man') the event of supreme and seminal importance in modern European history remains the emergence of the human individual in his modern idiom. The pursuit of individuality has evoked a moral disposition, an understanding of the office of government and manners of governing, a multiplicity of activity and opinion and a notion of 'happiness', which have impressed themselves indelibly upon European civilization. The onslaught of the 'mass man' has shaken but not destroyed the moral prestige of individuality; even the 'anti-individual', whose salvation lies in escape, has not been able to escape it. The desire of 'the masses' to enjoy the products of individuality has modified their destructive urge. And the antipathy of the 'mass man' to the 'happiness' of 'self-determination' easily dissolves into self-pity. At all important points the individual still appears as the substance and the 'anti-individual' only as the shadow.

THE ATAVISM OF SOCIAL JUSTICE*
F. A. Hayek

1

To discover the meaning of what is called 'social justice' has been one of my chief preoccupations for more than 10 years. I have failed in this endeavour – or, rather, have reached the conclusion that, with reference to a society of free men, the phrase has no meaning whatever. The search for the reason why the word has nevertheless for something like a century dominated political discussion, and has everywhere been successfully used to advance claims of particular groups for a larger share in the good things of life, remains, however, a very interesting one. It is this question with which I shall here chiefly concern myself.

But I must at first briefly explain, as I attempt to demonstrate at length in volume 2 of my *Law, Legislation and Liberty*, about to be published, why I have come to regard 'social justice' as nothing more than an empty formula, conventionally used to assert that a particular claim is justified without giving any reason. Indeed that volume, which bears the sub-title *The Mirage of Social Justice*, is mainly intended to convince intellectuals that the concept of 'social justice', which they are so fond of using, is intellectually disreputable. Some of course have already tumbled to this; but with the unfortunate result that, since 'social' justice is the only kind of justice they have ever thought of, they have been led to the conclusion that all uses of the term justice have no meaningful content. I have therefore been forced to show in the same book that rules of just individual conduct are as indispensable to the preservation of a peaceful society of free men as endeavours to realise 'social' justice are incompatible with it.

The term 'social justice' is today generally used as a synonym of what used to be called 'distributive justice'. The latter term

* The 9th R. C. Mills Memorial Lecture delivered at the University of Sydney on 6 October 1976.

perhaps gives a somewhat better idea of what can be meant by it, and at the same time shows why it can have no application to the results of a market economy: there can be no distributive justice where no one distributes. Justice has meaning only as a rule of human conduct, and no conceivable rules for the conduct of individuals supplying each other with goods and services in a market economy would produce a distribution which could be meaningfully described as just or unjust. Individuals might conduct themselves as justly as possible, but as the results for separate individuals would be neither intended nor foreseeable by others, the resulting state of affairs could neither be called just nor unjust.

The complete emptiness of the phrase 'social justice' shows itself in the fact that no agreement exists about what social justice requires in particular instances; also that there is no known test by which to decide who is right if people differ, and that no preconceived scheme of distribution could be effectively devised in a society whose individuals are free, in the sense of being allowed to use their own knowledge for their own purposes. Indeed, individual moral responsibility for one's actions is incompatible with the realisation of any such desired overall pattern of distribution.

A little inquiry shows that, though a great many people are dissatisfied with the existing pattern of distribution, none of them has really any clear idea of what pattern he would regard as just. All that we find are intuitive assessments of individual cases as unjust. No one has yet found even a single general rule from which we could derive what is 'socially just' in all particular instances that would fall under it – except the rule of 'equal pay for equal work'. Free competition, precluding all that regard for merit or need and the like, on which demands for social justice are based, tends to enforce the equal pay rule.

2

The reason why most people continue firmly to believe in 'social justice', even after they discover that they do not really know what the phrase means, is that they think if almost everyone else believes in it, there must be something in the phrase. The ground for this almost universal acceptance of a belief, the significance of which people do not understand, is that we have all inherited from an earlier different type of society, in which man existed very much longer than in the present one, some now deeply ingrained instincts which are inapplicable to our present civilisation. In fact, man emerged from primitive society when in certain conditions increasing numbers succeeded by disregarding those very principles which had held the old groups together.

We must not forget that before the last 10,000 years, during which man has developed agriculture, towns and ultimately the 'Great Society', he existed for at least a hundred times as long in small food-sharing hunting bands of 50 or so, with a strict order of dominance within the defended common territory of the band. The needs of this ancient primitive kind of society determined much of the moral feelings which still govern us, and which we approve in others. It was a grouping in which, at least for all males, the common pursuit of a perceived physical common object under the direction of the alpha male was as much a condition of its continued existence as the assignment of different shares in the prey to the different members according to their importance for the survival of the band. It is more than probable that many of the moral feelings then acquired have not merely been culturally transmitted by teaching or imitation, but have become innate or genetically determined.

But not all that is natural to us in this sense is therefore necessarily in different circumstances good or beneficial for the propagation of the species. In its primitive form the little band indeed did possess what is still attractive to so many people: a unitary purpose, or a common hierarchy of ends, and a deliberate sharing of means according to a common view of individual merits. These foundations of its coherence, however, also imposed limits on the possible development of this form of society. The events to which the group could adapt itself, and the opportunities it could take advantage of, were only those of which its members were directly aware. Even worse, the individual could do little of which others did not approve. It is a delusion to think of the individual in primitive society as free. There was no natural liberty for a social animal, while freedom is an artifact of civilisation. The individual had in the group no recognised domain of independent action; even the head of the band could expect obedience, support and understanding of his signals only for conventional activities. So long as each must serve that common order of rank for all needs, which present-day socialists dream of, there can be no free experimentation by the individual.

3

The great advance which made possible the development of civilisation and ultimately of the Open Society was the gradual substitution of abstract rules of conduct for specific obligatory ends, and with it the playing of a game for acting in concert under common indicators, thus fostering a spontaneous order. The great gain attained by this was that it made possible a procedure through which all relevant information widely dispersed was made available to ever-increasing numbers of men in the form of the symbols which we call market prices. But it also meant that the incidence of the results on different persons and groups no longer satisfied the age-old instinct.

It has been suggested more than once that the theory explaining the working of the market be called catallactics from the classical Greek word for bartering or exchanging – *katalattein*. I have fallen somewhat in love with this word since discovering that in ancient Greek, in addition to 'exchanging', it also meant 'to admit into the community' and 'to change from enemy into friend'. I have therefore proposed that we call the game of the market, by which we can induce the stranger to welcome and serve us, the 'game of catallaxy'.

The market process indeed corresponds fully to the definition of a game which we find in *The Oxford English Dictionary*. It is 'a contest played according to rules and decided by superior skill, strength or good fortune'. It is in this respect both a game of skill as well as a game of chance. Above all, it is a game which serves to elicit from each player the highest worthwhile contribution to the common pool from which each will win an uncertain share.

The game was probably started by men who had left the shelter and obligations of their own tribe to gain from serving the needs of others they did not know personally. When the early neolithic traders took boatloads of flint axes from Britain across the Channel to barter them against amber and probably also, even then, jars of wine, their aim was no longer to serve the needs of known people, but to make the largest gain. Precisely because they were interested only in who would offer the best price for their products, they reached persons wholly unknown to them, whose standard of life they thereby enhanced much more than they could have that of their neighbours by handing the axes to those who no doubt could also have made good use of them.

4

As the abstract signal-price thus took the place of the needs of known fellows as the goal towards which men's efforts were directed, entirely new possibilities for the utilisation of resources opened up – but this also required wholly different moral attitudes to encourage their exploitation. The change occurred largely at the new urban centres of trade and handicrafts, which grew up at ports or the cross-roads of trade routes, where men who had escaped from the discipline of tribal morals established commercial communities and gradually developed the new rules of the game of catallaxy.

The necessity to be brief forces me here somewhat to over-simplify and to employ familiar terms where they are not quite appropriate. When I pass from the morals of the hunting band in which man spent most of his history, to the morals which made possible the market order of the open society, I am jumping over a long intermediate stage, much shorter than man's life in the small band, but still of much greater length than the urban and commercial society has enjoyed yet, and important because from it date those codifications of ethics which became embodied in the teaching of the monotheistic religions. It is the period of man's life in tribal society. In many ways it represents a transitional stage between the concrete order of the primitive face-to-face society, in which all the members knew each other and served common particular ends, and the open and abstract society, in which an order results from individuals observing the same abstract rules of the game while using their own knowledge in the pursuit of their own ends.

While our emotions are still governed by the instincts appropriate to the success of the small hunting band, our verbal tradition is dominated by duties to the 'neighbour', the fellow member of the tribe, and still regarding the alien largely as beyond the pale of moral obligation.

In a society in which individual aims were necessarily different, based on specialised knowledge, and efforts came to be directed towards future exchange of products with yet unknown partners, common rules of conduct increasingly took the place of particular common ends as the foundations of social order and peace. The interaction of individuals became a game, because what was required from each individual was observation of the rules, not concern for a particular result, other than to win support for himself and his family. The rules which gradually developed, because they made this game most effective, were essentially those of the law of property and contract. These rules in turn made possible the progressive division of labour, and that mutual adjustment of independent efforts, which a functioning division of labour demands.

5

The full significance of this division of labour is often not appreciated, because most people think of it – partly because of the classical illustration given by Adam Smith – as a designed intra-mural arrangement in which different individuals contribute the successive steps in a planned process for shaping certain products. In fact, however, co-ordination by the market of the endeavours of different enterprises in supplying the raw materials, tools and semi-finished products which the turning out of the final commodity requires, is probably much more important than the organised collaboration of numerous specialist workers.

It is in a great measure this inter-firm division of labour, or specialisation, on which the achievement of the competitive market depends, and which that market makes possible. Prices the producer finds on the market at once tell him what to produce and what means to use in producing it. From such market signals he knows that he can expect to sell at prices covering his outlays, and that he will not use up more resources than are necessary for the purpose. His selfish striving for gain makes him do, and enables him to do, precisely what he ought to do in order to improve the chances of any member of his society, taken at random, as much as possible – *but only if* the prices he can get are determined solely by market forces and not by the coercive powers of government. Only prices determined on the free market will bring it about that demand equals supply. But not only this. Free market prices also ensure that all of a society's dispersed knowledge will be taken into account and used.

The game of the market led to the growth and prosperity of communities who played it because it improved the chances for all. This was made possible because remuneration for the services of individuals depended on objective facts, all of which no one could know, and not on someone's opinions about what they ought to have. But it also meant that while skill and industry would improve each individual's chances, they could not guarantee him a specified income; and that the impersonal process which used all that dispersed knowledge set the signals of prices so as to tell people what to do, but without regard to needs or merits. Yet the ordering and productivity enhancing function of prices, and particularly the prices of services, depends on their informing people where they will find their most effective place in the overall pattern of activities – the place in which they are likely to make the greatest contribution to aggregate output. If, therefore, we regard *that* rule of remuneration as just which contributes as much as possible to increasing the chances of any member of the community picked out at random, we ought to regard the remunerations determined by a free market as the just ones.

6

But they are inevitably very different from the relative remunerations which assisted the organisation of the different type of society in which our species lived so much longer, and which therefore still governs the feelings which guide us. This point has become exceedingly important since prices ceased to be accepted as due to unknown circumstances, and governments came to believe they could determine prices with beneficial effects. When governments started to falsify the market price signals, whose appropriateness they had no means of judging (governments as little as anyone else possessing all the information precipitated in prices), in the hope of thereby giving benefits to groups claimed to be particularly deserving, things inevitably started to go wrong. Not only the efficient use of resources, but, what is worse, also the prospects of being able to buy or sell as expected through demand equalling supply were thereby greatly diminished.

It may be difficult to understand, but I believe there can be no doubt about it, that we are led to utilise more relevant information when our remuneration is made to depend indirectly on circumstances we do not know. It is thus that, in the language of modern cybernetics, the feedback mechanism secures the maintenance of a self-generating order. It was this which Adam Smith saw and described as the operation of the 'invisible hand' – to be ridiculed for 200 years by uncomprehending scoffers. It is indeed *because* the game of catallaxy disregards human conceptions of what is due to each, and rewards according to success in playing the game under the same formal rules, that it produces a more efficient allocation of resources than any design could achieve. I feel that in any game that is played because it improves the prospects of all beyond those which we know how to provide by any other arrangements, the result must be accepted as fair, so long as all obey the same rules and no one cheats. If they accept their winnings from the game, it is cheating for individuals or groups to invoke the powers of government to divert the flow of good things in their favour – whatever we may do outside this game of the market to provide a decent minimum for those for whom the game did not supply it. It is not a valid objection to such a game, the outcome of which depends partly on skill and particular individual circumstances and partly on pure chance, that the initial prospects for different individuals, although they are all improved by playing that game, are very far from being the same. The answer to such an objection is precisely that one of the purposes of the game is to make the fullest possible use of the inevitably different skills, knowledge and environment of different individuals. Among the greatest assets which a society can use in this manner for increasing the pool from which the earnings of individuals are drawn, are the different moral intellectual and material gifts parents can pass on to their children – and often will acquire, create or preserve only in order to be able to pass them on to their children.

7

The result of this game of catallaxy, therefore, will necessarily be that many have much more than their fellows think they deserve, and even more will have much less than their fellows think they ought to have. It is not surprising that many people should wish to correct this by some authoritative act of redistribution. The trouble is that the aggregate product which they think is available for distribution exists only *because* returns for the different efforts are held out by the market with little regard to deserts or needs, and are needed to attract the owners of particular information, material means and personal skills to the points where at each moment they can make the greatest contribution. Those who prefer the quiet of an assured contractual income to the necessity of taking risks to exploit ever-changing opportunities feel at a disadvantage compared with possessors of large incomes, which result from continual redisposition of resources.

High actual gains of the successful ones, whether this success is deserved or accidental, is an essential element for guiding resources to where they will make the largest contribution to the pool from which all draw their share. We should not have as much to share if *that* income of an individual were not treated as *just*, the prospects of which induced him to make the largest contribution to the pool. Incredibly high incomes may thus sometimes be just. What is more important, scope for achieving such incomes may be the necessary condition for the less enterprising, lucky, or clever to get the regular income on which they count.

The inequality, which so many people resent, however, has not only been the underlying condition for producing the relatively high incomes which most people in the West now enjoy. Some people seem to believe that a lowering of this general level of incomes – or at least a slowing down of its rate of increase – would not be too high a price for what they feel would be a juster distribution. But there is an even greater obstacle to such ambitions today. As a result of playing the game of catallaxy, which pays so little attention to justice but does so much to increase output, the population of the world has been able to increase so much, without the income of most people increasing very much, that we can maintain it,

and the further increases in population which are irrevocably
on the way, only if we make the fullest possible use of that
game which elicits the highest contributions to productivity.

8

If people in general do not appreciate what they owe to
catallaxy and how far they are even dependent on it for their
very existence, and if they often bitterly resent what they regard
as its injustice, this is so because they have never designed it
and therefore do not understand it. The game rests on a
method of providing benefits for others in which the individual
will accomplish most if, within the conventional rules, he
pursues solely his own interests – which need not be selfish in
the ordinary sense of the word, but are in any case his own.

The moral attitude which this order demands not only of the
entrepreneur but of all those, curiously called 'self-employed',
who have constantly to choose the directions of their efforts, if
they are to confer the greatest benefit on their fellows, is that
they compete honestly according to the rules of the game,
guided only by the abstract signals of prices and giving no
preferences because of their sympathies or views on the merits
or needs of those with whom they deal. It would mean not
merely a personal loss, but a failure in their duty to the public,
to employ a less efficient instead of a more efficient person, to
spare an incompetent competitor, or to favour particular users
of their product.

The gradually spreading new liberal morals, which the Open
or Great Society demanded, required above all that the same
rules of conduct should apply to one's relation to all other
members of society – except for natural ties to the members of
one's family. This extension of old moral rules to wider circles,
most people, and particularly the intellectuals, welcome as
moral progress. But they apparently did not realise, and
violently resented when they discovered it, that the equality of
rules applicable to one's relationship to all other men
necessarily implied not only that new obligations were
extended to people who formerly had no such claims, but also
that old obligations which were recognised to some people but
could not be extended to all others had to disappear.

It was this unavoidable attenuation of the content of our
obligations, which necessarily accompanied their extension,

that people with strongly ingrained moral emotions resented. Yet these are kinds of obligations which are essential to the cohesion of the small group but which are irreconcilable with the order, the productivity, and the peace of a great society of free men. They are all those demands which under the name of 'social justice' assert a moral claim on government that it give us what it can take by force from those who in the game of catallaxy have been more successful than we have been. Such an artificial alteration of the relative attractiveness of the different directions of productive efforts can only be counter-productive.

If expected remunerations no longer tell people where their endeavours will make the greatest contribution to the total product, an efficient use of resources becomes impossible. Where the size of the social product, and no longer their contributions to it, gives individuals and groups a moral claim to a certain share of that product, the claims of what deserve really to be described as 'free riders' become an unbearable drag on the economy.

9

I am told that there are still communities in Africa in which able young men, anxious to adopt modern commercial methods, find it impossible thereby to improve their position, because tribal customs demand that they share the products of their greater industry, skill or luck with all their kin. An increased income of such a man would merely mean that he had to share it with an ever-increasing number of claimants. He can, therefore, never rise substantially above the average level of his tribe.

The chief adverse effect of 'social justice' in our society is that it prevents individuals from achieving what they could achieve – through the means for further investment being taken from them. It is also the application of an incongruous principle to a civilisation whose productivity is high, *because* incomes are very unequally divided and thereby the use of scarce resources is directed and limited to where they bring the highest return. Thanks to this unequal distribution the poor get in a competitive market economy more than they would get in a centrally directed system.

All this is the outcome of the, as yet merely imperfect, victory of the obligatory abstract rule of individual conduct over the common particular end as the method of social co-ordination – the development which has made both the open society and individual freedom possible, but which the socialists now want to reverse. Socialists have the support of inherited instincts, while maintenance of the new wealth which creates the new ambitions requires an acquired discipline which the non-domesticated barbarians in our midst, who call themselves 'alienated', refuse to accept although they still claim all its benefits.

10

Let me, before I conclude, briefly meet an objection which is bound to be raised because it rests on a very widespread misunderstanding. My argument, that in a process of cultural selection we have built better than we understood, and that what we call our intelligence has been shaped concurrently with our institutions by a process of trial and error, is certain to be met by an outcry of 'social Darwinism'. But such a cheap way of disposing of my argument by labelling it would rest on an error. It is true that during the latter part of the last century some social scientists, under the influence of Darwin, placed an excessive stress on the importance of natural selection of the most able individuals in free competition. I do not wish to underrate the importance of this, but it is not the main benefit we derive from competitive selection. This is the competitive selection of cultural institutions, for the discovery of which we did not need Darwin, but the growing understanding of which in fields like law and language rather helped Darwin to his biological theories. My problem is not genetic evolution of innate qualities, but cultural evolution through learning – which indeed leads sometimes to conflicts with near-animal natural instincts. Nevertheless, it is still true that civilisation grew not by the prevailing of that which man thought would be most successful, but by the growth of that which turned out to be so, and which, precisely because he did not understand it, led man beyond what he could ever have conceived.

COLLECTIVE ENTITIES AND MORAL RIGHTS: PROBLEMS IN LIBERAL-DEMOCRATIC THOUGHT*
[The Journal of Politics, Volume 44, 1982]
Vernon Van Dyke

Those who espouse traditional liberal-democratic thought – whom I will call *liberals*, however conservative or progressive they may be – have problems in dealing with collective entities. Their ideology focuses on the individual. They are protective and solicitous of the individual, seeking conditions that make for individual self-fulfillment. In bills of rights and, more recently, in various international documents such as the covenants on human rights, they have secured the spelling out of rights for individuals and are making the promotion of these rights (or some of them) a major issue in the world.

But liberals and their historic doctrine neglect collective entities. They assert the rights of individuals against the state and, thus, in a sense admit that the state exists with obligations, but, at the same time, they fear that this is an instance of reification and tend to dissolve the state into the persons who hold public office. Some liberals acknowledge that nations and peoples exist, and champion the idea of self-determination for them, but they tend to think of a nation or people not as a collective entity but as an aggregation of individuals. Liberals are naturally pleased with the requirement of the Charter of the United Nations that members shall promote human rights "without distinction as to race, sex, language, or religion," but are in a quandary over the proper response to groups identified by race, language, or religion that want differential treatment in order to preserve characteristics that they cherish.[1]

* I wish to thank Lane Davis and Lance Stell for helpful suggestions.

[1]   Frances Svensson, "Liberal Democracy and Group Rights: The Legacy of Individualism and its Impact on American Indian Tribes," *Political Studies*,

Although the existence of a liberal dilemma is fairly obvious, I will include evidence of it in what follows. My more important aim, however, is to contribute toward a solution. The solution, like the dilemma itself, is fairly obvious, being intimated in much current practice. The solution lies in recognizing that certain kinds of collective entities exist, just as individuals do – perhaps not tangibly but not transcendentally either; that these collective entities have moral rights that are distinct from the rights of individual members; and that the frequent cases of conflict between the rights of individuals and the rights of collective entities, and between the rights of different collective entities, must be handled through a balancing process in which judgments are made about the relative urgency and importance of the various claims. Approximately the same standards can be employed in making these judgments as are already employed in connection with conflicts between the rights of individuals and the rights of states.

Some Definitions

The argument that certain kinds of collective entities have both legal and moral rights calls for the definition of crucial terms. By collective entities I mean groups that exist as units and not simply as aggregations of individuals. I call them units and not persons to avoid any intimation that they may be organic. I assume that they exist in the same sense that corporations do, it being understood that a corporation is an entity that has rights and obligations distinct from those of individual stockholders. The corporation is conceded rights mainly so that it can serve the interests of stockholders, but the rights do not come from the stockholders and cannot be reduced to the rights of stockholders. They are original to the corporation.

The types of collective entities I have in mind are restricted in number. I am not speaking generally of interest groups. This is not an inquiry into the question of whether interest groups have rights. Rather, the collective entities that I have in mind are sovereign states, nations or peoples, and ethnic (including

37 (September 1979), 421–430; Kenneth D. McRae, "The Plural Society and the Western Political Tradition," *Canadian Journal of Political Science*, 12 (December 1979), 675–688; Vernon Van Dyke, "The Individual, the State and Ethnic Communities in Political Theory," *World Politics*, 29 (April 1977), 343–369.

racial) communities. All of these terms have some vagueness about them, which suggests problems in the argument; but problems also attend the principle that individual persons have rights, for it is not always clear what organisms count as persons.

By a legal right I mean a claim or an entitlement that a government is bound to uphold and does seek to uphold, at least on occasion. (If the appeal is to international law, the obligation must be accepted by more than one government.) By a moral right I mean a claim or entitlement that ought to be honored if justice is to be done or the good promoted, regardless of the attitudes and actions of any government.

The Sources or Bases of Rights

The sources or bases of legal rights are so generally agreed upon that nothing need be said on the subject here, but disagreement exists concerning the sources or bases of moral rights. I accept what I take to be the dominant liberal view, that moral rights reflect a conception of human interests and needs: some interests and needs are so important that they should be said to give rise to rights. In other words, it is to be presumed (the presumption being rebuttable) that human beings have those rights that are essential to the pursuit of their most basic interests and the satisfaction of their most basic needs. The view is reflected in various works, for example, in *Taking Rights Seriously* by Dworkin. The individual, according to Dworkin, has a right to pursue his interests and goals in the absence of good reason to the contrary:

> Individuals have rights when, for some reason, a collective goal is not a sufficient justification for denying them what they wish, as individuals, to have or to do, or not a sufficient justification for imposing some loss or injury upon them. . . . The basic idea of a right-based theory is that distinct individuals have interests that they are entitled to protect if they so wish. . . . In most cases, when we say that someone has a "right" to do something, we imply that it would be wrong to interfere with his doing it, or at least that some special grounds are needed for justifying any interference.[2]

---

2   Ronald Dworkin, *Taking Rights Seriously* (Cambridge: Harvard University Press, 1977), xi, 176, 188.

A similar conception is reflected in a number of other books, for example, those by Benn and Peters, by Ginsberg, and by Flathman.[3]

The conception suggests two sorts of comments. In the first place, assuming that the object is to satisfy the interests and needs of individuals, it does not necessarily follow that the associated rights should go to individuals. Where the right should be located is a matter of practicality; and in some instances it is best, if not essential, to locate it in a collective unit. So far as legal rights are concerned, it is clear that this often happens, and I will argue that it ought to be acknowledged with respect to some moral rights as well. In the second place, the liberal theory raises the question whether some interests and needs cannot be better conceived as collective rather than individual. If so, the same logic that leads from interests and needs to rights for individuals also leads to rights for collective entities.

Illustrations of Collective Rights

The sovereign state is the most obvious illustration of a collective entity with rights. Sovereign states are persons in international law, and as such have legal rights. On this point everyone is agreed. The related point, which is perhaps more likely to be challenged, is that the rights of states are in many instances original to it, not derived from individuals. When the state imposes taxes, breaks up a monopoly, requires attendance at school, or conscripts a person and sends him into battle, it is not exercising rights taken over from individuals, for they never had such rights. Moreover, such rights could not reasonably be reduced to individual rights; they are necessarily and unavoidably the rights of a collective entity. Further, it is unsound to attribute such rights to "persons in public authority," as some do.[4] To be sure, persons in public authority make the decisions and do the acting, for the state is not an organic entity that can itself decide or act. Moreover, persons in public authority may deserve personal credit for

3   S. I. Benn and R. S. Peters, *The Principles of Political Thought: Social Foundations of the Democratic State* (New York: Free Press, 1965), 63; Morris Ginsberg, *On Justice in Society* (Ithaca, New York: Cornell University Press), 74; Richard E. Flathman, *The Practice of Rights* (Cambridge: Cambridge University Press, 1976), 43–47.

4   Flathman, 36–37.

what they do, or be held personally curable, as at Nuremberg. But whatever their personal accountability, the principle on whose behalf they act is also accountable. The rights exercised, and the obligations assumed, go with the office held, and not with the person. When Germany paid reparations after World War I, the money came out of the treasury of the state, not out of the pockets of those who made decisions on its behalf.

Acceptance of the state as a unit possessing legal rights does not necessarily entail its acceptance as a unit with moral rights. Ernest Barker demonstrates this, holding that ". . . in the moral world there are no group persons. . . ."[5] Once the state is incorporated, it has legal rights, but up to that moment, according to Barker, no group exists that has collective moral rights. Moreover, even after the state is organized, it should not be regarded as a moral person, for that would invite étatisme and "a philosophy of the total and engulfing State whose will is the peace – and the tomb of its members."[6]

Though the danger that Barker fears may be real, his position is untenable. It is illogical to hold, for example, that the people of a colony, who collectively acquire legal rights the moment they are granted independence, have no collective moral claim up to that moment. Moreover, whatever the law may be, states are always facing issues in the moral realm – for example, in connection with plans for the use of nuclear weapons. The General Assembly of the United States obviously regards states as entities that should observe moral standards, as it indicated when it adopted the Universal Declaration of Human Rights. If bad consequences might flow from accepting the state as an entity with moral rights and obligations, even worse consequences might flow from any other course.

If the case is good for saying that states have moral rights and obligations, the same is true of nations and peoples. They are everywhere said to have the right of self-determination, and the Covenant on Civil and Political Rights is worth citing on the question of whether the right belongs to a collective entity or to individuals. The Covenant includes an article on minorities, the statement being that "persons belonging to . . . minorities" shall not be denied certain rights. The clear intent is to avoid

---

5   Ernest Barker, *Principles of Social & Political Theory* (Oxford: Clarendon Press, 1951), 71.

6   *Ibid.*

giving minorities any basis for a claim of a collective right. But no such intent appears in connection with the assertion of the right of self-determination. This right is attributed to "all peoples" as such, not to persons belonging to peoples. Further, the General Assembly describes the possible outcomes of an exercise of self-determination as "the establishment of a sovereign and independent state, the free association or integration with an independent state, or the emergence into any other political status freely determined by a people" – language that does not suggest a reference to the rights of individual persons.[7]

I am aware of assertions that the right of a people to self-determination is somehow an individual right, but such assertions have no reasonable basis that I can see. For example, a note in the *Yale Law Journal* says that ". . . in its broad meaning self-determination must be viewed as the basic right of an individual to form his own associations in order to maximize his preferred interests."[8] But the author of that statement does not tell us how he leaps from the right of persons to freedom of association to the right of a people to independent sovereignty. Freedom of association does not imply for each individual the right to choose the sovereignty under which to live, and if individuals lack the right of choice they cannot delegate it. To repeat the statement already made: if individuals have any right in connection with self-determination, it is to participate in the decision of the group. The right belongs to the group, and it is the fate of the group that is determined.

Dov Ronen reflects a view similar to that in the *Yale Law Journal* when he says that ". . . the 'self' in self-determination is the singular, individual being and not any aggregation of human beings."[9] Now I grant that one of the interests basic to the right is that of individuals. The individual has an interest in being grouped with his own kind for purposes of government – an interest in being governed by those who share his values,

[7]   "Declaration on Principles of International Law Concerning Friendly Relations and Cooperation among States . . .," United Nations document A/Res. 2625 (xxv), 14 October 1970.

[8]   "The United Nations, Self-Determination and the Namibia Opinions," *Yale Law Journal*, 82 (January 1973), 534.

[9]   Dov Ronen, *The Quest for Self-Determination* (New Haven: Yale University Press, 1979), 8, 53, 59.

who accord him respect, and who fully accept him as an equal human being. But, as already pointed out, the fact that the interest is that of individuals does not necessarily mean that the related right goes to individuals. This does not follow either as a matter of logic or as a matter of practicality. Sometimes an interest of individuals can be best served, or only served, by allocating the related right to a group, and this is the case with self-determination. One of the reasons why some governments objected to the inclusion of the article on self-determination in the Covenants was that self-determination is for collectivities whereas the Covenants enumerated rights for individuals.

Perhaps simply as an elaboration of the meaning of self-determination, the General Conference of UNESCO asserts and assumes "the right of all countries and peoples to preserve their culture. . . ."[10] Similarly, a Declaration of the World Conference to Combat Racism and Racial Discrimination endorses "the right of indigenous peoples to maintain their traditional structure of economy and culture, including their language. . . ."[11] Such statements cannot reasonably be construed to affirm an individual right. It makes sense to speak of a right to preserve a culture only if the right is attributed to the cultural group as a whole. Further, it would be ridiculous to say that the right of a country or people to preserve its culture is the right of "persons in public authority." It is the right of a collective entity.

Where a country or people is sovereign, the right to preserve a culture is a legal right; at least, sovereign states are free to adopt laws designed to preserve a culture – laws having to do with education, for example. But surely in asserting the right of indigenous and other peoples to preserve their culture, the General Conference was not making legal pronouncements. Rather, it was proclaiming the existence of moral rights.

In addition to states and nations or peoples, ethnic communities in a number of countries have legal rights. Some of them are identified by religion, and claim freedom of religion. That freedom is not simply freedom for individuals. It is not the right of an individual to go into a closet and worship alone. It is a communal right, and it includes the right (widely

10   17C/Res.4.111., 15 November 1972. Cf. 14C/Res.8.1., 4 November 1966.

11   *Objective Justice*, 10 (Autumn 1978), 30.

recognized) to maintain the community. In the province of Alberta, Canada, schools are organized on a religious basis, with the minority religious community entitled to establish its own schools and impose a school tax on its members.[12] In West Germany the main churches are formally accepted as corporate bodies under public law, authorized to tax their members, with government collecting the tax.[13] Even in the individualistic United States the right to maintain the religious community is held to override the obligation to send children to school beyond a certain point.[14] Many other such illustrations could be cited. I do not contend that a moral right lies behind every legal right, nor that the specific arrangements existing in Alberta or elsewhere are the only possible ways of satisfying a moral claim. But the generalization is surely valid that some kind of a claim of moral right lies behind decisions to grant legal rights to religious communities.

Comparable statements apply to ethnic communities identified mainly by language.[15] If they want to maintain their identity, as they usually do, they are likely to demand (or insist on the preservation of) certain rights. In Switzerland, the linguistic communities are by custom conceded the right of territorial integrity; communes do not switch from one language to another regardless of the movement of people. Similarly, in Switzerland the linguistic communities are by custom assured of representation in the Federal Council. In Belgium, these same rights for linguistic communities are written into the constitution. The constitution explicitly says that the country consists of three cultural communities, and goes on to say that "each community enjoys the powers invested in it." Moreover, powers are in fact invested. Further, the Belgian cabinet must be made up of an equal number of French-speaking and Dutch-speaking ministers, and the law requires that a just equilibrium (interpreted as parity) must be maintained between the two principle communities in the civil

12 Charles Bruce Sissons, *Church and State in Canadian Education* (Toronto: Ryerson Press, 1959), 344; *Schmidt v. Calgary Bd.*, 6 W.W.R. (1976), 717.

13 Frederic Spotts, *The Churches and Politics in Germany* (Middletown, Connecticut: Wesleyan University Press, 1973), 194–198.

14 *Wisconsin v. Yoder*, 406 U.S. 205 (1972).

15 Vernon Van Dyke, "Human Rights Without Distinction as to Language," *International Studies Quarterly*, 20 (March 1976), 3–38.

service. Clearly these provisions do not grant rights to individuals. By implication, they concede rights to the linguistic communities as entities. And it is clear that the legal arrangements followed the acceptance of a moral claim.

Some ethnic communities are identified as indigenous, which implies that their members differ in a number of ways from members of the dominant society; they are likely to differ in language, in religion, in race, in level of development, and, most generally, in culture. The liberal's dilemma with respect to them is especially acute. If he stick to his principles, he treats them severally as individuals, respecting their individual rights. But all history shows that the indigenous are as a rule not capable of upholding either their rights or their interests in free and open individualistic competition with those who are more advanced. Thus, the liberal, moved by humane concerns, has to favor some kind of a special, protective regime for them – perhaps establishing territorial reserves from which others are excluded. But this is contrary to liberal doctrine, which is at least integrationist if not assimilationist; permanent communalism is unacceptable. And so the liberal is torn. What he usually does is to say that the special measures for the indigenous are transitory, pending developments that permit integration. But if independence is impractical, permanent communalism may be exactly what the indigenous want.

The liberal dilemma with respect to the indigenous is illustrated by ambiguities and contradictions in policies of the United States toward the American Indians. The reference is to policies for which liberals might plausibly offer an intellectual and moral defense, and not to acts of despoliation and genocide that are obviously indefensible. The kind of problem I have in mind did not arise as long as "the Indian nations" were clearly "distinct, independent political communities, retaining their original natural rights. . . ."[16] But after Congress forbade the conclusion of any further treaties with Indians (in 1871) and, above all, after it conferred citizenship on the Indians, liberals could only squirm. On the one hand, both their ideology and other considerations impelled them to want 'to break up reservations, destroy tribal relations, settle Indians on their own homesteads, incorporate them into the national life, and deal with them not as nations or tribes or bands but as

16   *Worcester v. Georgia*, 6 Pet, 515 (1832), at 559.

individual citizens."[17] On the other hand, they faced and still face the fact that many Indians do not want to be integrated into mainstream society. The outlook is expressed in the manifesto of the Indians who made the Longest Walk (1978): "How do we convince the U.S. government to simply leave us alone to live according to our ways of life? . . . We have the right to educate our children to our ways of life. . . . We have the right to be a people. These are inherent rights. . . . Our fight today is to survive as a people."[18] The trouble is that the liberal has no place in his theory for peoples as distinct political units within the state. Individuals are the units, and when individuals are divided up for governmental purposes, it must be on a territorial basis and not on the basis of ethnic differences.[19] Of course, sometimes ethnic communities are geographically concentrated, so territorial divisions may also be ethnic; but the liberal must say that it is geography, not ethnicity, that counts.

The same dilemma that American liberals face with respect to the Indians shows up in the Indigenous and Tribal Populations Convention.[20] The convention euphemistically speaks of conditions that prevent indigenous peoples "from enjoying the benefits of the general laws of the country to which they belong," and says that so long as such conditions persist "special measures shall be adopted for the protection of [their] institutions, persons, property, and labor." They are to be "allowed to retain their own customs and institutions." At the same time, "the primary objective . . . shall be the fostering of individual dignity, and the advancement of individual usefulness and initiative," and "progressive integration" must be the goal. There seems to be no place in the liberal's thought for the possibility that an indigenous population might want to

17 A Commissioner of Indian Affairs, as quoted by Frances Svensson, *The Ethnics in American Politics: American Indians* (Minneapolis: Burgess, 1973), 73.

18 *Congressional Record*, July 27, 1978, H7458.

19 Nathan Glazer, *Affirmative Discrimination: Ethnic Inequality and Public Policy* (New York: Basic Books, 1975), 22–25. Cf. Nathan Glazer, "Individual Rights Against Group Rights," in Eugene Kamenka and Alice Erh-Soon Tay, eds., *Human Rights* (London: Edward Arnold, 1978), 87–103.

20 International Labor Organization, *Conventions and Recommendations Adopted by the International Labor Conference, 1919–1966* (Geneva: International Labor Office), 901, Convention No. 107.

preserve its distinctive identity indefinitely. The Fijians, the Malays, the Maoris, and all other indigenous peoples are to be "integrated" whether they wish this or not.

Ethnic communities and nations or parts of nations are sometimes identified as minorities, and problems about them further illustrate the liberal's dilemma. The individualism of the liberal makes him quite willing to insist that members of minorities shall enjoy equal rights with other inhabitants and other citizens, and shall not be victims of discrimination. This is what international arrangements for minorities ordinarily provide, as in the minority treaties after World War I. Similarly, as noted already, the Covenant on Civil and Political Rights includes an article designed to protect "persons belonging to . . . minorities." The Covenant makes a gesture in the direction of acknowledging a group right in speaking of the possibility that these persons may want to act "in community with the other members of their own group," but an individual right of voluntary association or cooperation is not always enough. Minorities find it difficult, for example, to finance their own schools through voluntary contributions, especially when their members also have to pay taxes to support public schools, and they sometimes want the power to tax and otherwise to act as corporate entities. But this means political recognition and status, challenging the idea of national unity and suggesting a state within a state, and from this liberals draw back.[21] Focusing on concerns at the level of the individual and the level of the state, they have no answer to the question of how to provide for those conditions of human well-being that can be promoted effectively only through corporate organizations operating at an intermediate level.

Ethnic communities are sometimes identified by race and want to preserve a racial identity. This is true above all today

21   George Kaeckenbeeck, *The International Experiment of Upper Silesia: A Study in the Working of the Upper Silesian Settlement 1922-1937* (New York: Oxford University Press, 1942), 272; Oscar I. Janowsky, *Nationalities and National Minorities* (New York: Macmillan, 1945), 5, 129-132; Inis L. Claude, Jr., *National Minorities, An International Problem* (New York: Greenwood, 1969), 19-20; J. W. Bruegel, "A Neglected Field: The Protection of Minorities," *Revue des Droits de l'Homme [Human Rights Journal]*, Vol. IV, Nos. 2-3 (1971), 439; Cynthia H. Enloe, *Ethnic Conflict and Political Development* (Boston: Little, Brown, 1973), 59; Francesco Capotorti, "Study of the Rights of Persons Belonging to Ethnic, Religious and Linguistic Minorities," E/CN.4/Sub.2/384, Add. 2, 62, para. 90.

of the Whites of South Africa, and it leads to special problems. The special problems stem from the fact that insistence on the preservation of a racial identity has been associated historically with ideas of superiority and inferiority, and with privilege for the dominant rather than with concessions to the weak. As a matter of general principle, I see no reason why ethnic communities identified by race should not have rights just like other kinds of ethnic communities, but imputations of inferiority and the deliberate accentuation of advantage for those already strong are intolerable.

The Kinds of Entities Entitled to Rights: Standards of Judgment

In the preceding section I have cited numerous illustrations of collective entities with rights without identifying standards for differentiating between them and other groupings that lack rights. Now the standards should be identified, lest it be thought that a Pandora's box has been opened from which all sorts of groupings might spring, demanding rights. Identifying them should be regarded more as a work of analysis than of imagination, the aim being to discover the standards intimated by the practices followed. The eight standards listed below are the result. They give valuable guidance, but do not eliminate the need for ad hoc judgments.

1. A group has a stronger claim the more it is a self-conscious entity with a desire to preserve itself. There ought to be a sense of belonging together, a we/they sense, a sense of solidarity vis-à-vis outsiders, a sense of sharing a common heritage and a common destiny, distinct from the heritage and destiny of others.

2. A group has a stronger claim the more evident it is that it has a reasonable chance to preserve itself. The characteristics referred to above should be stable and enduring, and the group should be of sufficient size to make long-term survival possible. If the group clearly seems destined to remain a "permanent and distinct" constituent of a plural society, the case becomes very strong.[22]

3. A group has a stronger claim the clearer are the tests or criteria of membership, permitting all to know who are members and who are not. It may or may not be possible for a person to transfer membership from one group to another.

22 Glazer, "Individual Rights Against Group Rights," 98.

Where it is possible, the person attempting the transfer must meet whatever conditions the receiving group fixes. Among the tests or criteria are race, language, religion, citizenship, and, more generally, adherence to a given set of cultural norms and social mores.

4. A group has a stronger claim the more significant it is in the lives of its members and the more the members tend to "identify themselves – explain who they are – by reference to their membership."[23] Although a group may have great significance in the lives of its members if it is distinguished by only one characteristic, the chance of this is increased if it is distinguished by several – for example, not only by race but also by cultural characteristics such as language and religion.[24] The claim is especially strong if the group serves as a major socializing agency, shaping the personalities and values of the members, and when not only their identity but also their well-being and their pride depend at least in part on their membership.

5. A group has a stronger claim the more important the rights that it seeks or ought to have are to the interests of its members, and the lest costly or burdensome the grant of the rights is to others.

6. A group has a stronger claim the more clearly and effectively it is organized to act and to assume responsibilities, Formal organization, however, should not be regarded as imperative. Many a group – many a people – has succeeded in establishing its claim through the more or less spontaneous and uncoordinated actions of individual members.

7. A group has a stronger claim the more firmly established is the tradition of treating it as a group. By definition, groups with legal status as corporate entities have established their legal claim however good their moral claim may be. And groups that historically have been victims of discrimination have a prescriptive basis for any claim they choose to make for continued differential treatment designed to advance them toward the equal enjoyment of human rights.

23   Owen M. Fiss, "Groups and the Equal Protection Clause," *Philosophy & Public Affairs*, 5 (Winter 1976), 148.

24   On differentiation between groups according to the number of "dimensions or facets" that distinguish them, see Svensson, "Liberal Democracy and Group Rights," 434–435.

8. A group has a stronger claim the more clearly the status and rights that it seeks can be granted compatibly with the equality principle. The central requirements of that principle are that those affected get equal consideration, that like cases be treated in like manner, that the purpose pursued in differentiating between groups be legitimate, and that differences in treatment by justified by relevant differences and be proportionate to them.

These standards permit varying degrees of decisiveness in judging whether a group is entitled to status and rights, but they do not suggest any great proliferation of the kinds of groups to be recognized. In truth, I do not see that any kinds qualify other than those I have been discussing. What are commonly described as interest groups are clearly excluded. The question whether social classes might qualify is troublesome, but I would argue that their claims – and particularly those that are likely to be associated with an upper or privileged class – are rendered doubtful by the first standard and are ruled out by the third, fourth, fifth, and eighth.

The Equality Principle

The eighth standard – the equality principle – calls for comment. It requires that like cases be treated in like manner. First, I would argue that "like cases" may include those of groups as well as those of individuals. Thus, if the grant of a certain status and a certain set of rights to one group means that like groups cannot have a like status and a like set of rights, then the requirement of the equality principle is not met. No group in a plural society, for example, could be conceded monopoly control over government.

Second, given the need to consider whether like cases are treated in like manner, comparisons are necessary, and this requires a choice of the universe within which the comparisons should be made. When it is a question of a right under a constitution or law, the universe includes those in the relevant jurisdiction. Or, to put it more broadly, when it is a question of a right vis-à-vis an authoritative actor, the universe includes those to whom the authority extends. This principle is applicable even in connection with rights assured by treaty, such as those assured in the Covenant on

Economic, Social, and Cultural Rights. In binding the parties to recognize the right of everyone to education, for example, and to guarantee that the right is exercised without discrimination, the Covenant is assuming comparisons within the national framework. If a person in Ecuador has educational opportunities inferior to those available to a person in England, no violation of the legal right to equal treatment occurs. Whether the same proposition holds with respect to moral rather than legal rights is a question. Moral rights are supposed to be general and universal, and in the long run the proposition that people in Ecuador should be treated equally with those in England is surely the ideal. Even now it makes a difference whether the inferior treatment of people in Ecuador results from deliberate choices of the government there or from the exigencies of relevant circumstances, such as a scarcity of necessary resources in Ecuador as compared to England. On the one hand, not even a moral right exists to what is impossible or impracticable. On the other hand, given the equality principle, the question is whether those receiving inferior treatment may not have a just claim to some kind of international action – for example, a transfer of resources – designed to advance them toward equality of treatment according to an international standard.

The third comment on the equality principle overlaps with the second. It is that different standards are employed around the world in interpreting the principle, and that caution is indicated in any attempt to say what it means. The situation is illustrated in the field of voting and political representation. I take for granted Article 25 of the Covenant on Civil and Political Rights, providing that every citizen shall have the right to equal suffrage in genuine, free elections, but the article does not say how votes are to be grouped for electoral purposes – whether territorially or communally. Although every vote is no doubt to count as one in a numerical sense, the requirement of "equal" suffrage may or may not mean that the votes must have equal weight or value. Even the meaning of equal weight or value is uncertain. In the United States we compute the weight or value of votes in terms of the total population of electoral districts, but some other countries do it in terms of the number of eligible or actual voters. Further, granting that precise equality is unachievable, countries vary widely in the deviations that they permit, deviations of up to one-third being not at all uncommon.[25]

The problem of the relationship between the equality principle and rules relating to voting and representation is complicated still more if practices at the international level are considered. There the general rule is one state/one vote despite egregious differences in the populations of the states casting the votes. In the Security Council the rule is supplemented by another: that the five permanent members have a veto whereas the other ten do not. In the World Bank voting is adjusted to the relative amounts of capital that the different member countries contribute. For the European parliament, it turns out that Luxembourg gets one member for every 60,00 persons in its population, Ireland one for every 220,000, Italy one for every 700,000, and West Germany one for every 760,000.

I have not seen a careful study of the relationship between these various practical and the equality principle. Perhaps the conclusion to be drawn is simply that the principle is frequently violated, but this would assume a meaning for the principle that others might not share. Moreover, some of the seeming departures can be explained in terms of other principles. For example, the principle is widely, though not universally, accepted that special concessions should be made to the weak, which may be the full explanation of the seeming "over-representation" of the weaker countries in the European parliament. Similarly, the principle is good that the voting power and influence of any unit should be more or less proportionate to its importance to the functioning of the system of which it is a part, or to its ability to defy or disrupt the system. Gross disparities between voting power and other kinds of power are dangerous to any system, for those with the other kinds of power will be tempted to use it instead of relying on a voting system that only brings defeat.

In calling attention to problems with the equality principle, I do not mean to attack the principle. I leave it as the eighth standard, as stated above. But neither the eighth nor any of the other standards is stated in unconditional terms. The statement is that the claims of intermediate groups will be stronger the more clearly or fully they meet the standards.

[25]   Vernon Van Dyke, "One Man One Vote and Majority Rule as Human Rights," *Revue des Droits de l'Homme [Human Rights Journal]*, Vol. 6, no. 3-4 (1973), 453-459.

What Rights Should Groups Have?

A substantial consensus has developed on the rights that individuals should have, but no comparable consensus exists on rights for groups intermediate between the individual and the state. And even where seeming consensus exists, as in connection with the right of peoples to self-determination and to preserve their culture, the language employed is vague. I see no general solution to this problem. Groups and the circumstance in which they find themselves differ so much that any acceptable code of group rights would have to be stated in quite general terms, leaving considerable room for ad hoc judgment. Given this situation, my argument is simply that there ought to be greater readiness to adopt special measures that respond to the legitimate claims of ethnic communities. Criteria for judging the strength of such claims have been stated above. The following are among the special measures to consider:

1. The granting of self-determination. The right of a state to its integrity and to choose a centralized governmental structure should not always be held to override the right of ethnic communities within the state to choose secession or some degree of autonomy.

2. The acceptance of some form of political communalism, assuring ethnic communities of reasonable representation in the legislative, executive, and judicial branches of government, including the civil and military services. An exclusive focus on the individual is not appropriate where the fate and fortunes of distinctive communities are at stake.

3. The adoption of other arrangements designed to enable ethnic communities to preserve their identity. In the case of communities that are territorially concentrated, the arrangements might authorize them to bar outsiders as property owners or permanent residents. Where at all feasible, they might authorize minorities to operate their own schools, with tax support. And in appropriate ways they should assure that minority languages are protected and used.

4. Affirmative action. Though preferential treatment is unacceptable when its purpose is to preserve or promote special privilege for those already advanced and advantaged, as in South Africa, it should be employed when necessary to undo the effects of any past discrimination or to promote the equal enjoyment of human rights.

Problems and Countervailing Considerations

The course of action proposed involves problems that might as well be acknowledged. The right of self-determination is potentially explosive, and if given full rein might well transform the political map of the world. It might produce a large number of additional mini-states, breaking up existing states in the process, or it might produce civil wars as minorities try to secede; and it might force the decentralization of states whose international boundaries remain unquestioned. To accept communalism in any state would be to give up hope of assimilation or fusion and implicitly to emphasize social cleavages, perhaps even to encourage the emergence of new collectivities that demand status and rights. The record of communalism in Ceylon and India under the British is generally deplored, and communalism obviously has failed to solve the problems of Cyprus and Lebanon. In South Africa its distinctive application has been calamitous. Special measures designed to enable a minority to preserve its culture, and most particularly its language, would present problems too, for they would seem to militate against the development and preservation of unity within the state. Finally, problems relating to fairness to individuals in the more advanced communities obviously attend affirmative action on behalf of those in other communities.

A problem of a different sort relates to the impact on the rights of individuals of the proposed recognition of the rights of groups. Obviously, the impact might be entirely negative. The rights of individuals would no doubt be put in jeopardy. Where a conflict arises between the right of one person and the right of a group, the right of the group might always be held to prevail. Not only would this have practical significance for the fate of individuals, but it would mean that the proposals made here, instead of helping to solve a problem in liberal-democratic thought, would lead to the abandonment of a central feature of that thought – the stress on the freedom and rights of the individual.

The problems sketched in the above two paragraphs are real and are not to be dismissed. Nevertheless, considerations going in the opposite direction need to be taken into account too. Where is it written that the continued unity and even the peace of every existing state is the paramount value? Suppose that one nation or people within a state is dominant, and uses government mainly for its own advantage, consigning another nation or people or ethnic community to second-class status and governing oppressively. Suppose that those who emphasize unity and seek homogeneity are in effect taking the view that certain minorities simply do not count, or are demanding that the minorities abandon their language and their culture and take on the language and culture of the dominant community. Suppose that the dominant community magnanimously extends equal treatment to individuals in a minority, safe in the knowledge that the minority is too small to obtain representation in government. Suppose that the weaker people or the weaker ethnic community is indigenous and is threatened by an immigrant people that is more advanced, as in Fiji, Malaysia, New Zealand, and some other countries. Suppose that, even if social harmony is threatened by granting status and rights to a nation or a people or an ethnic community within the state, it is also threatened by a refusal of status and rights. After all, Northern Ireland has not achieved peace by insisting on individualism and by pretending that the population is homogeneous; and if the kind of communalism tried in Cyprus and Lebanon has not worked, this does not prove that individualism and majority rule would have worked better. A sizeable number of states in addition to those mentioned immediately above follow policies of the sort proposed here, whether on the basis of formal enactment or informal practice, including Belgium, Canada, Finland, India, West Germany, Switzerland, the USSR, and Zimbabwe. Even the individualistic United States follows such policies in limited measure – for example, in connection with the Indians and the indigenous inhabitants of American Samoa. How long Zimbabwe will continue its special measures for the Whites remains to be seen, but the others can be expected to continue their policies indefinitely and perhaps to extend them.

Implications for Political Theory

Liberal political theory has been based on implausible assumptions. Hobbes and Locke had no basis for assuming that individuals were the only significant units, or the crucial units, in the state of nature. And John Rawls has nothing but his imagination to go on in assuming that those in the "original position" are individuals who speak only for themselves and their immediate relatives.[26] Had Hobbes and Locke conceived the state of nature in a plausibly different way, their theories would have been different, and so would the theories of Rawls if he had assigned those in the original position plausibly different roles.[27] After all, it is highly unlikely that individuals in a state of nature or in an original position would be the only units that count, or that they would speak only for themselves and their relatives. Individuals are not self-sufficient. Everything we know suggests that in a state of nature, or in an original position, they would be joined not only in families but also in other collectivities of various kinds. They would be joined in groups identified by race, language, or religion, by social custom and convention, or more broadly by culture. They would make up tribes or communities or peoples. The development of their personalities and talents, their philosophies of life, and perhaps their very existence would depend on the community of which they are a part. Given these assumptions, it is incredible that in a state of nature or in an original position they would be concerned only with individuals. They also surely would be concerned about the community on which so much depends, and on its relationships both with individuals and with other communities. And these concerns surely would affect the terms of the contract reached and the nature of the rules adopted.

It would be wrong to say that all liberal political theorists, or all who write about political theory, focus on individuals to the exclusion of any examination of the role and the claims of groups,[28] but surely anyone who goes over the relevant literature must be struck by pronounced tendencies going in this direction. Rawls illustrates the point. So do both Roland Pennock and Carl Cohen, writing on democracy.[29] Dworkin,

26 John Rawls, A Theory of Justice (Cambridge: Belknap Press of Harvard University Press, 1971), 128, 136-150.

27 Vernon Van Dyke, "Justice as Fairness: For Groups?," American Political Science Review, 69 (June 1975), 607-614.

28 Note, for example, the treatment of "The Obligations of Oppressed Minorities" in Michael Walzer, Obligations, Essays on Disobedience, War, and Citizenship (Cambridge: Harvard University Press, 1970), 46-70.

29 J. Roland Pennock, Democratic Political Theory (Princeton: Princeton University Press, 1979); Carl Cohen, Democracy (New York: Free Press, 1971).

in the statement quoted earlier, grants a role to collective "goals," and in a brief footnote he says that ". . . a political theory that counts special groups, like racial groups, as having some corporate standing within the community may therefore speak of group rights";[30] but this is only a glance in the direction of a subject that deserves much fuller attention. Actually, to stress individualism in a democracy and to ignore or neglect the claims of groups is to fight the battle of any ethnic community that happens to be in a majority. Those in a majority community can insist on individualism and the nondiscriminatory treatment of individuals, and can decry any differentiation based on race, language, or religion, knowing that this formula assures their dominance. If the less numerous ethnic communities are to preserve their identity and their culture, and even if they are simply to be assured of a fair consideration of their interests, it may well be imperative to grant them special rights as collective entities.

[30] Dworkin, 91.

CAPITALISM, CITIZENSHIP
AND COMMUNITY*
By Stephen Macedo

Introduction

The authors of *Habits of the Heart* (Robert N. Bellah, Richard Madsen, William M. Sullivan, Ann Swindler, and Steven M. Tipton; hereafter, simply Bellah) charge that America is losing the institutions that help "to create the kind of person who could sustain a connection to a wider political community and thus ultimately support the maintenance of free institutions."[1] Bellah fears that "individualism may have grown cancerous – that it may be destroying those social integuments that Tocqueville saw as moderating its more destructive potentials, that it may be threatening the survival of freedom itself."[2]

Proponents of the liberal free market order should, I will argue, take seriously the concerns that motivate Bellah and company: citizens of a liberal regime cannot live by exchanges alone. Liberal constitutionalism depends upon a certain level and quality of citizen virtue. But while the need for virtue is often neglected by liberal theorists, it is far from clear that the actual workings of liberal institutions have drastically undermined virtue in the way Bellah's dire account suggests. That analysis serves, moreover, as the springboard for a radically transformist argument that seeks, not so much to elevate and shape, but to transcend and deny, the self-interestedness that the free market exercises. Having argued against Bellah's analysis and prescriptions, I shall attempt to show how the

* For their helpful comments on an earlier draft I would like to thank Jack Crittenden, Hannes Gissurarson, Rob Rosen, Jeremy Shearmur, Shannon Stimson, my fellow participants in the Liberty Fund seminar on "Capitalism and Socialism," and the editors of this journal.

[1] Robert N. Bellah, Richard Madsen, William M. Sullivan, Ann Swindler, and Steven M. Tipton, *Habits of the Heart* (Berkeley: University of California Press, 1985), p. vii.

[2] *ibid.*

phenomena he describes are open to an interpretation that is
happier from the point of view of a concern with virtue. I shall
end by using Tocqueville to suggest that combining liberal
capitalism with intermediate associations like voluntary groups
and state and local government helps elevate and shape self-
interest, promoting a citizenry capable of and insistent upon
liberal self-government.

I. Toward a Communitarian Critique of Capitalism

Much of the normative apparatus deployed by Bellah is lifted
directly from Alasdair MacIntyre, Michael Sandel, Charles
Taylor, and other communitarians.³ *Habits*, for example, is a
lament about "modernity" that often sounds like MacIntyre at
his most dire: "Progress, modernity's master idea, seems less
compelling when it appears that it may progress into the
abyss."⁴ And, echoing the "atomistic" complaint of Taylor and
Sandel, *Habits* warns that "in our day . . . separation and
individuation have reached a kind of culmination."⁵

While *Habits* develops several important communitarian
themes, it also helps us see that some elements of the
communitarian critique of liberalism are misguided.
MacIntyre, for example, claims that modern Western societies
are characterized by basic moral disagreement. "The most
striking feature of contemporary moral utterance," says
MacIntyre, "is that so much of it is used to express
disagreements. . . ."⁶ And this is, in part, because all we have
are "fragments" of genuine morality: the "language and
appearances of morality" without the "integral substance."⁷
MacIntyre's main evidence for his disintegration thesis is the
rampant disagreement among moral philosophers and others
about how to justify correct positions on issues such as just war

³ See Alasdair MacIntyre, *After Virtue* (Notre Dame: University of Notre
Dame Press, 1981); Michael Sandel, *Liberalism and the Limits of Justice*
(Cambridge: Cambridge University Press, 1982); Charles Taylor, *Hegel
and Modern Society* (Cambridge: Cambridge University Press, 1979), and
Taylor's two volumes of *Philosophical Papers: Human Agency and
Language* and *Philosophy and the Human Sciences* (Cambridge: Cambridge
University Press, 1985).

⁴ Bellah, *Habits*, p. 277.

⁵ *ibid.*, p. 275; and see Taylor, "Atomism," in *Papers*, vol. 2.

⁶ MacIntyre, *After Virtue*, p. 6.

⁷ *ibid.*, p. 5.

and abortion. These disagreements seem to come to a head in metaethical disputes among "incommensurable" moral paradigms: "deontology," the varieties of consequentialism, perfectionism, and so on.[8] If MacIntyre is right, the problem for a polity like America must be to acquire rather than revise a moral identity.[9]

The evidence presented in *Habits* suggests that it would be hard to sustain the claim that incoherence is the leading characteristic of political culture in America. The authors of *Habits* find that "beneath the sharp disagreements" animating our politics, "there is more than a little consensus . . . [Americans] all to some degree share a common moral vocabulary . . . the 'first language' of American individualism." We share, as others have put it, an "American ethos," a vision of what, in the abstract, we stand for at our best, a vision centered around liberal/capitalist values.[10]

The concern of *Habits*, then, is not with the existence of a coherent political culture, but with its substance and sustainability. Is materialism bred by economic freedom destroying the "civic culture" that supports liberal democratic institutions?[11]

One leading complaint shared by many communitarians and Bellah is that ends and purposes tend to be regarded as matters of choice, matters about which our liberal public morality

---

8 *ibid.*, pp. 8–21.

9 MacIntyre's claim is doubly odd. Only philosophers argue about methaethics, yet philosophical communities appear to thrive on such debates. Few in broader political communities are even aware of the distinction between deontology and consequentialism. The practical consensus that sustains actual political communities probably draws on both "rights-based" and "goods-based" considerations (as well as interests, apathy, and other attitudes that have nothing to do with morality). For an interesting discussion of the plurality of ultimate sources of moral value see Thomas Nagel, "The Fragmentation of Value," *Mortal Questions* (London: Cambridge University Press, 1981).

10 See Herbert McClosky and John Zaller, *The American Ethos: Public Attitudes Toward Capitalism and Democracy* (Cambridge: Harvard University Press, 1984), esp. chapter 1.

11 On the connection between a participatory civil culture and the health of liberal democracy see Gabriel A. Almond and Sidney Verba, *The Civic Culture: Political Attitudes and Democracy in Five Nations* (Princeton: Princeton University Press, 1963), chapter 11; Sidney Verba and Norman H. Nie, *Participation in America: Political Democracy and Social Equality* (Chicago: University of Chicago Press, 1987), *passim.*

provides little guidance. And so, Sandel complains that liberalism posits an "unencumbered self": "the values and relations we have are the products of choice, the possessions of a self given prior to its ends."[12]

MacIntyre, likewise, bemoans what he terms the "emotivist" moral character of our age: "the self as presented by emotivism . . . cannot be simply or unconditionally identified with *any* particular moral attitude or point of view (including that of those *characters* which socially embody emotivism) just because of the fact that its judgments are in the end criterionless."[13] Lacking any ultimate criteria of choice, "the self is 'nothing', is not a substance but a set of perpetually open possibilities."[14] Without "objective and impersonal" criteria of morality, people come to hold that any moral principle is "in the end an expression of the preferences of an individual . . . ."[15] And so, even when Americans are bound up in valuable associations and personal relationships, according to *Habits*, they tend to regard these as basically "arbitrary."[16]

Because they consider the ends of purposes of life to be arbitrary, Americans pursue mere "means" such as material prosperity.

> Americans tend to think of the ultimate goals of a good life as matters of personal choice. The means to achieve individual choice, they tend to think, depend on economic progress. This dominant American tradition of thinking about success does not, however, help very much in relating economic success to our ultimate success as persons and our ultimate success as a society.[17]

But consider the example of Brian Palmer, discussed in *Habits*, who threw off his frenetic careerism to embrace a "devotion to marriage and children." This is, to Bellah, all for the good, but Palmer is incapable of explaining why,

> his current life is, in fact, better than his earlier life. . . . Both are justified as idiosyncratic preference rather than as

12   Sandel, *Liberalism*, p. 176.

13   MacIntyre, *After Virtue*, p. 30, emphasis in original.

14   *ibid.*, p. 31.

15   *ibid.*, pp. 20–21.

16   Bellah, *Habits*, p. 21.

17   *ibid.*, p. 22.

representing a larger sense of the purpose of life. . . . What is good is what one finds rewarding. If one's preferences change, so does the nature of the good.[18]

Lacking in substantive justification, Bellah further suggests, personal commitments rest on a "fragile foundation. . . . [Brian Palmer] lacks a language to explain what seem to be the real commitments that define his life, and to that extent the commitments themselves are precarious."[19] The stability of shared commitments and associations requires, for Bellah, articulateness about real human goods.

A couple of points should be noted here. First, the alleged precariousness of Palmer's commitments is not the problem of detachment complained of by Sandel.[20] Brian Palmer cannot easily cast off his old values and ways by a sovereign act of unencumbered choice. His commitments partly constitute his identity. But his wife's decision to divorce him provokes a personal crisis and a good bit of soul-searching and hard thinking: he reads, reflects, reexamines, and only painfully alters and revises his sense of priorities.[21] Palmer's case is typical of those discussed by Bellah: middle-class Americans are, apparently, capable of reflecting upon and revising their moral values and commitments, but they are not "unencumbered selves" choosing in abstract isolation.[22]

Brian Palmer is not unencumbered by his values and ends, but he does lack an articulate account of ultimate human goods. Does this imply that he lacks any sense of real goods, as Bellah suggests? Simon Weil and Iris Murdoch (among others) argue that apprehending the good is more a matter of "seeing" than "saying," a matter of loving attention to "a magnetic but inexhaustible reality."[23] Inarticulateness is not necessarily a

18   ibid., pp. 5–6.

19   ibid., 6 and 8.

20   See Sandel's discussion of the "voluntarist notion of agency," *Liberalism*, p. 59.

21   Bellah, *Habits*, p. 4.

22   The point that liberalism does not depend upon an unencumbered conception of the self is developed at greater length in my *Liberal Virtue: A Liberal Theory of Citizenship, Virtue, and Community* (Oxford: Oxford University Press: forthcoming).

23   Iris Murdoch, *The Sovereignty of the Good* (London: Ark, 1986), p. 42, and see *Simon Weil: An Anthology*, ed. Sian Miles (New York: Weidenfeld and Nicholson, 1986).

sign of the arbitrariness of one's commitments: real human goods may be hard to articulate.

If inarticulateness is not necessarily a sign of arbitrariness, neither is it obviously a sign of the fragility of commitments, or clearly the reason why Palmer's commitments may have become more fragile. Fragility may be a consequence of any number of things: recognition of the plurality of ways of participating in human goods, greater tolerance of diversity, or a greater tendency to think critically about traditional patterns of life. People have become more willing to divorce, for example, rather than live with an unhappy marriage. Bellah does not show that such changes are either bad or the consequence of an inability to articulate what the components of a good life are.

It seems clear that Brian Palmer has learned something from the experiences and reflections surrounding his divorce: "That exclusive pursuit of success now seems to me not a good way to live. . . . I have just found that I get a lot of personal reward from being involved in the lives of my children."[24] Palmer seems to have come to appreciate the real value of family life, and it is simply not clear that his inability to articulately account for his moral progress renders his new commitments more fragile or arbitrary than they would otherwise be.

Bellah, like communitarians generally, tends to avoid objective moral claims, favoring instead the local route to community provided by our shared "social identity."[25] And so he argues that our preferences are "detached from any social or cultural base that could give them broader meaning."[26] Our problem, apparently, is that "American cultural traditions" leave individuals "suspended in glorious but terrifying isolation."[27]

The isolation of the self is exhibited in our public life by the dominance of managerial expertise, and in private by a therapeutic model of relationships. In public the question is what means will most effectively realize ends arbitrarily chosen by individuals. In private the question is how to get in close touch with your own "feelings" so that you do what you

24   Bellah, *Habits*, p. 6.

25   Especially Michael Walzer, *Spheres of Justice* (New York: Basic Books, 1983), and "Philosophy and Democracy," *Political Theory*, vol. 9 (Aug. 1981), pp. 379–399.

26   Bellah, *Habits*, p. 7.

27   *ibid.*, p. 6.

"really' want to do, where what you really want to do is arbitrary, personal, and not discussable; it is discovered "down deep" inside yourself rather than in some form of "reason-giving moral argument" or social "conversation."[28] Modern liberalism's moral condition is, as another communitarian has put it, a "mixture of private Romanticism and public utilitarianism."[29]

Relationships, Bellah finds, are modelled on a "therapeutic" quest for self-clarification, self-acceptance, and self-expression: the therapist takes "each person's values as given or self-defined," as "self-set values."[30] The task of therapy is simply to achieve "clarity" about one's "personal preferences" so that they can better be realized.[31] Bellah worries that this conception of "healthy" personal relationships implies an ultimately isolated self-reliance. "In the end," according to Margaret Oldham (another Bellah interviewee), "you're really alone and you really have to answer to yourself . . . ."[32]

Both MacIntyre and the authors of *Habits* are concerned to emphasize the importance of understanding our choices as choices among options defined by inherited ideals and traditions. Perhaps our culture does elevate self-expression at the expense of tradition, but traditionalism becomes mere conventionalism unless it is supported by a critical account of which among our many inherited practices have real value.

Neither liberalism nor capitalism depends on keeping personal choices detached from inherited ideals and traditions. The defense of liberal freedom supposes that we are inheritors of many ideals and traditions, and that mature persons have a right to choose among a plurality of conceptions of the good life. Liberals would also want to emphasize that persons are quite properly critical interpreters of inherited ideals and traditions, and that this process of criticism properly leads to the rejection of patterns of life based on mere habit, prejudice, or stereotype (patterns based on maxims such as "a woman's place is in the home"). Indeed, it is not clear how one would go

28 *ibid.*, p. 140.

29 Taylor, *Hegel and Modern Society*, p. 126. But for a more positive view of Romanticism, see Nancy Rosenblum's excellent study, *Another Liberalism* (Cambridge: Harvard University Press, 1987).

30 Bellah, pp. 127–128.

31 *ibid.*, p. 15.

32 *ibid.*

about distilling a valuable tradition from the welter of our inherited practices without the capacity for critical judgment of the sort that liberalism elevates.[33]

What Bellah tends to portray as a general value skepticism in America appears actually to be carefully focused and embedded in a set of substantive values. Brian Palmer, for example, is not skeptical about the value of giving everyone the equal right to pursue their choices. Palmer praises California:

> By and large, the rule of thumb out here is that if you've got the money, honey, you can do your own thing as long as your thing doesn't destroy someone else's property, or interrupt their sleep, or bother their privacy, then that's fine.[34]

Palmer's vision of tolerance, for Bellah, implies that freedom is a matter of being left alone, of "freedom as freedom *from* the demands of others [which] provides no vocabulary in which . . . Americans can easily address common conceptions of the ends of a good life . . . ."[35] And liberal justice, for Bellah as for Sandel, yields a public preoccupation with mere "procedures."[36] But Palmer's statements could equally well be interpreted as a set of ultimate substantive commitments which are partly, though not completely, constitutive of the good of all: liberal freedoms place a premium on peace, choice, and prosperity, the resolution of differences through persuasion rather than coercion, the value of reflectiveness and self-control, and an openness to change. And Palmer's freedom is not the freedom of an isolated individual: the self-examination provoked by his divorce leads him to read, reflect, and talk things over with his children, to whom he is devoted.[37] Liberal freedom of choice can, in general, be understood as the freedom to choose among associations and communities.

33 Sotirios A. Barber develops the notion that reasoned criticism is central to the task of distilling a tradition from mere history; see his *On What the Constitution Means* (Baltimore: Johns Hopkins University Press, 1984), pp. 84–5. I develop the argument that liberalism does not depend upon an instrumental notion of rationality in *Liberal Virtues*.

34 Bellah, *Habits*, pp. 6–7.

35 *ibid.*, p. 24.

36 See Michael Sandel, "The Procedural Republic and the Unencumbered Self," *Political Theory*, vol. 12 (1984), p. 93.

37 Bellah, *Habits*, p. 4.

Bellah himself does not really press the charge, in any case, that our pubic life is wholly given over to the pursuit of material gain, or that our politics is merely procedural, or that freedom stands for isolation. *Habits* is a profoundly ambivalent book: its authors, despite their misgivings, recognize that many Americans continue to participate in politics and various voluntary associations and to affirm that a wide range of common involvements is crucial to living a good life:

> If there are vast numbers of a selfish, narcissistic "me generation" in America, we did not find them, but we certainly did find that the language of individualism, the primary American language of self-understanding, limits the ways in which people think.[38]

All this leads one to ask, finally: To what extent has individualism undermined associations in America? And what kinds of political and economic reforms are called for?

Bellah notes that America remains the most religious of Western nations. According to a recent Gallup poll, 57 percent of Americans say that religion can answer "all or most of today's problems," 55 per cent say religion is "very important" in their lives, and another 30 percent say "fairly important."[39] Seven in ten Americans are church members.[40] These figures have remained constant over the last five years, while materialistic yuppiedom has come into it own[41] The continuing vitality of religion in America suggests not only that many people value association, but also that many would not regard the ends of life as arbitrary in the ways Bellah has suggested.

Volunteerism was at least as prevalent in 1986 as at any time in the previous decade: 36 percent reported being *currently* engaged in private charitable activity, up from 27 percent in 1977.[42] Indeed, volunteerism rose disproportionately among 18–29 year olds (again, yuppies). And Bellah himself found

[38]   *ibid.*, p. 290.

[39]   *The Gallup Report*, § 259, April 1987, p. 10.

[40]   *ibid.*, p. 35.

[41]   *ibid.*, p. 13. "Yuppies," young, upwardly mobile professionals, are usually regarded as the vanguard of materialism and self-centeredness.

[42]   *The Gallup Report*, § 248, May 1986, p. 14.

evidence that tolerant cosmopolitan yuppiedom can be combined with civic activism and responsibility.[43]

Americans are still participators: significantly more Americans belong to associations and are active in them than citizens of other industrial countries.[44] There have, undoubtedly, been changes over the longer run: participation seems to decline with urbanization, but to increase with education and socioeconomic status.[45] In their classic study of participation in America, Verba and Nie argue that while the personal proclivity to participate is increasing (with education and status) the opportunities for effective participation may be declining somewhat (with urbanization).[46] The issue of participation is worth addressing, but the evidence does not suggest that an associative ethos has been destroyed or that we face an impending crisis.

If, at the personal level, people nowadays feel somewhat more uncertain about their ultimate goals and values and about the stability of their personal relationships, perhaps this has something to do with the apparent lessening of social pressures to marry, the more widespread acceptance of divorce, and the far greater range of options open to women.

Economic progress has also encouraged mobility, and rendered communities and extended family ties less stable. And so, Bellah comes back, over and over, to the complaint that the "commercial dynamism at the heart of the ideal of personal success . . . undermines community involvement. . . . The rules of the competitive market, not the practices of the town meeting or the fellowship of the church, are the real arbiters of living."[47] But it is not merely avarice, or the desire for gain, that "estranges" one from community and "the public household" (as Bellah puts it).[48] The trade-offs between remaining in a familiar community setting and moving on for some new challenge raise hard and genuine problems (as any academic ought to appreciate). The interviews reported in *Habits* suggest, in fact, that people are often thrilled by the prospect of

---

43   See the discussion of Mary Taylor at *Habits*, pp. 192–5.

44   See Verba and Nie, *Participation*, chapter 11, Tables 1 and 9.

45   *ibid.*, p. 20 and chapter 13 generally.

46   *ibid.*, p. 264.

47   Bellah, *Habits*, p. 251.

48   *ibid.*, p. 197.

a promotion, a new job, and a new environment: "moving on" is often stimulated by a search for new challenges and a desire to avoid becoming "bored" and "stale."[49] It is wrong, then, to write off the attractions of change and mobility as the products of mere grasping ambition, as Bellah often seems to do.

People seem well aware of the genuine and difficult trade-offs between new career challenges and settled commitments. "Practically everyone we talked to would agree," say the authors of *Habits*,

> that two of the most basic components of a good life are success in one's work and the joy that comes in serving one's community. And they would also tend to agree that the two are so closely intertwined that a person cannot usually have one without having the other.[50]

And so it seems, on Bellah's own testimony, that Americans are fairly self-conscious about the choices they are making, that people continue to value family, participation, and association while making hard choices among these and competing goods that really are to some degree incompatible. Bellah presents no real evidence to show that America has experienced a critical, or even significant, decline in group participation.

Why does the theme of impending crisis recur so frequently in *Habits* when the stories Bellah relates seem hardly to support a fear of immediate social collapse? The crisis theme has more to do with Bellah's desired prescriptions than with the actual state of individualism in America.

While the conception of freedom of many Americans is resistant to "overt forms of political oppression," it also "leaves them with a stubborn fear of acknowledging structures of power and interdependence in a technologically complex society dominated by giant corporations and an increasingly powerful state.[51] In the face of "predatory capitalists," and the "untrammelled pursuit of wealth without regard to social justice," the "old moral order" that governed small-town America has proved ineffective. The "crucial change" in American life has been the shift from economic and social relationships that were "visible and . . . morally interpreted as

[49]   *ibid.*

[50]   *ibid.*, p. 196.

[51]   *ibid.*, p. 25.

parts of a larger common life – to a society vastly more interrelated and integrated economically, technically, and functionally."[52]

Lamentably for Bellah, Americans continue to look at the problems of corporate giants like Chrysler in terms of the presence or absence of "small-town" virtues: "To maintain their moral balance, town fathers have to pretend they live in a kind of community that no longer exists."[53] They ignore their "dependence on a complicated national and international political economy."[54]

For Bellah the American way represents not an assertion of a set of guiding values, but the inability of the "language of individualism" to "make sense of human interaction."[55] In order to "minimize 'cognitive dissonance,' many individuals tend not to deal with embedded inequalities of power, privilege, and esteem in a culture of self-proclaimed moral equality."[56] Those who see threats to the "viability" of middle-class American values from "poor people who have never learned any self-restraint" are simply falling back on "highly personal and moralistic rhetoric with no clue to the understanding of large-scale structures and institutions."[57]

So hegemonic is the American ethos of individualism that even those progressive souls in the Campaign for Economic Democracy are really moved by a "conception of community as a voluntary gathering of autonomous individuals [which] is not radically different from the views of the others" interviewed by the Bellah team. So, in a sense, Americans may share too many values, they may be too homogeneous in their expectations about behavior and their beliefs about virtue:

> Americans, it would seem, feel most comfortable in thinking about politics in terms of a consensual community of autonomous individuals, and it is to such a conception that they turn for the cure of their present ills. . . . [S]uch a

52   ibid., p. 43.

53   ibid., p. 175.

54   ibid., p. 176. For an excellent argument about the prohibitive costs involved in trying to compensate people for a variety of forms of bad luck, see Richard A. Epstein's contribution to this volume.

55   ibid., p. 204.

56   ibid.

57   ibid., p. 205.

society is really constituted only of autonomous middle-class individuals.[58]

Americans, apparently, share a rather thick set of expectations about personal independence and responsibility, and they tend to be judgmental when people fail to measure up. If groups persist in poverty that "must be someone's fault . . . perhaps because their culture is defective, and they lack a 'work ethic.' "[59]

But just when Americans might seem, from a communitarian perspective, to be getting it right, behaving like a "substantive" cultural community, with expectations and standards of conduct and united by more than "relativistic tolerance," Bellah simply scoffs. Americans have "difficulty coming to terms with genuine cultural or social differences . . . [and] even more difficulty coming to terms with large impersonal organization and institutions."[60]

Americans, unlike sociologists and economists, cannot see the "invisible complexity" of society, little less make " moral sense of significant cultural, social, and economic differences between groups."[61] In the "moral vacuum" of their ignorance, Americans tend to "translate group claims and interests into the language of individual rights."[62] But this will not do, because there are "individuals and groups or categories of individuals" who "insist" that "they are owed or entitled to certain benefits, assistance, or preference as a matter of right" and "such claims are not readily accepted as matters of justice. . . . They begin to be treated instead simply as competing wants. . . . [and are] interpreted in terms of power."[63]

So Americans continue to lodge their confidence in market competition, and to respect personal effort. The criteria of

[58] ibid., p. 206. See Louis Hartz's discussion, *The Liberal Tradition in America* (New York: Harcourt Brace Jovanovich, 1955), esp. ch. 8.

[59] ibid.

[60] ibid., p. 207.

[61] ibid.

[62] ibid.

[63] ibid. The "moral"egalitarianism of Bellah and his cohorts turns out, after all, to be a rather thin patina glossing a thoroughly intellectual elitism (economists and sociologists understand the complexity "invisible" to most Americans). Bellah is, finally, derisive about middle-class American values (the work ethic, suspicion of politics, and insistence on independence). Middle-class attitudes are systematically reduced to a failure "to come to terms" with reality.

inclusion in America's political community include, apparently economic self-support and responsibility: classical liberal, bourgeois virtues that make people resistant to democratizing and socializing the economy. Americans are unwilling to "accept" cultural groups that they consider lazy or irresponsible, and they insist on a distinction between rights and welfare entitlements.

Do Americans go too far in emphasizing economic independence and personal responsibility? That proposition is arguable, but largely beyond the scope of this paper. It should be emphasized, however, that the popular attitudes and economic conditions that Bellah considers most troubling seem hardly new. The attitudes resemble Weber's "protestant ethic."[64] The conditions (economic complexity and invisible interdependence, uncertainty, risk, and inequality) are not recent features of capitalism; they are the characteristics of the commercial order that Adam Smith described in the *Wealth of Nations*.[65] Apart from asserting what now seems patently false (that we have reached the limits of economic growth, a "zero-sum" society in which liberal capitalism can no longer sustain itself),[66] Bellah and company, as I have noted, really present no evidence to show that these attitudes and conditions have taken a new, self-destructive turn. And so, the quest for transformation that underlies *Habits* has less to do with contemporary conditions than with the nature of liberal capitalism as such.

The ultimate political ambition of Bellah and company is to "transform" a society that they find deeply flawed.

> What has failed at every level – from the society of nations to the national society to the local community to the family – is integration. . . . We have put our own good, as individuals, as groups, as a nation, ahead of the common good.[67]

All that Bellah can hope for is:

> A conception of society as a whole composed of widely different, but independent, groups might generate a language of the common good that could adjudicate between conflicting wants and interests, thus taking the pressure off the over-

---

64 Max Weber, *The Protestant Ethic and the Spirit of Capitalism*, trans. Talcott Parsons (New York: Scribner's 1930).

65 See especially Book 1.

66 Bellah, *Habits*, pp. 185–189.

67 *ibid.*, p. 285.

strained logic of individual rights. But such a conception would require coming to terms with the invisible complexity that Americans prefer to avoid.[68]

Since our moral turpitude springs, in great part, from our free market individualism, redemption must lie in "economic democracy and social responsibility."[69] We must "give up our dream of private success for a genuinely integrated societal community."[70] Without the "transformation," Bellah warns, "there may be very little future to think about at all."[71]

To revitalize our "social ecology," Bellah proposes to increase taxes and raise welfare benefits, thus reversing "Reaganomics." The aim would be to alter the relationship between work and reward, substituting vocationalism for careerism: "If the extrinsic rewards and punishments associated with work were reduced, it would be possible to make vocational choices more in terms of intrinsic satisfactions."[72] Nobler motives and deeper satisfactions are, it seems, suppressed by capitalist avarice and cupidity: "The social wealth that automation brings, if not siphoned off into the hands of a few, can be used to pay for work that is intrinsically valuable, in the form of a renewal of crafts . . . and in the improvement of social services."[73] It would take a very deep social transformation indeed to get corporate lawyers and longshoremen to transfer their energies and aspirations to "crafts" (pot throwing? basket weaving?) and social work.

Bellah wishes to avoid the "soft despotism" that Tocqueville feared lurks behind an increasingly powerful regulatory/

68 *ibid.*

69 *ibid.*, p. 287.

70 *ibid.*, p. 286.

71 *ibid.*

72 *ibid.*, p. 288. Bellah's critique of market relations seems more than a little indebted to Marx, especially the discussions of money as the universal "pimp" of mankind, and of commodity fetishism, in the *Economic and Philosophical Manuscripts*, and *Capital*, vol. 1, respectively; *The Marx-Engels Reader*, 2nd ed., ed. Robert C. Tucker, (New York: Norton, 1978, pp. 101-105, 319-329. Besides tax increases, Bellah proposes that government promote this moral transformation via economic democracy, measures establishing the "social responsibility" of corporations, and a "revitalized party system"; see *Habits*, p. 287. He offers few details. Would revitalizing the party system, for example, require reversing the "democratic" reforms of the early 1970s?

73 *ibid.*, p. 288.

welfare state.[74] Because he opposes further centralization and bureaucratization, he must hope for a moral transformation of the polity broadly; a revival of "civil virtue" centered on a "substantive" conception of the common good and on a new awareness of our intricate economic "connectedness and interdependence."[75] This new politics will involve not so much the altruistic subordination of personal concerns to a larger good as the identification of one's interest with a polity committed to common deliberation and dialogue:

> Politics . . . is a forum within which the politics of community, the politics of interest, and the politics of the nation can be put into a new context of wider possibilities for accommodation and innovation. This view of politics depends upon a notion of community and citizenship importantly different from the utilitarian individualist view. It seeks to persuade us that the individual self finds its fulfilment in relations with others in society organized through public dialogue.[76]

There would seem to be more than little wishful thinking built into Bellah's proposals. He wants a more substantial sense of national purpose, but not one imposed from Washington.[77] Bellah wants people to work for pleasure rather than pay – raising income taxes, he hopes, will lead people to embrace intrinsically "meaningful" work, not make them lazy and listless. But do we have any good reason to really expect the emergence of a more substantial sense of the common good? And have socialist countries been successful in dissociating work and reward? Bellah presents no hard evidence to suggest that his high hopes are anything more than that.

Bellah's frequent recurrence to the abyss theme suggests a desperate need to frighten people into accepting his bitter

74 See Tocqueville's famous discussion in *Democracy in America*, trans. G. Lawrence, ed. J. P. Mayer (Garden City: Anchor, 1986), pp. 690–695.

75 Bellah, *Habits*, p. 256, 289. Sandel, I might add, also suggests moving against capitalism to shore up community by allowing states to enact plant closing laws "to protect their communities from the disruptive effects of capital mobility and sudden industrial change." See Michael Sandel, "Morality and the Liberal Ideal," *The New Republic*, May 7, 1984, pp. 15–17.

76 Bellah, *Habits*, p. 218.

77 As in the bumper-sticker: "Think Globally – Act Locally."

medicine, and perhaps a hope that moral renewal will emerge from a sense of crisis:

> In the late twentieth century, we see that our poverty is as absolute as that of the poorest of nations. We have attempted to deny the human condition in our quest for power after power. It would be well for us to rejoin the human race, to accept our essential poverty as a gift, and to share our material wealth with those in need.[78]

Must we, one must wonder, pin our hopes on Bellah's exasperated pleas for a radical transcendence of pluralism and self-interest?

On Bellah's account, many Americans adhere to the paradigm of associationism that is compatible with the acceptance of economic self-interest and the value of self-support. Bellah disparages these attitudes and practices, but the phenomena he describes are open to a happier interpretation than the one he presents.

II. Capitalism and Community

Bellah finds evidence that government welfare may displace the efforts of private association and, so, the impetus toward voluntary public involvement. Jim Reichart, another *Habits* interviewee

> muses that his loss of commitment is "probably caused by too much government. The government's like a domineering mother." It takes away all the people's incentive and tries to do everything for them. You know what it's like for children who have been dominated all their lives by a strong, powerful mother. They become damn near vegetable cases. It's the same with the government.[79]

One reason why government programs may discourage Americans from participation is not hard to find. Americans, according to Bellah, value success based on personal effort: "It is only insofar as they can claim that they have succeeded *through their own efforts* that they can feel they have deserved that achievement."[80] And earned success is not all they value; they also value voluntary service because it is voluntary:

[78] Bellah, *Habits*, p. 296.

[79] *ibid.*, p. 197.

[80] *ibid.*, p. 198, emphasis in original.

truly to deserve this joy, one has to make a personal, voluntary effort to "get involved." But one of the greatest sources of unhappiness for most Americans is the sense of being involuntarily involved – "trapped" – in constraining social relationships. Those with whom we talked tend to think of themselves as deserving joy only if they make such a commitment beyond having to do so.[81]

The thread that unifies the emphasis on earned achievement and voluntary service is free, responsible action, and the satisfaction derived from individual effort.

Americans understand the good life as a balance between these two types of free action: "without some individually deserved success, an individual would have little voluntarily to contribute to his choosen community."[82] And "practically all those we talked with are convinced, at least in theory, that a selfish seeker after purely individual success could not live a good, happy, joyful life."[83]

The authors of *Habits*, aside from their concern with greater equality, have two main objections to the vision of voluntary community implicit on liberal capitalism. First, liberalism implies that "community is a voluntary association of neighbors who personally know one another and freely express concern for one another, an essentially private, rather than public, form of association."[84] This objection is crucial, for it is the main reason why Bellah also rejects the "Welfare Liberalism" of Democrats like Ted Kennedy: "the Welfare Liberal vision articulated by Kennedy shares with Neocapitalism a fundamental assumption about the relationship between public and private life. .. [It] offers only what Neocapitalists such as Reagan offer: 'compassion,' the subjective feeling of sympathy of one private individual for another."[85]

---

[81]   *ibid.*

[82]   *ibid.*, p. 199.

[83]   *ibid.*

[84]   *ibid.*, p. 263.

[85]   *ibid.*, p. 265. And so, between Neocapitalists and Welfare Liberals, the Debate "is over procedures to achieve fairness for each, not about the substantive meaning of justice for all." In Hegelian terms, Neocapitalists and Welfare Liberals stand for different versions of *moralitat*, or civil society, while Bellah pursues a vision of *sittlichkeit*, a substantive ethical community; see *Hegel's Philosophy of Right*, trans. T. M. Knox (Oxford: Oxford University Press, 1967), third part.

This objection seems to rest, in part, on an extremely narrow conception of what counts as a *public* association. It is wrong to identify an emphasis on voluntarism with the elevation of merely personal or private concerns. The Red Cross, the National Audubon Society, the Salvation Army, and the Moral Majority are just as much constituted by "public" concerns as NASA or the Commodity Futures Trading Commission or the local sanitation department. We certainly have no reason to think that voluntary associations are inherently incapable of forming "constitutive" features of a person's identity: certainly religious commitments often do so. For purposes of passing judgment about the "communal" character of people's involvements, one must consider the purposes, motives, and membership criteria of voluntary associations before simply writing them off as "private."

Bellah also objects that proponents of voluntary community are unwilling to grasp and take hold of the large-scale economic forces shaping their lives.

> [W]hen they think of the kind of generosity that might redeem the individualistic pursuit of economic success, they often imagine voluntary involvements in local, small-scale activities such as a family, club, or idealized community in which individual initiatives interrelate to improve the life of all. They have difficulty relating this ideal image to the large-scale forces shaping their lives.[86]

This unwillingness to extend political control over the economy is consistent with the American preference for voluntarism, but this makes it "difficult to address the problems confronting us as a whole."[87] The preference for voluntarism is coupled with an antipolitical bias: "For a good number of those we talked to, politics connotes something morally unsavory, as though voluntary involvement were commendable up to the point at which it enters the realm of office holding, campaigning, and organized negotiation."[88]

But Americans are not against politics per se, or at least not equally against all politics. They appreciate and support,

---

[86] Bellah, *Habits*, p. 199.

[87] *ibid.*, p. 250.

[88] *ibid.*, p. 199. And see Robert Lane, "Market Justice and Political Justice," *American Political Science Review*, vol. 80, no. 2 (June 1986), pp. 383–402.

according to Bellah, a politics of local deliberation and moral consensus, and are suspicious of interest-group politics, the politics of "adversarial struggles, alliance building, and interest bargaining."[89] Americans, on moral grounds, prefer the market whose "legitimacy rests in large part on the belief that it rewards individuals impartially on the basis of fair competition."[90]

Besides local consensus politics and interest group bargaining, there is a politics of "national order and purpose," sustained by "patriotism" and a "revered Constitution."[91] For Bellah this positive politics of the nation "is a notion that bypasses the reality of utilitarian interest bargaining by appealing for legitimacy to . . . the vision of consensual, neighborly community."[92]

This idea for liberal/capitalist community has room for a limited conception of politics. Foreign policy making often transcends narrow interests. Domestic issues like civil rights involve matters of principle that also transcend interest bargaining.[93] People sometimes pursue a national good, most evidently during wartime, but also at other times, as during the Civil Rights movement.[94]

Bellah associates this alternative vision of community with Ronald Reagan. Reagan certainly represents a bridge with the past, a "community of memory" of the sort that *Habits* espouses.[95] His political credo encourages the economic energy that Tocqueville saw as the animating feature of democracy in

---

89   Bellah, *Habits*, p. 201.

90   *ibid.*, p. 200. Robert Lane also reports that Americans view the market as more "fair and wise" than political processes; see Lane, "Market Justice," p. 385.

91   Bellah, *Habits*, pp. 201–202.

92   *ibid.*, p. 202.

93   Bellah notes, at page 252 of *Habits*, that the civil rights movement drew on "strength and vitality still latent in the sense of the public good Americans have inherited." Well it did, until it turned into claims for affirmative action and special privileges which a majority of American oppose.

94   "But social movements quickly lose their moral edge if they are conceived as falling into special pleading, as when the Civil Rights movement was transformed into 'Black Power.' Then we are back in the only semilegitimate realm of the politics of interest." See Bellah, *Habits*, pp. 202–203.

95   *ibid.*, p. 263.

America.[96] But he links this energy with traditional groups like the family. "Work and family are the center of our lives, the foundation of our dignity as a free people."[97] And Reagan links economic self-support with a call for voluntarism: "It's time to reject the notion that advocating government programs is a form of personal charity. Generosity is a reflection of what one does with his or her resources – and not what he or she advocates the government do with everyone's money."[98]

If we leave aside Bellah's poorly substantiated claims that liberal capitalism in America is self-destructing, we might turn from his transformative program and consider other ways of invigorating opportunities for association and participation within a liberal-capitalist framework. If voluntary association is important for promoting a self-reliant, energetic citizenry, then we should be willing to accept some inefficiency in the delivery of some public benefits for the sake of providing opportunities for the exercise of the capacity for spontaneous association.

Since state and local governments provide more numerous, varied, and accessible opportunities for participation than the federal government, a concern with the popular capacity for self-government provides a reason to favor concentrating political activity at the lowest level of government possible. Perhaps we should resist, for example, the progressive federalization of education, a traditional preserve of state and local governments, and a great source of local concern and involvement.

Of course, one might worry that a "new federalism" could become a front for the old states-rights opposition to the Bill of Rights. One way to help insure that individuals will continue to be able to appeal to the federal government for protection of

---

96   In the relative prosperity of the last several years, people's satisfaction with their own lives and the state of the union has, according to some measures at least, been quite high. *The Gallup Report* § 246, March 1986, informs us that, when asked whether they are satisfied or dissatisfied "with the way things are going in the United States at this time," the ratio of responses was 66–30% in March of 1986, as compared with 12–84% in August of 1979. These figures vary considerably from one month to another, and the latter figure is a real low point, but the change has been substantial and is closely related to people's financial outlook.

97   Bellah, *Habits*, p. 263.

98   *ibid.*, p. 263.

their basic constitutional rights would be to avoid linking federalism with judicial restraint. Judges actively committed to the enforcement of individual rights might themselves reconsider the constitutional limitations on the powers of Congress.

Article 1, Section 8 of the Constitution enumerates Congress's powers, but that enumeration has become all but a dead letter. There enumerated powers speak to the legitimacy of national policies regarding commerce and national security broadly understood. Section 8 concludes with an "elastic clause": Congress may "make all laws necessary and proper for carrying into execution the foregoing powers. . . ." But the very fact that powers are enumerated and means sometimes specified implies that some things not enumerated must be beyond Congress's power. Article 1 provides judges with a critical perspective for examining the legitimacy of further federal encroachments on the political responsibilities of states and localities.[99]

Voluntarism speaks to the need for a citizenry capable of energetic, spontaneous action. Federalism speaks to the value of opportunities to participate in self-government.[100] And liberal constitutionalism provides a vision of the good of our political whole: it attempts to preserve the overarching norms of mutual respect for basic liberal rights that makes ours a union of liberal communities. The principles of liberal constitutionalism are, of course, more abstract than the principles of communities united around particular religious, ethnic, or local visions. But liberal constitutionalism has helped promote an open, diverse, tolerant, and prosperous national community.

Is liberal constitutionalism a mere legal framework, incapable of constituting a polity united by a shared identity? The uncommon patriotism of Americans, focused on our constitutional heritage, suggests that an ongoing historical struggle for the establishment and extension of liberal values

[99]   I deal with these issues at somewhat greater length in *The New Right v. The Constitution*, 2nd ed. (Washington, DC: Cato Institute, 1987); much more needs to be said.

[100]   Once liberals recognize that the preservation of our constitutional arrangements depends on a certain active quality of citizenship, they should take more seriously the principle of "subsidiarity," discussed in John Finnis, *Natural Law and Natural Rights*, (Oxford: Oxford University Press, 1980), p. 146 and passim.

can create and support a shared and robust identity, one that leaves room for certain norms of universal respect and critical reflection on more particular attachments.[101]

We should, in any case, be leery of attachments which displace critical reflection by constituting one's identity too fully or deeply. Liberal constitutionalism embraces a kind of integration, but not one that seeks to overcome all divisions and tensions within individual lives or society as a whole. We live in a diverse society, situated in a world composed of a dizzying array of cultural and religious communities. We need, in our political arrangements with one another and with other societies, to cultivate not an exclusive attachment to our own ways, but a reflective willingness to pay others their due. Liberal justice, established through our constitutional structures, emphasizes the importance of a reflective respect for legitimate diversity. But one whose character is too "thickly" constituted by more narrowly partisan commitments may lose precisely the ability to distance the self from one's "own kind." and with it the ability to respect those who are different.

All of this suggests (albeit quite sketchily) a certain division of political responsibilities, and a three-pronged program to promote liberal virtues, citizenship, and community: greater emphasis on voluntarism to promote citizen initiative, federalism to beef up the possibilities for local diversity and participation, and a national politics of rights enforcement (and certain limited common ends like national security) to protect the liberal right to choose.

III. A Tocquevillean Perspective

Bellah depicts himself as embracing and extending the project of Tocqueville's *Democracy in America*. But does *Habits* preserve the central features of Tocqueville's analysis of democratic capitalism? I would suggest not: in two crucial respects, *Democracy in America* lends support to the model of voluntary community that I have advanced as an alternative to Bellah's egalitarian/communitarian vision.

First, Tocqueville understood that liberal rights in a free market order provide Americans with a vision of the political whole that is uniquely "graspable" by average people, because

---

[101]   These themes are discussed at much greater length in my 'Liberal Virtues'.

it is not far removed from their interests. Second, Tocqueville's discussion suggests that a liberal vision of economic independence and voluntary community helps sustain self-government by speaking not only to our interests, but also to our pride: it speaks to our pride by cultivating self-esteem based on individual responsibility, earned achievement, and voluntary action.[102]

Tocqueville was not an uncritical friend of democratic capitalism, but he certainly perceived the particular virtues of a liberal form of democracy. Free enterprise disperses power and sets property in motion.[103] It animates the ambition of every man by holding out the prospect of economic betterment. Tocqueville argued that the last thing democracies need to worry about is the old fear of being consumed by the heat of demagogic passion or anarchy. The danger, rather, is the loosening of individual attachments to those decentralized institutions and associations that support individuality by bolstering personal self-confidence in the face of mass opinion and a centralizing, paternalistic state. "Breathless cupidity" might, indeed, consume the mind of democratic man, were it not for the existence of a complex variety of mechanisms that check, constrain, temper, and broaden the pursuit of self-interest in America: local self-government, voluntary associations, religion, respect for rights, law, and education, the federal Constitution, and family life. All of these support liberal democracy by warding off its worst tendency: personal isolation and anxiety leading to the passive acquiescence to a "soft despotism."

Associations mediate men's relations with, and strengthen them in the face of, "public opinion": that form of majority tyranny that "leaves the body alone and goes straight for the soul."[104] Association relieves the nervous anxiety that forms beneath the restless animation and uncertainty of vast, ever-changing market societies. People need, on Tocqueville's

---

[102]   As Harvey C. Mansfield, Jr.'s, recent excellent discussion of American conservatism suggests, Bellah is not alone is failing to take adequate account of the interplay of interests and pride that helps sustain liberal constitutionalism; see "Pride versus Interest in American Conservatism Today," *Government and Opposition*, vol. 22, no. 2 (Spring 1987), pp. 194–205.

[103]   Tocqueville, *Democracy*, p. 52.

[104]   *ibid.*, p. 255.

account, the stable moorings of religious belief, a "caring" sphere of family life, and a variety of ties to intermediate groups to sustain their confidence in their own ability to manage and direct their individuality – an individuality that, for Tocqueville, is far more fragile than that found in Mill's classic defense of liberty.[105]

Associative supports for individuality help nurture the capacity for, and confidence in, self-government, broadly understood as governing one's own life and participating in the management of politics. Trust in one's capacity for self-government is necessary to sustain liberty because, without self-trust, anxiety-ridden individuals will be all too willing to choose equality in a safe and secure slavery, handing power over to a paternalistic state that promises to manage their interests better than they can themselves. By failing actively to exercise their capacity for "self-government," Tocqueville suggests, people will lose confidence in that capacity and will cease to insist on their right to freedom.

But the collapse of self-government is as much a triumph of integration as the failure of it. Tocqueville's good form of democracy is characterized by something more ethically substantial than "integration" or "community"; it is characterized by liberty. Not, to be sure, mere "negative" liberty, but liberty as the realized, exercised, self-confident capacity for self-direction and self-government, exercised through economic activity, politics, and associations. The confident sense of one's capacity for self-government sustains the demand for actual political liberty and independence.

The virtues prompted by liberal capitalism, then, help sustain liberal self-government by addressing man's interests, and gently turning these outward toward the good of larger wholes. People take an interest in property rights partly because they have some property; they take an interest in local

[105] The contrasts between Mill and Tocqueville (on religion, for example) are striking. The confidence, so striking in Mill, in an inner core of individuality needing only to be liberated and stimulated by diversity in order to flourish is lacking in Tocqueville. Compare Tocqueville's discussion in *Democracy*, pp. 429–436 with John Stuart Mill, *On Liberty* (New York: Norton, 1975), pp. 27–38 and 46–50. And for an interesting similarity with Tocqueville, see Adam Smith's discussion of religious sects in *An Inquiry into the Nature and Causes of the Wealth of Nations*, ed. R. H. Campbell, A. S. Skinner, and W. B. Todd (Oxford: Oxford University Press, 1979), vol. 2, pp. 794–796.

government because everyone has an interest in the mundane concerns of local governments, such as roads and schools. Tocqueville seeks to contain and shape economic self-interest in a variety of ways; he does not seek to deny "self interest rightly understood."[106] And so, "In the United States there is hardly any talk of the beauty of virtue. But they maintain that virtue is useful and prove it every day."[107]

Indeed, far from disparaging the profit motive, Tocqueville praises the character of the entrepreneur as holding out a model of virtue and honor appropriate to democratic ages:

> The American will describe as noble and estimable ambition which our medieval ancestors would have called base cupidity. He would consider as blind and barbarous frenzy that ardor for conquest and warlike spirit which led the latter every day into new battles. In the United States fortunes are easily lost and gained again. The country is limitless and full of inexhaustible resources. . . . Boldness in industrial undertakings is the chief cause of their rapid progress, power, and greatness. . . . Such a people is bound to look with favor on boldness in industry and honor it. . . . The Americans, who have turned rash speculation into a sort of virtue, can in no case stigmatise those who are rash.[108]

Indeed, the associative zeal of Americans, as Tocqueville portrays it, is an extension of the same brash power, the same "spirit of liberty," that animates the entrepreneur. In both cases people are motivated by tangible, "local" benefits, whether profits in the one case, or good schools and good roads in the other.[109] "He trusts fearlessly in his own powers, which seem to him sufficient for everything." When such a man conceives an idea for public improvement, "It does not come into his head to appeal to public authority for its help. He publishes his plan, offers to carry it out, summons other individuals to aid his efforts, and personally struggles against all obstacles."[110] Here, then, Tocqueville speaks not only to the interests, but also the pride that energetic, enterprising men take in the active exercise

106   Tocqueville, *Democracy*, p. 526.

107   *ibid.*, p. 525.

108   *ibid.*, p. 622.

109   *ibid.*, p. 92.

110   *ibid.*, p. 95.

of their powers: pride, Tocqueville says, is the "vice" that most needs to be nurtured in democratic peoples.[111] If Tocqueville is right, it makes sense not to separate economic energy and voluntary effort on behalf of shared goods, but to promote them together, recognizing that they combine to promote an ideal of virtue accessible to a free democratic nation.

It is, of course, absolutely crucial to Tocqueville's whole scheme that the individual become active in conditions of real opportunity, where "the idea of progress comes naturally into each man's mind," and where "the desire to rise swells in every heart at once."[112] And the crucial background condition of this attitude is faith in the attainability of advancement through personal effort: "Nowhere does he see any limit placed by nature to human endeavor; in his eyes something which does not exist is just something that has not been tried yet." The active liberal citizen, as Tocqueville depicts him, could not flourish in the zero-sum society, since to sustain his energy he needs actually to see the results of his efforts, and that means he needs a growing economy replete with opportunity.

In its preoccupation with distributive justice, with the "fair sharing" of "social wealth," and its anxiety in the face of change with no promise of growth, the zero-sum society would seem much more conducive to the "debased taste for equality, which leads the weak to want to drag the strong down to their level."[113]

Indeed, the political ambitions of *Habits* could not animate and sustain the sort of energy that Tocqueville discusses. Tocqueville's citizens are animated by plans for local roads, schools, church projects; their "ambition is both eager and constant, but in general it does not look very high. For the most part life is eagerly spent in coveting small prizes within reach."[114] Local activism gives men a tangible sense of accomplishment. But how many people could feel they are successfully participating in shaping large issues of economic justice and social planning? In transforming a national "social ecology"? The remoteness of the large "structural" economic issues that worry Bellah and his colleagues argues against their

[111] *ibid.*, p. 632.
[112] *ibid.*, p. 629.
[113] *ibid.*, p. 57.
[114] *ibid.*, p. 629.

ability to engage personal ambition. And were ambitions engaged, the diversity of groups in our society, each with its own vision of an ideal order, will help ensure that the energies of most will be frustrated.

Tocqueville, finally, gives a central place to voluntarism. It is especially valuable, says Tocqueville, for people to act voluntarily to promote public projects because relying on government discourages direct popular attention to, and responsibility for, their own affairs.[115] And so, anticipating Brian Palmer, Tocqueville warns that government action will "crowd out" private initiative: "The more government takes the place of associations, the more will individuals lose the idea of forming associations and need the government to come to their help. This is a vicious circle of cause and effect."[116]

Voluntary association does not, for Tocqueville, serve our interests more effectively than government action. Centralized administration could achieve many common purposes more efficiently than private activity. The case for voluntarism speaks not to our interests (not, at least, to a "cowardly love of immediate pleasures") but to our pride as free, independent persons, doing things for ourselves.[117] Again, only in exercising our capacity for free action with others do we retain confidence in our capacity for freedom.

Self-trust is undermined when the government does things for people that they might do for themselves: "It would resemble parental authority if, fatherlike, it tried to prepare its charges for a man's life, but on the contrary, it only tries to keep them in perpetual childhood."[118] Whether government produces some genuine "public good" or not is irrelevant: Tocqueville's point is that the pride of free men is undermined by being provided for, by being made happy rather than securing their own happiness: "it daily makes the exercise of free choice less useful and rarer, restricts the activity of free will within a narrower compass, and little by little robs each citizen of the proper use of his own faculties."[119] An active central government may promote people's interests, but in doing so

115   *ibid.*, pp. 514–517.

116   *ibid.*, p. 515; and see pp. 681–683.

117   *ibid.*, p. 645.

118   *ibid.*, p. 692.

119   *ibid.*, p. 692.

too readily it will undermine their pride, their self-confident independence, their insistence on liberty, thus promoting the 'soft despotism' Tocqueville feared.

Tocqueville's insights were fashioned over 150 years ago: applying his ideas to contemporary America is, obviously, not unproblematic. The economy has changed drastically since Tocqueville's day: the labor force has shifted away from agriculture and small towns to urban manufacturing and now toward a service economy. Families are no longer the same sources of stability they once were.

Tocqueville did foresee certain changes, such as the weakening of religion. In response he stressed that rights were all the more important: if, he said, "you do not succeed in linking the idea of rights to personal interest, which provides the only stable point in the human heart, what other means will be left to you to govern the world, if not fear?"[120] It must be admitted, as well, that Tocqueville feared that the rise of great industries would create a permanent and deep inequality. Like Adam Smith, he feared that workers incessantly performing monotonous tasks would become degraded and intellectually enervated: "he no longer belongs to himself, but to his choosen calling. . . . As the principle of the division of labor is ever more completely applied, the worker becomes weaker, more limited, and more dependent."[121] The worker loses, in short, his capacity for self-government.[122]

Liberty, then, is threatened by the loss of the confident capacity for self-government: the feeling of impotence before large forces that makes people feel incapable of running their own affairs.[123] If is precisely excessive attention to personal interests that makes people too anxious and weak, and too attentive to their immediate comforts, to sustain free self-government.

For Tocqueville the survival of liberty depends upon the possession of a sufficient measure of the right kind of virtue: virtue as the insistence on one's equal rights as a chooser. This

[120] ibid., p. 239.

[121] ibid., p. 556. And see Adam Smith's discussion in *Wealth of Nations*, pp. 782, 787–788.

[122] On the other hand, Tocqueville defended the Bank of the United States, and argued that opposition to its power was motivated by the levelling equality he feared; *Democracy*, pp. 178, 388–389.

[123] ibid., p. 642.

virtue is not of a very "high" sort: it is not a saintly submission of self and interests to the divine, or the heroic identification of one's interests with the glory of the polity. It is self-interest elevated and shaped by the attachment to freedom and its active exercise. All of the supports for liberty that Tocqueville praises (local self-government, free association, law and courts) are designed to retain that measure of virtue that free democratic peoples are capable of. And that measure is "love of independence"[124] and liberty:

> I am firmly convinced that one cannot found an aristocracy anew in this world, but I think that associations of plain citizens can compose very rich, influential, and powerful bodies, in other words, aristocratic bodies.[125]

I do not mean to argue, in any case, that Tocqueville's analysis and prescriptions should be applied wholesale to the United States. But if Tocqueville's depiction of the psychological condition of citizens of a liberal capitalist polity remains important (as I believe it does), then economic freedom needs to be supplemented with opportunities for voluntary association and local participation. The liberal virtues compatible with, and not far removed from, the energies unleashed by economic liberty, find their expression in the American ethos of voluntary community that was advanced above as an alternative to Bellah.

Conclusion

The suggestions advanced in this article, while far from complete or conclusive, speak largely against Bellah's positive programme for the reformation of our economic system and political culture.[126] This is not to say, however, that Bellah's concern with the social supports and cultural setting of liberal individuality is frivolous. In their preoccupation with arguments about rights and liberty, liberals too often neglect the

---

[124]   *ibid.*, p. 667.

[125]   *ibid.*, p. 697.

[126]   I am all too conscious that much more needs to be said about the variety of ways one might attempt to support the popular capacity for self-government. Joshua Cohen, for example, provides some very powerful arguments for a bevy of measures I would want to resist; see his "The Economic Basis of Deliberative Democracy," *Social Philosophy and Policy*, vol. 6, no. 2 (Spring 1988).

forms of virtue and citizenship necessary to maintain liberal democracy. If Tocqueville's depiction of the human condition in liberal capitalist societies is still cogent, then the readiness to associate spontaneously to accomplish common projects and the willingness to participate in the practices of self-government are among the virtues that liberal polities depend upon.

Liberal constitutionalism presupposes and exercises capacities for reflective self-government that embody a genuine form of virtue. Taking pride in the active exercise of one's capacity for self-government (broadly understood as running one's own life and taking a hand in politics) is the higher form of life that democratic citizens are capable of. Liberals have a hard time discussing "high" and "low" forms of life of character.[127] The levelled understanding of personality deployed by most liberals finds its alternative in Tocqueville.

Liberal theorists are often equally unwilling to make use of the idea of pride. But without the idea of pride it would be hard to appreciate the stubborn insistence on choice and independence that Bellah and his colleagues found in America, and that Tocqueville emphasized 150 years ago. Contemporary studies confirm that participation in the market and small primary groups are the principle sources of self-esteem for Americans.[128] If Tocqueville was right, then it is crucial to displace the idea of interests as the sole support for liberty: liberty may not be in our "interests"; it may be the hard road, the road that requires effort, discipline, and self-control, a road that is sometime the less efficient means to achieving satisfaction, the road that requires the acceptance of a certain amount of risk, uncertainty, and material inequality.

Liberals who take Tocqueville seriously should be concerned about people's connections with larger wholes that sustain their

---

127 Precursors of certain variants of today's liberal thought, such as Hobbes and Bentham, heaped scorn and cynicism on the idea that qualitative discriminations could be made about the value of different ways of life. The hegemony of these ideas is also transmitted through the influence of economics: *homo economicus* has interests only, and his motto is *de gustibus non est disputandum*. Bentham's famous maxims are illustrative: "pushpin is as good as poetry," and "better a pig satisfied than Socrates dissatisfied." See his *The Principles of Morals and Legislation* (New York: Hafner, 1948) and Thomas Hobbes, *Leviathan* (Harmondsworth: Penguin, 1981).

128 See Lane, "Market Justice," p. 385, and "Government and Self-Esteem," *Political Theory*, vol. 10 (1982), pp. 5–31.

allegiance while supporting their individuality, their liberty, and their capacity for self-government. It is not enough to hold out a vision of selfless social harmony that is incapable of attracting the energetic support of people as we know them. But neither is it enough to preserve people's economic freedom if they lose, as a consequence, the strength to insist on liberty. Contemporary defenders of democratic virtue (like Bellah) need to think more about interests; both they and liberal skeptics need to think more about pride and virtue.

The strongest defense of liberalism and the free market must be complex. It would stress liberalism's unique ability to combine interests, freedom, pride, and virtue – a kind of virtue that is not especially noble, but that is attainable and conducive to peace and prosperity. That is how I have interpreted Tocqueville's claim: liberal virtue equals the proud exercise of the capacity for self-government in public and private life. By refusing to take this claim seriously, defenders of capitalism may surrender their most effective weapons against communitarian and republican critics of liberalism.

Political Science, Harvard University

LIBERALISM AND THE POLITICIZATION
OF ETHNICITY
Will Kymlicka

Most liberal democracies exhibit cultural pluralism, that is, citizens of the same country belong to various cultural communities, and so speak different languages, read different literatures, practice different customs. Most contemporary liberal political philosophy, on the other hand, assumes that countries are "nation-states". Citizens of the same state are assumed to share a common nationality, speak the same language, develop the same culture. My concern in this paper is how liberals have adapted their principles to deal with cultural pluralism.

1. *Multination States and Polyethnic States*

There are many different forms of cultural pluralism, and many different ways of labelling them, so some preliminary distinctions are required. There are two main sources of cultural pluralism. One source is the co-existence within a given state of more than one culture, where "culture" means a historical community, more or less institutionally complete, occupying a given territory or homeland, sharing a distinct language and history. A "culture" in this sense is closely related to the idea of a "nation" or of a "people" – indeed, these terms are often defined in terms of each other. A country which contains more than one culture is, therefore, not a nation-state but a multination state, and the smaller cultures form "national minorities", or "minority cultures". The incorporation of different cultures into a single state may be involuntary, as occurs when one cultural community is invaded and conquered by another, or when its homeland is simply overrun by colonizing settlers who maintain their old culture. But the formation of a multination state may also arise voluntarily, when different cultures agree to form a federation for their mutual benefit.

The second source of cultural pluralism is immigration. A country will exhibit cultural pluralism if it accepts large numbers of individuals and families from other cultures as immigrants, and allows them to maintain some of their ethnic particularity. Under these circumstances, immigrants are expected to integrate into the public institutions of the existing culture(s), but they are not required or expected to shed all aspects of their distinctive heritage and assimilate entirely to existing cultural norms. Immigrants may associate with each other to pursue their ethnic preferences, but such groups are not nations, and do not constitute cultures. Their distinctiveness is manifested in their private lives, and does not affect their institutional integration: they still participate within the dominant culture and speak the dominant language. A country with extensive immigration of this sort will have a number of "ethnic groups" as loosely aggregated subcultures, and so exhibit "polyethnicity".

A single country may be both multinational (as a result of colonizing, conquest, or confederation) and polyethnic (as a result of immigration). Indeed, all of these patterns are present in Canada – the Indians were overrun by French settlers, the French were conquered by the English – although the current relationship between the two can be seen as a voluntary federation, and both the English and French have accepted immigrants who are allowed to partially maintain their ethnic particularity. So Canada is both multinational and polyethnic. Those labels are less popular than the term "multicultural". But that term can be confusing, precisely because it is ambiguous between multinational and polyethnic. Thus some French-Canadians have opposed the Canadian government's "multiculturalism" policy because they think it reduces their claims of nationhood to the level of mere ethnicity. Other people had the opposite fear (or hope) that the policy was intended to treat immigrant groups as nations, and hence support the development of institutionally complete cultures alongside the French and English. In fact, neither fear was justified, since "multiculturalism" is a policy of supporting polyethnicity within the national institutions of the English and French cultures. As Burnet says,

> culture, including language, can only be maintained and developed when it is employed in all areas of life. So far as

this is so, it cannot have been the intention of the framers of the policy to promote multiculturalism: that there was to be a bilingual - English and French - framework makes this evident. Rather, the policy makers wished to endorse polyethnicity.[1]

Since "multicultural" invites this sort of confusion, I will use the terms "multinational" and "polyethnic" to refer to the two main forms of cultural pluralism.

In culturally plural countries, an important area of conflict concerns the way ethnicity should be recognized by the state, e.g., which languages should be recognized in the parliaments, bureaucracies and courts: should each nation or ethnic group have publicly funded cultural institutions and education in their mother-tongue; should state benefits be distributed by national or ethnic organizations; should political offices be reserved for members of particular nations or ethnic groups, or distributed in accordance with a principle of national or ethnic proportionality; should nations have veto power over culture-affecting decisions on immigration, communication, education, etc.?

These are all questions about what we might call the "politicization of ethnicity". We can distinguish two broad categories of political claims, to correspond with the two categories of cultural pluralism. In multination states, the component nations are inclined to demand some form of political autonomy or territorial jurisdiction so as to ensure the free development of their culture. At the extreme, nations may wish to secede, if they think their self-determination is impossible within the larger state.[2] In polyethnic states, ethnic groups demand the right to freely express their particularity (e.g., in private ethnic associations and presses), without it hampering their success in the economic and political institutions of the dominant culture, and are inclined to demand state

---

1   J. Burnet, "Multiculturalism, Immigration, and Racism: A Comment on the Canadian Immigration and Population Study" (1975) 7 Canadian Ethnic Studies 35 at 36.

2   For surveys of minority rights claims worldwide, see J. Sigler, *Minority Rights: A Comparative Analysis* (Westport: Greenwood Press, 1983); V. Van Dyke, "The Individual, the State, and Ethnic Communities in Political Theory" (1977) 29 World Politics 343; F. Caportorti, *Study on the Rights of Persons Belonging to Ethnic, Religious and Linguistic Minorities*, UN Doc. E/CN 4/Sub.2/384 Rev. 1 (New York: United Nations, 1979).

support for these actions (e.g., cultural exchanges and festivals, ethnic studies in schools, bilingual education). At the extreme, ethnic groups may demand that political offices be reserved for their members according to their proportion of the population, and that state benefits be distributed through ethnic organizations.[3]

2. The Current Liberal Orthodoxy

These questions form much of the substance of the political life of pluralist countries, both in the day-to-day administration of state policy, and in the historical moments of constitutional commitments and crises. Yet they are almost entirely ignored in contemporary liberal political philosophy. Liberal philosophers rarely discuss the difference between nation-states and polyethnic or multination states, and apparently do not think of cultural plurality as raising important questions for liberal politics. Despite this theoretical vacuum, a certain view about the salience of ethnicity has come to be accepted as the orthodox liberal position. And while this view is rarely articulated explicitly, we can construct its basic outline.

Contemporary liberals, insofar as they discuss the issue, treat culture in the same way as religion, as something which people should be free to pursue in their private life, but which is not the concern of the state. Just as liberalism precludes the establishment of an official religion, so too there cannot be official cultures which have preferred status over other possible cultural allegiances. In a liberal society "the state sets before itself the model that [cultural] group membership is purely private, a shifting matter of personal choice and degree".[4] The state does not oppose the freedom of people to express their particular cultural attachments, but nor does it nurture such expression – rather, to use Glazer's phrase, it responds with "benign neutrality". Ethnic groups "are protected against discrimination and prejudice, and they are given the liberty, as

---

[3] A comprehensive quota system is ultimately incompatible with genuine polyethnicity, for it reproduces within every group the same educational and employment patterns, whereas "historically specific cultures necessarily produce historically specific patterns of interest and work" [M. Walzer, "Pluralism in Political Perspective" in M. Walzer, ed., The Politics of Ethnicity (Cambridge: Harvard University Press, 1982) at 23-24].

[4] N. Glazer, "Individual Rights Against Group Rights", in A. Tay and E. Kamenka, eds. Human Rights (London: Edward Arnold, 1978) 87 at 98.

all individuals and groups are, to maintain whatever part of an ethnic heritage or a distinct identity they wish, as long as that does not transgress on the rights of others."[5] But their efforts are purely private, and it is not the place of public agencies to attach legal identities or disabilities to cultural membership or ethnic identity. The state adheres to the "principle of the separation between state and society which makes religion and ethnic communities a voluntary and private matter. The separation between state and society in this sense is what liberal democracy is all about."[6] Since ethnicity is a private matter, liberals tend to oppose "any legal or governmental recognition" of ethnic groups, and prohibit the use of "ethnic criteria" in the distribution of rights, resources, and duties.[7]

There is an immediate problem, however, with official languages. Surely the state is giving at least partial establishment to a culture when it decides which language is to be used in public schooling, or in the provision of state services. This is a significant embarrassment for the "benign neutrality" view, and it is remarkable how rarely language rights are discussed in contemporary liberal theory. But there have been attempts to reconcile official languages with benign neutrality. According to Knopff, language has two functions: it can function as the vehicle for the transmission of a particular culture, but it can also function as "a culturally neutral, or utilitarian means of communication which allows those of different cultures to participate in the same political community."[8] By placing the

[5] N. Glazer, *Ethnic Dilemmas: 1964-1982* (Cambridge: Harvard University Press, 1983) at 124.

[6] H. Brotz, "Multuculturalism in Canada: A Muddle" (1980) 6 Canadian Public Policy 41 at 44. Cf. Glazer, *supra*, note 5 at 124.

[7] M. Gordon, "Toward a General Theory of Racial and Ethnic Group Relations", in N. Glazer and D. Moynihan, eds. *Ethnicity, Theory and Experience* (Cambridge: Harvard University Press, 1975) 84 at 105. *See also* J. Porter, "Ethnic Pluralism in Canada", in *ibid* 267 at 295; P. van den Berghe, "Protection of Ethnic Minorities: A Critical Appraisal" in R. Wirsing, ed., *Protection of Ethnic Minorities: Comparative Perspectives* (New York, Pergamon Press, 1981) 343 at 347; J. Ajzenstat, "Liberalism and Assimilation: Lord Durham Revisited" in S. Brooks, ed. *Political Thought in Canada: Contemporary Perspectives* (Toronto, Irwin Publishers, 1984) 239 at 251-52.

[8] R. Knopff, "Language and Culture in the Canadian Debate: The Battle of the White Papers" (1979) 6 Canadian Review of Studies in Nationalism 66 at 67; cf. D. Segal, "Nationalism, Comparatively Speaking" (1988) 1 Journal of Historical Sociology at 312.

emphasis on the utilitarian function, governments "can enact official languages without at the same time legislating official cultures . . . in enacting 'official languages', one does not necessarily imply that the cultures which these languages transmit and represent thereby become 'official cultures' ".[9] Culture "remains a purely private affair", for while English and French have official backing as the "utilitarian" languages, all languages compete on equal terms for "cultural" allegiance. It is the

> task of the individual members of a culture to show the excellence of their product on the cultural marketplace, as it were. If they succeed, the language of that culture will become attractive to others. . . . If [a] culture, and hence, language, cannot show itself to be worthy of choice in the light of standards of the good, then it deserves to disappear.[10]

Although this distinction between the utilitarian and cultural functions of language is questionable, we now have the basic outline of the current liberal orthodoxy on ethnicity. Liberals have invoked the ideal of benign neutrality in attacking the entire range of proposals for the politicization of ethnicity in Canada, whether it be the national rights claims of French Canadians,[11] the national and aboriginal rights claims of the Inuit and Indian peoples,[12] or the demands of ethnic groups to

9   Knopff, *supra*, note 8 at 67.

10   *ibid.* at 70.

11   R. Knopff, "Liberal Democracy and the Challenge of Nationalism in Canadian Politics" (1982) 9 Canadian Review of Studies in Nationalism 23 at 29-39; J. Ajzenstat, *The Political Thought of Lord Durham* (Kingston: McGill-Queen's University Press, 1988) c. 8: F. L. Morton, "Group Rights Versus Individual Rights in the Charter: The Special Cases of Natives and the Quebecois" in N. Nevitte, A. Kornberg, eds. *Minorities and the Canadian State* (Oakville: Mosaic Press, 1985) 71 at 77-83.

12   Morton, *supra*, note 11 at 73-77; B. Schwartz, *First Principles, Second Thoughts: Aboriginal Peoples, Constitutional Reform and Canadian Statecraft* (Montreal: The Institute for Research on Public Policy, 1986) c. 1. Cf. M. Asch, *Home and Native Land: Aboriginal Rights and the Canadian Constitution* (Toronto: Methuen, 1984) at 75-88, 100-104; S. Weaver, "Federal Difficulties with Aboriginal Rights in Canada" in M. Boldt & J. Long, eds. *The Quest for Justice: Aboriginal Peoples and Aboriginal Rights* (Toronto: University of Toronto Press, 1985) at 141-42; G. Dacks, *A Choice of Futures: Politics in the Canadian North* (Toronto: Methuen, 1981) at 63-79; J. Ponting & R. Gibbins, *Out of Irrelevance: A Socio-political Introduction to Indian Affairs in Canada*

state benefits under the mutliculturalism policy.[13] This conflict between the requirements of liberalism and the demand for public recognition of cultural groups has led to a schizophrenia in the way Canadian politicians and courts deal with ethnicity. Our political culture and institutions recognize both liberal equality and minority rights, yet each has been weakened by the other.[14]

3. Ethnicity and the Liberal Tradition

But are liberals committed to this view of ethnicity? It is part of the current orthodoxy that liberals have always opposed politicizing ethnicity, and that demands for the political recognition of cultural groups are a recent and illiberal deviation from long-established liberal practice.[15] This is not true. Minority rights were an important part of liberal theory and practice between the world wars. Hobhouse, for example, said that "the more liberal statesmanship" of his day had recognized the necessity of minority rights to ensure "cultural equality".[16] There is more than one way to meet the legitimate demands of national minorities, but "[c]learly it is not achieved by equality of franchise. The smaller nationality does not merely want equal rights with others. It stands out for a certain life of its own".[17] One manifestation of this liberal commitment was the minority protection scheme set up under the League of Nations for various European national minorities.

Some liberals gave a more qualified endorsement of minority rights, seeing them as consistent with, but not required by, liberalism. Hoernle, for example, thought that "assimilation",

(Toronto: Butterworth, 1980) at 327-31; R. Barsh & J. Henderson, "Aboriginal Rights, Treaty Rights and Human Rights: Indian Tribes and Constitutional Renewal" (1982) 17 Journal of Canadian Studies 53 at 69-70.

13 Brotz, *supra* note 6 at 44-45; L. Roberts & R. Clifton, "Exploring the Ideology of Multiculturalism" (1982) 8 Canadian Public Policy 88 at 90-93.

14 I discuss this tension in W. Kymlicka, *Liberalism, Community, and Culture* (Oxford: Oxford University Press, 1989) c. 7.

15 See, for example, Ajzenstat, *supra*, note 11 at 91-92.

16 L. T. Hobhouse, *Social Development: Its Nature and Conditions* (London: George Allen and Unwin, 1966) at 297, 299.

17 L. T. Hobhouse, *Social Evolution and Political Theory* (New York: Columbia University Press, 1928) at 146-47.

"separation", and "parallel development" were all consistent with the requirements of liberal equality, since "each offers a realization of the ideal of an 'area of liberty', or in other words, of a free society for free men".[18] But, like Hobhouse, he believed that developing the pluralist options was the greatest challenge facing English liberalism if its appeal was to move beyond the boundaries of its (culturally homogeneous) homeland.[19]

Some liberals did oppose minority rights, but not because of a commitment to the principle of "benign neutrality". Their concern was stability, not justice. They believed, with Mill, that free institutions are "next to impossible" in a multination state:

> Among a people without fellow-feeling, especially if they read and speak different languages, the united public opinion necessary to the workings of representative institutions cannot exist. . . . [It] is in general a necessary condition of free institutions that the boundaries of governments should coincide in the main with those of nationalities.[20]

For liberals like Mill, democracy is government "by the people", but self-rule is only possible if "the people" are "a people": a nation. The members of a democracy must share a sense of political allegiance, and common nationality was said to be a precondition of that allegiance. Thus T. H. Green argued that liberal democracy is only possible if people feel bound to the state by "ties derived from a common dwelling place with its associations, from common memories, traditions and customs, and from the common ways of feeling and thinking which a common language and still more a common literature embodies."[21] According to this stream of liberal

18 R. F. A. Hoernle, *South African Native Policy and the Liberal Spirit* (Cape Town: Lovedale Press, 1939) at 181.

19 Hoernle, *supra*, note 18 at 123-25, 136-8; Hobhouse, *supra*, note 17 at 146.

20 J. S. Mill, "Considerations on Representative Government" in H. Acton, ed., *Utilitarianism, Liberty, Representative Government* (London: J. M. Dent and Sons, 1972) 171 at 361, 363. But see Lord Acton's response that Mill's demand for homogeneity threatens liberty ["Nationality" in J. Figgis R. Laurence, eds. *The History of Freedom and Other Essays* (London: Macmillan, 1922), 270 at 285-90].

21 T. H. Green, *Lectures on the Principles of Political Obligation* (London: Longmans, Green & Co., 1941) at 130-31. *Cf.* P. Rich, "T. H. Green, Lord Scarman and the Issue of Ethnic Minority Rights in English Liberal Thought" (1987) 10 Ethnic and Racial Studies 149 at 155.

thought, since a free state must be a nation-state, national minorities must be dealt with by coercive assimilation or the redrawing of boundaries, not by minority rights.[22]

So the current liberal orthodoxy obscures the diversity of earlier liberal positions on minority rights. Notice also that *none* of these earlier positions endorses the current view that the state should treat ethnicity as a purely private matter. On the contrary, the first two views endorse the legal recognition of minority cultures, and the third rejects minority rights not because it rejects the idea of an official culture, but precisely because it believes there should only be *one* official culture.

This is just a quick sketch of the way many earlier liberals viewed ethnicity – a fuller account would probably reveal an even greater range of views. But we now have a rough sense of both the current orthodoxy and the range of earlier views it supplanted, and we can begin to look at the causes of this change. One possible explanation is that liberalism is only now working out the full implications of its "abstract individualism". Earlier liberals tacitly drew on pre-liberal ideas of culture, but modern liberals have been more consistent in their individualism, basing their theories on a conception of the individual as a solitary atom who is independent of, and prior to, her cultural environment. On this view, liberals ignore the political significance of cultural membership and ethnic identity because their individualism ignores its significance entirely. This explanation of the liberal view of ethnicity has become almost as much of an orthodoxy in the literature as the position it criticises,[23] and it is echoed in communitarian claims

22 Glazer, *supra*, note 5 at 298. The need for cultural homogeneity remains a much-debated issue. For a current representative of Mill's school, see P. van de Berghe, *The Ethnic Phenomenon* (New York: Elsevier, 1981) c 2. For the opposite view that cultural pluralism and minority rights help guarantee a free society, see Sigler, *supra* note 2 at 188–92.

23 E.G., J. Deganaar, "Nationalism, Liberalism, and Pluralism" in J. Butler, ed., *Democratic Liberalism in South Africa: Its History and Prospect* (Middletown: Wesleyan University Press, 1987) 236 at 242; F. Svensson, "Liberal Democracy and Group Rights: The Legacy of Individualism and its Impact on American Indian Tribes" (1979) 27 Political Studies 421 at 425; H. Adam, "The Failure of Political Liberalism" in H. Adam & H. Giliomee, eds. *Ethnic Power Mobilized: Can South Africa Change?* (New Haven: Yale University Press, 1979) 258 at 265–67; H. Dickie-Clark, "On the Liberal Definition of the South African Situation" in P. van den Berghe, ed., *The Liberal Dilemma in South Africa* (New York: St. Martin's Press, 1979) 48 at 51–52; P. Rich, "Liberalism and Ethnicity in South African Politics: 1921-1948" (1976) 35 African Studies 229 at 239–40.

that liberalism depends on a notion of the self which is unencumbered by social attachments, whose freedom is exercised precisely by abstracting itself from its cultural situation.[24]

I believe the explanation lies elsewhere. The new liberal orthodoxy is the result, not of the inexorable working out of liberalism's individualistic premises, but of the convergence of a number of post-way political changes. Three features of the post-war world have conspired to suppress or distort questions of ethnicity, and have led liberals to adopt a misplaced antagonism towards the politicization of ethnicity. These three factors are (a) disillusionment with the minority rights scheme of the League of Nations, (b) the American racial desegregation movement, and (c) the "ethnic revival" amongst immigrant groups in the United States. While none of these events or movements are distinctively Canadian, each has contributed to the formation of a new liberal orthodoxy that has been adopted, perhaps unwittingly, by Canadian liberals. I will discuss each of these in turn, to see how they have helped create this new liberal orthodoxy.

4. The Failure of the Minority Treaties

The first important change in liberal views came with the failure of the League's minority protection scheme, and its role in the outbreak of World War Two. The scheme gave international recognition to the German-speaking minorities in Czechoslovakia and Poland, and the Nazis encouraged them to make demands and lodge complaints against their governments. When the Polish and Czech governments were unwilling or unable to meet the escalating demands of their German minorities, the Nazis used this as a pretext for aggression. This Nazi manipulation of the League scheme, and the cooperation of the German minorities in it, created "a strong reaction against the concept of international protection" of national minorities. The "hard fact was that statesmen, generally backed by public opinion which was deeply impressed by the perfidy of irredentist and disloyal minorities, were disposed to

---

24   A. MacIntyre, *After Virtue* (London: Duckworth, 1981) c. 15; M. Sandel, *Liberalism and the Limits of Justice* (Cambridge: Cambridge University Press, 1982) at 150–65.

curtail, rather than to expand, the rights of minorities."[25] This curtailing of minority rights was done, not in the interest of justice, but by people "within whose frame of reference the interests of the national state ranked as supreme values. . . . [The majority nationality] has an interest in making the national state secure and its institutions stable, even at the cost of obliterating minority cultures and imposing an enforced homogeneity upon the population."[26]

This "frame of reference" is similar to the earlier liberal view that freedom requires cultural homogeneity, although it differs in emphasis. Whereas Mill and Green were concerned with domestic stability, post-war statesmen were primarily concerned with international peace. But the effect was the same – questions about the fairness of minority rights were subordinated to the higher demands of stability. There was an explicit desire to leave the issue of minority rights off the United Nations agenda, and the U.N. has only recently agreed to reconsider the legitimacy of minority rights claims.[27] The fear that national minorities will be disloyal (or simply apathetic) continues to inhibit discussion of the justice of these claims, both internationally and in the domestic politics of many countries.[28]

5. Racial Desegregation in the United States

The modern liberal rejection of minority rights began with worries about political stability, but it acquired the mantle of justice when it was linked to racial desegregation. In *Brown v Board of Education*, the American Supreme Court struck down the system of segregated educational facilities for black and

[25] I. Claude, *National Minorities: An International Problem* (Cambridge: Harvard University Press, 1955) at 57, 69.

[26] *supra*, note 25 at 80-81.

[27] L. Sohn, "The Rights of Minorities" in L. Henkin, ed., *The International Bill of Rights: The Covenant on Civil and Political Rights* (New York: Columbia University Press, 1981); P. Thornberry, "Is There a Phoenix in the Ashes? International Law and Minority Rights" (1980) 15 Texas International Law Journal 421.

[28] D. Maybury-Lewis, "Living in Leviathan: Ethnic Groups and the State" in Maybury-Lewis, ed., *The Prospects for Plural Societies* (Washington: American Ethnological Society, 1984) at 222-27; J. Clayton, "Internationally Uprooted People and the Transnational Protection of Minority Cultures" (1978) 24 New York Law School Review 125 at 138.

white children in the South. This decision, and the civil rights movement generally, had an enormous influence on American views of racial equality. The new model of racial justice was "colour-blind laws", replacing "separate but equal treatment", which was now seen as the paradigm of racial injustice. But the influence of *Brown* was soon felt in areas other than race relations, for it seemed to lay down a principle which was equally applicable to issues of ethnicity. According to this principle, injustice is a matter of arbitrary exclusion from the dominant institutions of society, and equality is a matter of non-discrimination and equal opportunity to participate. Viewed in this light, legislation providing separate institutions for minority cultures seems no different than the segregation of blacks. The natural extension of *Brown*, therefore, was to remove the separate status of minority cultures, and encourage their equal participation in mainstream society. This reasoning underlies the Canadian government's 1969 proposal to remove the special constitutional status of Indians,[29] and *Brown* was cited by the Canadian Supreme Court when striking down a law enacted under that status.[30] *Brown*'s formula for racial justice was also invoked against the rights of American Indians, and the rights of national minorities in international law.[31]

But the actual judgment in *Brown* does not support this application of the colour-blind formula to the rights of national minorities. The Court was simply not addressing the issue of national rights, like the right of a culture to the autonomous institutions needed to be able to freely develop itself within a multination state. Segregationists were not claiming that whites and blacks formed different cultures with different languages and literatures. On the contrary, the whole burden of their case

29 "Statement of the Government of Canada on Indian Policy", in R. Bowles et al., eds., *The Indian: Assimilation, Integration or Separation?* (Scarborough: Prentice-Hall, 1972) 201 at 204 ("separate but equal services do not provide truly equal treatment") and at 202 ("the ultimate aim of removing the specific references to Indians from the constitution . . . is a goal to be kept constantly in view").

30 *Regina* v. *Drybones* [1970] S.C.R. 282 at 300 ("The social situations in *Brown* v. *Board of Education* and in the instant case are, of course, very different, but the basic philosophic concept is the same.")

31 R. Barsh and J. Henderson, *The Road: Indian Tribes and Political Liberty* (Berkeley: University of California Press, 1980) at 241–48; V. Van Dyke, *Human Rights, Ethnicity and Discrimination* (Vernon, Conn.: Greenwood Press, 1985) at 194.

was that the education received by blacks in their segregated facilities was *identical* to that of whites. The question was whether racial groups could be given separate facilities so long as the facilities were identical. And the Court ruled that *under those circumstances* segregation was inherently unequal, since it would be seen as a "badge of inferiority", as a sign of racism.

Nothing in the judgment warrants the claim that national rights are incompatible with liberal equality. Indeed, the judgment, examined more closely, may argue *for* the recognition of national rights. Consider the situation of American Indians, whose separate institutions came under attack after *Brown*:

Where blacks have been forcibly *excluded* (segregated) from white society by law, Indians – aboriginal peoples with their own cultures, languages, religions and territories – have been forcibly *included* (integrated) into that society by law. That is what [is] meant by coercive assimilation – the practice of compelling, through submersion, an ethnic, cultural and linguistic minority to shed its uniqueness and identity and mingle with the rest of society.[32]

Integrated education for the Indians, like segregated education for the blacks, is a "badge of inferiority" for it fails "to recognize the importance and validity of the Indian community".[33] In fact, the "integration of Indian children in white-dominated schools had the same negative educational and emotional effects which segregation was held to have in *Brown*", so the "underlying principle" which struck down the segregation of blacks (i.e. that racial classifications harmful to a minority are prohibited) should also strike down legislated integration of Indians.[34]

The point is not that Indians don't need protection against racism. But whereas racism against blacks comes from the denial by whites that blacks are full members of the community, racism against Indians comes primarily from the denial by whites that Indians are distinct peoples with their own cultures and communities. Unfortunately, the centrality of the

---

[32]   M. Gross, "Indian Control for Quality Indian Education" (1973) 49 North Dakota Law Review 237 at 244.

[33]   *Ibid.* at 242.

[34]   *Ibid.* at 245, 248.

246 Group Rights

civil rights movement has prevented people from seeing the distinctive issues raised by the existence of national minorities.[35]

6. Polyethnicity and the American Ethnic Revival

The belief that minority rights are unfair and divisive was confirmed, for many liberals, by their role in the ethnic revival which rocked the United States in the 1960's and 1970's. This revival began with the claim that it was legitimate (not "un-American") for ethnic groups to express their distinctive characteristics. At the time, the explicit aim of immigration policy was "anglo-conformity", i.e. converting immigrants to the cultural norms of the country's English heritage. Those groups which were considered incapable of making this adjustment faced immigration restrictions, and whoever was admitted was expected to give up their previous ethnic ties. These restrictions and expectations were progressively abandoned in the 1960's and 1970's, in both the U.S. and Canada, as governments accepted the existence of "unmeltable ethnics" among the immigrants.[36]

35 As Thomas Berger notes, "The American media penetrates Canadian life so completely, we have a tendency sometimes to think that our own issues of race relations must be defined in the same way as they are in the United States. Thus many of our legal scholars and political scientists think only in terms of replicating American experience. In 1969, the Government of Canada adopted a policy of integration and assimilation for Canada's Native population that was based on American policy, developed in the 1960's, towards blacks" ["Towards the Regime of Tolerance" in S. Brooks, ed., Political Thought in Canada: Contemporary Perspectives (Toronto: Irwin Publishers, 1984) 83 at 94].

36 This shared commitment to anglo-conformity is obscured by the misleading contrast between the American "melting-pot" and the Canadian "ethnic mosaic". While "ethnic mosaic" carries the ideological connotation of respect for the integrity of ethnic cultures, in practice it simply meant that immigrants to Canada had a choice of two dominant cultures to assimilate to. But while Canada is bi-national, the "uneasy tolerance which French and English were to show towards each other was not extended to foreigners who resisted assimilation or were believed to be unassimilable" [J. Porter, The Measure of Canadian Society (Toronto: Gage, 1979) at 154]. Conversely, the "melting pot" referred primarily to the biological fusing of various ethnic groups through intermarriage, not the fusing of their cultural practices. As Theodore Roosevelt explained, "the representatives of many old-world races are being fused together into a new type", but "the crucible in which all the new types are melted into one was shaped from 1776 to 1789, and our nationality was definitely fixed in all its essentials by the men of Washington's day" [Theodore Roosevelt quoted in M. Gordon, Assimilation in American Life: The Role

But the ethnic revival in the United States soon moved on to new demands. One result of the more open expression of ethnic identity was that ethnic groups became more conscious of their status *as a group*. It became common to measure the distribution of income or occupations in terms of ethnicity, and those groups which were faring less well demanded group-based ameliorative action, such as extensive quotas in education and employment. Other groups, less concerned with success in the dominant institutions of society, emphasized cultural self-determination, and the need for separate institutions in which to develop their own culture. In these and other ways, ethnicity became increasingly salient in American political culture and public policy.

American liberals have had an ambiguous relationship to this ethnic revival. Most liberals accepted the initial demand for the abandonment of the anglo-conformity model, even though earlier liberals strongly supported the old model which emphasized shared cultural allegiance as the basis of political allegiance.[37] But as ethnic demands escalated, liberal support diminished. I will look at two discussions of the ethnic revival to see how worries about the politicization of immigrant groups in America has influence liberal views of ethnicity in general.

A. Nathan Glazer

Glazer believes that the politicization of ethnicity in America is a new and disturbing trend. Ethnicity has not been the traditional basis of American politics because the federal division of the United States "preceded the creation of much of our great ethnic diversity" (275):

> [I]n the absence of ethnic and racial concentrations dominating one or more states, and of ethnic concentrations that could claim national rights on the basis of settlement on

of *Race, Religion, and National Origin* (New York: Oxford University Press, 1964) at 121–22].

[37] *Supra*, note 5 at 99. For an important exception to this earlier American liberal support for anglo-conformity, see R. Bourne, "Transnational America" in C. Resek, ed. *War and the Intellectuals: Essays by Randolph S. Bourne, (1915–1919)* (New York: Harper and Row, 1964). See also Horace Kallen's critique of the way his fellow American liberals supported "Americanization" policies [*Culture and Democracy in the United States* (New York: Boni and Liveright, 1924) at 145–47].

American territories before they became part of the United States, it became difficult for most groups to envisage claims to national rights – for example, the right to use their language in a state's government, or to establish institutions reflecting their distinctive ethnic culture, or to secede.[38]

This American pattern of dispersed and intermingled ethnicity, which he calls "new world ethnic diversity", is fundamentally different from the multination states of the old world. American groups "rarely put forward concrete ethnic demands of the type we might see in nations where ethnic groups formed more compact, self-conscious, culture-maintaining entities" (283).

The fact that ethnic groups in America don't make national claims is not evidence of racism, for ethnic groups have no ground for such claims. In the case of mother-tongue education, for example, most Americans

> had come to this country not to maintain a foreign language and culture but with the intention . . . to become Americanized as fast as possible, and this meant English language and American culture. They sought the induction to a new language and culture that the public schools provided – as do many present-day immigrants, too – and while they often found, as time went on, that they regretted what they and their children had lost, this was *their* choice, rather than an imposed choice (149).

When immigrants chose to leave their culture and come to America, they voluntarily relinquished their national membership, and the national rights which go with it. This is in contrast to national minorities in the old world, where the denial of national rights, like mother-tongue education, is "an imposed choice".

The heart of Glazer's argument against the politicization of ethnicity in America is this distinction between old-world countries which are "a federation of peoples", and immigrant countries which are composed of "dispersed, mixed, assimilated [and] integrated" ethnic groups (227). And I think this *is* a significant distinction.[39] Surely immigrant groups

---

38   *Supra*, note 5 at 276–77. References to this work are in parenthesis in the text.

39   Of course, there will be some cultural groups which do not fit neatly into either the "national minority" or the "voluntary immigrant" camp. For

cannot claim the same rights as national minorities. If I and others decide to emigrate to China, we have no right that the Chinese government provide us with public services in our mother-tongue. We could argue that a government policy that provided English-language services would benefit everyone, by enriching the whole cultural environment. But we have no *right* to such policies, for in choosing to leave Canada, we relinquish the rights that go with membership in our cultural community. Public subsidization of the ethnic activities of voluntary immigrant groups is best seen as a matter of policy, which no one has a right to, or a right against.[40]

As the ethnic revival escalated, however, some immigrant groups in the United States adopted the language and attitudes of colonized nations or peoples (110–11). They labelled social pressures for assimilation as "oppression", and demanded their "right" to state recognition of ethnicity, and state support for separate ethnic institutions. But this adoption of nationalist rhetoric by immigrant groups is, Glazer argues, totally unwarranted. The new demands are unjustified, since immigration was not an imposed choice. They are also divisive, since each group will resent any special rights given to other groups (228–29), and impracticable, since American ethnic groups are too dispersed and assimilated to exercise collective autonomy. Moreover, any attempt to turn ethnic groups into the "compact, self-conscious, culture-maintaining entities' necessary for collective autonomy would require coercion since many immigrants desire integration (124). Implementing the

example, the Doukhobours immigrated to Canada, not voluntarily as individuals, but en masse, precisely in order to preserve their culture, since they were being persecuted in Russia. Other groups (e.g. the Hutterites and Ukrainians) came voluntarily, but on the explicit promise from Canadian immigration officials that they would be able to retain their culture and social structures. In neither case can they be said to have freely chosen to relinquish the rights that go with membership in their cultural community. The special tax arrangements for Hutterite colonies show that our legal system recognizes that some cultural groups do not fit neatly into the categories of national minority or voluntary immigrant group, and so require some intermediate status. See K. Z. Paltiel, "Group Rights in the Canadian Constitution and Aboriginal Claims to Self-Determination" in R. J. Jackson, ed., *Contemporary Canadian Politics: Readings and Notes* (Scarborough: Prentice-Hall, 1987) at 28.

[40] Evelyn Kallen, however, argues that ethnic groups in a polyethnic society have a right to public support ["Ethnicity and Collective Rights in Canada" in L. Driedger, ed., *Ethnic Canada* (Toronto: Copp Clark, 1987) at 325–31].

extensive demands of the ethnic revival would, therefore, be unjust, impracticable, divisive, and coercive.

This is Glazer's argument against the politization of ethnicity in America, and it is a recognizably liberal argument, for it is focused on the role of choice in immigrant assimilation, and coercion in the assimilation of minority nations. But notice that this argument, whatever its validity, is not an argument against national rights.[41] Glazer's point is that ethnic groups in America are not national minorities, not that national minorities don't have any rights. Yet, as with the *Brown* judgment, there has been a tendency for liberals to generalize the conclusions to all issues of ethnicity. Indeed, Glazer himself twists his arguments so as to make them apply to national minorities. He notes that even in the United States there are exceptions to the new world ethnicity pattern – American Indians, Mexican-Americans, blacks, Puerto Ricans etc. In respect to many of these groups, the United States is (or at least was) "a federation of peoples". When the Southwest joined the United States, Spanish-Americans were recognized as a distinct culture entitled to special rights, although these were taken away when anglophone settlers achieved majority status (277),[42] and Indians and Puerto Ricans continue to be federated to the American state as distinct peoples with special political status.

Glazer recognizes that these groups "possess much more in the way of national characteristics" (283–84), and that they are demanding national rights on just the grounds that he emphasizes are inapplicable to immigrant groups:

> Both blacks and the Spanish-speaking point to a distinctive political situation: the blacks were brought as slaves, and the Mexicans and Puerto Ricans were conquered. The American Indians were also conquered. The white ethnic groups,

---

41   It is also not an argument against existing "multiculturalism" policies, so long as these are not seen as matters of national rights or collective autonomy. Glazer, however, thinks that the risks of coercion and divisiveness are so great that even modest forms of support for polyethnicity are bad policy (*supra*, note 5 at 124).

42   This parallels the fate of the Métis, whose national rights were recognized when Manitoba entered Confederation, then taken away when English settlers became the majority in the province. See J. Weinstein, *Aboriginal Self-Determination off a Land Base* (Kingston: Institute for Intergovernmental Relations, 1986) at 46–47.

however, came as free immigrants. Thus the blacks, the Spanish-speaking groups, the American Indians, and perhaps some other groups can make stronger claims for public support of their distinctive cultures than can European groups (118).

So Glazer recognizes that his argument against the politicization of immigrant ethnicity actually argues for the recognition of some national rights.[43] He cannot avoid accepting that "there is a good deal of weight" in this point (119).

Yet Glazer opposes recognising the rights of America's national minorities. Instead, his hope is that "these groups, with proper public policies to stamp out discrimination and inferior status and to encourage acculturation and assimilation, will become not very different from the European and Asian ethnic groups, the ghost nations, bound by nostalgia and sentiment and only occasionally coalescing around distinct interests" (284). In the end, Glazer insists that "benign neutrality" is appropriate for national minorities as well, even though this contradicts Glazer's own argument for benign neutrality, i.e., the difference between the coerced assimilation of minority nations and the voluntary assimilation of immigrants.

Why does Glazer reject the implications of his own argument for national rights? In places he seems to say that the American commitment to benign neutrality is essentially arbitrary. The legitimacy of national rights is not, after all, a question of justice: "Whether or not a nation elects to handle multi-ethnic diversity by formally ignoring it or by formally recognizing it has no bearing on whether . . . we consider that nation responsive to human rights and to civil rights."[44] The reason Americans reject minority rights is not justice, but simply that there is

such a thing as a state ideology, a national consensus, that shapes and determines what attitude immigrant and minority groups will take toward the alternative possibilities of group

---

43 American blacks do not fit either the new world ethnicity pattern or the national minority pattern. They did not choose to leave their original cultures, and they were not allowed to preserve those cultures, or create a national community, within the United States. As a result, their claims for group rights have centred more on compensatory justice than national rights.

44 Glazer, *supra*, note 4 at 98.

maintenance and group rights on the one hand, or individual integration and individual rights on the other. . . . The United States, whatever the realities of discrimination and segregation, had as a national ideal a unitary and new ethnic identity, that of American.[45]

So Glazer's claim is not that minority rights are excluded from the national consensus because they are unfair. Rather, they are unfair because they are excluded from the national consensus.

But this is no argument (at least not a liberal argument). What if the national consensus is built on ignorance of or insensitivity to the interests of minority nations (as his own argument suggests)? In any event, Glazer's description of the national consensus is biased. He says the consensus must either accept or reject the politicization of ethnicity. But why can't the national consensus emphasize what Glazer himself emphasizes: the difference between immigrant groups and national minorities? The national ideal may recognize the legitimate rights of minority cultures while denying the illegitimate claims of immigrant groups. Indeed, this is close to the actual practice and national consensus in both the U.S. and Canada; our laws give Indians, Inuit, French-Canadians, and Puerto Ricans a special political status that other ethnic groups do not have. So glazer has no argument of justice *or* convention to support his commitment to benign neutrality towards national minorities. Why then is he opposed to the rights of national minorities? After asserting that the "proper" policy is to assimilate the Indians, he goes on to note "a final complication":

> If the public policy gets turned around to the point where, rather than trying to suppress or ignore the existence of the ethnic group as a distinctive element in American society and polity, it acknowledges a distinctive status for some groups and begins to attach rights in public law to membership in them, will that not react on the others, halfway toward assimilation, and will they not begin to reassert themselves so that they will not be placed at a disadvantage? (284)

Here is the crux of the matter for Glazer. Indians who desire recognition of their national rights may have both justice and convention on their side, but

45 *Ibid.* at 100.

Our problem is that we are not a federation of peoples (like Canada or the Soviet Union) but of states, and our ethnic groups are already too dispersed, mixed, assimilated, integrated to permit without confusion a policy that separates out some for special treatment. But if we try, then many other groups will join the queue, or try to, and the hope of a large fraternity of all Americans will have to be abandoned. . . . In a multiethnic society, such a policy can only encourage one group after another to raise claims to special treatment for its protection. . . . The demand for special treatment will lead to animus against other groups that already have it, by those who think they should have it and don't. (227–29)

In other words, recognizing the legitimate demands of Indians would make European and Asian ethnic groups demand illegitimate and divisive benefits, and there by jeopardize the "larger fraternity of all Americans".

It is worth pausing to consider how weak this argument is. Firstly, Glazer's argument is hypocritical. It rests on the importance of distinguishing national minorities and ethnic groups, but he then denies that this distinction can be drawn. Secondly, his argument is ethnocentric. He says there is a "national consensus" in favor of assimilation, but he clearly means by this a consensus amongst European and Asian ethnic groups, since he admits that other groups do want national rights. He says that this consensus has produced a "fraternity of all Americans", even though he admits that it has excluded blacks, Indians, Hispanics and Puerto Ricans. He says that national rights should be rejected in order to avoid mutual resentment. But what he really hopes to avoid is (unjustified) resentment amongst European and Asian ethnic groups, since he admits that national minorities are already (and legitimately) resentful at the denial of their national rights. Immigrant groups have illegitimately adopted the language of national rights, and in order to fight this divisive tendency, Glazer denies Indians the legitimate use of that language.

It is hard to avoid the conclusion that Indians are pawns being sacrificed to preserve Glazer's real concern, viz., the fraternity of immigrant groups in America. The beliefs of ethnic groups are taken by Glazer to be definitive of the "national" ideal, of what "all Americans" feel. As a result, the claims of Indians are evaluated, not in terms of their intrinsic merits, but in terms of their potential effect on the "fraternity" of immigrant groups. Glazer's commitment to colour-blind laws, which was presented as the defining feature of liberal justice, [46] is in fact defended through arbitrary and ethnocentric fiat, and through the explicit subordination of the interests of national minorities to the fraternity of ethnic groups. Glazer's rejection of national rights, therefore, is not the product of his liberal principles.

B. Michael Walzer

While Walzer and Glazer are on different ends of the American liberal spectrum – Walzer a social democrat, Glazer a conservative – they have remarkably similar views of ethnicity. Like Glazer, Walzer begins by insisting on the distinctive features of "new world ethnic diversity". Unlike the Old World,

> pluralism in the New World originated in individual and familial migration. . . . The Old World call for self-determination had no resonance here; the immigrants (except for the black slaves) had come voluntarily and did not have to be forced to stay (indeed, many of them returned home each year), nor did different groups have any basis for or any reason for secession.[47]

This process of assimilating voluntary immigrants was unlike Russification, which was aimed at

> intact and rooted communities, at nations that, with the exception of the Jews, were established on lands they had occupied for many centuries – In the United States, by contrast, Americanization was aimed at peoples far more susceptible to cultural change, for they were not only uprooted; they had uprooted themselves. Whatever the pressures that had driven them to the New World, they had chosen to come, while others like themselves, in their own families, had chosen to remain (9)

[46] N. Glazer, *Affirmative Discrimination: Ethnic and Public Policy* (New York: Basic Books, 1975) at 220.

[47] *Supra*, note 3 at 6–7. Subsequent references to this work are in parenthesis in the text. Cf. M. Walzer, "States and Minorities" in C. Fried, ed., *Minorities: Community and Identity* (Berlin: Springer-Verlag, 1983) 224.

Thus immigrants had no reason for rejecting English as the public language, and when they did resist Americanization "their resistance took a new form. It was not a demand that politics follow nationality, but rather that politics be separated from nationality – as it was already separated from religion. It was not a demand for national liberation, but for ethnic pluralism" (10–11).

Unfortunately, the ethnic revival has broken this pattern, as ethnic leaders adopt attitudes that are only appropriate for old world minorities. So Walzer's argument against the demands of the ethnic revival, like Glazer's, rests on the fact that immigrant groups are not minority nations. Yet Walzer, like Glazer, twists his argument to attack the rights of minority cultures. Consider his treatment of American Indians, who are an exception to this common approach, this "unity" (18), concerning the political role of ethnicity. The logic of Walzer's argument suggests that Indians should not be forced to accept an approach which is "not primarily the product of their experience" (6), but rather is "adapted to the needs of immigrant communities" (27). Indeed, the Indians' situation is the opposite of that which justifies the depoliticization of immigrant ethnicity.

Yet Walzer opposes the recognition of their national rights. His hope is that "this kind of equity, adapted to the needs of immigrant communities, can successfully be extended to the racial minorities now asserting their own group claims" (27). But he gives no argument for endorsing this "extension". Like Glazer, his response to minority cultures that are claiming national rights is not to consider the merits of the claim (which his own arguments endorse), but rather to arbitrarily apply the immigrant model instead. Rather than argue against the legitimacy of their claims, Walzer suggests that Indians don't really want national rights: "Racism is the great barrier to a fully developed pluralism and as long as it exists American Indians and blacks, and perhaps Mexican Americans as well, will be tempted by [national rights]" (27). These national rights claims would not be tempting if Indians had the "same opportunities for group organization and cultural expression" available to immigrant groups (27). But there is no evidence that Indians only desire national rights because they have been prevented from becoming just another ethnic group. On the contrary, Indians have often been pressured to become just another ethnic group, but they have resisted that pressure and fought to protect their distinct status. Indians are indeed subject to racism, but the racism they are most concerned with is the racism denial that they are distinct peoples with their own cultures and communities.

Since Walzer has no argument against minorities which demand national rights rather than polyethnicity, he instead suggests that no one really wants national rights. It is hard to believe that he actually thinks this, for it is completely at odds with the history of Indian tribes in America or Canada.[48] In any event, the fact that Indians might choose to become an ethnic group like all the others does not show that they don't have the right to choose otherwise (nations can choose not to exercise their legitimate rights). Walzer's claim is not only insensitive to the real aspirations of American Indians, it is irrelevant to the question of the legitimacy of their national rights.

So nothing in Walzer's argument supports the claim that national rights are unfair. In the end, Walzer, like Glazer, resorts to the idea of a national consensus. He says that the question of national rights within a multination state "must itself be worked out politically, and its precise character will depend upon understandings shared among the citizens about the value of cultural diversity, local autonomy, and so on. It is to these understandings that we must appeal when we make our arguments".[49] And in America, the larger political community sees national rights as "inconsistent with our historical traditions and shared understandings – inconsistent, too, with contemporary living patterns, deeply and bitterly divisive."[50] In other words, the dominant culture, adapted to the needs of immigrant ethnicity, is paramount, and Indians can't be allowed to interfere with its "shared understandings", or have rights that would be "divisive". But, like Glazer, Walzer provides no argument why a consensus adapted to immigrant ethnicity should define what is legitimate for national minor-

---

48   This recalls Thurgood Marshall's claim that Indians want colour-blind laws but "they just have not had the judgment or the wherewithal to bring lawsuits" [in L. Friedman, ed., *Argument: The Oral Argument Before the Supreme Court in Brown v. Board of Education* (New York: Chelsea House, 1969) at 50].

49   M. Walzer, *Spheres of Justice: A Defence of Pluralism and Equality* (Oxford: Blackwell, 1983) at 29.

50   *Ibid.* at 151.

ities, and he ignores the fact that the national consensus in the U.S. (and Canada) does accept the special status of national minorities.

Walzer's argument exhibits the same faults as Glazer's. Both switch between emphasizing and ignoring the distinction between ethnic groups and national minorities, depending on whether the distinction helps or hinders their cause.[51] Both make ad hoc appeals to a "national consensus", which they equate with the aspirations of European and Asian immigrants, and which they describe in simplistic terms. Both assert the importance liberalism attaches to the separation of state and ethnicity, but the reasons they give for rejecting national rights have nothing to do with liberal principles, and indeed are in conflict with them.

[51] American delegates to the U.N. manifest the same tendency to switch between emphasizing and ignoring the difference between immigrant groups and national minorities when opposing the international protection of minority rights. See Sohn, *supra*, note 27 at 272, 279; W. McKean, *Equality and Discrimination Under International Law* (Oxford: Oxford University Press, 1983) at 70-71, 142-43.

ARE THERE ANY CULTURAL RIGHTS?
Chandran Kukathas
Australian Defence Force Academy

I

I shall advance the thesis that if there are any moral rights at
all, it follows that there is at least one natural right, the equal
right of all men to be free.
        – H. L. A. Hart, "Art There Any Natural Rights?"

At least since the American civil rights movement, many
people have become more aware of the harm suffered by ethnic
or cultural minorities laboring under discriminatory practices
or inequities which have developed over decades, if not
centuries. The conditions of the American black and the
American Indian, the Canadian Inuit, the New Zealand Maori,
and the Australian Aborigine have been the subject of various
administrative and legislative initiatives. And the political
claims of the Basques in Spain, the French Canadians in
Canada, and the Tamils in Sri Lanka have been gaining wider
prominence. In more recent times, however, one particular
concern has begun to receive greater attention: the cultural
health of some of these ethnic minorities. Increasingly, the
impact of the larger society on the cultural integrity and
durability of ethnic minorities has come to be a matter of
debate, if not concern. And to a significant extent, it is cultural
integrity which now forms the basis of the moral claims, and
political demands, advanced by these minorities. In particular,

Author's Note: I wish to thank audiences at Bowling Green State University
and the Federalist Society of the University of Toledo Law School where
versions of this essay were first read. For helpful comments and suggestions I
am grateful to Richard Mulgan, Philip Pettit, Brian Beddie, John Gray,
Stephen Macedo, Emilio Pacheco, and Robert Goodin. I am especially
indebted to William Maley for his criticism and advice. I would like to
acknowledge the generous support of the Institute for Humane Studies through
its F. Leroy Hill Fellowship. Thanks are also due to the Social Philosophy and
Policy Center at Bowling Green State University for providing the collegial but
interruption-free environment in which work on this essay was completed.

some of those who describe themselves as "indigenous peoples" swamped by settler cultures – Polynesian Fijians, Maori New Zealanders, and American Indians, for example – call not simply for improvements in their economic conditions but for protection of their cultural practices.

These developments have not been without significance for political theory, and liberal theory in particular. In the light of this modern "ethnic revival," many have come to question the relevance of liberal political thinking. Liberalism, with its stubborn insistence on viewing society in individualist terms, is said to be incapable of coping with the phenomena of group loyalty and cultural reassertion. The disdain for liberal thinking is forcefully expressed by Anthony Smith in the introduction to his study of *The Ethnic Revival*:

> The dissolution of ethnicity. The transcendence of natio-nalism. The internationalisation of culture. These have been the dreams, and expectation, of liberals and rationalists in practically every country, and in practically every country they have been confounded and disappointed. . . . Today the cosmopolitan ideals are in decline and rationalist expectation have withered. Today, liberals and socialists alike must work for, and with, the nation state and its increasingly ethnic culture, or remain voices in the wilderness.[1]

Much of this criticism has emerged in the wake of a growing conviction that there is no prospect of individuals abandoning their particular loyalties for a universalist humanism. Thus one has to accept the conclusion "well known to great masses of people for a long time but not to generations of elite humanist scholars and strivers for human perfectibility: namely, that our tribal separatenesses are here to stay. . . . They are not about to dissolve into any new, larger human order."[2] The problem with liberalism, it is held, is that its individualist outlook leads it to neglect those communal interests which are so much more important than liberals recognize. Vernon Van Dyke, for

1   Anthony D. Smith, *The Ethnic Revival* (Cambridge: Cambridge University Press, 1980), 1. Liberal hopes are described as "delusions," resting "on a systematic underestimation of one of the fundamental trends of the last two centuries."

2   Harold R. Isaacs, *Idols of the Tribe: Group Identity and Political Change* (New York: Harper & Row, 1975), 216.

example, has argued in a series of papers that "the liberal emphasis on the individual precludes a proper theory of the state, which suggests in principle that liberalism cannot be trusted to deal adequately with the question of status and rights for ethnic communities."[3] Frances Svensson, drawing on Van Dyke's work, similarly complains that "liberal democratic theory, in its almost exclusive emphasis on individual rights and its neglect of communal interests, has created a context in which no balance has been possible between the claims of individuals and multidimensional communities."[4]

Reservations about liberalism have been expressed by its friends as much as by its detractors. John Gay, for example, suggests that liberal thinking makes a fatal error in regarding people not as "Sikhs or Poles, Palestinians or Israelis, Blacks or Wasps, but merely persons, rights-bearing (and, doubtless also, gender-neutral) ciphers."[5] Indeed, he maintains that "the sustaining myths of liberal modernity – myths of global progress, of fundamental rights and of a secular movement to a universal civilization – cannot be maintained even as useful fictions in the intellectual and political context of the last decade of our century."[6] For Gray, this means that we should abandon liberalism and look to other, more coherent ways of theorizing.

A somewhat different response comes from Will Kymlicka in his important study, *Liberalism, Community, and Culture.* Kymlicka too concedes that liberalism, "as commonly interpreted . . . gives no independent weight to our cultural membership, and hence demands equal rights of citizenship, regardless of the consequences for the existence of minority

---

3   Vernon Van Dyke, "The Individual, the State, and Ethnic Communities in Political Theory," *World Politics* 29 (April 1977): 343–69, at 344. See also "Justice as Fairness: For Groups?," *American Political Science Review* 69 (June 1975); 607–14; "Collective Entities and Moral Rights: Problems in Liberal Thought," *Journal of Politics* 44 (1982): 21–40; *Human Rights, Ethnicity, and Discrimination* (Westport and London: Greenwood, 1985).

4   Frances Svensson, "Liberal Democracy and Group Rights: The Legacy of Individualism and Its Impact on American Indian Tribes," *Political Studies* 27 (1979): 421–39, at 438.

5   John Gray, "Mill's and Other Liberalisms," in his *Liberalisms: Essays in Political Philosophy* London and New York: Routledge, 1989), 217–38, at 234.

6   Ibid., 235.

cultures."[7] Yet he proposes to reinterpret the liberal tradition, to show that a respect for minority rights is indeed compatible with liberal equality: "Post-war liberal clichés need to be rethought, for they misrepresent the issue, and the liberal tradition itself."[8]

In this essay, I propose to take issue with these writers. I shall argue that while we are right to be concerned about the cultural health of minority communities, this gives us insufficient reason to abandon, modify, or reinterpret liberalism. Far from being indifferent to the claims of minorities, liberalism puts concern for minorities at the forefront. Its very emphasis on *individual rights or individual* liberty bespeaks not hostility to the interests of communities but wariness of the power of the majority over minorities. There is thus no need to look for alternatives to liberalism or to jettison the individualism that lies at its heart. We need, rather, to reassert the fundamental importance of individual liberty or individual rights and question the idea that cultural minorities have collective rights.

It ought, however, to be emphasized that to take this view is not to imply that groups or cultural communities do not have interests or, indeed, that particular peoples cannot have legitimate grievances which need to be addressed as a matter of justice. The primary thesis advanced here is not that groups do not matter but rather that there is no need to depart from the liberal language of *individual* rights to do justice to them.

To defend this thesis, I begin, in the next section, to put the case for the liberal standpoint, taking issue with those who challenge its individualist premises. The third section then turns to develop my case in response to those who wish to see liberal theory modified to take cultural claims into consideration, after which the fourth section takes on the question of what such a view amounts to and attempts to account for the place of cultural minorities in liberal society. The fifth section reviews various important objections before the conclusions of this essay are given a final formulation.

---

7 Will Kymlicka, *Liberalism, Community, and Culture* (Oxford: Oxford University Press, 1989), 152.

8 Ibid., 211: "A government that gives special rights to members of a distinct cultural community may still be treating them *as individuals*; the provision of such rights just reflects a different view about how to treat them as individuals."

II

Liberal political theories, it is widely held, assume or argue that the good society is one which is not governed by particular common ends or goals but provides the framework of rights or liberties or duties within which people may pursue their various ends, individually or cooperatively. It is a society governed by law and, as such, is regulated by right principles. These are principles of justice, which do not themselves presuppose the rightness or betterness of any particular way of life. Although liberals are not commonly skeptics about questions about the good life, they emphasize that no one should be forced to accept any particular ideal of the good life. The liberal response to the multiplicity of religious and moral traditions in modern society has thus been to advocate toleration, as far as possible, of different ways of living.

This response has received a variety of justifications from liberal thinkers, who have founded their conclusions on claims of natural right or arguments about original contracts or calculations of utility. Despite this variety, there is a core of common assumptions to be found in liberal arguments.[9] First, liberal theory is *individualist* in asserting or assuming the moral primacy of the person against the claims of any social collectivity; second, it is *egalitarian* because it confers on all such individuals "the same moral status and denies the relevance to legal or political order of differences in moral worth among human beings"; and third, it is *universalist* because it affirms the moral unity of the human species and accords "a secondary importance to specific historic associations and cultural forms."

These characteristically liberal assumptions – particularly the first and third – have long been the targets of criticism from communitarian quarters. Typically, these criticisms have made the point that liberalism's individualist premises are unacceptable because any conception of an individual presupposes some view of society and community since individuals are social beings. This objections has acquired a more distinctive flavor, however, in an argument that groups occupy an intermediate position between the individual and the state and deserve special moral recognition. Vernon Van Dyke in

---

[9]   In the account that follows, I borrow freely from John Gray's discussion in *Liberalism* (Milton Keynes: Open University Press, 1985), x.

particular has objected that "modern liberal political theorists focus on relations between the individual and the state as if no groups count that are intermediate.[10] He takes to task for this neglect a variety of contemporary theorists from John Plamenatz and John Rawls to Carole Pateman and Hanna Pitkin.[11] Making the point that, as a matter of political fact, ethnic groups of all sorts are indeed accorded "rights" in many countries, Van Dyke offers a number of reasons why it is important that, "alongside the principle that individuals are right-and-duty-bearing units, a comparable principle should be accepted for the benefit of ethnic communities."[12] His argument is worth noting.

Stressing the importance of individual and equal treatment, Van Dyke argues, promotes the view that it is improper even to think about differences of race, except to combat discrimination and so tends to promote blindness to group differences and an assumption that societies should properly be regarded as homogeneous.[13] If group differences were recognized and communities were accepted as right-and-duty-bearing units, there would be a greater chance of developing a coherent set of doctrines to respond to real-world problems. Theory would be more sensitive to collective sentiment and group loyalties.[14] This would make a difference to the fate of "nondominant" communities and to the psychological health of their members. Individualism, however, "combined with the usual stress on personal merit, is destructive of cultures other than the majority or dominant culture."[15] If ethnic communities were accepted as right-and-duty-bearing, it would become easier to take "affirmative action" to compensate communities which have suffered discrimination. This would supply a "more satisfactory doctrinal basis for some actual practices."[16] For example, in the case of the Old Order Amish in Wisconsin, the Supreme Court gave the community the right not to send their

---

10 Van Dyke, "The Individual, the State," 361.

11 Ibid., 363–4. See also his paper on Rawls, "Justice as Fairness."

12 Van Dyke, "The Individual, the State," 363.

13 Ibid.

14 Ibid., 364.

15 Ibid., 365.

16 Ibid., 366.

children to public schools beyond the eighth grade on the basis of the first amendment guarantee of freedom of religion. But while the Amish won this fight for the survival of their community, their victory left untouched the presumption "that nonreligious ethnic communities do not have a comparable right."[17] Van Dyke concludes by suggesting that, in principle, granting status and rights to ethnic communities should extend justice by giving minorities their due. This is conducive to peace, for justice is one of the conditions of peace.[18]

The point of all this, it should in fairness be emphasized, is not to belittle the idea of individual rights. Van Dyke's concern is to ensure that the "right of the community to preserve itself"[19] is not neglected. His suggestion is that many individual rights should be understood as flowing from the community's right of self-preservation. For example, individual freedom of expression can often be interpreted in terms of the right of a linguistic community to preserve its language. But taking individual rights as exhaustive of all rights would not allow us to defend the interests of communities, and particularly their interest in self-determination. This view tends to see communities as needing to be assimilated rather than liberated and to regard permanent communalism as unacceptable.[20]

Van Dyke, like many others, is right to say that liberal theory subordinate the claims of the community to those of the individual. But subordination is not neglect. What needs to be established now is that liberal theory does have good reason for elevating the individual, yet does not go so far as to disparage the interests of communities – interests which cannot be reduced to the interests of individuals. That is the task of the rest of this section. It ought now to be made clear, however, that in advancing the arguments that follow I am in fact not only defending liberal theory *simpliciter* but developing *a particular* liberal theory.

[17]   Ibid., 367.

[18]   Ibid., 368.

[19]   Ibid., 369.

[20]   "Thus, the liberal, moved by humane concerns, has to favour some kind of a special, protective for them – perhaps establishing territorial reserves from which others are excluded. But this is contrary to liberal doctrine, which is at least integrationist if not assimiliationist; permanent communalism is unacceptable." Vernon Van Dyke, "Collective Entities and Moral Rights," 29.

Contrary to a commonly held and often expressed view, liberal theory does not begin with the assumption that the world is made up of isolated, atomistic individuals. (Even the most individualistic of thinkers, Hobbes, was moved to put forward his political theories by the actions of particular groups or interests in society – the warring actions during the upheavals of the 1640s.) Individuals invariably find themselves members of groups or associations which not only influence their conduct but also shape their loyalties and their sense of identity. There is no reason for any liberal theorist to deny this. What has to be denied, however, is the proposition that fundamental moral claims are to be attached to such groups and that the terms of political association must be established with these particular claims in mind.

The primary reason for rejecting the idea of group claims as the basis of moral and political settlements is that groups are not fixed and unchanging entities in the moral and political universe. Groups are constantly forming and dissolving in response to political and institutional circumstances. Groups or cultural communities do not exist prior to or independently of legal and political institutions but are themselves given shape by those institutions.[21] As Donald Horowitz has put it, "Ethnic identity is not static; it changes with the environment."[22]

The importance of this point cannot be too strongly emphasized. Scholars, like Anthony Smith, who are critical of liberalism have insisted on "the 'naturalness' of ethnicity" and criticize recent scholarship for starting "from the premiss that nations and nationalism are peculiarly modern phenomena, and that there is nothing 'natural' or inborn about national loyalties and characteristics."[23] Yet the work of Horowitz shows quite clearly that this criticism is mistaken. There is an "interactive quality" to the variables related to group identity: culture, boundaries, conflict, and the policy outcomes of

[21] A finer distinction needs to be made with regard to certain cultural groups such as the American Indians or the New Zealand Maori that did, in some sense, exist as cultural groups before European political institutions were established in their territories. This distinction is discussed further on in the essay.

[22] Donald L. Horowitz, *Ethnic Groups in Conflict* (Berkeley: University of California Press, 1985), 589.

[23] Smith, *The Ethnic Revival*, 85.

conflict.[24] Ethnic identity has a contextual character: Group boundaries "tend to shift with the political context."[25]

For example, in the former Indian state of Madras, cleavages within the Telugu population were not very important. Yet as soon as a separate Telugu-speaking state was carved out of Madras, Telugu subgroups quickly emerged as political entities. Similarly, many ethnic groups were the product of subgroup amalgamation in the colonial period in Asia and Africa. The Malays in Malaysia, for example, emerged as a "distinct" group only after colonialists created specific territories out of loose clusters of villages and regions; much the same can be said for the Ibo in Nigeria and the Moro in the Philippines. Indeed, Horowitz suggests that some "such groups were 'artificial' creations of colonial authorities and missionaries, who catalyzed the slow merger of related peoples into coherent ethnic entities. They did this by the way they categorized those they encountered and by the incentives they established to consummate the amalgamation."[26] Of course, it was not only colonialism that shaped these identities. The Malays, for instance, despite the fact that their numbers were drawn from island peoples as far away as Sumatra, Sulawesi, Borneo, and Java, as well as Malaya, developed their highly cohesive identity partly because of the appearance of *Chinese* immigrants.[27] But the important point remains: Group formation is the product of environmental influences, and among these environmental factors are political institutions.

This is not to say that culture is unimportant, but it is not fundamental, even for the constitution of group identity. Legal rights can themselves be important determinants. In the late 1960s in Assam, Bengali Muslims found it advantageous to declare Assamese their language in part to become eligible for land reserved for indigenes.[28] As Horowitz observes, "Culture is important in the making of ethnic groups, but it is more important for providing *post facto* content to group identity

[24]   Horowitz, *Ethnic Groups in Conflict*, 73; see also chap. 2 passim.

[25]   Ibid., 66.

[26]   Ibid., 66–67.

[27]   Ibid., 68. See also Alfred P. Rubin, *The International Personality of the Malay Peninsula: A Study of the International Law of Imperialism* (Kuala Lumpur: Penerbit Universiti Malaya, 1974).

[28]   Horowitz, *Ethnic Groups in Conflict*, 195.

than it is for providing some ineluctable prerequisite for an identity to come into being.[29]

Now, the causes of group formation do not render group interests illegitimate. But they do point to why it may not be appropriate to try to answer questions about what political institutions are defensible by appealing to the interests of existing groups. Often, those interests exist, or take their particular shape, only because of certain historical circumstances or because particular political institutions prevail and not because they are a part of some natural order. There is no more reason to see particular interests as fixed than there is to see particular political arrangements as immutable. Liberal political theories thus typically take as their starting points the existence of a plurality of interests – often competing, if not in actual conflict – and ask how or by what principles a political order might adjudicate between or accommodate competing claims. But recognizing that many interests, cultural or otherwise, might have well-founded claims, liberal theory tries to look at the problem of divining political rules from a standpoint which owes its allegiance to no particular interest – past, current, or prospective.

For this reason, liberal theory looks at fundamental political questions from the perspective of the individual rather than that of the group or culture or community. Such collectives matter only because they are essential for the well-being of the individual. If the condition of the community or the culture made no difference to the life of any individual, then the condition of the collective would not matter.[30] None of this implies that there is such a thing as "the individual" in the abstract. Individuals do not exist in the abstract any more than interests do. But interests *matter* only because individuals do. Thus, while groups or cultures or communities may have a character or nature which is not reducible to the nature of the individuals who inhabit them, their moral claims have weight

---

[29] Ibid., 69.

[30] A more detailed defence of this individualist standpoint may be found in Chandran Kukathas and Philip Pettit, *Rawls: A Theory of Justice and its Critics* (Oxford: Polity Press, 1990), 12–16. For a contrary view, see Charles Taylor, "Irreducibly Social Goods," in *Rationality, Individualism and Public Policy*, edited by Geoffrey Brennan and Cliff Walsh (Canberra: Australian National University, 1990), 45–63; but see the reply by Robert E. Goodin, "Irreducibly Social Goods: Comment 1," 64–79.

only to the extent that this bears on the lives of actual individuals, now or in the future.[31] Liberal political theories rest on the assumption that while the interests given expression in groups, cultural communities, or other such collectives do matter, they matter ultimately only to the extent that they affect actual individuals.

So groups or communities have no special moral primacy in virtue of some natural priority. They are mutable historical formations – associations of individuals – whose claims are open to ethical evaluation. And any ethical evaluation must, ultimately, consider how actual individuals have been or might be affected, rather than the interests of the group in the abstract. It is not acceptable to evaluate or choose political institutions or to establish legal rights on the basis of the claims or interests of cultural communities because those very institutions or rights will profoundly affect the kinds of cultural communities individuals decide to perpetuate or to form. Groups may generate entitlements, but entitlements can also create groups. Historical priority does not confer on a community the right to continued existence (even though it may be the source of other valid claims – to which I return later).

This last (unqualified) sentence would be challenged immediately by a defender of cultural rights, raising the following objection. If institutions or legal rights are to be established, why not choose conservatively and protect existing cultural communities? Granted that the choice of laws and institutions can indeed alter the composition of groups, is there not a case for establishing rights that protect actual cultural communities on which individuals depend? After all, the breakdown or disintegration of such communities, bringing social dislocation and anomie, is scarcely a good – for group or individual. So, there appears to be good reason to recognize the right of groups to guard themselves against the intrusions of the outside world and to determine their own destiny.

Yet this case is not as straightforward as it appears, for reasons that have much to do with the mutable nature of cultural communities. In recognizing this, it is important to note not only that group composition changes over time but

---

[31] Note that I have not made the stronger assertion that it is only the lives of individuals *within* the group that can relevantly be taken into account.

that most groups are not homogeneous at any given moment. Within cultural communities there may be important differences and conflicts of interest. Internal divisions can take two forms: divisions between subgroups within the larger community and divisions between elites and masses, which may have quite different interests. Differences of interest between subgroups might be observed, for example, in the experiences of groups such as the Yoruba of Nigeria, the Lozi of Zambia, and the Bakongo of Zaire, Angola, and Congo (Brazzaville). In each of these cases, the group was formed in response to internal differentiation among subgroups, many of whom fought each other. It was only in opposition to colonialism that their leaders sought to minimize subgroup cultural differences, standardize language, and take other measures to assimilate the many interests into a united association with political strength. Although many of these movements of assimilation met with great success, subgroup identities have remained, and in some cases, subgroup conflict persists.[32]

The more important conflict of interest within groups, however, is that between the masses and elites. This conflict is starkly revealed within ethnic cultural communities confronted by modernization. Under these circumstances, elites have "distinctive interests that relate to modernity: good jobs, urban amenities, access to schools, travel, prestige."[33] In some cases, there is no doubt that elites use their advantages to further their personal ends, in some cases manipulating ethnic sentiment in pursuit of their career aspirations.[34] In others, however, matters are more complex. Aboriginal representatives on the National Aboriginal Consultative Committee established by the Australian Commonwealth government were often suspected by their people of succumbing to "white" patronage, even when they were innocent.[35] To some extent this was the product of ignorance: In many cases, Aborigines did not understand agreements entered into on their behalf by their

32   On this, see Horowitz, *Ethnic Groups in Conflict*, 71.

33   Ibid., 101. Bitter jokes about the two most dangerous tribes in Africa, the Wabenzi (those who drive Mercedes cars) and the Bintu (those who have "been to" Europe and America) suggest that there is an awareness of the differences of interest.

34   Ibid., 225, and more generally chap. 5.

35   See Judith Wright, *We Call for a Treaty* (Sydney: Collins/Fontana, 1985), 292–99.

"representatives." And it is not always easy for those uninitiated into the ways of bureaucracies to understand how difficult it is to avoid being "swallowed up."[36] Yet these cases also reveal the real gap that sometimes exists between the interests of the elite and the interests of the mass of group members.

This poses a particular dilemma for cultural minorities seeking self-determination within the larger society and wishing to preserve their cultural integrity. To be self-determining in the larger society requires a measure of political power, and this means becoming involved in the political processes of the nation. Elites from minority cultures must invariably mix with the educated elites from other minorities and from the dominant society. But in this process, the interests of the minority elite become further removed from those of their cultural community. If their cultural community itself undergoes changes, however, the prospect of preserving cultural integrity diminishes.

The cultural community and its elite may, of course, share a common interest in the symbolic standing of the group as a whole. If both gain from the growth of collective self-esteem, then the masses might welcome the prestige derived from the success of wealthier or higher-status group members. One Malay leader has, in fact, defended policies of preferential treatment in these terms, arguing that although the benefits fall disproportionately to the Malay elite, the masses, knowing of Malay group success, enjoy a vicarious satisfaction more highly prized than personal material gain.[37] Yet while it may indeed be the case that "the distribution of prestige is a real and rational object of conflict"[38] among ethnic groups, securing this goal can serve to heighten the divisions within the community.

36   A complaint made by a senior Aboriginal public servant, Charles Perkins, responding to Aboriginal complaints about his ineffectiveness. See Scott Bennett, *Aborigines and Political Power* (Sydney: Allen & Unwin, 1989), 103.

37   "With the existence of the few rich Malays at least the poor can say their fate is not entirely to serve rich non-Malays. From the point of view of racial ego, and this ego is still strong, the unseemly existence of Malay tycoons is essential." Mahathir bin Mohamad, *The Malay Dilemma* (Kuala Lumpur: Federal Publications, 1981), 44. See also Thomas Sowell, *Preferential Policies: An International Perspective* (New York: Morrow, 1990), 48-51.

38   Horowitz, *Ethnic Groups in Conflict*, 226.

Indeed, it could be argued that the masses may be more interested in jobs and economic progress whereas the elites, who already enjoy these material benefits, have a greater interest in symbolic traditionalism.[39]

From a liberal point of view, the divided nature of cultural communities strengthens the case for not thinking in terms of cultural rights. Cultural groups are not undifferentiated wholes but associations of individuals with interests that differ to varying extents. So within such minorities are to be found other, smaller minorities. To regard the wider group as the bearer of cultural rights is to affirm the existing structures and therefore to favor existing majorities. Minorities within a cultural community which might over time have formed quite different coalitions with other interests may find that their interests are to a significant degree subject to control by the larger rights-bearing community. More important, it restricts the opportunity of minorities within the group to reshape the cultural community, whether directly or through its interaction with those outside the group. Liberal theory is generally concerned to avoid entrenching majorities or creating permanent minorities.

To say this is to recognize that it is not always the case that the entire cultural community is eager, or even willing, to preserve cultural integrity at any price. Often, individuals or groups within the community wish to take advantage of opportunities which have produced the unintended consequence of changing the character of the community. Thus, for example, while Aboriginal elites have argued that land rights granted to Aborigines as a people ought to reserve those lands for Aboriginal communities in perpetuity, some individual Aborigines argue that those communities should be free to use the land as an economic asset to be bought and sold.[40] Here, there is undeniably a conflict between the interests of the

[39] I owe this point to Richard Mulgan, who suggests that the urbanized Maori in New Zealand might provide an example of elite interests.

[40] One Aboriginal businessman thus complained: "Land is granted to appease the non-Aboriginal conscience in the large cities, but Aborigines are not allowed to use it freely because paternalists do not think the black man is sufficiently mature to behave responsibly. For example, Aborigines are prohibited from selling, leasing or trading their land – thus shut out of the activities that would make their land an economic asset." Bob Liddle, "Aborigines Are Australian too," in *A Treaty with the Aborigines?*, edited by Ken Baker (Melbourne: Institute for Public Affairs, 1988), 14.

cultural community as a whole – at least as conceived by elites within it – and those of (groups of) individual members. Liberal theory does not look to give precedence to the views of those who claim to speak in the interests of the cultural community as a whole, even if they are in the majority, because the interests of the minority cannot be discounted.

In the end, liberalism views cultural communities more like private associations or, to use a slightly different metaphor, electoral majorities. Both are the product of a multitude of factors, and neither need be especially enduring, although they can be. The possibility that they might be, however, does not justify entrenching the interests they manifest.

One significant objection raised here is that this individualist view is fundamentally an assimilationist one which is destructive of minority cultures because it ignores their need for special protection. The more forceful assertion of this criticism of liberalism has been Van Dyke's, and it is worth expounding more fully. Liberal doctrine, he argues, is at least integrationist if not assimilationist and finds permanent communalism unacceptable. The trouble is, permanent communalism may be exactly what some groups, notably "indigenous peoples," actually want.[41] Liberal "ideology," however, is inclined to "break up reservations, destroy tribal relations, settle Indians on their own homesteads, incorporate them into the national life, and deal with them not as nations or tribes or bands but as individual citizens," despite the fact that "many Indians do not want to be integrated into mainstream society."[42] Van Dyke quotes from the manifesto of the Indians who made the Longest Walk (1978): " 'How do we convince the U.S. government to simply leave us alone to live according to our ways of life? . . . We have the right to educate our children to our ways of life. . . . We have the right to be a people. These are inherent rights. . . . Our fight today is to survive as a people.' "[43]

All this leaves Van Dyke in no doubt that the individualist perspective, as he characterizes it, "gives an advantage to

41   Van Dyke, "Collective Entities," 29.

42   Ibid., 29. The internal quotation is from a Commissioner of Indian Affairs, as quoted by Frances Svensson, *The Ethnics in American Politics: American Indians* (Minneapolis: Burgess, 1973), 73.

43   Ibid., 29. The internal quotation is from *Congressional Record*, July 27, 1978, H7458.

members of the dominant group" who find it easier to establish rapport with those with influence and power and "tend to obtain disproportionate representation in the various elites."[44] (Elite members co-opted from minorities, he adds, tend not to be "representative," often because they have abandoned the culture from which they sprang.[45]) Moreover, individualism, "combined with the usual stress on personal merit," tends to be destructive of minority cultures because the schools are likely to promote the dominant culture and undermine all others. The minority person is likely to find his culture disparaged: "The whole attitude is an attack on the existence of the group and the self-respect of its members. It means oppression, and perhaps exploitation as well."[46]

But this outlook is mistaken both in its characterization of the liberal view, and in its assertions about liberalism's implications. There is no reason why liberals should press for assimilation or integration of cultures or find communalism unacceptable. Nor is there a good case, from a liberal point of view, for destroying tribal communities to force Indians to enter the mainstream of national life. This is not to say that no liberal thinker has defended views which might be used to justify such intentions, but there is no good reason to suppose that any liberal must go along with them. On the contrary, there is every reason, from a liberal point of view, to accede to the Indians request to "leave us alone to live according to our ways of life." What follows is the outline of a liberal point of view which does precisely this, without invoking claims about group rights.

From a liberal point of view the Indians' wish to live according to the practices of their own cultural communities has to be respected not because the culture has the right to be preserved but because individuals should be free to associate: to form communities and to live by terms of those associations. A corollary of this is that the individual should be free to dissociate from such communities. If there are any fundamental rights, then there is at least one right which is of crucial importance: the right of the individual to leave a community or association by the terms of which he or she no longer wishes to

---

44   Van Dyke, "The Individual, the State," 365.

45   Ibid., 365.

46   Ibid.

live. Cultural communities should, then, be looked on in this way: as associations of individuals whose freedom to live according to communal practices each finds acceptable is of fundamental importance.

This view appears to place great weight on the nature of cultural communities as *voluntary* associations. To some extent, this is so – but to a very small extent. Most cultural communities are not voluntary associations in any strong sense. Membership is usually determined by birth rather than by deliberate choice, and in many cases, there is no option of entry for those born outside – even though, as we have seen, groups will seek to redefine the boundaries of membership (and of group identity) when circumstances are propitious. Cultural communities may be regarded as voluntary associations to the extent that members recognize as legitimate the terms of association and the authority that upholds them. All that is necessary as evidence of such recognition is the fact that members choose not to leave. Recognition in these austere terms would, of course, be meaningless without the individual having one important right against the community: the right to be free to leave. That has to be the individual's fundamental right; it is also his only fundamental right, all other rights being either derivative of this right, or rights granted by the community.[47]

This view of the rights of the individual gives a great deal of authority to cultural communities. It imposes no requirement on those communities to be communities of any particular kind. It does not require that they become in any strong sense "assimilated," or even "integrated" into the mainstream of modern society. It in no sense requires that they be liberal societies; they may indeed be quite illiberal. There is thus no justification for breaking up such cultural communities by, for example, driving tribes off their lands or forcibly resettling them. The wider society has no right to require particular standards or systems of education within such cultural groups

[47] There are also rights which the individual might have as a member of the wider society. Some of these might be exercised by an individual while living in a cultural community within that society; other rights might not be open for the individual to take up without leaving his cultural community. For example, an individual might not be free to exercise the right to marry whomsoever she wishes if such a right is recognized by the wider society but not by her religious community – unless she chooses to leave her religion. This issue is discussed more fully later.

or to force their schools to promote the dominant culture. If members of a cultural community wish to continue to live by their beliefs, the outside community has no right to intervene to prevent those members acting within their rights.

Yet at the same time, this view does not give the cultural community any fundamental right. The basis of the community's authority is not any right of the culture to perpetuation, or even existence, but the acquiescence of its members. Those members have the inalienable right to leave – to renounce membership of – the community. This right is more potent than it might at first appear because it implies that in many circumstances, individuals within the cultural community are free to leave *together or in association with others* and to reconstitute the community under modified terms of association. Cultural communities without the broad support or commitment of their members will thus wither; yet communities within which there are only isolated pockets of discontent with its cultural norms might well prevail.

This version of the liberal individualist standpoint seeks, then, to strike a balance between the claims of the individual and the interests of the community. It recognizes the existence of cultural groups but denies that they are in any sense "natural," regarding them rather as associations of individuals drawn together by history and circumstance. As such, they have certain acquired interests, but these are in no way equivalent to the interests of all their members. The mutability of such communities reflects their nature as associations of individuals with different interests. The interests of the community as a whole and the interests of particular (groups of) individuals within may well conflict. The liberal individualist view outlined here, by regarding the group as having its moral basis in the acquiescence of individuals with its cultural norms, rejects the idea that the group as such has any right to self-preservation or perpetuation. Nonetheless, by seeing the right of association as fundamental, it gives considerable power to the group, denying others the right to intervene in its practices – whether in the name of liberalism or any other moral ideal.

But the thesis, as it stands, will be subjected to numerous objections from defenders of cultural rights and liberals alike and needs to be refined and given more careful expression. Some especially prominent criticisms are addressed in the following sections.

III

Criticisms of the standpoint expounded here come from two general directions: from those who think culture has been given too little recognition and from those who think it has been given too much. These objections have to be met. Somewhat fortuitously, they both appear in Will Kymlicka's recent study, *Liberalism, Community, and Culture*, that argues for a liberalism which gives special weight to claims of cultural membership. So I shall try to meet the criticisms in question by addressing some of the arguments advanced in Kymlicka's work.

Kymlicka maintains that liberals have been wrong to regard the idea of collective rights for minority cultures as theoretically incoherent and practically dangerous.[48] In his view, liberals can and should embrace the idea of cultural rights without denying liberalism's individualist premises – individualist premises of the kind I discussed earlier.[49] The right way to look at the issue, he suggests, is not to see a conflict between individual rights and group rights, or "respect for the individual" and "respect for the group." The real conflict, which does indeed pose a dilemma, is between two kinds of respect for the individual. Individuals might be due respect as members of a distinct cultural community – in which case "we must recognize the legitimacy of claims made by them for the protection of that culture" – or they might be due respect as citizens of the common political community – in which case "we must recognize the importance of being able to claim the rights of equal citizenship."[50] The demands of citizenship and the demands of cultural membership can pull in different directions because "differential citizenship rights may be needed to protect a cultural community from unwanted disintegration."[51] For Kymlicka, the solution to this dilemma lies not in rejecting liberalism but in reconciling minority rights with "liberal equality," thereby providing an individualist

[48] Kymlicka, *Liberalism*, 144.

[49] Thus the question that Kymlicka poses himself (on p. 162) is "How can we defend minority rights within liberalism, given that its moral ontology recognizes only individuals, each of whom is to be treated with equal consideration?"

[50] Ibid., 151.

[51] Ibid., 151–52.

justification of differential (cultural) rights.[52] And this means showing "that membership in a cultural community may be a relevant criterion for distributing the benefits and burdens which are the concern of a liberal theory of justice."[53]

In trying to show this, Kymlicka in effect mounts a case for thinking that culture has been given too little recognition in liberal theorizing. Certainly, the protection he wishes to give cultural communities exceeds that given them by the liberal theory advanced earlier in this essay. So the two considerations on which he defends cultural rights call for careful examination. The first consideration is the value of culture and cultural membership. Culture matters, Kymlicka argues, because the range of options open to us to choose is determined by our cultural heritage. It is within cultures, through examples and stories, that we learn about the kinds of life it is possible to lead, and we "decide how to lead our lives by situating ourselves in these cultural narratives, by adopting roles that have struck us as worthwhile ones, as ones worth living (which may, of course, include the roles we were brought up to occupy)."[54] Cultural structures are thus important because they provide "the context of choice."[55] The fundamental reason for supporting cultural membership is "that it allows for meaningful individual choice."[56] Liberals should be concerned with the fate of cultural structures because it is "only through having a rich and secure cultural structure that people can become aware, in a vivid way, of the options available to them, and intelligently examine their value."[57] Concern for the cultural structure thus "accords with, rather than conflicts with, the liberal concern for our ability and freedom to judge the value of our life-plans."[58]

The second consideration on which Kymlicka bases his defense of cultural rights is liberal equality. Cultural minor-

---

52 Ibid., 164: "Aboriginal rights, at least in their robust form will only be secure when they are viewed, not as competing with liberalism, but as an essential component of liberal political practice."

53 Ibid., 162.

54 Ibid., 165.

55 Ibid., 178.

56 Ibid., 197.

57 Ibid., 165.

58 Ibid., 167.

ities, such as the Inuit, he argues, suffer a particular disadvantage inasmuch as they "can face inequalities which are the product of their circumstances or endowment, not their choices or ambitions."[59] Their cultural communities are often undermined by decisions of people outside the community. Cultural minorities, compared with the majority culture, operate in unequal circumstances, and this, Kymlicka insists, is the case for all members of such minorities; thus "all Inuit people face the same inequality in circumstances."[60] His conclusion is that "only if we ground collective rights in unequal circumstances can we distinguish the legitimacy of Aboriginal rights from the illegitimacy of attempts of assorted racial, religious, class, or gender groups to gain special status for their preferred goals, and practices."[61]

Although Kymlicka's outlook is also a liberal individualist one, his position is clearly quite different from that advanced in this essay. While I have tried to play down concern for group rights by describing cultural communities as having their legitimate basis in individual freedom of association, Kymlicka wishes to emphasize group interests and sees them as having their basis in liberal concerns about choice and equality. Like Van Dyke, he is motivated by a concern for the plight of ethnic minorities, and "indigenous" peoples in particular. This theory is, however, untenable both from a liberal point of view and from the perspective of someone concerned with the interests of cultural minorities.

The problem stems from the attempt to justify cultural rights, which need to be given some foundation consistent with liberal theory. Kymlicka's foundation is essentially an argument about the primary importance of individual *autonomy*. Cultural rights protect autonomy. They do this inasmuch as they look to guarantee the stability of the cultural environment within which the individual is able to exercise the capacity to make meaningful choices. Unfortunately, many cultures do not place such importance on choice. This is an ideal which finds especial favor among the adherents of the liberalism of J. S. Mill. As Kymlicka himself notes, "For Mill the conditions under which people acquired their ends were important: it

[59]   Ibid., 190.

[60]   Ibid., 240.

[61]   Ibid., 241.

mattered whether their education and cultural socialization opened up or closed off the possibility of revising their ends."[62] Yet many cultures, including those of a number of the "indigenous peoples" referred to, do not place such value on the *individual's* freedom to choose his ends. Often, the individual and his interests are subordinated to the community. Moreover, the individual might be expected to accept uncritically the long-standing practices of the cultural group. Critical reflection need play no part in their conceptions of the good life.

Consider, for example, the following account by Kenneth Maddock of the nature of Australian Aboriginal society:

> On Anderson's view of freedom we would have to say either that Aboriginal society traditionally was servile in spirit or that it was not the kind of society in which attitudes of servility and independence could arise. Now the absence of opposition and criticism cannot be explained by an absence of inequality or disenfranchisement. It seems rather that explanation must be sought in the Aboriginal acceptance of a utopian conception of society according to which an order having been laid down all that remains to do is to conform to it. This anti-historical view of how things have come to be as they are is bound up with the disjoining of creativity, which is imputed to the powers, and tradition, fidelity to which is urged upon humans. When ideas like this take root – and the initiatory process is calculated to ensure they do – all prospect of opposition and criticism vanishes.[63]

Here we have a society in which the values of order and conformity are inculcated through ritual, with creativity and critical reflection on the fundamental nature of individual commitment to these values thereby extinguished. If these practices are to be allowed to continue in the wider society, the

62   Ibid., 19. See J. S. Mill, *On Liberty in Utilitarianism: On Liberty; Essay on Bentham*, edited with an introduction by Mary Warnock (London: Fontana, 1985), chap. 3.

63   Kenneth Maddock, *The Australian Aborigines: A Portrait of Their Society* (Ringwood: Penguin, 1972), 193–94. John Anderson's account of freedom, referred to at the beginning, suggested that freedom in a community is measured by the degree to which its ruling order meets with opposition and its ruling ideas with criticism, and that the servility of a community is measured by the extent to which political opposition is suppressed. This is discussed by Maddock on 192–93.

justification cannot be one which emphasizes the importance of preserving the context of choice. If choice and critical reflection are most highly valued, then it is cultural interference rather than cultural protection that is required. If we disdain interference, then choice ceases to be a consideration.

Having embraced choice as critically important, Kymlicka is drawn down the path of interference. This is revealed in his response to the problem of the Pueblo Indians raised by Svensson.[64] The problem arose when some members of this culture, following conversion to Christianity, chose to withdraw from certain communal functions while continuing to demand their "share" of community resources. The result was the ostracizing of, and denial of resources to, those apostates who had thus violated Pueblo religious norms. Objecting to this treatment, the Christian converts appealed to the "Indian Bill of Rights" (Title II, added to the 1968 Civil Rights Act) for religious protection. Other Indians objected to the extension of the Indian Bill of Rights to the Pueblos as destructive of their traditions, in which religion was an integral part of community life. Kymlicka's response is that "the restriction on religious liberty *couldn't* be defended on [his] account of minority rights" because, first, "there is no inequality in cultural membership to which if could be viewed as a response" and, second, the "ability of each member of the Pueblo reservation . . . to live in that community is not threatened by allowing Protestant members to express their religious beliefs."[65] To complaints by scholars like Svensson that for many of the Pueblos, "violation of religious norms is viewed as literally threatening the survival of the entire community."[66] Kymlicka responds that the only real evidence for such a claim is the dislike that the majority feels for the dissident practice. In this regard, he likens the complaint to Lord Devlin's claim that the acceptance of homosexuality undermines the English community. The mistake made here by people like Devlin, he suggests, is that of seeing anything that changes the *character* of the community as *undermining* the community.

Kymlicka makes the basis for his own view very clear: "If the goal is to ensure that each person is equally able to lead their

64 Svensson, "Liberal Democracy," 430–34.
65 Kymlicka, *Liberalism*, 196.
66 Svensson, "Liberal Democracy," 434.

chosen life within their own cultural community, then restricting religion in no way promotes that."[67] He is in no doubt that were the theocracy ended, each majority member of the Pueblo would still have "as much ability to use and interpret their own cultural experiences," and that "supporting the intolerant character of a cultural community undermines the very reason we had to support cultural membership – that it allows for meaningful individual choice."[68]

Yet the important question is, why make "meaningful individual choice" the basis for supporting cultural membership – particularly when this value is not recognized as such by the culture in question? Many cultural minorities besides the Pueblo Indians do not place individual autonomy or choice high in the hierarchy of values. To the extent that they have had to go so far as to defend their cultural integrity against invasion or exploitation, they have invoked the independence of their community's way of life and the importance of retaining their *identity*.[69] By insisting that the cultural community place a high value on individual choice, the larger society would in effect be saying that the minority culture must become much more liberal.

Kymlicka does not reject this conclusion, arguing that "finding a way to liberalize a cultural community without destroying it is a task that liberals face in every country, once we recognize the importance of a secure cultural context of choice."[70] Yet from the perspective of persons seeking to preserve the group identity or the cultural integrity of the minority community, this is surely unacceptable. First, they might raise an objection that Hume noted: that it is all too easy to judge societies by standards they do not recognize.[71] More

67   Kymlicka, *Liberalism*, 196.

68   Ibid., 196–97.

69   I have discussed the importance of identity with regard to the Australian Aborigines in *Without Oppression or Disputation: Aboriginal Identity and the Origins and Growth of the Protest Movement of the 1960s* (Canberra: B.A. Honors thesis, Department of History, Australian National University, 1978).

70   Kymlicka, *Liberalism*, 170. Elsewhere, Kymlicka writes of "helping the culture to move carefully towards a fully liberal society" (p. 170) and promoting "the longer-term idea of full liberal freedoms" (p. 171).

71   "There are no manners so innocent or reasonable, but may be rendered odious or ridiculous, if measured by a standard unknown to the persons; especially if you employ a little art or eloquence, in aggravating some

important, however, they would surely object that to elevate individual choice and suggest the course of "liberalizing" their cultures "without destroying them" is to fail to take their culture seriously. If their culture is not already liberal, if it does not prize individuality or individual choice, then to talk of liberalization is inescapably to talk of undermining their culture. Culture is not simply a matter of colourful dances and rituals, nor is it even a framework or context for individual choice. Rather, it is the product of the association of individuals over time, which in turn shapes individual commitments and gives meaning to individual lives – lives for which individual choice or autonomy may be quite valueless. To try to reshape it in accordance with ideals of individual choice is to strike at its very core.

Furthermore, it is not clear why it should be permissible to intervene in existing cultural practice even if the result is not the destruction of the culture but "merely" the reshaping of its "character." What many cultural communities are asking for, as the American Indian manifesto quoted earlier suggests, is to be left alone.[72] Moreover, they wish the reshaping of their community to take place, as far as possible, by the terms set by their own practices. If the change in character takes place as a result of dissident members of the minority community invoking "rights" granted them by the dominant culture, then the change constitutes not a response of the community to the new circumstances confronting it but a change enforced by the wider society interfering in its internal practices.

Although these arguments may justifiably be put against Kymlicka, it must also be borne in mind that none of this is to suggest that cultural communities can be insulated from the wider society. As T. S. Eliot suggested, this is an illusion which

circumstances, and extenuating others, as best suits the purpose of your discourse." David Hume, "A Dialogue," in Hume, *Enquiries Concerning Human Understanding and Concerning The Principles of Morals*, edited by L. A. Selby-Bigge, revised by P. H. Niddith (Oxford: Clarendon, 1975), 330.

[72] It must, in fairness, be noted that Kymlicka is not suggesting that there is any reason to think that there is always a case for practical intervention by, say, the courts in cultural community affairs. He notes in the case of the Pueblo Indians, for example, that the dispute may be best resolved by tribal courts "if that is the consensus among the Pueblo." See *Liberalism*, 197. What precisely is meant here by consensus, however, is perhaps in need of fuller explanation.

can only be maintained "by a careful fostering of local 'culture,' culture in the reduced sense of the word, as everything that is picturesque, harmless and separable from politics, such as language and literature, local arts and customs."[73] There must, of necessity, be some political contact between the dominant and the minority culture, and change is inescapable for both. The problem here is to establish the principles that account for the place of minority cultures within the larger society. The problem is not that of finding ways to insulate minority cultures against change.

The argument against Kymlicka is that his account of the place of cultural minorities seeks to entrench cultural rights on a basis which itself undermines many forms of cultural community, specifically those that fail in their practices to conform to liberal norms of tolerance and to honour the liberal ideal of autonomy. Cultural minorities are given protection – provided they mend their ways. In the end, it is only culture in Eliot's "reduced sense of the word" that is protected. Thus from the perspective of a defender of the interests of cultural minorities, Kymlicka's view has to be found wanting.

But his position is also inadequate from a liberal point of view. Here the problem stems from his desire to give cultural minorities differential rights on the basis of liberal equality. His contention is that cultural minorities are specially disadvantaged because they can face inequalities which are the result of circumstance rather than choice and that, in cases such as that of the Inuit, all members of the minority face the same inequality of circumstances as compared with the majority culture. Yet both parts of this contention look dubious in the extreme. First, there is no good reason to think that only minorities can face inequalities which are not the product of their choices. Anyone born physically or mentally disabled, for example, could make this claim no matter what his culture, as indeed might anyone born into poverty. If there is a reason to give cultural minorities special rights, lack of control over circumstances surely is not one of them.

Second, the idea that *all* minority members face the *same* inequality of circumstances seems absurd. Even if the Australian Aborigines are collectively and, on average, the worst

---

[73] T. S. Eliot, *Notes Towards the Definition of Culture* (London: Faber, 1962), 93.

off in the society (and they are if we look to the standard range of social indicators – from infant mortality to rates of imprisonment), there are many (even if, arguably, not enough) Aborigines who are better off – richer, better educated, more powerful– than the majority of Australians. So, why not give other disadvantaged Australians the same rights? Again, there seems to be no case here for special cultural rights.

If these two empirical propositions are the basis of Kymlicka's call for cultural rights, then that call looks extremely dubious from the point of view of the liberal idea of equal treatment.

In sum, Kymlicka's theory seems both to grant cultural minorities too much recognition and to give them too little. It gives them too much insofar as liberal equality does not appear to sanction special rights, and it gives them too little insofar as regarding choice or autonomy as the fundamental liberal commitment disregards the interests of cultural communities which do not value the individual's freedom to choose. If so, then it cannot mount a serious liberal challenge to the individualist view elaborated in this essay.

IV

Now it might, at this point, be objected that it is odd to criticize Kymlicka – or any other liberal view which seeks to incorporate cultural rights – for failing to respect some minority cultures, because the theory advanced in this essay maintains that cultures should not be given special protection, that there are no cultural rights. It is therefore worth reiterating that the point of this essay is not to disparage the interests of minorities but to argue that it is not necessary to abandon or modify liberal theory to do justice to their concerns. It is on the basis of this objective that Kymlicka's theory was questioned and found wanting from the perspectives of both cultural minorities and liberalism. The problem now is to explain more carefully what this liberalism amounts to and how it accounts for the place of cultural minorities in the wider society.

What should have become clear from the criticisms raised against Kymlicka is that the liberal view advanced here is individualist in quite a different way from some others. It begins with the relatively innocuous, shared assumption that moral evaluation is individualistic in the sense that what counts, ultimately, is how the lives of actual individuals are affected. "It is individual, sentient beings whose lives go better or worse, who suffer or flourish, and so it is their welfare that is the subject-matter of morality."[74] But unlike some other liberal views, including Kymlicka's, it does *not* go on to impose severe restrictions on what is to count as (a legitimate form of) human flourishing. It does not go on to suggest that human flourishing requires that the individual be capable of autonomy or have the capacity to choose his or her way of life on the basis of critical reflection on a range of options. Rather, it is content to accept that what matters most when assessing whether a way of life is legitimate is whether the individuals taking part in it are prepared to acquiesce in it.

These premises are somewhat austere. They may be more austere even than those on which Loren Lomasky chooses to defend his own conception of liberal basic rights: the idea of individuals as project pursuers.[75] Lomasky is critical of the idea of grounding liberal rights in the ideal of individual autonomy – and for good reason: With the defense of autonomy often comes a disregard for actual practices and ways of life.[76] For this reason, he argues that what is most important and requires recognition is that individuals are project pursuers. Projects may not be chosen: "A person's commitments may be unarticulated and not at all the product of conscious deliberation culminating in a moment of supreme decision. They may rather be something that he has gradually and imperceptibly come to assume over time in much the same way that one takes on distinctive vocal inflections or the cast of one's face."[77] Nonetheless, project pursuit is "partial." "To be committed to a long-term design, to order one's activities in light of it, to judge one's success or failure as a person by reference to its fate: these are inconceivable apart from a frankly partial attachment to one's most cherished ends." Thus, Lomasky maintains, an "individual's projects provide him with a *personal* – an intimately personal – standard of value to choose his actions

74 Kymlicka, *Liberalism*, 242.
75 Loren Lomasky, *Persons, Rights, and the Moral Community* (Oxford: Oxford University Press, 1987).
76 Ibid., 248–50.
77 Ibid., 42.

by. His central and enduring ends provide him reasons for action that are recognized as his own."[78]

But even to take personal project pursuit as fundamental to our nature excludes a part of human practice because some cultures are not able to accept the idea that *individual* projects can provide any sort of standard of value. Consider, once again, Maddock's portrait of Australian Aboriginal society:

> If we take human culture to be humanly created, then we are forced to the conclusion that there is among Aborigines a profound resistance to crediting themselves with their own cultural achievements. Their plan of life is held to have been laid down during The Dreaming by the powers and occasionally to have been modified since by the intervention of these powers, as when one appears to a man in a dream and communicates a new song or rite. Aborigines claim credit only for fidelity to tradition or, as they put it, for "following up The Dreaming". It is powers alone who are conceived as creative, men being passive recipients of unmotivated gifts. As men deny the creativity which is truly theirs, they can account for their culture only by positing that to create is to be other than human. To be human is to reproduce forms.[79]

In such a society, it would seem, individuals are not project pursuers; although they might be said to display commitments, they do not regard themselves as possessing *personal* goals.[80] Nonetheless, there may be enough reason to respect that way of life into which they have been inducted and which is the only life they know.

The theory advanced here looks to recognize as legitimate cultural communities which do not in their own practices conform to individualist norms or recognize the validity of personal projects. Yet at the same time, it is a liberal theory inasmuch as it does not sanction the forcible induction into or

---

[78]   Ibid., 27–8.

[79]   Maddock, *The Australian Aborigines*, 129.

[80]   Here I am not sure how strongly Lomasky wants to insist that projects are what provide personal standards by which individuals make choices. Elsewhere in his book he seems to suggest that any display of commitment may be taken as evidence of the existence of a project. See, for example, p. 45 where he says that all "patterns of motivated activity that form the structure of a scrutable life . . . merit recognition as projects." If so, there may be less reason for disagreement between us.

imprisoning of any individual in a cultural community. No one can be *required* to accept a particular way of life. Thus if, as has often happened, some members of a particular culture on making contact with the wider society wished to forsake their old ways, they would be free to do so, and the objections of their native community would not be recognized. In this respect, minorities within cultural minorities receive some protection. On the other hand, if those members wished not to leave their community but to assert rights recognized by the wider society but not by their culture, they receive no recognition. What is given recognition first and foremost is individual freedom of association (and dissociation). The practices of communities of individuals, the majority of whom accept the legitimacy of the association, must also be accepted, the views of dissidents notwithstanding.

The implications of this view deserve to be spelled out in concrete terms. In the case of the Old Order Amish of Wisconsin, raised by Van Dyke, for example, it means that they would have the right to live by their traditional ways. Their right not to send their children to public schools beyond the eighth grade would be grounded not in the First Amendment guarantee of freedom of religion but in the principle of freedom of association. (Indeed, the obligation of Amish parents to send their children to public schools at all becomes questionable.)

A similar conclusion would be defended in the case of gypsy children. Section 39 of the British Education Act of 1944 makes it an offense for a parent not to send a child to school regularly but includes a special provision for gypsy children of no fixed abode. Because their parents move constantly in search of seasonal work, they are required to attend only half the number of school sessions. But because gypsy custom does not value schooling, the parents believing they can educate a child satisfactorily through informal instruction in the ways of their culture, only a minority of children receive any formal primary education. Their freedom to associate and live by their own ways, however, would, by my argument, make this permissible. The argument put by Sebastian Poulter that because "at present many gypsy children are being denied the sort of education which would fit them to make a rational choice of lifestyle as adult," there may be reason to convict the parents under the Education Act and override "this particularly harmful aspect of gypsy tradition and culture"[81] would be rejected. There is no more reason to insist that gypsy parents offer their children a "rational choice" of life-style through public education than there is to require that other parents offer their children the opportunity to become gypsies.

In the case of the Pueblo Indians, it means that if the community refuses to accept the conversion of some of its individual members to Protestant Christianity, those individuals have to choose between abiding by the wishes of the community or ceasing to be a part of it. They may, of course, seek to change the Pueblo stance from within, but they may not appeal to any outside authority. As members of American society, they have freedom of religion; as Pueblo, they do not. The case of the individual Muslim wishing to deny that there is no other god but Allah and that Muhammad is his messenger is precisely analogous. As a citizen of a liberal society, he has the right of free speech; as a Muslim, however, he has no right to challenge Islam's fundamental tenet or to deny that the Quran was a part of God's essence by, say, embracing the metaphysical doctrines of the Mu'tazila.[82] The individual would therefore have to choose between being a part of the Muslim community and retaining his right of free speech. The community would be entitled to ostracize the individual who refuses to conform to its norms; it would not, however, be entitled to inflict any greater penalty.[83]

As these examples illustrate, the liberal view advanced here gives communities a considerable amount of power over the individuals who constitute their membership. Despite the individualist premises, some very strong "communitarian" conclusions have been reached. Communities undoubtedly are important, but it is not necessary to reject individualist

[81] Sebastian Poulter, "Ethnic Minority Customs, English Law and Human Rights," *International and Comparative Law Quarterly*, 36 (1987): 589–615, at 600–1.

[82] The Mu'tazila were an eighth-century Arab-Muslim school whose "larger philosophy, developed under the influence of Greek thought, betrayed the majority sentiment of the Arab-Muslim milieu about the nature of God and his creation. For other Muslims, Muhammad and the Quran, not reason, were the central experiences of Islam." See Ira M. Lapidus, *A History of Islamic Societies* (Cambridge: Cambridge University Press, 1988), 107 and 105–108 more generally.

[83] Certainly not the death penalty, as *some* Muslims have advocated in the case of Salman Rushdie.

premises so as to give them some recognition. To do this, however, the primacy of freedom of association is all-important; it has to take priority over other liberties – such as those of speech or worship – which lie at the core of the liberal tradition. Otherwise, "illiberal" communities cannot perpetuate themselves or even form.

This last point perhaps indicates more sharply what kind of liberal theory is being defended here. It is a theory which sees a liberal society as one that need not be made up of liberal communities. If society is, in Rawls's phrase, a "social union of social unions,"[84] there is no necessity that these all be liberal social unions. What is of crucial importance, however, is that each community enjoy a certain amount of independence and integrity: that they are in fact the social unions *of those individuals* and not simply the categories within which society places particular groups. For each social union to have any significant measure of integrity, it must *to some extent* be impervious to the values of the wider liberal society.

Yet the qualification "to some extent" is an important one. No community within a wider society can remain entirely untouched by the political institutions and the legal and moral norms of the whole. (One of the weaknesses of Robert Nozick's conception of utopia is that it suggests the possibility of a society of wholly independent communities unaffected by the workings of the other social unions or the society as a whole.[85]) For a number of reasons, most cultural communities will be profoundly affected by the wider community. The most important reason is the very fact of the society recognizing the freedom of the individual to leave his community. Once the individual has the option to leave, the nature of his community is transformed, particularly if the formal right comes with substantive opportunities.

The case of the New Zealand Maori provides an illustration of this point. Maori society before contact with Europeans was, as Richard Mulgan explains, a very strongly non-individualist culture. Groups and their welfare were the prime values, and individuals found their identity as part of the group, existing to serve collective ends. Individuals could

---

[84] John Rawls, *A Theory of Justice* (Oxford: Oxford University Press, 1971), 527–30.

[85] See Robert Nozick, *Anarchy, State and Utopia* (Oxford: Blackwell, 1974), part 3.

justifiably be subordinated or sacrificed for the good of the community. Yet today, Maori social life is much less collectively oriented, with many Maori living in urban areas away from their tribal settings. Indeed, Maori identity has become much more a matter of individual personal choice. The cause of this change was the possibility of leaving the community. A precontact Maori would never have contemplated leaving the clan or village, but this is no longer the case. As Mulgan remarks, "Once the possibility of leaving with impunity becomes a practicable and the fact of staying becomes a deliberate decision the ethical balance between individual and group has shifted irrevocably in the individual's direction. Total loyalty to the group and submersion in its activities and purposes can never be recovered."[86]

In the theory defended here, although cultural communities may seek to protect themselves against the intrusions of the wider society, they may not take any action they like to enforce group loyalty. Thus, in recognizing the right of exist, they would also have to abide by liberal norms forbidding slavery[87] and physical coercion. More generally, they would be bound by liberal prohibitions on "cruel, inhuman or degrading treatment."[88] Cultural groups that persisted in violating such norms would therefore disappear as their dissident members exercised their enforceable claims against the community.

Cultural communities, however much they tried to distance themselves from the larger society, would be affected by it to the extent that their ways of life might have external effects. Even communities that are geographically separate and remote might generate environmental externalities. In such cases, they would not be able to invoke the right of free association as a defense against prosecution for damages, for example. This, again, might well have the effect of fundamentally altering the practices within the community.

[86]   Richard Mulgan, *Maori, Pakeha and Democracy* (Auckland: Oxford University Press, 1989), 64.

[87]   This would include "voluntary slavery." For an argument showing why the individual has no right to sell himself into slavery, see Thomas W. Pogge, *Realizing Rawls* (Ithaca and London: Cornell University Press, 1989), 48–50.

[89]   See Poulter, "Ethnic Minority Customs," 602, for a discussion of this notion as it has affected British legislation through European Convention, Art. 3 and the International Covenant on Civil and Political Rights, Art. 7.

Indeed, cultural communities would be more profoundly affected by the wider society to the extent that they opt to coexist more closely with it. For example, an Indian immigrant community which had chosen (whether separately or collectively) to settle in the midst of English society might be determined to retain certain customs or practices but would be subject to established legal provisions for, say, testator's family maintenance. In this respect, such communities would be open to legal challenge by their own members who dissent from the rulings of the community. It would also affect the community's understanding of the marriage contract and possibly its understanding of the obligations of children to their parents.

The idea of accounting for the claims of minority cultural communities by taking freedom of association, and the corollary right of exit for a community, as fundamental may perhaps now be seen in fuller light. Although formulated earlier as a freedom which seems to offer purely formal guarantees, it is clearly one that has some substantive bite. Thus without establishing cultural rights, it may be possible to account for the legitimate claims of cultural minorities in a liberal social order. Before pressing this conclusion any more strongly, however, it is necessary to look at some lingering worries and to say a little more about the nature of the society which provides the context for this theory.

V

Doubts and reservations about the liberal view advanced here will come, as ever, from two directions. First, there will be those who argue that the interests of cultural communities have been given too little recognition; and second, there will be those who maintain that they have been given too much.

Writers, like Van Dyke, have a number of reasons for complaining that liberal theory gives groups too little prominence. Two merit further attention. The first is that the liberal view does not recognize group claims to self-determination; and the second is the related concern that without special entitlements, such groups will not be able to take action to protect their identity. Van Dyke suggests that self-determination is vitally important and " is essentially the moral right of a group."[89] The initial defense he offers for this view, that "the

---

[89]   Van Dyke, "The Individual, the State," 360.

existence of needs implies a right to act (within limits) to meet them, or that a conception of the good has a corresponding implication,"[90] is not especially robust, as little is said to explain how needs imply rights. But Van Dyke offers two other considerations: first, that sometimes "an interest of individuals can be best served, or only served, by allocating the related right to a group, and this is the case with self-determination."[91] In the face of "free and open individualistic competition with those who are more advanced," history shows us, groups such as indigenous peoples are not capable of defending their interests.[92] Second, he argues that as a matter of empirical fact, many societies, including international society through such agencies as UNESCO and the United Nations, have chosen to recognize the right of peoples to self-determination or to preserve their culture.[93] This only makes sense in the context of a conception of group or collective rights of self-determination. Unless we think in terms of group rights, a large part of modern practice cannot be justified.

In response to this, a number of things need to be said. First, and most generally, it has to be recognized that there are considerable limits to the extent to which collective self-determination is possible. Once cultures come into contact with others and trade and other forms of social intercourse develop, it is very difficult for the community to preserve its ways.[94] As Richard Mulgan has pointed out, once there is the possibility of the individual leaving the group with impunity, the balance changes, and some practices can never be recovered. While it is true to say that many cultural minorities find it difficult to preserve their ways in the midst of an alien culture, there is little reason to think that giving rights to the group will change the fundamental nature of the problem.

90   Ibid.; see also 350.
91   Van Dyke, "Collective Entities," 26.
92   Ibid., 28–29.
93   Ibid., 27.
94   This point is discussed by Karl Popper in his account of the development of the "open society" and the breakdown of tribalism. See his *The Open Society and Its Enemies. Volume I: The Spell of Plato* (London: Routledge & Kegan Paul, 1977), chap. 10, esp. 176–77. See also F. A. Hayek, *The Fatal Conceit: The Errors of Socialism*, edited by W. W. Bartley III (London: Routledge, 1989), esp. chap 3.

Second, even if self-determination were possible, groups are not always united. Often, as was pointed out early in this essay, communities form and acquire an identity only after cultural invasion (whether by immigrants or colonialists). The desire for collective self-determination is in many instances forged by elites seeking to unify disparate groups that did not always claim a collective identity. Thus the Maori, for example, did not exist as a single people in the precolonial period, consisting of different subtribes grouped together in larger *iwi*, or tribes.[95] They began to perceive a common identity after European settlement. Yet even so, there is considerable ambiguity in the matter of Maori identity because of generations of intermarriage, with many undecided about which group they belong to. With the Maori, as with many other cultures, self-determination is problematic because there is considerable internal disagreement about the direction it should take.

Third, it ought always to be borne in mind that to give any community the right of self-determination is never a matter of giving it the power of determining its own destiny alone. As Donald Horowitz has put it, "To encourage some groups to determine their own future may also mean allowing them to determine the future of others."[96] If power is to be devolved in such ways, it ought to be done with great care, partly because it can adversely affect the peace and stability of the larger society but also because it will also have serious repercussions within the smaller cultural community that is acquiring the so-called power of self-determination. This latter concern is particularly important when some of the self-proclaimed indigenous minorities are involved. The devolution of political power, as Horowitz has shown, tends to push conflict away from the major centers and into the subgroups.[97] The result is the exacerbation of subethnic divisions. While this may benefit the larger society which will no longer bear the brunt of ethnic confrontation, it may be highly destructive within some, relatively fragile, ethnic communities. The case of the Salish

[95]   See Mulgan, *Maori, Pakeha and Democracy*, 12.

[96]   Horowitz, *Ethnic Groups in Conflict*, 591.

[97]   "Where groups are territorially concentrated, devolution may have utility, not because it provides 'self-determination,' but because, once power is devolved, it becomes somewhat more difficult to determine who the self is." Horowitz, @*Ethnic Groups in Conflict*, 617.

fishing communities provides a striking – but tragic – example of this.[98]

This brings us to our fourth point: Van Dyke's objection that unless we think in terms of group rights, much of modern practice cannot be justified. Here he has in mind the fact that many polities and international practices give recognition to groups. Lebanon, for example, from the National Pact of 1943 to the civil war that began in 1975–76, had an electoral system that required interethnic coalitions and "prevented the crystallization of allegiances around the overarching affiliations of Muslim and Christian."[99] This was accomplished by recognizing and institutionalizing ethnic claims. For example, all major offices were reserved: the presidency for the Maronites, the prime ministership for the Sunnis, the speakership for the Shiites, and so on. On the liberal view, Van Dyke would object, such practices would not be acceptable.

One initial observation must be made: Such attempts to regulate and contain ethnic conflict do not always succeed; Lebanon's case has, after all, had only limited success to say the least. Nonetheless, there may sometimes be good reason to design political institutions to take into account the ethnic or cultural composition of the society. Yet there is no reason to see this as inconsistent with liberal theory, which, at least since

98   The Salish people sought protection for their traditional culture through the legal process, winning special rights enabling them to continue traditional fishing practices. Indeed, the courts chose to recognize the cultural importance of traditional fishing and provided greater fishing opportunities on the basis of treaty rights. But the implementation of the decision exacerbated hitherto unimportant divisions within Salish society between riparian and marine fisherfolk. This made for the disintegration of that cultural community to the extent that it has seen the development of new inequalities, several lawsuits, and even open hostility between tribes. On this see Michael R. Anderson, "Law and the Protection of Cultural Communities: The Case of Native American Fishing Rights," *Law and Policy* 9 (April 1987): 125–42. Anderson's sobering conclusion is that, of the factors explaining the "decay of traditional cultural community" among the Salish,

of greatest importance .. was the pre-existing cultural divisions within other tribes which encouraged treaty fishers to take advantage of their expanded fishing rights in distinctly different ways. While equal before the law in terms of treaty rights, the Salish were and are culturally diverse: traditional and capitalist marine fishers have different values and ways of viewing the world. It is perhaps not surprising that expanded opportunities accorded a culturally diverse group only reinforced the diversity. (Pp. 139–40).

99   Horowitz, *Ethnic Groups in Conflict*, 633.

Montesquieu, has recognized the importance of the institutions conforming to the nature of the social order. While the guiding principle of respect for *individual* rights or liberties has to be upheld, the question of what institutional mechanisms are necessary to protect individual rights and provide for the stability of the social order is, to some extent, an independent one. The choice of electoral systems, for example, will vary according to any of a number of factors, ranging from the structure of the wider political system to the geographical concentration of populations to the country's political history.

One of the factors that has to be considered when constructing – or reconstructing – institutional mechanisms is the power of significant groups within the polity. A political structure that ignored the power of a significant minority could run the risk of minority disaffection developing into separatist demands and breakdown into civil war; here the case of Sri Lanka springs to mind. Equally, a structure that was unmindful of the power of the majority group could bring about similarly unpleasant results. There is no need, however, to appeal to the rights of groups to justify designing mechanisms to cope with, and temper the exercise of, political power.

Indeed, it is often vitally important that group rights play no part in the justification of the mechanisms that uphold the modus vivendi. For such mechanisms to succeed, it is crucial that they be sensitive to the changing group composition of the political order and capable of adjusting the formal powers devolved toward particular groups in accordance with their actual power. (One of the reasons for the collapse of the Lebanese state was that the changing demographic structure produced by differential birth rates led to changes in the balance of power which some groups felt were not reflected in their formal standing.[100]) If groups are recognized as having rights *as groups*, it is must more difficult to justify mechanisms that vary their political entitlements with their size and influence. It is far better then to maintain an emphasis on the rights and liberties of the individual, while conceding that institutions have to be designed with a view to protecting those

---

[100] On this, see John P. Entelis, " 'How Could Something So Right Go So Wrong? The Collapse of Lebanon's Ethnoconfessional Democracy'," in *A Way Prepared: Essays on Islamic Culture in Honor of Richard Bayly Winder*, edited by Farhad Kazemi and R. D. McChesney (New York and London: New York University Press, 1988), 216–40.

liberties by accommodating (and guarding against) the vagaries of group power.[101]

Thus far, the objections of those who wish to see greater recognition of group rights have been addressed. From another quarter, however, would come objections that even the individualist view defended here gives too much weight to the interests of cultural minorities. The fundamental concern of those who hold this view is well expressed by Poulter in his discussion of toleration of immigrant cultures. "Cultural tolerance," he writes, "obviously cannot become 'a cloak for oppression and injustice within the immigrant communities themselves,' neither must it unduly strain and endanger the integrity of the 'social and cultural core' of English values as a whole."[102] Here is a clear statement of the view that minority cultural communities must conform to the standards of morality and justice of the wider society – first, for the sake of justice within the minority community, and second, for the sake of the stability and social unity of the society as a whole. Does the view defended in this essay run the risk of upholding injustice within minority communities – perhaps to the extent that this will undermine the stability of society as a whole?

If to do justice is to give each person his or her due, the answer to the first part of this question depends on what we think a person is due. The problem is that different cultural communities have different conceptions of what individuals are due or entitled to, and in many cases, these conceptions will not value those freedoms and equalities which figure prominently in liberal conceptions of justice. Here, then, it has to be admitted that by liberal standards there may be injustice within some cultural communities: Freedom of worship may not be

---

101   It is perhaps in this way that we should look to deal with some of the problems confronting Aboriginal and Indian communities who have claims based on past injustice. The solution is not to be found in recognizing group rights. Rather, it is to be found in specifying the entitlements of particular historical communities who were the victims of past injustice. Once the validity of their claims has been established (and I have said nothing here about how past injustice should be established or about the principles by which it should be treated), we can turn to the question of the institutional mechanisms needed to satisfy legitimate claims and rectify the injustice. If the granting of land rights is deemed an appropriate solution, this would open up the issue of the form which these rights should take, given the interests of the individuals in question and their communities.

102   Poulter, "Ethnic Minority Customs," 593.

respected; women may have opportunities closed off to them; and the rights of individuals to express themselves may be severely restricted.

Yet it must also be borne in mind that the probability and the extent of "injustice" is tempered by two factors. The first is that the acceptability of cultural norms and practices depends in part on the degree to which the cultural community is independent of the wider society. Tribal communities of Indians or Aborigines which are geographically remote and have little contact with the dominant society might well live according to ways which betray little respect for the individual. Yet cultural communities that are more fully integrated into the mainstream of society would not find it so easy because their members will also be a part of the larger legal and political order. They might, for example, be tied to that order not only by the fact of citizenship but by the fact that they own property, trade, and use public services. This makes it more difficult to maintain different standards of justice partly because community members (especially of the younger generation) may reject them in favor of the societywide norms but also because individuals are not free to change their cultural allegiances as convenient. We cannot choose to be Quakers only in wartime.

To take a practical example, people from the Indian subcontinent settling in Britain, may not be entitled to enforce the arranged marriages of unwilling brides. Under section 12 of the Matrimonial Causes Act of 1973, a marriage can be annulled if it took place under "duress," and the case of *Hirani v. Hirani* in 1982 established that the threat of social ostracism could place the individual under duress to a sufficient degree to determine that the marriage was not entered into voluntarily.[103] The immigrant community, while entitled to try to live by their ways, have no right here to expect the wider society to enforce those norms against the individual.[104]

The second factor tempering the probability and the extent of "injustice" is the principle upholding individual freedom of association and dissociation. If an individual continues to live in a community and according to ways that (in the judgment of

[103] Ibid., 599–600.

[104] The community would, of course, continue to ostracize the dissenting member. It is perhaps impossible to prevent the oppression and injustice resulting from the withdrawal of love or affection or social acceptance.

the wider society) treat her unjustly, even though she is free to leave, then our concern about the injustice diminishes. What is crucially important here, however, is the extent to which the individual does enjoy a *substantial* freedom to leave. As was indicated at the end of the preceding section, the freedom of the individual to dissociate from a community is a freedom with considerable substantive bite. Yet there are certain conditions which make this possible, and these ought, in conclusion, to be brought out more explicitly, for they go a little way further to indicating what kind of social and political order is upheld by the theory advanced here.

The most important condition which makes possible a substantive freedom to exit from a community is the existence of a wider society that is open to individuals wishing to leave their local groups. A society composed of tribal communities organized on the basis of kinship, for example, would not make the freedom of exit credible: The individual would have to choose between the conformity of the village and the lawlessness (and loneliness) of the heath. Exit would be credible only if the wider society were much more like a market society within which there was a considerable degree of individual independence and the possibility of what Weber called social closure was greatly diminished.

More important still, the wider society would have to be one in which the principle of freedom of association was upheld, and this seems unlikely in a social order in which the other liberal freedoms were not valued. This suggests that it may be necessary that the wider society itself be one that could be described as embodying a liberal political culture.

Chandran Kukathas is Lecturer in Politics at University College, University of New South Wales, at the Australian Defence Force Academy. He is author of *Hayek and Modern Liberalism* (Oxford University Press, 1989) and *Rawls: A Theory of Justice and Its Critics,* coauthored with Philip Pettit (Stanford University Press, 1990), and has also written for such journals as *Philosophical Quarterly* and *Political Studies*. He is currently writing a book on cultural diversity and political institutions.

THE CIVIL SOCIETY ARGUMENT
Michael Walzer

I

My aim here is to defend a complex, imprecise and, at crucial points, uncertain account of society and politics. I have no hope of theoretical simplicity, not at this historical moment when so many stable oppositions of political and intellectual life have collapsed; but I also have no desire for simplicity, since a world that theory could fully grasp and neatly explain would not, I suspect, be a pleasant place. In the nature of things, then, my argument will not be elegant, and though I believe that arguments should march, the sentences following one another like soldiers on parade, the route of my march today will be twisting and roundabout. I shall begin with the idea of civil society, recently revived by Central and East European intellectuals, and go on to discuss the state, the economy and the nation, and then civil society and the state again. These are the crucial social formations that we inhabit, but we do not at this moment live comfortably in any of them. Nor is it possible to imagine, in accordance with one or another of the great simplifying theories, a way to choose among them – as if we were destined to find, one day, the best social formation. I mean to argue against choosing, but I shall also claim that it is from within civil society that this argument is best understood.

The words 'civil society' name the space of uncoerced human association and also the set of relational networks – formed for the sake of family, faith, interests and ideology – that fill this space. Central and East European dissidence flourished within a highly restricted version of civil society, and the first task of the new democracies created by the dissidents, so we are told, is to rebuild the networks: unions, churches, political parties and movements, cooperatives, neighbourhoods, schools of thought, societies for promoting or preventing this and that. In the West, by contrast, we have lived in civil society for many years without knowing it. Or, better, since the Scottish

Enlightenment, or since Hegel, the words have been known to the knowers of such things, but they have rarely served to focus anyone else's attention. Now writers in Hungary, Czechoslovakia and Poland invite us to think about how this social formation is secured and invigorated.

We have reasons of our own for accepting the invitation. Increasingly, associational life in the 'advanced' capitalist and social democratic countries seems at risk. Publicists and preachers warn us of a steady attenuation of everyday cooperation and civil friendship. And this time it is possible that they are not, as they usually are, foolishly alarmist. Our cities really are noisier and nastier than they once were. Familial solidarity, mutual assistance, political likemindedness – all these are less certain and less substantial than they once were. Other people, strangers on the street, seem less trustworthy than they once did. The Hobbesian account of society is more persuasive than it once was.

Perhaps this worrisome picture follows – in part, no more, but what else can a political theorist say? – from the fact that we have not thought enough about solidarity and trust or planned for their future. We have been thinking too much about social formations different from, in competition with, civil society. And so we have neglected the networks through which civility is produced and reproduced. Imagine that the following questions were posed, one or two centuries ago, to political theorists and moral philosophers: what is the preferred setting, the most supportive environment, for the good life? What sorts of institution should we work for? Nineteenth- and twentieth-century social thought provides four different, by now familiar, answers to these questions. Think of them as four rival ideologies, each with its own claim to completeness and correctness. Each of them is importantly wrong. Each of them neglects the necessary pluralism of any *civil* society. Each of them is predicated on an assumption I mean to attack: that such questions must receive a singular answer.

II

I shall begin, since this is for me the best-known ground, with two leftist answers. The first of the two holds that the preferred setting for the good life is the political community, the democratic state, within which we can be citizens: freely engaged, fully committed, decision-making members. And a citizen, on this view, is much the best thing to be. To live well is to be politically active, working with our fellow citizens, collectively determining our common destiny – not for the sake of this or that determination but for the work itself, in which our highest capacities as rational and moral agents find expression. We know ourselves best as persons who propose, debate and decide.

This argument goes back to the Greeks, but we are most likely to recognize its neoclassical versions. It is Rousseau's argument, or the standard leftist interpretation of Rousseau's argument. His understanding of citizenship as moral agency is one of the key sources of democratic idealism. We can see it at work in liberals like John Stuart Mill, in whose writings it produced an unexpected defence of syndicalism (what is today called 'workers' control') and, more generally, of social democracy. It appeared among nineteenth- and twentieth-century democratic radicals, often with a hard populist edge. It played a part in the reiterated demand for social inclusion by women, workers, blacks and new immigrants, all of whom based their claims on their capacity as agents. And this same neoclassical idea of citizenship resurfaced in the 1960s in New Left theories of participation, where it was, however, like many latter-day revivals, highly theoretical and without local resonance.

Today, perhaps in response to the political disasters of the late 1960s, 'communitarians' in the United States' struggle to give Rousseauian idealism a historical reference, looking back to the early American republic and calling for a renewal of civic virtue. They prescribe citizenship as an antidote to the fragmentation of contemporary society – for these theorists, like Rousseau, are disinclined to value the fragments. In their hands, republicanism is still a simplifying creed. If politics is our highest calling, then we are called away from every other activity (or, every other activity is redefined in political terms); our energies are directed towards policy formation and decision-making in the democratic state.

I don't doubt that the active and engaged citizen is an attractive figure – even if some of the activists that we actually meet carrying placards and shouting slogans aren't all that attractive. The most penetrating criticism of this first answer to the question about the good life is not that the life isn't good but that it isn't the 'real life' of very many people in the modern world. This is so in two senses. First, though the power of the democratic state has grown enormously, partly (and rightly) in response to the demands of engaged citizens, it cannot be said that the state is fully in the hands of its citizens. And the larger it gets, the more it takes over those smaller associations still subject to hands-on control. The rule of the *demos* is in significant ways illusory; the participation of ordinary men and women in the activities of the state (unless they are state employees) is largely vicarious; even party militants are more likely to argue and complain than actually to decide.

Second, despite the singlemindedness of republican ideology, politics rarely engages the full attention of the citizens who are supposed to be its chief protagonists. They have too many other things to worry about. Above all, they have to earn a living. They are more deeply engaged in the economy than in the political community. Republican theorists (like Hannah Arendt) recognize this engagement only as a threat to civic virtue. Economic activity belongs to the realm of necessity, they argue; politics to the realm of freedom. Ideally, citizens should not have to work; they should be served by machines, if not by slaves, so that they can flock to the assemblies and argue with their fellows about affairs of state. In practice, however, work, though it begins in necessity, takes on value of its own – expressed in commitment to a career, pride in a job well done, a sense of camaraderie in the workplace. All of these are competitive with the values of citizenship.

III

The second leftist position on the preferred setting for the good life involves a turning away from republican politics and a focus instead on economic activity. We can think of this as the socialist answer to the questions I began with; it can be found in Marx and also, though the arguments are somewhat different, among the utopians he hoped to supersede. For Marx, the preferred setting is the cooperative economy, where we can all be producers – artists (Marx was a romantic), inventors and craftsmen. (Assembly-line workers don't quite seem to fit.) This again is much the best thing to be. The picture Marx paints is of creative men and women making useful and beautiful objects, not for the sake of this or that object but for the sake of creativity itself, the highest expression of our 'species-being' as *homo faber*, man-the-maker.

The state, in this view, ought to be managed in such a way as to set productivity free. It doesn't matter who the managers are so long as they are committed to this goal and rational in its pursuit. Their work is technically important but not substantively interesting. Once productivity is free, politics simply ceases to engage anyone's attention. Before that time, in the Marxist here and now, political conflict is taken to be the superstructural enactment of economic conflict, and democracy is valued mainly because it enables socialist movements and parties to organize for victory. The value is instrumental and historically specific. A democratic state is the preferred setting not for the good life but for the class struggle; the purpose of the struggle is to win, and victory brings an end to democratic instrumentality. There is no intrinsic value in democracy, no reason to think that politics has, for creatures like us, a permanent attractiveness. When we are all engaged in productive activity, social division and the conflicts it engenders will disappear, and the state, in the once-famous phrase, will wither away.

In fact, if this vision were ever realized, it is politics that would wither away. Some kind of administrative agency would still be necessary for economic coordination, and it is only a Marxist conceit to refuse to call this agency a state. 'Society regulates the general production', Marx wrote in *The German Ideology*, 'and thus makes it possible for me to do one thing today and another tomorrow . . . just as I have a mind'. Since this regulation is non-political, the individual producer is freed from the burdens of citizenship. He attends instead to the things he makes and to the cooperative relationships he establishes. Exactly how he can work with other people and still do whatever he pleases is unclear to me and probably to most other readers of Marx. The texts suggest an extraordinary faith in the virtuosity of the regulators. No one, I think, quite shares this faith today, but something like it helps to explain the tendency of some leftists to see even the liberal and democratic state as an obstacle that has to be, in the worst of recent jargons, 'smashed'.

The seriousness of Marxist anti-politics is nicely illustrated by Marx's own dislike of syndicalism. What the syndicalists proposed was a neat amalgam of the first and second answers to the question about the good life: for them, the preferred setting was the worker-controlled factory, where men and women were simultaneously citizens and producers, making decisions and making things. Marx seems to have regarded the combination as impossible; factories could not be both democratic and productive. This is the point of Engels's little essay on authority, which I take to express Marx's view also. More generally, self-government on the job called into question the legitimacy of 'social regulation' or state planning, which alone, Marx thought, could enable individual workers to devote themselves, without distraction, to their work.

But this vision of the cooperative economy is set against an unbelievable background – a non-political state, regulation without conflict, 'the administration of things'. In every actual experience of socialist politics, the state has moved rapidly into the foreground, and most socialists, in the West at least, have been driven to make their own amalgam of the first and second answers. They call themselves *democratic* socialists, focusing on the state as well as (in fact, much more than) on the economy and doubling the preferred settings for the good life. Since I believe that two are better than one, I take this to be progress. But before I try to suggest what further progress might look like, I need to describe two more ideological answers to the question about the good life, one of them capitalist, the other nationalist. For there is no reason to think that only leftists love singularity.

IV

The third answer holds that the preferred setting for the good life is the marketplace, where individual men and women, consumers rather than producers, choose among a maximum number of options. The autonomous individual confronting his, and now her, possibilities – this is much the best thing to be. To live well is not to make political decisions or beautiful objects; it is to make personal choices. Not any particular choices, for no choice is substantively the best: it is the activity of choosing that makes for autonomy. And the market within which choices are made, like the socialist economy, largely dispenses with politics; it requires at most a minimal state – not 'social regulation', only the police.

Production, too, is free even if it isn't, as in the Marxist vision, freely creative. More important than the producers, however, are the entrepreneurs, heroes of autonomy, consumers of opportunity, who compete to supply whatever all the other consumers want or might be persuaded to want. Entrepreneurial activity tracks consumer preference. Though not without its own excitements, it is mostly instrumental: the aim of all entrepreneurs (and all producers) is to increase their market power, maximize their options. Competing with one another, they maximize everyone else's option too, filling the market place with desirable objects. The market is preferred (over the political community and the cooperative economy) because of its fullness. Freedom, in the capitalist view, is a function of plenitude. We can only choose when we have many choices.

It is also true, unhappily, that we can only make effective (rather than merely speculative or wistful) choices when we have resources to dispose of. But people come to the marketplace with radically unequal resources – some with virtually nothing at all. Not everyone can compete successfully in commodity production, and therefore not everyone has access to commodities. Autonomy turns out to be a high-risk value, which many men and women can only realize with help from their friends. The market, however, is not a good setting for mutual assistance, for I cannot help someone else without reducing (for the short term, at least) my own options. And I have no reason, as an autonomous individual, to accept any reductions of any sort for someone else's sake. My argument here is not that autonomy collapses into egotism, only that autonomy in the marketplace provides no support for social solidarity. Despite the successes of capitalist production, the good life of consumer choice is not universally available. Large numbers of people drop out of the market economy or live precariously on its margins.

Partly for this reason, capitalism, like socialism, is highly dependent on state action – not only to prevent theft and enforce contracts but also to regulate the economy and guarantee the minimal welfare of its participants. But these participants, in so far as they are market activists, are not active in the state: capitalism in its ideal form, like socialism again, does not make for citizenship. Or, its protagonists conceive of citizenship in economic terms, so that citizens are transformed into autonomous consumers, looking for the party or programme that most persuasively promises to strengthen their market position. They need the state, but have no moral relation to it, and they control its officials only as consumers control the producers of commodities, by buying or not buying what they make.

Since the market has no political boundaries, capitalist entrepreneurs also evade official control. They need the state but have no loyalty to it; the profit motive brings them into conflict with democratic regulation. So arms merchants sell the latest military technology to foreign powers and manufacturers move their factories overseas to escape safety codes or minimum wage laws. Multinational corporations stand outside (and to some extent against) every political community. They are known only by their brand names, which, unlike family names and country names, evoke preferences but not affections or solidarities.

V

The fourth answer to the question about the good life can be read as a response to market amorality and disloyalty, though it has, historically, other sources as well. According to the fourth answer, the preferred setting is the nation, within which we are loyal members, bound to one another by ties of blood and history. And a member, secure in his membership, literally part of an organic whole – this is much the best thing to be. To live well is to participate with other men and women in remembering, cultivating and passing on a national heritage. This is so, on the nationalist view, without reference to the specific content of the heritage, so long as it is one's own, a matter of birth, not choice. Every nationalist will, of course, find value in his own heritage, but the highest value is not in the finding but in the willing: the firm identification of the individual with a people and a history.

Nationalism has often been a leftist ideology, historically linked to democracy and even to socialism. But it is most characteristically an ideology of the right, for its understanding of membership is ascriptive; it requires no political choices and no activity beyond ritual affirmation. When nations find themselves ruled by foreigners, however, ritual affirmation is not enough. Then nationalism requires a more heroic loyalty:

self-sacrifice in the struggle for national liberation. The capacity of the nation to elicit such sacrifices from its members is proof of the importance of this fourth answer. Individual members seek the good life by seeking autonomy not for themselves but for their people. Ideally, this attitude ought to survive the liberation struggle and provide a foundation for social solidarity and mutual assistance. Perhaps, to some extent, it does: certainly the welfare state has had its greatest successes in ethnically homogeneous countries. It is also true, however, that once liberation has been secured, nationalist men and women are commonly content with a vicarious rather than a practical participation in the community. There is nothing wrong with vicarious participation, on the nationalist view, since the good life is more a matter of identity than activity – faith, not works, so to speak, though both of these are understood in secular terms.

In the modern world, nations commonly seek statehood, for their autonomy will always be at risk if they lack sovereign power. But they don't seek states of any particular kind. No more do they seek economic arrangements of any particular kind. Unlike religious believers who are their close kin and (often) bitter rivals, nationalists are not bound by a body of authoritative law or a set of sacred texts. Beyond liberation, they have no programme, only a vague commitment to continue a history, to sustain a 'way of life'. Their own lives, I suppose, are emotionally intense, but in relation to society and economy this is a dangerously free-floating intensity. In time of trouble, it can readily be turned against other nations, particularly against the internal others: minorities, aliens, strangers, Democratic citizenship, worker solidarity, free enterprise and consumer autonomy – all these are less exclusive that nationalism but not always resistant to its power. The ease with which citizens, workers and consumers become fervent nationalists is a sign of the inadequacy of the first three answers to the question about the good life. The nature of nationalist fervour signals the inadequacy of the fourth.

VI

All these answers are wrong-headed because of their singularity. They miss the complexity of human society, the inevitable conflicts of commitment and loyalty. Hence I am uneasy with the idea that there might be a fifth and finally correct answer to the question about the good life. Still, there is a fifth answer, the newest one (it draws upon less central themes of nineteenth- and twentieth-century social thought), which holds that the good life can only be lived in civil society, the realm of fragmentation and struggle but also of concrete and authentic solidarities, where we fulfil E. M. Forster's injunction 'only connect', and become sociable or communal men and women. And this is, of course, much the best thing to be. The picture here is of people freely associating and communicating with one another, forming and reforming groups of all sorts, not for the sake of any particular formation – family, tribe, nation, religion, commune, brotherhood or sisterhood, interest group or ideological movement – but for the sake of sociability itself. For we are by nature social, before we are political or economic, beings.

I would rather say that the civil society argument is a corrective to the four ideological accounts of the good life – part-denial, part-incorporation – rather than a fifth to stand alongside them. It challenges their singularity, but it has no singularity of its own. The phrase 'social being' describes men and women who are citizens, producers, consumers, members of the nation and much else besides – and none of these by nature or because it is the best thing to be. The associational life of civil society is the actual ground where all versions of the good are worked out and tested . . . and proven to be partial, incomplete, ultimately unsatisfying. It cannot be the case that living on this ground is good-in-itself; there isn't any other place to live. What is true is that the quality of our political and economic activity and of our national culture is intimately connected to the strength and vitality of our associations.

Ideally, civil society is a *setting of settings*: all are included, none is preferred. The argument is a liberal version of the four answers, accepting them all, insisting that each leave room for the others, therefore not finally accepting any of them. Liberalism appears here as an anti-ideology, and this is an attractive position in the contemporary world. I shall stress this attractiveness as I try to explain how civil society might actually incorporate and deny the four answers. Later on, however, I shall have to argue that this position too, so genial and benign, has its problems.

Let's begin with the political community and the cooperative economy, taken together. These two leftist versions of the good life systematically undervalued all associations except the demos and the working class. Their protagonists could imagine conflicts between political communities and between classes, but not within either; they aimed at the abolition or transcendence of particularism and all its divisions. Theorists of civil society, by contrast, have a more realistic view of communities and economies. They are more accommodating to conflict – that is, to political opposition and economic competition. Associational freedom serves for them to legitimate a set of market relations, though not necessarily the capitalist set. The market, when it is entangled in the network of associations, when the forms of ownership are pluralized, is without doubt the economic formation most consistent with the civil society argument. This same argument also serves to legitimate a kind of state, liberal and pluralist more than republican (not so radically dependent upon the virtue of its citizens). Indeed, a state of this sort, as we will see, is necessary if associations are to flourish.

Once incorporated into civil society, neither citizenship nor production can ever again be all-absorbing. They will have their votaries, but these people will not be models for the rest of us – or they will be partial models only, for some people at some time of their lives, not for other people, not at other times. This pluralist perspective follows in part, perhaps, from the lost romance of work, from our experience with the new productive technologies and the growth of the service economy. Service is more easily reconciled with a vision of man as a social animal than with *homo faber*. What can a hospital attendant or a school teacher or a marriage counsellor or a social worker or a television repairman or a government official be said to *make*? The contemporary economy does not offer many people a chance for creativity in the Marxist sense. Nor does Marx (or any socialist thinker of the central tradition) have much to say about those men and women whose economic activity consists entirely in helping other people. The helpmate, like the housewife, was never assimilated to the class of workers.

In similar fashion, politics in the contemporary democratic state does not offer many people a chance for Rousseauian self-determination. Citizenship, taken by itself, is today mostly a passive role: citizens are spectators who vote. Between elections, they are served, well or badly, by the civil service. They are not at all like those heroes of republican mythology, the citizens of ancient Athens meeting in assembly and (foolishly, as it turned out) deciding to invade Sicily. But in the associational networks of civil society, in unions, parties, movements, interest groups, and so on, these same people make many smaller decisions and shape to some degree the most distant determinations of state and economy. And in a more densely organized, more egalitarian civil society they might do both these things to greater effect.

These socially engaged men and women – part-time union officers, movement activists, party regulars, consumer advocates, welfare volunteers, church members, family heads – stand outside the republic of citizens as it is commonly conceived. They are only intermittently virtuous; they are too caught up in particularity. They look, most of them, for many partial fulfilments, no longer for the one clinching fulfilment. On the ground of actuality (unless the state usurps the ground), citizenship shades off into a great diversity of (sometimes divisive) decision-making roles; and, similarly, production shades off into a multitude of (sometimes competitive) socially useful activities. It is, then, a mistake to set politics and work in opposition to one another. There is no ideal fulfilment and no essential human capacity. We require many settings so that we can live different kinds of good lives.

All this is not to say, however, that we need to accept the capitalist version of competition and division. Theorists who regard the market as the preferred setting for the good life aim to make it the actual setting for as many aspects of life as possible. Their singlemindedness takes the form of market imperialism; confronting the democratic state, they are advocates of privatization and *laissez-faire*. Their ideal is a society in which all goods and services are provided by entrepreneurs to consumers. That some entrepreneurs would fail and many consumers find themselves helpless in the marketplace – this is the price of individual autonomy. It is, obviously, a price we already pay: in all capitalist societies, the market makes for inequality. The more successful its imperialism, the greater the inequality. But were the market to be set firmly within civil society, politically constrained, open to communal as well as private initiatives, limits might be fixed on its unequal outcomes. The exact nature of the limits would depend on the strength and density of the associational networks (including, now, the political community).

The problem with inequality is not merely that some individuals are more capable, others less capable, of making their consumer preferences effective. It's not that some individuals live in fancier apartments than others, or drive better-made cars, or take vacations in more exotic places. These are conceivably the just rewards of market success. The problem is that inequality commonly translates into domination and radical deprivation. But the verb 'translates' here describes a socially mediated process, which is fostered or inhibited by the structure of its mediations. Dominated and deprived individuals are likely to be disorganized as well as impoverished, whereas poor people with strong families, churches, unions, political parties and ethnic alliances are not likely to be dominated or deprived for long. Nor need these people stand alone even in the marketplace. The capitalist answer assumes that the good life of entrepreneurial initiative and consumer choice is a life led most importantly by individuals. But civil society encompasses or can encompass a variety of market agents: family businesses, publicly owned or municipal companies, worker communes, consumer cooperatives, non-profit organizations of many different sorts. All these function in the market though they have their origins outside. And just as the experience of democracy is expanded and enhanced by groups that are in but not of the state, so consumer choice is expanded and enhanced by groups that are in but not of the market.

It is only necessary to add that among the groups in but not of the state are market organizations, and among the groups in but not of the market are state organizations. All social forms are relativized by the civil society argument – and on the actual ground too. This also means that all social forms are contestable; moreover, contests can't be won by invoking one or another account of the preferred setting – as if it were enough to say that market organizations, in so far as they are efficient, do not have to be democratic or that state firms, in so far as they are democratically controlled, do not have to operate within the constraints of the market. The exact character of our associational life is something that has to be argued about, and it is in the course of these arguments that we also decide about the forms of democracy, the nature of work, the extent and effects of market inequalities, and much else.

The quality of nationalism is also determined within civil society, where national groups coexist and overlap with families and religious communities (two social formations largely neglected in modernist answers to the question about the good life) and where nationalism is expressed in schools and movements, organizations for mutual aid, cultural and historical societies. It is because groups like these are entangled with other groups, similar in kind but different in aim, that civil society holds out the hope of a domesticated nationalism. In states dominated by a single nation, the multiplicity of the groups pluralizes nationalist politics and culture; in states with more than one nation, the density of the networks prevents radical polarization.

Civil society as we know it has its origin in the struggle for religious freedom. Though often violent, the struggle held open the possibility of peace,. 'The establishment of this one thing', John Locke wrote about toleration, 'would take away all ground of complaints and tumults upon account of conscience.' One can easily imagine groundless complaints and tumults, but Locke believed (and he was largely right) that tolerance would dull the edge of religious conflict. People would be less ready to take risks once the stakes were lowered. Civil society simply is that place where the stakes are lower, where, in principle, at least, coercion is used only to keep the peace and all associations are equal under the law. In the market, this formal equality often has no substance, but in the world of faith and identity, it is real enough. Though nations do not compete for members in the same way as religions (sometimes) do, the argument for granting them the associational freedom of civil society is similar. When they are free to celebrate their histories, remember their dead, and shape (in part) the education of their children, they are more likely to be harmless than when they are unfree. Locke may have put the claim too strongly when he wrote that 'There is only one thing which gathers people into seditious commotions, and that is oppression', but he was close enough to the truth to warrant the experiment of radical tolerance.

But if oppression is the cause of seditious commotion, what is the cause of oppression? I don't doubt that there is a materialist story to tell here, but I want to stress the central role played by ideological single-mindedness: the intolerant universalism of (most) religions, the exclusivity of (most) nations. The actual experience of civil society, when it can be had, seems to work against these two. Indeed, it works so well, some observers think, that neither religious faith nor national identity is like to survive for long in the network of free associations. But we really don't know to what extent faith and identity depend upon coercion or whether they can reproduce themselves under conditions of freedom. I suspect that they both respond to such deep human needs that they will outlast their current organizational forms. It seems, in any case, worthwhile to wait and see.

VII

But there is no escape from power and coercion, no possibility of choosing, like the old anarchists, civil society alone. A few years ago, in a book called *Anti-Politics*, the Hungarian dissident George Konrad described a way of living alongside the totalitarian state but, so to speak, with one's back turned towards it. He urged his fellow dissidents to reject the very idea of seizing or sharing power and to devote their energies to religious, cultural, economic and professional associations. Civil society appears in his book as an alternative to the state, which he assumes to be unchangeable and irredeemably hostile. His argument seemed right to me when I first read his book. Looking back, after the collapse of the communist regimes in Hungary and elsewhere, it is easy to see how much it was a product of its time – and how short that time was! No state can survive for long if it is wholly alienated from civil society. It cannot outlast its own coercive machinery; it is lost, literally, without its firepower. The production and reproduction of loyalty, civility, political competence and trust in authority are never the work of the state alone, and the effort to go it alone – one meaning of totalitarianism – is doomed to failure.

The failure, however, has carried with it terrible costs, and so one can understand the appeal of contemporary anti-politics. Even as Central and East European dissidents take power, they remain, and should remain, cautious and apprehensive about its uses. The totalitarian project has left behind an abiding sense of bureaucratic brutality. Here was the ultimate form of political singlemindedness, and though the 'democratic' (and, for that matter, the 'communist') ideology on which it rested was false, the intrusions even of a more genuine democracy are rendered suspect by the memory. Post-totalitarian politicians and writers have, in addition, learned the older anti-politics of free enterprise – so that the *laissez-faire* market is defended in the East today as one of the necessary institutions of civil society, or, more strongly, as the dominant social formation. This second view takes on plausibility from the extraordinary havoc wrought by totali-tarian economic planning. But it rests, exactly like political singlemindedness, on a failure to recognize the pluralism of associational life. The first view leads, often, to a more interesting and more genuinely liberal mistake: it suggests that pluralism is self-sufficient and self-sustaining.

This is, indeed, the experience of the dissidents; the state could not destroy their unions, churches, free universities, illegal markets, *samizdat* publications. None the less, I want to warn against the anti-political tendencies that commonly accompany the celebration of civil society. The network of associations incorporates, but it cannot dispense with the agencies of state power; neither can socialist cooperation or capitalist competition dispense with the state. That's why so many dissidents are ministers now. It is indeed true that the new social movements in the East and the West – concerned with ecology, feminism, the rights of immigrants and national minorities, workplace and product safety, and so on – do not aim, as the democratic and labour movements once aimed, at taking power. This represents an important change, in sensibility as much as in ideology, reflecting a new valuation of parts over wholes and a new willingness to settle for something less than total victory. But there can be no victory at all that does not involve some control over, or use of, the state apparatus. The collapse of totalitarianism is empowering for the members of civil society precisely because it renders the state accessible.

Here is the paradox of the civil society argument. Citizenship is one of many roles that members play, but the state itself is unlike all the other associations. It both frames civil society and occupies space within it. It fixes the boundary conditions and the basic rules of all associational activity (including political activity). It compels association members to think about a common good, beyond their own conceptions of the good life. Even the failed totalitarianism of, say, the Polish communist state had this much impact upon the Solidarity union: it determined that Solidarity was a Polish union, focused on economic arrangements and labour policy within the borders of Poland. A democratic state, which is continuous with the other associations, has at the same time a greater say about their quality and vitality. It serves, or it doesn't serve, the needs of the associational networks as these are worked out by men and women who are simultaneously members and citizens. I will give only a few obvious examples, drawn from American experience.

Families with working parents need state help in the form of publicly funded day-care and effective public schools. National minorities need help in organizing and sustaining their own educational programmes. Worker-owned companies and consumer cooperatives need state loans or loan guarantees; so (even more often) do capitalist entrepreneurs and firms. Philanthropy and mutual aid, churches and private universities, depend upon tax exemptions. Labour unions need legal recognition and guarantees against 'unfair labour practices'. Professional associations need state support for their licensing procedures. And across the entire range of association, individual men and women need to be protected against the power of officials, employers, experts, party bosses, factory supervisers, directors, priests, parents, patrons: and small and weak groups need to be protected against large and powerful ones. For civil society, left to itself, generates radically unequal power relationships, which only state power can challenge.

Civil society also challenges state power, most importantly when associations have resources or supporters abroad: world religions, pan-national movements, the new environmental groups, multinational corporations. We are likely to feel differently about these challenges, especially after we recognize the real but relative importance of the state. Multinational corporations, for example, need to be constrained, much like states with imperial ambitions; and the best constraint probably lies in collective security, that is, in alliances with other states that give economic regulation some international effect. The same mechanism may turn out to be useful to the new environmental groups. In the first case, the state pressures the corporation; in the second it responds to environmentalist pressure. The two cases suggest, again, that civil society requires political agency. And the state is an indispensable agent – even if the associational networks also, always, resist the organizing impulses of state bureaucrats.

Only a democratic state can create a democratic civil society; only a democratic civil society can sustain a democratic state. The civility that makes democratic politics possible can only be learned in the associational networks; the roughly equal and widely dispersed capabilities that sustain the networks have to be fostered by the democratic state. Confronted with an overbearing state, citizens, who are also members, will struggle to make room for autonomous associations and market relationships (and also for local governments and decentralized bureaucracies). But the state can never be what it appears to be in liberal theory, a mere framework for civil society. It is also the instrument of the struggle, used to give a particular shape to the common life. Hence citizenship has a certain practical pre-eminence among all our actual and possible memberships. That's not to say that we must be citizens all the time, finding in politics, as Rousseau urged, the greater part of our happiness. Most of us will be happier elsewhere, involved only sometimes in affairs of state. But we must have a state open to our sometime involvement.

Nor need we be involved all the time in our associations. A democratic civil society is one controlled by its members, not through a single process of self-determination but through a large number of different and uncoordinated processes. These need not all be democratic, for we are likely to be members of many associations, and we will want some of them to be managed in our interests, but also in our absence. Civil society is sufficiently democratic when in some, at least, of its parts we are able to recognize ourselves as authoritative and responsible participants. States are tested by their capacity to sustain this kind of participation – which is very different from the heroic intensity of Rousseauian citizenship. And civil society is tested by its capacity to produce citizens whose interests, at least sometimes, reach further than themselves and their comrades, who look after the political community that fosters and protects the associational networks.

VIII

I mean to defend a perspective that might be called, awkwardly, 'critical associationalism'. I want to join, but I am somewhat uneasy with, the civil society argument. It cannot be said that nothing is lost when we give up the singlemindedness of democratic citizenship or socialist cooperation or individual autonomy or national identity. There was a kind of heroism in those projects – a concentration of energy, a clear sense of direction, an unblinking recognition of friends and enemies. To make one of them one's own was a serious commitment. The defence of civil society does not quite seem comparable. Associational engagement is conceivably as important a project as any of the others, but its greatest virtue lies in its inclusiveness, and inclusiveness does not make for heroism. 'Join the associations of your choice' is not a slogan to rally political militants, and yet that is what civil society requires: men and women actively engaged – in state, economy and nation, and also in churches, neighbourhoods and families, and in many other settings too. To reach this goal is not as easy as it sounds; many people, perhaps most people, live very loosely within the networks, a growing number of people seem to be radically disengaged – passive clients of the state, market drop-outs, resentful and posturing nationalists. And the civil society project doesn't confront an energizing hostility, as all the others do; its protagonists are more likely to meet sullen indifference, fear, despair, apathy, and withdrawal.

In Central and Eastern Europe, civil society is still a battle cry, for it requires a dismantling of the totalitarian state and it brings with it the exhilarating experience of associational independence. Among ourselves what is required is nothing so grand; nor does it lend itself to a singular description (but this is what lies ahead in the East too). The civil society project can only be described in terms of all the other projects, against their singularity. Hence my account here, which suggests the need (1) to decentralize the state, so that there are more opportunities for citizens to take responsibility for (some of) its activities; (2) to socialize the economy so that there is a greater diversity of market agents, communal as well as private; and (3) to pluralize and domesticate nationalism, on the religious model, so that there are different ways to realize and sustain historical identities.

None of this can be accomplished without using political power to redistribute resources, and to underwrite and subsidize the most desirable associational activities. But political power alone cannot accomplish any of it. The kinds of 'action' discussed by theorists of the state need to be supplemented (not, however, replaced) by something radically different: more like union organizing than political mobilization, more like teaching in a school than arguing in the assembly, more like volunteering in a hospital than joining a political party, more like working in an ethnic alliance or a feminist support group than canvassing in an election, more like shaping a co-op budget than deciding on national fiscal policy. But can any of these local and small-scale activities ever carry with them the honour of citizenship? Sometimes, certainly, they are narrowly conceived, partial and particularist; they need political correction. The greater problem, however, is that they seem so ordinary. Living in civil society, one might think, is like speaking in prose.

But just as speaking in prose implies an understanding of syntax, so these forms of action (when they are pluralized) imply an understanding of civility. And that is not an understanding about which we can be entirely confident these days. There is something to be said for the neoconservative argument that in the modern world we need to recapture the density of associational life and relearn the activities and understandings that go with it. And if this is the case, then a more strenuous argument is called for from the Left: we have to reconstruct that same density under new conditions of freedom and equality. It would appear to be an elementary requirement of social democracy that there exist a *society* of lively, engaged, and effective men and women – where the honour of 'action' belongs to the many and not to the few.

Against a background of growing disorganization – violence, homelessness, divorce, abandonment, alienation and addiction – a society of this sort looks more like a necessary achievement than a comfortable reality. In truth, however, it was never a comfortable reality, except for the few. Most men and women have been trapped in one or another subordinate relationship, where the 'civility' they learned was deferential rather than independent and active. That is why democratic citizenship, socialist production, free enterprise, and nationalism were all of them liberating projects. But none of them has yet produced a general, coherent or sustainable liberation. And their more singleminded adherents, who have exaggerated the effectiveness of the state or the market or the nation and neglected the networks, have probably contributed to the disorder of contemporary life. The projects have to be relativized and brought together, and the place to do that is in civil society, the setting of settings, where each can find the partial fulfilment that is all it deserves.

Civil society itself is sustained by groups much smaller than the *demos* or the working class or the mass of consumers or the nation. All these are necessarily pluralized as they are incorporated. They become part of the world of family, friends, comrades and colleagues, where people are connected to one another and made responsible for one another. Connected and responsible: without that, 'free and equal' is less attractive than we once thought it would be. I have no magic formula for making connections or strengthening the sense of responsibility. These are not aims that can be underwritten with historical guarantees or achieved through a single unified struggle. Civil society is a project of projects; it requires many organizing strategies and new forms of state action. It requires a new sensitivity for what is local, specific, contingent – and, above all, a new recognition (to paraphrase a famous sentence) that the good life is in the details.